Natural
Enemies

Natural Enemies

The
Notre Dame–Michigan
football
feud

JOHN KRYK

ANDREWS AND McMEEL
A Universal Press Syndicate Company
Kansas City

Library of Congress
Cataloging-in-Publication Data

Kryk, John.
Natural enemies : the Notre Dame–Michigan
football feud / John Kryk.
p.   cm.
ISBN 0-8362-8072-5 : $18.95
1. University of Notre Dame—Football—History.
2. University of Michigan—Football—History.
I. Title.
GV958.N6K79   1994
796.332'63'0977289—dc20   94-22284
CIP

To my wife Sandee,
for enduring four years
of a football widow's
ultimate nightmare

Contents

Acknowledgments

I hope I haven't forgotten anybody, but here goes.

You probably wouldn't be reading this book if it weren't for Murray Sperber. I met Murray in July 1991, during one of my many research trips to Notre Dame. We were both wading through the school's vast and seldom-perused athletic correspondence, circa 1909–28. By chance, I beat Murray by only eight months to this "golden mountain" of information, as he called it.

Murray and I hit it off right away and shared some thoughts, some information, some laughs. I didn't know squat about the publishing industry, but Murray enlightened me. And lucky for me, he put me on to his outstanding agent and friend, John Wright of New York. The result is this book, which comes out a year after Murray's *Shake Down The Thunder: The Creation of Notre Dame Football*—the most accurate, most detailed book ever written solely about the Fighting Irish. Murray, from one Canuck to another . . . thanks, eh?

John Wright believed in me and believed in my book. Then he found me a publisher. No long-suffering New York Rangers fan deserves a Stanley Cup more than you, John.

To Donna Martin and everybody at Andrews and McMeel, thanks, too, for believing. It was also my good fortune to have Matt Lombardi as copy editor.

This book was researched mainly at the University of Michigan's Bentley Historical Library and at the University of Notre Dame Archives. I cannot possibly overstate how incredibly helpful everybody was at both schools.

At Michigan, I wish to single out Nancy Bartlett, Karen L. Jania, and Greg Kinney for their prompt assistance and exuberant interest throughout this project.

At Notre Dame, Dr. Wendy Clauson Schlereth, Charles Lamb, Peter Lysy, Jennifer A. Webber, and Sharon Sumpter all catered to my every request, whether during my brief, hectic research trips or after my many frantic phone calls. I bugged Charles the most, and I thank him sincerely for his keen insight and professionalism.

Jethrow Kyles, the former curator of the Joyce International Sports and Games Collection at Notre Dame, continually put himself out on my behalf during the first year or so of this project. For your assistance, and especially for your encouragement—thanks, Jethrow.

Barb Pietraszewski, Jethrow's assistant in 1990 and '91, undertook several freelance research assignments for me, and as usual she was impeccably thorough.

The Notre Dame and Michigan sports information departments found time to help me out at every step of the way. John Heisler of Notre Dame and Bruce Madej of Michigan arranged interviews, helped me locate former players and coaches, and provided a wealth of statistical information. John gave me full access to all his department's files, which was a tremendous asset. Don Lund at Michigan also helped arrange interviews.

Others I wish to thank for their research help: retired NCAA statistician and Notre Dame stats historian Steve Boda, Jr.; Nancy Meister of Whitman College; Carl C. and Janet C. Cowen of Indianapolis; and Emily Clark of the Chicago Historical Society.

For their encouragement, or assistance, I am grateful also to Mike Riter of the National Championship Foundation; to Bob Lipson; to Jeff DeFran; and especially to Radio's Best Friend, and one of mine, Art Vuolo, Jr.

Those who granted me interviews for this book were gracious with their time and thoughts, all 32 of them.

The sports editor at the *Toronto Sun,* Scott Morrison, was especially patient during the final stages of this project. Thanks for the advice, too, Scott. And thanks to Sheila Chidley for covering for me so often.

Bill Harris, an outstanding journalist and copy editor in the *Toronto Sun* sports department, was the first to read over my entire manuscript. Not a big fan of the sport, Bill would always return his keenly edited portions by saying, "You do realize that, once again, every sentence is about college football." Yes I do, Bill, just as I hope you realize that your catches, your corrections, and your suggestions made this book infinitely better.

Then there's my best friend, Steve Sapardanis. What can I say about "The Ber"? Ten years later, the dream—our dream—is reality. For your suggestions, your "careful" editing, your unflagging encouragement when I was ready to pack it all up, and for your awesome friendship . . . all I can say is, you're *it*!

Various relatives in Windsor, Ontario, baby-sat my boys or put us up so I could hop across the border to do research. Thanks Louanne and Julie, Sue and Chris, Joan and Cliff, and Mom and Dad Carson.

Nana Ambrose, my grandmother, was the first person to turn me on to Michigan football and the first to encourage me to get into sports journalism. When I was determined to be an engineer, she was just as sure I was missing my calling. Thanks for the nudge, Nana, and for all your love.

To Nana Harris Kryk, thanks for your support and prayers.

My brother, Jason, is the most talented young photo journalist in Canada. At first, I viewed his taking photos for my book as a convenience. Now I view it as a genuine privilege.

My Mom and Dad, Pat and Lewis Kryk, have always been there for me—and they typically provided guidance and encouragement at every stage of this project. I love you both very much.

To my wife, Sandee, I vow never, ever to research and write another book in my part time. Throughout this four-year ordeal, you have been more understanding than any man could ever expect from his wife. For so long, you sacrificed so much—just so I could try to realize a boyhood dream, with no guarantees. You're incredible. I have accomplished so much so soon in life because of you, and I love you with every fiber of my heart.

To my two sons, I vow to be a better father. My oldest boy, Russell, was 16 months old when I decided to tackle this project. He starts kindergarten this fall, and my other son, Carson, is now two and a half. Occasionally, perhaps on a Sunday morning, a Tuesday afternoon, or a Thursday night, one of the boys would come tugging at Daddy's pant legs, on the verge of tears, begging me to come play. "Sorry," I'd say. "Daddy has to keep working."

But not anymore. I'm shutting off the computer, and I'm coming to play.

Preface

Who was I, an unpublished kid from Canada, to write a book on a hallowed slice of Americana, anyway?

That's the question I continually wrestled with while pondering the idea of fulfilling my teenage dream—to write a book on the Notre Dame–Michigan football rivalry.

I grew up in Windsor, Ontario (which borders Detroit), and by watching the Wolverines on TV and attending two or three games a year, I became the most crazed Michigan fan in South Windsor, circa 1978–86. Actually, that title was shared by my best friend who lived down the street, Steve Sapardanis. Together, "The Ber" and I lived for Michigan football in the fall—and consequently died almost every New Year's Day. As it happened, our devout fanhood was born the same year as the modern Michigan–Notre Dame series. So to us, this was always a red-letter game.

But my interest in this rivalry soon extended beyond that of just a rabid fan. I became genuinely intrigued by the fact that these nearby schools, both dripping with tradition, had hardly ever played each other.

Obsession was, and still is, my middle name, and by the mid-1980s I had gotten my hands on every book available on Michigan football. My curiosity exploded after I read John Behee's *Fielding Yost's Legacy to the University of Michigan.* Behee briefly mentioned there had been a heated feud between Michigan's Fielding Yost and Notre Dame's Knute Rockne, and that this was probably responsible for their teams never meeting on the gridiron in the 1920s.

It was also around this time that I bought Bill Cromartie's *The Big One: Michigan vs. Ohio State,* a game-by-game chronicle of that storied series. I wondered if Cromartie would ever write such a book on Michigan–Notre Dame . . . but then I realized a game-by-game chronicle of this more-off-than-on rivalry would produce little more than a pamphlet. If someone ever were to write a book on this rivalry, I thought, it would have to focus on the behind-the-scenes relations between the two schools, rather than mere games.

By 1985 I had compiled my own little series history, culled from every morsel of information in my possession. All told it was eight pages long and left more questions unanswered than a Reagan press conference. When I embarked on a career in journalism in 1986, I vowed to one day dig up all the answers and write this book—but not until I was an experienced-enough writer and reporter to do a credible, impartial job.

In early 1990, shortly after joining the copy-editing and layout desk in the *Toronto Sun* sports department, I felt I was ready.

Behee's revealing, scholarly book on Yost had relied on the massive athletic correspondence archives at the University of Michigan, so that's where I began. Similar archives existed at Notre Dame, but I discovered no authors of Fighting Irish football books had ever bothered to peruse them extensively.

As for my concern about not being taken seriously because of my nationality, it was quickly dispelled. No one ever turned me down for an interview and no one at either university was anything less than completely helpful.

Now, almost four grueling years after this immense research project began, I am satisfied I have turned over every rock that can be turned over. In addition to all the revelations about this rivalry, this book corrects many long-repeated inaccuracies about both Notre Dame's and Michigan's football pasts. At Notre Dame I gained a perspective on Michigan football that no book on the Wolverines researched solely at Michigan could ever provide—and vice versa. Knowledgeable Wolverines and Fighting Irish fans will be surprised by what they read.

Deep down I am still a Michigan fan, but I am confident my personal allegiance does not peek through. Had any such bias been a problem, I would have abandoned this project long ago—for it was clear, early on, that Michigan's reputation would not emerge untainted.

All I have done here is report the facts as revealed in surviving evidence. Only rarely did I go out of my way to play judge and jury, mainly because there were two valid arguments to just about every controversy that arose. You, the reader, can pick sides depending on whether your blood runs Michigan blue or Irish green.

Yet no matter what side you're on (if any), the facts surrounding this rivalry are as fascinating as they are revelatory.

And for this obsessive fan turned obsessive reporter, that is the most gratifying aspect of realizing a life's dream.

—John Kryk
December 29, 1993

Overview

1

Notre Dame and Michigan are natural enemies. Always have been, probably always will be.

No other major college football rivalry has been aflame as long, or has produced flames as long, as this scorcher. For more than 100 years the Wolverines and Fighting Irish have been at each other's throats, but most of the wrangling and attempted strangling has occurred off the gridiron.

Indeed, while their modern-day series is as intense, and as important, as any in college football—it's the September Super Bowl—Notre Dame and Michigan hardly ever played before 1978. In fact, between 1910 and 1977 they met on the field but twice.

The dormant years were hallmarked by contempt, connivance, and, in some periods, pure hatred. The roaringest days were in the Roaring Twenties, when Notre Dame's coaching immortal Knute Rockne and Michigan's legendary Fielding Yost were the bitterest of adversaries.

Little has been written about these age-old feuds, however. Francis Wallace, the late Fighting Irish football historian, pointed out some 40 years ago that "there is quite a bit of Notre Dame–Michigan tradition, though mostly submerged, like icebergs."

This book raises them all to the surface.

Generations of football followers were disappointed by the long break-offs, as there always have been compelling reasons for these schools to play:

First and foremost, Notre Dame and Michigan have long been the two most tradition-laden schools in college football. Today they rank either first or second all-time in all the important categories: winning percentage, victories, national championships, All-Americans, and AP poll appearances. (See Appendix III.) But tradition is more than mere numbers, and Michigan and Notre Dame measure up by every other barometer; their respective fight songs, marching bands, stadiums, and helmets are as legendary and as identifiable as any in the sport.

Another compelling factor for these schools to play is that they're only 150 miles apart. In fact, before Michigan State joined the Big Ten in 1949, Notre Dame was closer to Michigan than any conference school.

A final factor is that their series predates *every major college foot-*

ball rivalry in the country. When Michigan and Notre Dame first
played in 1887, Army had yet to play Navy, and the following schools
had yet even to take up the sport: Oklahoma, Nebraska, Penn State,
Ohio State, Florida State, Miami, Alabama, Auburn, Texas, Texas A&M,
Georgia, Georgia Tech, USC, UCLA . . . the list goes on.

For all these reasons, proponents of a Notre Dame–Michigan game
have forever been labeling it a "natural."

The game has certainly been a natural from Notre Dame's perspective. It was Michigan, king of the midwestern hill, which led the
Fighting Irish to the path of big-time football (by teaching them how
to play), which nudged them in the right direction (by sending them
their first coach)—and which later provided the inspiration for Notre
Dame's fight song and stadium. "We owe a lot to Michigan," summed
up the late Moose Krause, longtime Notre Dame athletic director.

Perhaps the biggest favor the Wolverines ever did the Fighting
Irish, though, was to shun them. After the turn of the century, when
the Wolverines felt their diligent Notre Dame pursuers tugging at
their heels, they began leaving roadblocks and planting land mines. A
boycott in the 1910s by Michigan and other Big Ten schools was
intended to blast the Irish permanently off course. But Notre Dame
looked elsewhere for opposition, and in 1913 whipped Army—a game
that catapulted the forward pass and the Irish forever into prominence. Ever since, Notre Dame and Michigan have battled one another
for midwestern, and ultimately national, supremacy.

While most schools generally consider themselves lucky, even honored, to play Notre Dame in football, no such feelings have ever existed
at Michigan. In fact, Michigan, without exception, has always been the
one to break off the series. Remarkably, Wolverine officials each time
cited the same basic reason: whenever they perceived the Fighting
Irish as having a competitive advantage, which was most of the time,
they refused to play them. Notre Dame always thought Michigan's
motives were more devious—namely, athletic jealousy or anti-Catholic
prejudice.

Michigan is the only active school that owns a winning record
against Notre Dame (14–10–1 after 1993), a huge point of pride among
Wolverine fans. But Notre Dame has won 10 of the last 17 games, a
huge point of pride among Fighting Irish fans. To be sure, competitive
pride runs very deep at both schools. When you sift everything else
out, competitiveness is the crux of the Michigan–Notre Dame relationship.

It developed at these schools long before the first footballs were
kicked. Notre Dame and Michigan, the universities, have always strived

for nothing short of excellence in every endeavor, be it a football game, a debate, ground-breaking research—whatever. This desire was simply a product of each school's size. Michigan, as occasionally the largest university in the country in the late 1800s, felt it should also be the nation's leader in just about everything, athletics included. Likewise Notre Dame, the largest Catholic university in the country back then. So size begot self-assuredness, which in turn begot success. Thus was born "Michigan spirit" and "Notre Dame mystique."

Critics be damned, this aura at each school is an intangible yet very real entity revered by players, students, and fans alike. This sense of tradition instills in the players a confidence, an expectation of victory, that simply cannot be fully understood nor fully achieved at most other schools. That's why you saw Lou Holtz sternly promising his players, "We'll come back! We'll come back!" when Michigan took a 10-point lead in the 1990 game; and Notre Dame did come back. That's why, to this day, Michigan sizes up every opponent, including Notre Dame, with the attitude indoctrinated almost a century ago by Fielding Yost: "Who are *they* that they should beat a Michigan team?"

Simply put, competitiveness at these schools exceeds rational thought. "Let me explain my attitude toward total victory," Frank Leahy, Notre Dame's coaching great in the 1940s, once wrote. "There is no other attitude to take. . . . Unless you have total commitment to excellence, you have a flawed attitude toward life."

You see, second best just doesn't cut it at Notre Dame and Michigan—especially when it means finishing second best to the other. And that, more than anything, is the common thread running through all you are about to read.

Prehistory

2

The schools

The University of Michigan and the University of Notre Dame make an intriguing pair. They always have been stark contrasts of one another.

Michigan, the university, is actually older than Michigan the state.

Originally situated in Detroit, the school was chartered in 1817 as the "Catholepistemiad of Michigania" by the Territory of Michigan. The cofounders were John Monteith, a Presbyterian divine, and Gabriel Richard, a Catholic priest. Four years later the school was renamed the University of Michigan and restructured to accept persons of every religious denomination as trustees.

When Michigan entered the union in 1837, the university was issued a new charter and moved some 40 miles west of Detroit, to Ann Arbor.

The new University of Michigan drew many of its aspiring scholars from the two nearby metropolitan centers, Detroit to the east and Chicago about 200 miles to the west. This strategic location afforded the Ann Arbor campus the opportunity of mass enrollment. Michigan quickly became the largest university in the Midwest—or the West, as easterners termed everything left of the Allegheny Mountains—and would soon hold the distinction as the largest, most liberal college on the continent. Michigan's academic standing grew proportionately with its enrollment, to the extent that it was widely renowned as the Harvard of the West.

By contrast, Notre Dame has always been a comparatively tiny, strictly run school. Even today, it accommodates about only 10,000 students, compared to Michigan's 36,000. Notre Dame was founded by the Congregation of Holy Cross and to this day remains a private school, although it's no longer run solely by the congregation.

It was a young Holy Cross priest from France, Rev. Edward Frederick Sorin, who founded the school in 1842 along with several brothers from the Holy Cross order. A year earlier they had set up at a missionary station near Vincennes, Indiana, but Sorin moved the mission north to a plot of land on the northern fringe of South Bend. It was a flat, wooded area nestled around two small lakes, subsequently named St. Mary's and St. Joseph's. In 1844 the state of Indiana chartered the school as the University of Notre Dame Du Lac, meaning "Our Lady of the Lake."

Father Sorin patterned his school after those in France, making Notre Dame markedly different from traditional universities. As a denominational school, Notre Dame was strictly for males—boys, teens, and young men alike (it didn't become college-level only until 1921 and coed until 1972). What's more, the French system of education did not clearly differentiate between grade school, high school, and college. For example, a Bachelor of Arts degree required six years of study, some of it prep level. Hence, professors at the large state-run universities in the Midwest—such as Michigan—would positively scoff at the crude academics being offered at such a denominational school.

By 1887 Notre Dame had become the largest Catholic school in the country, so it was already America's school to America's ever-growing Catholic population. Students were coming from all 38 states in the union.

Champions of the West

The very first champion of the West in football, fittingly, was Michigan.

American football was only 10 years old when, on May 30, 1879, Michigan battled Racine College of Wisconsin at Chicago's White Stocking Park. It was the first game played in the West, and Michigan won 1–0, by virtue of a touchdown and a "goal."

The victorious Wolverines were instantly anxious to prove their mettle against the best teams around. Problem was, there weren't any. Football, or "rugby football" as it was more commonly called, was slow to catch on in the West. One reason may have been that the easterners were continually introducing drastic changes, including, by 1884, a system of downs for advancing the ball, a line of scrimmage, new scoring values, and an oblong ball instead of a round one.

Later in 1879, Michigan found a strong team about 300 miles to the northeast, the University of Toronto, and proceeded to play the Varsity Blues to a scoreless tie. The Wolverines won the follow-up game in 1880, 13–6.

These cross-border successes prompted the Wolverines in 1881 to line up the first intersectional games in college football history. Michigan traveled east to play the best teams anywhere—the mighty trio of Yale, Harvard, and Princeton. The Wolverines lost to all three, but the scores were respectable, especially considering the games were played within the span of a week. The easterners, in fact, were so impressed they later invited Michigan to join the Eastern College League, but

Michigan's faculty would not permit the Wolverines to join such a faraway association for mere athletics.

Another foray east in 1883 proved less successful (two losses, including a 46–0 pulverization by Yale), so Michigan resolved to spend the rest of the decade bolstering its status as champion of the West.

Accordingly, the Wolverines steamrolled into the 1887 season on an eight-game, three-and-a-half-year winning streak.

Carefully taught:
1887–88

I. Fall term, '87

Before November 23, 1887, this was football at Notre Dame:

A hundred boys to a side, all scrambling to get a round ball over the opponent's fence by any means. Kick it, toss it, slap it—whatever. If you want to get technical, it was part soccer and part rugby, but mostly it was pure pandemonium.

The first echo wasn't awakened until the University of Michigan's team dropped by to teach—literally teach—Notre Dame to play rugby football.

In this spirit, the rivalry began as a marriage made in football heaven. The hellish divorce was still years away.

Three men deserve all the credit for arranging what was really only a demonstration game. Former Notre Dame students George DeHaven and Billy Harless, as members of the '87 Wolverine varsity, set things up from the Michigan end, while Patrick Connors did likewise at Notre Dame. That DeHaven and Harless were born and raised in nearby Chicago, and Connors was an Irish holyman, certainly is fitting from a Notre Dame perspective.

Even more fitting, though, is the character exhibited on both sides to see the game through. Those at Notre Dame had the courage to do what no Notre Damers had done before, while those at Michigan embraced the adventurous and overcame a series of daunting obstacles—all qualities much in vogue in the 1880s.

It was a decade that saw Americans adopt a "can-do" mentality: a newfound mixture of confidence, resolve, and daring. People from all walks of life suddenly uprooted the boundary posts of reality and chucked them over the horizon. They invented light bulbs, built skyscrapers, organized themselves as never before, and even ventured off to explore the nether regions of the planet.

The post–Civil War baby boomers, now entering adulthood, made adventurism their way of life. The Michigan–Notre Dame story kicked off when two of them, Harless and DeHaven, hooked up in the fall of 1884.

William Warren Harless was beginning his first year at Notre Dame when he befriended George Winthrop DeHaven, Jr., who was already in his sixth year at the school. Considering what these rambunctious teens had in common, it's not surprising they hit it off. DeHaven was 18, Harless 17; both came from Chicago's downtown; and both were studying in the Commercial program, a high-school-level course emphasizing math and business.

But their strongest bond of all may have been a love for sports. Both were exceptional athletes, and lucky for them intramural sports dominated on-campus recreation at Notre Dame—a tradition that thrives to this day. Harless and DeHaven achieved their first tandem glory in rowing, as members of the campus-champion six-man team. They also played baseball together.

Like all sports-minded students, DeHaven and Harless were indebted to Connors, the key promoter of campus athletics around this time. Born in Ireland, Patrick Connors had been at Notre Dame as a member of the Brothers of the Holy Cross since 1867. Though not ordained like priests, the brothers were entrusted with integral roles at Notre Dame, and Connors—who went by his religious name of Brother Paul—was a prefect of the senior department, for students 17 and older. He would always go to bat for, and get bats for, ever-grateful pupils of all ages. And because he himself was only in his mid-30s, it's no surprise Brother Paul was one of the most well-liked religious men on campus. He and DeHaven apparently hit it off exceptionally well.

In Brother Paul's impressive intramural program, baseball and rowing were the most popular sports, but lawn tennis and handball were beginning to flourish. And so was that chaotic game the students called football.

Fate left it for DeHaven and Harless to go and discover the genuine version and bring it back to Notre Dame.

They left after the 1885–86 school year. Academic records do not list either as having received his Commercial diploma, but both had become, essentially, high school graduates. DeHaven was 20, Harless 19. Their parents back in Chicago were apparently well-to-do, because they had the luxury of pursuing a higher education elsewhere—and perhaps broadening their athletic horizons at the same time. So in the fall of 1886, Harless and DeHaven together enrolled in the arts department at the University of Michigan.

In Ann Arbor they found a wholly different learning atmosphere from that at Notre Dame. The Michigan student body was four times as large (1,600 to Notre Dame's 400), the curricula far wider in scope, the discipline not anywhere near as rigid. On the latter point, the *Cornell Sun* printed a stinging criticism of Michigan that fall: "The absence of government in Michigan University was so notorious that some wag was tempted to say that the University had but two rules: 1) No student shall set on fire any of the college buildings; 2) Under no circumstances shall any student kill a member of the faculty."

Suffice it to say, DeHaven and Harless were entering a more liberal setting. With the chains off, as it were, they apparently did not apply themselves liberally to their arts studies, because they didn't graduate from Michigan, either. Perhaps their minds too often drifted away from their books and onto the playing fields, where both continued to excel.

Harless was a star in the U of M's annual fall and spring "field days," winning the shot put and hammer throw events as a freshman. Harless also was a good wrestler, but in that sport DeHaven was unbeatable. A robust man, DeHaven was the campus wrestling champion in each of his four years at Michigan.

That first autumn, Harless tried out for the varsity football team and made it, albeit as a "scrub," or substitute. DeHaven's only football experience in '86 came in the loosely regulated class games, or "rushes," which were like the mass pushing and shoving matches at Notre Dame.

In the fall of 1887, DeHaven joined his best friend on the Michigan varsity, and that's when the ball really got rolling. Both were good enough to start—Harless at center, DeHaven at left rush end.

DeHaven, as one might expect of a wrestling champion, took an instant liking to the rugged opportunities in rugby football, even before the '87 Wolverines had played an outside game. At the time, Michigan was playing only two or three contests a season, usually late in the autumn following a couple of months of rigorous preparation. This year Michigan was gearing up for a Thanksgiving Day trip to Chicago, ostensibly to play Northwestern.

DeHaven's enthusiasm was to Notre Dame's everlasting benefit. He still had pen pals back at Notre Dame, and in mid-October he wrote Brother Paul about this wonderful new game and Michigan's pending journey west.

New game, huh? Brother Paul, ever open to fresh athletic challenges for the boys, was interested, not just in learning how to play the sport, but in actually pitting a campus team against Michigan. That was a radical idea because Notre Dame had never before been party to an intercollegiate athletic contest. But this was the 1880s, when radicalism was in and conservativism was out.

Brother Paul wrote back to his friend at Michigan and asked if DeHaven and Harless could convince the Wolverines to make a stop at Notre Dame, on their way to Chicago, and teach some seniors this rugby brand of football. DeHaven said he'd try, and this morsel of hope thrilled the Notre Dame campus. "If matters can be properly adjusted," the student newspaper, *The Scholastic,* announced on October 29, "a match game of football will take place on the senior campus about the 27th of next month. . . . The Ann Arbor boys hold the championship of the West, and are such fine players that they will probably contend with the leading Eastern teams next spring for the college championship of the United States. However, there is good material here for a fine team, and the boys will undoubtedly give the Michigan players a hard 'tussle.'"

By the middle of November the tussle was confirmed; DeHaven and Harless had bent enough arms. Michigan would visit Notre Dame on Wednesday, November 23—a day before the Wolverines' big Thanksgiving Day contest with Northwestern in Chicago. (Imagine, *Northwestern* the red-letter game, not Notre Dame.)

Brother Paul then initiated the tradition of ensuring that Notre Dame's athletes were well prepared and at their fighting best. He immediately obtained a copy of the eastern rules, and may also have secured one of the egg-shaped balls used by the rugbians. Six days before the game he rounded up a group of seniors who painstakingly, and awkwardly, tried learning from the book. They found little success. To Brother Paul's disappointment, Notre Dame was as ready as it was going to get. So, too, was Michigan after a 32–0 pasting of Albion.

Then the fateful trip was almost sacked.

A few days before Michigan was to embark, Northwestern chickened out of the Turkey Day game. Evidently, the Wolverines had sent a man to Chicago ahead of time to properly teach the Northwestern boys rugby football, but this rough-and-tumble version was not to the liking of the mild-cats, and they immediately wired their cancellation.

Suddenly the Wolverines had no big game to look forward to. No one could have blamed them if they scrapped the trip right then and there. But enough money had already been raised to cover the trip's expenses—$150 by students, plus the usual donations by Ann Arbor merchants. And the Wolverines hadn't been practicing two months for nothing. So on the Monday before Thanksgiving they decided to send a representative to Chicago to schedule any football team he could find, and on that adventurous premise the trip was on.

And what a crazy trip it would be. Not that Notre Dame was out of the way; the Michigan Central Rail Road passed through Niles, a city in Michigan that hugs the Indiana border just a few miles north of Notre Dame. The problem was in logistics. The Wolverines wanted to reach Chicago by Wednesday evening, for a good night's rest before the mystery game. That meant their brief visit to Notre Dame would have to be made on Wednesday morning, and that meant leaving Ann Arbor late Tuesday and traveling through the night. Still, it must have all sounded like good fun to these venturesome young men, especially with the added persuasion from DeHaven and Harless.

After Tuesday's last classes before the Thanksgiving break, the Wolverines slogged through mud and freshly fallen snow and congregated at the Ann Arbor station. Of course, only on such a brisk night would the train be an hour late. When it finally arrived, the damp, weary players hit the sack, and the train steamed on into the night.

At dawn, they pulled into Niles. There was no time to spare because their connection to Chicago was due to pass through at three o'clock that afternoon. So after a quick breakfast, the Wolverines changed cars and arrived at the Notre Dame depot at about nine. They were greeted by a reception committee of students, who shuffled them off on a tour of the campus.

There wasn't a whole lot to see. Notre Dame, Indiana, consisted of the domed administration building (even then it was golden), the Sacred Heart church, a barn, several school halls and boarding houses, and three playing fields. About all that awed the Michiganders was the elegant artwork and valuables inside many of the buildings. A show-case of rare coins and medals then on display in the library was a particular highlight.

It must have been an odd sight, this tour. Reports indicate the hosts couldn't have been more gracious, nor the visitors more appreciative. One would suspect if tea had been served, pinkies everywhere would have been pointing skyward.

Two hours of touring later, the point of the trip was remembered. Right, football! The Wolverines changed into their spotless white uniforms, the Notre Damers into their usual outdoor gear, and together they made their way to the senior campus field.

Michigan's lineup this day consisted entirely of students. That needs to be said because this was the heyday of the "ringer"—when local ruffians not associated with a school were wantonly played. Just about every school was playing them, and, at least before the 1890s, nobody seemed particularly to mind. A behemoth of a lineman named J.H. Duffie was apparently the only ringer Michigan used in 1887. Duffie didn't accompany the Wolverines to Notre Dame but would meet up with the team later that day in Chicago. (He might well have been the man sent ahead to find the replacement opponent.)

The stars on the Michigan team were the Duffy brothers, James E. and John L. Both had great speed and were exceptional kickers; in fact, in 1891 James would tie the American football record by booting a 55-yard field goal.

The best athlete from the Notre Dame team, unquestionably, was halfback Harry Jewett. He would soon become the world champion in both the 100-yard dash and the 220-yard run, and would also set a national record in the hop, step, and jump (triple jump).

Waiting to cheer on all the players was the entire Notre Dame student body, now more than 500 in number. As no grandstand existed, the boys simply surrounded the senior field en masse. If that wasn't enough school spirit, the campus band assembled for the game. The Notre Dame Victory March would not be written for 21 more years, yet here was the band firing up the crowd to set another famous precedent from the get-go.

The only downer was the condition of the field. Melting snow was turning it into a bog. "There was no necessity of oiling the grounds," *The Scholastic* wryly noted.

At about 11 o'clock the elevens trotted onto the slop, which we can only assume was somehow marked to proper proportions. Before the players were set to have at it, Brother Paul informed DeHaven that the Notre Dame boys—several of them former classmates of DeHaven's and Harless's—had had trouble playing by the book. Brother Paul then suggested the teams at first be mixed for a brief period of hands-on instruction. The Wolverines agreed.

"So we played gently with them that day," DeHaven recalled, ". . . and carefully taught Notre Dame how to play modern football."

When the Notre Dame players learned just how physical this game was, they took to it with reckless abandon. Too reckless, actually. One student in attendance recalled DeHaven and company having to caution their eager pupils against playing too violently.

After this brief tutorial, the players segregated into their proper squads and played a 30-minute game. When both sides finished slipping, rolling, and tumbling in the mud, Michigan tallied two touchdowns to win 8–0. (Touchdowns were worth four points. More about methods of scoring will follow shortly.) It was said the Notre Dame players, as well as the students in attendance, appreciated the fact the Wolverines did not try to run it up on their disadvantaged hosts.

Both Michigan scores were unconverted because, of course, there were no goalposts. Nowhere was it recorded who made the touchdowns, but that's understandable considering the informality of the occasion. "We always thought of it as just a practice game," recalled Frank Fehr, a Notre Dame lineman. "But then years later, they decided it was Notre Dame's first intercollegiate football game. I guess that made us historic, but we never thought of it that way."

Afterward, both teams quickly cleaned up and changed back into their dry garments. The players were allowed a short rest, and then "footballists" and students alike marched toward the massive dining hall.

Following a hearty meal, the Wolverines were escorted to a reception parlor, where they were introduced to the Notre Dame president, Rev. Thomas Walsh. His "kindly manor put all at ease," wrote one of the Wolverines the next week in the Michigan student newspaper, *The Chronicle*. Then Walsh assured the Wolverines "of the cordial reception that would always await them at Notre Dame," *The Scholastic* recorded.

It was now one o'clock, and the Wolverines wanted to get going back to Niles, in the event their connection to Chicago arrived early. The entire visit had lasted only four hours.

"After a hurried handshaking," wrote *The Chronicle*'s correspondent, "we were loaded into carriages, which were in waiting through the courtesy of our hosts, and the road for Niles taken amid hearty cheers and with the kindliest feelings for our friends of Notre Dame."

Encouraging start, or what!

The remainder of the Wolverines' trip was equally splendid, if you discount the weather.

After arriving in Chicago, Michigan learned that the Harvard School would be the next day's opponent. No, not the Ivy League juggernaut. Nor the local ad-hoc team of Harvard and Yale alumni, although this has been erroneously reported many times over the years. The Harvard School was in fact a school, a renowned Chicago prep school at that. Northwestern probably suggested this foe because it had played Harvard the previous year. And there was an element of prestige at stake, because this Harvard had never lost a game of football.

But even with the help of a few ringers from the crowd, Harvard's teenage boys were no match for the champions of the West that Thanksgiving Day. Michigan won 26–0. The game was played in pouring rain and finished in the bitter chill of darkness. That night the Wolverines might have wondered just how much they had to be thankful for, after having played two games in as many days in utterly dreadful conditions. While some Wolverines hopped a train back to Ann Arbor that night, most of the conquering heroes returned home on Friday.

Back at Notre Dame, rugby football was the new rage.

"We had been playing what we called football on the campus," Fehr said, "but we could see after the Michigan visit that we had to become more organized. The trouble was that we didn't really know much about it, just that it was a game that would be fun."

Ah, but then that can-do mentality took over.

Beginning the following Tuesday, a series of meetings led to the formation of the Rugby Football Association at Notre Dame. Brother Paul was elected president. A report in the next *Scholastic* revealed to what football heights Notre Dame instantly aspired: "Great enthusiasm was manifested in the meetings, and prospects are bright for a football team which will be able to cope with any eleven in the West." Champions of the West included, and soon the Notre Dame boys would get another crack at the Wolverines, this time for real.

Meantime, as 1887 wound down, rugby football was played almost daily on the athletic fields at Notre Dame. The campus was taking to the game with a serious passion.

Perhaps too serious. A few more cautions from the Wolverines might have been in order.

"The football teams are taking advantage of the pleasant weather to keep up the enthusiasm," wrote *The Scholastic* on December 17. "Liniments and soothing ointments will be acceptable for Christmas donations."

II., III. Spring term, '88

The winter of 1888 was brutal, one of the harshest in American history. When it finally showed signs of subsiding in March, Notre Dame's footballists instantly burrowed out of hibernation.

Hey, why wait until fall to play again?

About the only thing on campus that hadn't been in a deep freeze was the burning passion for football. Fanning the flames was the ever-energetic Brother Paul. He had organized the Rugby Football Association's fundraisers to buy new balls and proper uniforms, and he was now planning a course outline for the spring—a follow-up to Football 101 as conducted by the Michigan Wolverines the previous fall.

The same teachers were sought for spring term. "Notre Dame challenged us to a game in South Bend and another the day following at Notre Dame," George DeHaven remembered.

Unlike last time, though, DeHaven and mate Billy Harless didn't have to bend any arms. "Mr. DeHaven writes from Ann Arbor that the boys of the University of Michigan have such pleasant remembrances of their Thanksgiving game here that they are anxious to play here again," reported *The Scholastic* on March 24.

The games were soon confirmed: for Friday, April 20, in South Bend, and Saturday the 21st on the Notre Dame campus. The first was arranged solely to help cover the Wolverines' costs (as there would be a price of admission).

Neither side had much time to prepare.

At Notre Dame, lingering snowstorms kept the first-string team (the "Specials") from squaring off against the backups (the "Anti-Specials") until the end of March. As per the plan, the Specials' weaknesses were spotlighted in a sluggish 20–0 win over the scrubs. One glaring need was to get into shape. "Our footballists are endeavoring to raise the wind by running around the lake several times a day," *The Scholastic* recorded.

This stepped-up training regimen plus a slew of mixed-squad games did the trick, because in their final tune-up on April 12, the Specials mashed the Anti-Specials 32–6. That was more like it. "It is the opinion of most of the students that our special team will give the Ann Arbor boys a hard struggle," *The Scholastic* observed.

Struggle was the catchword back in Ann Arbor. DeHaven and Billy Harless were unable, after all, to round up all of last autumn's team. Even worse, three starters who had committed to the trip were on the "hospital list": Royal Farrand's knee was in a cast, and Ernest Sprague and Fred Townsend were hurt in the final days of practice.

"We were totally unprepared," DeHaven remembered, "but I got five starters to go, and with Harless and I (we wanted to see some South Bend friends) and four of our friends, who had never played, and a referee, we went."

The starters from the '87 team included the Duffy brothers and the ringer, J.H. Duffie. A note of infamy for the record: Duffie and two of the friends DeHaven referred to—nonstudents G. Briggs and E. Rhodes—apparently were the only ringers ever to play in a Michigan–Notre Dame contest.

Outside help notwithstanding, this patchwork Michigan squad was cut from a lesser cloth than the one sent to Notre Dame the previous fall. That didn't matter to the Michigan student body, which expected the Wolverines to return from Notre Dame not only victorious but unscored upon, to keep intact a four-year string of shutting out the opposition.

As the Wolverines' train pulled into South Bend, it was plain for all to see that Old Man Winter still hadn't finished with the Michiana region. The ground was lightly covered by snow—as rare a sight on April 19 as football games would become.

Some 300 to 400 South Benders braved the unseasonable elements and showed up Friday afternoon at Green Stocking Ball Park. "The football craze has even affected our local dude," *The Scholastic* deduced.

A foot race, 100 yards in length, preceded the game and was open to members of both teams. James Duffy of Michigan and Notre Dame's Harry Jewett, the world-class-sprinter-to-be, took the challenge. So did Notre Dame's Joe Hepburn and an unidentified South Bend runner. Jewett stumbled at the start and, even with his great speed, was not able to catch the fleet Duffy.

At 3:20 the game was initiated by Sprague, the injured Michigan player serving as referee. There was no need for the Wolverines to provide any pregame instruction this time because the Notre Dame Specials—eight of whom had started in last fall's inculcation—were especially ready.

The first 30-minute half was interrupted several times while the teams dickered over the rules, a common occurrence back then. There was no argument, however, as to which was the better team in that opening half. Michigan completely dominated play, giving the pro–Notre Dame crowd little reason to cheer.

Three minutes and 28 seconds into the game, James Duffy scored a touchdown. His older brother, John, missed the conversion, so it was 4–0, Michigan.

Now, about those four-point touchdowns.

The scoring system back then was as radically different as the game itself. Touchdowns counted four, conversions two, and field goals five points. You had three downs to gain five yards, forward passes were illegal, and the riskiest, most wide-open plays were—get this—end runs.

Perhaps the best way to illustrate how much this game has evolved since then is to explain how touchdowns and conversions were scored.

Until 1900, a rule required the scoring player to touch the ball down on the ground after crossing the goal line—hence the term *touchdown*. If he crossed over the goal but fumbled to the defensive team before touching the ball down, it was a touchback.

The conversion was another adventure. It was a free placekick that could be attempted from any distance; the challenge lay in getting favorably aligned with the goal posts. You had two options after scoring your touchdown. The first was to take an automatic placement anywhere along the end-zone–to–end-zone line of the touchdown spot. When you scored in the middle of the field, you gladly took this option and attempted the conversion from the middle of the field. When you scored nearer to the sidelines, however, you gave your kicker a harsh angle, and that's when you'd exercise the second option. From the precise touchdown spot behind the goal line, you could punt out to the field of play, and wherever a member of your team caught the ball is where the kicker tried the conversion—a placement hopefully closer to the middle of the field. This "punt-out" stuff was tricky business, so the idea was to score your touchdowns as near to the goal posts as possible. The touchdown requisite and the first option on conversions derived from rugby, in which both still apply.

Only Michigan had to concern itself with such rules as the first half continued. William Ball, Duffie, and James Duffy scored additional touchdowns (John Duffy converting only two of them) to give the Wolverines a 20–0 lead. You'd expect if the Notre Dame boys weren't tired out by halftime they sure must have been Duffied out.

The second period began much like the first, with Michigan dominating. Ball scored and John Duffy converted to make it 26–0. So much for any Notre Dame threat, Michigan must have thought. This was a blowout.

Ah, but soon came the first sign of greatness for Notre Dame. It instantly turned the tide of this weekend doubleheader, to say nothing of the future of the university and the game of football itself. One of the Notre Dame linemen, Frank Springer, somehow secured the ball from a Wolverine and took off with it, crossing the Michigan goal line and touching the ball down for, apparently, Notre Dame's first-ever score. The team and the crowd went wild. Only one problem: referee Sprague claimed Springer had interfered with the Wolverine runner before stripping away the ball, and the score was nullified.

No matter.

Fueled by the excitement of this play, the Specials pressed on. A few minutes later, the speedy Jewett got the ball and sent the first volley cheer on high by scoring on a dazzling run. This one counted, and the proud Wolverines were utterly shocked. DeHaven recalled that Jewett "broke through nearly our entire team" en route to what we now call the end zone. To top it off, Ed Prudhomme converted to cut Michigan's lead to 26–6.

"Little fine play was shown after that," reported *The Scholastic,* and the 26–6 score stood.

The moral victory was Notre Dame's, however. The Specials had played the Wolverines to a tie in the second half and had slashed Michigan's four-year shutout string. All thoughts at Notre Dame, then, turned to Saturday's rematch.

All thoughts for many of the bettors in attendance turned to despair, or worse, because the smart money had ND failing to score at all. It wasn't the last time Notre Dame bucked the odds.

🏈   🏈   🏈

A worried, weary group of Wolverines carriaged into the Notre Dame campus on Saturday morning. The Michiganders had good reason to fear this game.

Not only was momentum clearly on Notre Dame's side, but James Duffy was called home Friday night for an unknown reason, thereby depriving the Wolverines of their speedy halfback. Worse, lineman Robert Babcock was hurt in Friday's game and could not play. "We were so badly shaken up," DeHaven recalled, "we played our 120-pound referee." Indeed, Ernest Sprague—last week's casualty and yesterday's official—was today's lineman. Michigan brought no other substitutes, so the game would have to be played with only 10 men to a side. Babcock would serve as referee.

Before the teams met on the senior campus field, the ever-gracious Notre Dame hosts took the Wolverines on a tour similar to that of last fall's—an inspection of various buildings and their rare artwork. After a pregame meal, the players were then taken on a short boat ride around St. Joseph's Lake.

Rest assured, such pregame rituals no longer take place when Michigan visits Notre Dame. Can you imagine Gary Moeller inspecting . . . never mind.

At two o'clock, the Specials and the Wolverines took the field. Kickoff was delayed so a South Bend photographer could snap pictures of each team.

The Wolverines' worst fears were realized immediately after the kickoff, as Notre Dame methodically pushed the ball downfield. The Wolverines managed to gain possession near their goal line, but Harless knealt down in the end zone for a safety touchdown (a safety). For the first time, Notre Dame led a football game, 2–0.

Play remained deep in Michigan territory. John Duffy gave up another safety touchdown to make it 4–0 for Notre Dame. Now the Wolverines were hanging on for dear life.

With two minutes left in the half, the most controversial play of the weekend unfolded. Michigan scored a highly questionable touchdown, as *The Scholastic* explained: "Sprague took the ball, while the others players were settling some dispute, and made a touchdown for his side, and a goal kick by Duffy gave them two more points. Notre Dame claimed the touchdown was illegal, asserting that Sprague neglected to put the ball in play, and furthermore went out of bounds on his way to the goal. The referee, however, could not see it in this light."

Like Sprague the day before, Babcock was anything but a hometown referee. So Michigan led 6–4 at the half.

The Wolverines composed themselves after the intermission and played much better. Harless scored a legitimate touchdown, Duffy missing the conversion, to increase Michigan's lead to 10–4.

To nail down the victory, though, the Wolverines later needed more help from their referee. Jewett scored an apparently legal touchdown for Notre Dame, but Babcock, for some reason, disallowed it. Final score: Michigan 10, Notre Dame 4.

Notre Dame passed these weekend tests with flying colors, even if Michigan taught little about fair play. Had Jewett's touchdown been counted and Sprague's disallowed, Notre Dame might well have wound up an 8–4 winner. "By many it is believed Notre Dame won the game," contended *The Scholastic*. In fact 21 years later, a campus prefect remembered that Notre Dame had indeed split the weekend series.

DeHaven had a somewhat different recollection of the Saturday game: "They were so rude to us we narrowly escaped defeat."

Unsurprisingly, however, these disputes were left on the gridiron. This was another tradition carried over from rugby. Besides, Notre Dame found so much consolation in the two moral victories there was no room left for bitterness. "The record of Ann Arbor was badly broken, and they have not had as hard a tussle for some time as they experienced (here)," *The Scholastic* later beamed.

But know this: It was the last time Notre Dame ever felt so much as a smidgen of joy after losing to Michigan.

There was no rest for the weary after the game. The teams quickly cleaned up and wolfed down some dinner before a group of Notre Damers escorted the Wolverines back to Niles, where their connection back to Ann Arbor was due to leave at five o'clock. "Poor DeHaven," *The Scholastic* quipped, "almost had his arm talked off whilst waiting for the train."

And DeHaven and his teammates almost had their ears booed off whilst deboarding the train. "It was a badly battered team that landed in the crowded Ann Arbor depot," DeHaven recounted, "and we received a proper razzing for breaking a four-year record."

And this apparently was in response to the news of only Friday's 26–6 score. It seems no Wolverine dared mention a word about Saturday's tight struggle, because the next edition of Michigan's *Chronicle* reported only Friday's victory. In fact more than half a century would pass before the 10–4 triumph was recorded in Michigan football annals. But that story will be dealt with later.

The next week's *Scholastic*, meanwhile, raved at length about the Wolverines' second visit. "They made a favorable impression by their manly bearing and courteous conduct, and we hope that next year may bring with it another friendly contest for football honors."

Having been tutored by Michigan three times in six months, Notre Dame had every reason to expect such visits on a regular basis. But it would be 54 years before a Michigan football team again set foot on the Notre Dame campus. And it wasn't until 1898 that these teams played again anywhere.

The Michigan–Notre Dame series was now on ice—just another victim of the winter of '88.

🏈   🏈   🏈

The three founders of this series may never have crossed paths again.

Oddly, DeHaven's playing days at Michigan ended with these games, while Harless suited up only sporadically in 1889 and '90. Despite failing to earn their Michigan degrees, both earned passing grades in the insurance business. And despite having gone their separate ways, Harless and DeHaven remained lifelong friends.

Harless planted his roots back in dear old Chicago. After serving as a captain in the Seventh Cavalry during the Spanish-American War of 1898, Harless set about ingraining another sport into the nation's conscience: golf. It became his great passion, and he earned renown as a player and as secretary of the Western Golf Association. Harless died in 1923 at age 56.

DeHaven ran insurance businesses in Buffalo and Philadelphia before heading west and setting up similar shop in Hollywood. There he retired among the stars, dying in 1948 at 82.

Brother Paul might have remained a vibrant force on the Notre Dame campus for decades to come, but he succumbed to illness only five years later, in 1893. He was 43.

His role has often been either undervalued or ignored by Notre Dame football historians. But it was this Irishman who fought the hardest to entrench football at Notre Dame.

Indeed, the Fighting Irish owe their start, if not their nickname, to this man.

Michigan and its pesky kid brother: 1888–1900

Homebodies

Although Notre Dame and Michigan didn't play over the next 10 years, it sure wasn't for a lack of trying on somebody's part.

Take the late '80s. Notre Dame directed almost all of its scheduling energies toward Ann Arbor, only to have the Wolverines rebuff every attempt.

The first snub came on Thanksgiving weekend 1888. Michigan had again trekked to Chicago but this time suffered its first loss in five years: 26–4 at the hands of a team of beefy Ivy League grads. Complained *The Scholastic* of Notre Dame: "Quite an effort was made to have the Ann Arbor eleven stop over on their way to Chicago last Wednesday and meet the Notre Dame team. In response to several urgent requests for a game, Capt. [James] Duffy of Ann Arbor replied that extra time could not be secured until after the Thanksgiving game in Chicago, and then the team would be in no condition to meet our eleven, as several of its members would leave for their homes after the Chicago contest."

Undaunted, Notre Dame tried to convince Michigan to drop by the following spring. The Specials had even bought a new set of uniforms in anticipation of a contest, but it never materialized. "Michigan backed squarely out when asked to play, alleging various thin excuses," erupted *The Scholastic* on April 20. "The secret of the matter probably is that their best men have left the team and it is in a weak state. They have not yet recovered from the defeat in Chicago, which served to displace some of their vanity."

When autumn 1889 rolled around, Michigan again turned a cold shoulder. "Will Ann Arbor dare to meet Notre Dame this fall?" wondered *The Scholastic* on November 2. "She crows loudly over Albion, but keeps a discreet silence as to our eleven, and perhaps does not want to hear from ND."

The truth of the matter probably was that the Wolverines couldn't have cared less about ND. Around this time, rival colleges were always trading shots in their student newspapers, on academic matters, on athletic matters . . . on just about anything. Stinging broadsides seldom went unanswered, but the Michigan *Chronicle*'s guns remained silent following *The Scholastic*'s biting barrages.

Why? Because in Michigan's eyes, Notre Dame was just the pesky kid brother who refuses to understand he can't always hang out with the big boys. And when kid brother goes off whining to the other small fry on the block, well, big brother couldn't care less.

But kid brother was determined to prove he belonged. Indeed, for the next two decades, Notre Dame aspired to be everything that mighty Michigan already was in athletics. Whenever the Wolverines appeared on the schedule of any Irish athletic team, that game was automatically one of the biggest—most times *the* biggest—of the year.

This feeling was seldom mutual, however. Playing Michigan might mean everything to Notre Dame, but playing Notre Dame meant little or nothing to the champions of the West. And this was always a sore spot with Notre Dame.

Michigan's football brush-offs in 1888 and '89 were particularly devastating. While the Specials waited in vain for Michigan to accept their offers, they played only twice—victories over the Harvard Preps and Northwestern.

Consequently, football fever waned at Notre Dame, to the extent that the sport became strictly a campus activity in 1890 and '91.

                        ◉   ◉   ◉

Midwestern football was still in diapers in the early 1890s.

There were no long-standing series or feuds, simply because (1) the game was so young and (2) there were no coaches or athletic directors to carry on such traditions. As football players came and went, contacts and relations with other schools—good or bad—went with them.

Therefore, it should come as no surprise that Michigan came knocking on Notre Dame's door in 1891. Purdue had also issued a challenge. "Ann Arbor's has been accepted," *The Scholastic* reported on October 31. "Training will commence Monday." It appears a game with Michigan was even scheduled for November 25, but for some unexplained reason it never came off.

This was typical for the times, when games were arranged or canceled on the spur of the moment.

                        ◉   ◉   ◉

When football returned to intercollegiate status at Notre Dame in 1892, prospects for resuming the Michigan series anytime soon were bleak. That's because Notre Dame was now chained to the campus: no road games allowed.

Perhaps the Holy Cross fathers had been turned off by chants of "Kill the fighting Irish! Kill the fighting Irish!" during Notre Dame's only road game against Northwestern in Chicago in 1889. Finances may have also played a part, as athletics were run in the red at Notre Dame until the 1910s, and road trips may have been deemed an unnecessary expense.

The homebody rule was in effect until 1897, and the Notre Dame hierarchy permitted only two exceptions—for short junkets to the Windy City to play the University of Chicago. So the only way there could have been a Michigan–Notre Dame game from 1892 to '97 was if the Wolverines were willing, and able, to travel to Notre Dame.

In 1894 they were willing, indeed asking, to meet Notre Dame halfway—in Battle Creek, Michigan. But the homebody rule prevented the Notre Damers from accepting.

There is no surviving record to indicate the Wolverines were willing to play at Notre Dame, although from '95 to '97 they had a good reason for not dropping by. At that time Michigan, too, found itself more or less grounded by its faculty.

Football had gotten out of hand at Michigan. After the debacles of the late '80s, the Wolverines had vowed never to be so disorganized, nor so disgraceful, ever again. They took the vow too far, however. By 1892 they had arranged a 12-game schedule that took them through six states: Minnesota, Wisconsin, Illinois, Indiana, Ohio, and New York. Their frequent-rider mileage added up again in '93, to such an extent that the Michigan faculty felt compelled to derail them. The fact that the Wolverines were always taking ringers along with them, as many as seven starters at a time, was just as much a concern. So after the '93 season, the Faculty Board in Control was instituted to clean up athletics. By '95 the crackdown was firm: The Michigan varsity was allowed only two or three single-game trips a year. And no more ringers. Thus, the precious traveling opportunities now had to be reserved for the powerhouses, such as Harvard (yes, *the* Harvard), Chicago, and Minnesota.

Notre Dame didn't approach the stature or prowess of that crowd. So here you had the Notre Damers unable to leave home and the Wolverines more or less unable to visit. Hence the continuing hiatus.

Carefully coached

Athletic relations between the schools were actually quite friendly during the '90s. Correspondences were warm and cordial, and the Michigan–Notre Dame baseball series thrived.

But perhaps the best indication of mutual goodwill is that Michigan sent Notre Dame its very first football coach in 1894.

Notre Dame had been desiring quality instruction for years. Back in 1892 a campus instructor, James Kivlan, had even written American football's founding father, Walter Camp, for pointers.

In 1894 Notre Dame's football manager, T.D. Mott, Jr., remarked to Michigan's graduate manager of athletics, Charles Baird, that "we have good material and only require the services of a good coach to make a first-class team."

So Baird found Notre Dame a coach: James Laury Donaldson Morrison, a tackle on the previous year's Wolverine team. A contractual arrangement was ironed out, and Morrison arrived at Notre Dame on October 6. He immediately went to work, and the next day gave Baird a progress report, which revealed just how much growing up kid brother had to do:

Dear Charly:
Thanks old man for this position. I arrived here yesterday morning and found about as green a set of football players as ever donned a jacket. And I am afraid it will be a very hard matter to get up a good team.

You can imagine the kind of crowd it is when I tell you that Jacob Rosenthal, that big lump of guts that was at Michigan last year, is the most promising candidate for center. I am informed however that there will be some good men here during the coming week.

We play our first game next Saturday with Hillsdale, Mich. I am afraid we will get swiped unmercifully as I have a hard set to train. They want to smoke, and when I told them that they would have to run and get up some wind they thought I was rubbing it in on them.

Why yesterday I started them to dropping on the ball, and one big, strong cuss remarked that it was too much like work. Well maybe you think I didn't give him hell! I bet you a hundred no one ever makes a remark like that again.

But Charly, I wish I could describe this place to you. It is about as damned a place as I ever fell into. But to tell you the truth, I am in love with it. The college is about three miles from town. And I don't intend to go outside of the grounds while I am here.

I have a contract with them for two weeks at $40.00 + expenses. If you can give me any pointers in regard to plays be sure and do so.

Give my love to all the old boys, and tell them we who are not so fortunate as to be with them expect wonders of them.

Your old friend, J.L.D. Morrison.

After a few more days, Morrison himself was performing wonders, according to *The Scholastic:* "He has been indefatigable in teaching the men their plays and duties. Not content with explaining on the field the movements of the different players, he has assembled them in the evening before a blackboard and instructed them by chalk diagrams. If the men follow out his orders, we'll trail the banners of our antagonists in the dust."

Despite Morrison's initial fears, Notre Dame dusted off Hillsdale 14–0. Then the Notre Damers tied Albion 6–6 before Morrison's two-week contract expired. Hillsdale must have been impressed with Morrison's coaching acumen, because the small Michigan college whisked him away the next week.

Notre Dame hired another ex-Wolverine as head coach the following year, a fact that has eluded all Notre Dame historians. Harry Graydon Hadden, who went by his initials, was the coach of record in 1895, even though he was in charge for only one of Notre Dame's four games—an 18–0 loss to Indianapolis Artillery. Hadden played the latter part of that game at tackle, inserting himself into the lineup after Indianapolis Artillery had sent in some ringers.

Unlike Morrison, however, Hadden didn't come to Notre Dame with Michigan's blessings. A tackle on the 1894 Michigan team, Hadden told the Wolverines in early October '95 that he couldn't return to Ann Arbor because his parents wouldn't let him leave Chicago. Then he immediately took off with the Chicago Athletic Club on a tour of the East, and when he returned he took over as coach of the Notre Dame team. A powerful Michigan alumnus caustically remarked that Hadden had "deserted his colors."

H.G. Hadden actually holds a unique place in the Michigan–Notre Dame rivalry. Nobody wore more hats than he. Hadden not only played for Michigan and coached Notre Dame, but he went on to become an assistant coach with the Wolverines in 1899, then served the next year as umpire in the Michigan–Notre Dame game.

The Naughty Nineties

Recruiting scandals. Scholastic skulduggery.

How sad that the cancers of college football in the 1890s still malign in the 1990s. Only then it was worse, and Notre Dame and Michigan were as afflicted as anyone.

As outraged academics were quick to point out, football had become far too naughty by the mid-nineties. At many schools the game now was controlled by students and alumni, who basically allowed their teams to face who they wanted, when they wanted, and with whatever players they wanted.

Some of the larger schools in the Midwest, such as Michigan, had already begun cracking down when the Western Conference—later known as the Big Ten—formed in January 1896. The mandate: to restore academic integrity to college sports, especially football. The original conference members were Chicago, Illinois, Michigan, Minnesota, Northwestern, Purdue, and Wisconsin. (Indiana and Iowa joined in 1899, Ohio State in 1912.)

The conference's first sweeping legislation was to place intercollegiate athletics at all member schools under the control of a faculty board. What's more, only bona fide, full-time students who were not "delinquent" in their studies would be allowed to play, and their careers would be limited to four years. From now on, ringers, hired hulks, and tramps (those who hopped from school to school to major only in football) were history. At least that was the plan.

Notre Dame, too, decided to clean up its act, despite having been rejected in its attempt to join the Western Conference. The purity of Notre Dame's athletic teams apparently left a lot to be desired in the mid-nineties. The *South Bend Tribune* later reported that "previous to '96, Notre Dame had little respect for amateurs, and the students became discouraged because of the professional men who were annually being played." It had actually decayed to the point where most students didn't even bother trying out anymore for either football or baseball, the *Tribune* noted.

Notre Dame president Rev. Andrew Morrisey set the reform movement in motion, and by 1897 coach Frank Hering, a former quarterback under Amos Alonzo Stagg at Chicago, was starting to weed out the ringers. It helped that the Commercial Athletic Club had just been formed in South Bend, and that Hering was also its coach, because on this team he probably welcomed the local louts and nomads who otherwise would have gone knocking on Notre Dame's door. In 1898 Notre Dame created its own Faculty Board of Control, in an attempt to cement its commitment to purity. Although not all of the Western Conference rules were adopted, athletes now had to maintain a 75 percent average to remain eligible.

These moves put Notre Dame a rung above other small schools in the Midwest that continued to solicit vagabond help.

But nobody was above reproach. Conference schools soon discovered they could not purify everything over night. For instance, Michigan learned after the '97 season that a Wolverine football player had registered in only two classes—ones he had already passed—and, worse, had left school right after the season ended.

Indeed, it was all well and good that the Western Conference had pioneered the sweeping changes, but there was also a matter of enforcement. And for decades to come, that would be the biggest single knock against the Big Ten: that member schools were hypocritical, always pointing fingers everywhere but at their pompous, guilty selves.

Notre Dame would get this "point" over and over again.

IV. Michigan . . . convincingly, '98

Because the powerhouses of college football were now playing almost exclusively at home, the Holy Cross fathers must have realized the travel ban had to go if Notre Dame was ever to go anywhere in football. It might have helped that Hering's '97 team had shown signs of greatness in going 4–1–1.

So at long last, the chains were removed in 1898.

The goal now at Notre Dame was to hit the road, play the best teams in the West, beat them, and thus become one of them. The first priority was to play the best of the best, Michigan, and the Wolverines agreed to an immediate resumption of the series—in Ann Arbor, of course.

The reunion was set for Saturday, October 22. That the game was not played in November means Michigan did not consider it very important. Back then, leading teams always tried to sequence their opponents from worst to best. The ideal season would allow them to experiment against patsies in early October, fine-tune against decent teams in midseason, then peak for the toughest foes in late November.

Yet when fall rolled around, the Wolverines were taking no chances against the ever-improving Notre Damers. *The Michigan Daily* reported this might well be the Wolverines' toughest game all year.

It was an even bigger game to the folks back at Notre Dame—as big as any in the school's short athletic history. "Notre Dame feels that she has a team that deserves recognition among the important teams of the West, and will make every effort to clinch her claim," reported the *South Bend Tribune*. Some midwestern pundits thought Notre Dame could win, and several South Bend bettors were said to be giving 2–1 odds that Michigan wouldn't so much as score.

Hardly.

The Wolverines played a stellar defensive game that afternoon and cashed in on Notre Dame's incredible generosity to win decisively, 23–0, before a crowd of 1,500 at muddy Regents' Field.

Michigan guard William Caley jumped into the backfield to score three touchdowns, while halfback Clifford Barabee scored the other five-pointer. (The value of the touchdown had increased to five points, while the conversion had dropped to one.) Neil Snow was true on three of four conversion placekicks.

The Notre Damers couldn't have been more feeble. They lost five fumbles in their own end and picked up only one first down all afternoon. The highlight for them came in the final minute, when Charles Fleming attempted a rare play in the West—a field goal. His 35-yarder was wide left by two yards.

But the smartest play by Notre Dame actually came a week after the game. Rev. John Cavanaugh of the Notre Dame Faculty Board of Control wrote Michigan to apologize for the conduct of right halfback George Lins during the game.

Lins admitted to Notre Dame authorities that he had slugged a Wolverine, but pleaded "that he had been repeatedly held by the Michigan quarterback, and that his protests to the officials were unavailing." Cavanaugh informed Michigan officials that Lins was being held out of Notre Dame's next game against DePauw as disciplinary action. "Though I am not authorized to do so," Cavanaugh wrote, "I may inform you that the exclusion of Lins, coupled with our large 'hospital list,' makes it extremely likely that we shall lose today's game with DePauw."

Although Notre Dame won 32–0, the gesture was greatly appreciated in Ann Arbor. Witness this editorial in *The Michigan Daily:*

> The Athletic Board of Notre Dame is greatly to be commended for the stand it has taken. . . . This action is the more praiseworthy for the reason that it was done voluntarily, and without any complaint on the part of the Michigan authorities. . . . Up to last year Notre Dame usually played some professional men on its teams, but has this year been making great efforts to raise her standard of amateurism. That her efforts and promises in this direction have been sincere has now been clearly evidenced by the honest and manly action in the case of her offending player.

Michigan athletic director Charles Baird must have been impressed, too. Good thing. He handled all football negotiations, and he scheduled Notre Dame for a return visit in 1899. He would do so again in 1900.

V. Getting a line on Notre Dame, '99

With athletics at Notre Dame having been returned to the students, enthusiasm reached new heights. The Notre Dame baseball and track teams were now among the best in the West, and the footballists weren't far behind. *The Scholastic* noted the epoch with a specific reference to the track team, but one which certainly held for football as well: "It is [no longer] a question of where we will find the man for the position, but which man shall we choose?"

It was believed Notre Dame had a great chance to beat the Wolverines on Wednesday, October 18. Before the game, experts were rating the Notre Damers among the tops in the West. That would certainly be true if they could beat Michigan, the defending Western Conference champion. The *South Bend Tribune* reported that coaches Frank Hering and James McWeeney had, "with a grim determination," drilled the Notre Damers all season long in the sole purpose of taming the Wolverines. *The Michigan Daily* somberly observed that if Notre Dame "has a team that is anywhere near as strong as it is claimed to be, there should be little difficulty in the way of her winning."

Oh, but there was. Michigan, a loaded team that underachieved all year, was good enough just long enough to score two touchdowns against Notre Dame's weakened team and won 12–0 at soggy Regents' Field.

It was advertised as the "Businessmen's Game" because Ann Arbor merchants closed their shops and joined students and other townspeople in the stands. Even rarer was the presence of so many women among the crowd of nearly 2,000.

The story of this game was line play. Going in, the Notre Damers knew their ends and guards were weaker than Michigan's. Their hope was that their hefty tackles, Frank Hanley and Earl Wagner, could shore up the outside while mountainous center John Eggeman, a six-foot-four, 250-pounder, plugged up the middle. But Eggeman was injured and didn't play a down. His absence left Notre Dame completely outclassed between the tackles, and that's exactly where Michigan continually attacked, with considerable success. Leo Keena and John McLean scored the Wolverines' touchdowns, both of which were converted by Neil Snow.

Michigan finished its season 8–2. Notre Dame wound up 6–3–1, including a very respectable 2–2–1 mark against Western Conference schools. That rose Notre Dame's star a little higher in the midwestern sky. Not high enough for its liking, of course. Michigan, Chicago, and Wisconsin remained the Big Three of the West, and the Notre Damers desperately craved that status. For the second straight year they had blown their big chance to attain it.

"Regents' Field at Ann Arbor must have a hoodoo secreted somewhere behind the grandstand or bleachers," *The Scholastic* reasoned. "There is something there that goes against our players and keeps us from getting a victory."

The turn of the century did not halt the hex.

VI. Another slipup, '00

The first year of the twentieth century was a turning point for the rivalry, because it was obvious Michigan now felt Notre Dame was too strong to play early on. The 1900 contest was played on Saturday, November 17, at Regents' Field.

Big brother was getting wary.

Both Notre Dame and Michigan went into this game banged up, mentally and physically, and this was reflected in the action. The teams played conservatively and Michigan barely hung on for a 7–0 victory, before a few hundred shivering fans on a brisk, windy afternoon. A midweek snowfall had left the field a sloppy, slushy, slippery mess. But what else was new? This was the sixth game in series history, and for the sixth time the teams played in a veritable quagmire.

Michigan's scores, as usual, came as the result of untimely Notre Dame miscues. Arthur Redner scored a touchdown after Notre Dame fumbled deep in its territory, and the Wolverines registered a safety on an errant Irish punt snap. Notre Dame, however, dominated the second half, successfully hammering away at the Wolverine line and keeping play almost exclusively in Michigan territory. Two goal-line stands sealed the win for the Wolverines.

Notre Dame freshman Louis (Red) Salmon was the star of the second half. He "punted in excellent form, carried the ball and handled punts in the backfield like a veteran," *The Scholastic* reported. "And [he] battered the Michigan line into smithereens. Time and again Captain [George] Kuppler called the fullback signal, and few were the times that [Salmon] failed to make his distance."

The Wolverines ended their season 7–2–1. The Notre Damers finished 6–3–1 and could not improve on their second-rung status in the West. The monumental victory continued to elude them.

🏈　🏈　🏈

It was such an incidental remark.

At a Notre Dame–Michigan track meet in March 1900, Ann Arborites generously applauded the defeated ND athletes, and *The Scholastic* observed: "This goes to show that the relations between Michigan and Notre Dame are very friendly."

It would be almost 40 years before the same could be said again.

Undercurrents of ill will: 1901–08

Fielding H. Yost

1901 saw the arrival in Ann Arbor of Fielding Harris (Hurry Up) Yost, the man who over the next 40 years would shape Michigan athletics and become the central figure in the Michigan–Notre Dame rivalry.

Yost coached the Wolverines for all but one year through 1926, and was athletic director from 1921 to 1941. He is most renowned for producing the "Point-A-Minute" teams of 1901–05, arguably the most dominant in college football history. In that era the Wolverines posted a 55–1–1 record, outscored the opposition 2,821 to 42, and won four national titles. The National Championship Foundation credits Yost with having won two other titles, in 1918 and 1923, giving him six in all—more than any other coach.

Yost was born and raised on a farm in Fairview, West Virginia. He grew into a man of rugged proportions for his day—six foot, 200 pounds—and was a star lineman for both West Virginia and, as a ringer, for Lafeyette. In 1897, with a law degree from West Virginia in hand, Yost began his long, successful coaching career. In his attempt to see as much of the country as possible, he jumped from Ohio Wesleyan, to Nebraska, to Kansas, to Stanford in consecutive years, compiling a 31–6–2 record along the way.

Anxious to plant some roots in 1901, the 29-year-old Yost sought a return to the Midwest. He applied to Illinois but was referred to Michigan, where athletic director Charles Baird made him a highly paid, high-profile coach.

Michigan and other western schools had been hiring "coaches" only since the early 1890s. In the beginning most were hired seasonally, others—like J.L.D. Morrison and H.G. Hadden at Notre Dame—for just weeks at a time. They often held little power, even less than the team's captain and trainer. But when schools discovered just how closely tied a team's success was to its coach, the power base shifted. The coach's stature, influence, and wages skyrocketed. Yost was one of the first to assume such prominence in the West.

He became one of college football's most colorful and controversial figures. According to legendary writer Ring Lardner, Yost had "more personality than any other man I have ever met."

He was an intriguing character, indeed. Yost's most fascinating—and irritating—trait was his unrestrained penchant for bragging. He was an "unabashed ham" who positively adored the spotlight. Writer Edwin Pope reported that the "surest way to find a camera was to put your hand on Yost's shoulder, close your eyes, and follow him." Yost was forever downplaying his opponents' accomplishments and boasting about those of his own team, an approach diametrically opposed to today's coaching wisdom that you never say anything to upset an opponent.

But braggadocio was an instinctive characteristic in Yost; it was one thing he did not do for effect, and only rarely did he do it to disparage somebody else. This incessant desire to impress had a childlike naïveté, and perhaps that's why Yost endeared himself to as many people as he outraged.

This was a large part of Yost's country-bumpkin persona, which is best exemplified in an anecdote by J. Fred Lawton in his book, *"Hurry Up" Yost in Story and Song*. In 1908 Lawton was a candidate for the Michigan varsity, and one afternoon during a break from preseason training, he volunteered to row while Yost fished for bass on Whitmore Lake, near Ann Arbor:

> Dressed in an old, sloppy suit, wearing a beat-up old hat, and chewing a stogie, [Yost] stood in the boat, telling me stories, and singing bits of a song between casts. . . . He told the story of the Buffalo substitute, who had had enough. Casting his frog far from the boat, he drawled, "Y'see, Buffalo only brought 15 players, so we gave 'em permission to play their men over and over—we broke the rules in their favor, y'know (he's smiling generously). The score was about a hundred to nothin', when a Buffalo player comes a walkin' by the Meeshegan bench. He's wearin' patent leather pumps, and carryin' his football shoes. So our team hollers, 'Where are ye goin'?' He says, 'I'm goin' home! Our coach told us we were comin' daown here to get experience, and I've had enough!'" Here Yost chuckled, tongued his stogie, then drawled, "I reckon he'd had enough experience t'last him a lifetime, y'know!" Then, he broke into a laugh, and kept repeating, "Sure, y'know," almost under his breath, looking into my eyes to make sure I got the full humor of the situation.

But this boundless pride rankled a lot of foes. The only thing worse than getting whipped by a Yost team was hearing him gloat about it afterward. And if ever you were fortunate enough to beat the "Yost-men," or if ever you sacked Yost's pride in any way, he could be indignant, irrational—downright mean, even. It was this side of his personality that would surface so often in his relations with Notre Dame.

Yost was a devout Methodist, a successful southern businessman, a teetotaler, a much-in-demand speaker, and most of all, a man who took football as seriously as anyone who ever strolled a sideline. Said Grantland Rice: "No other man has ever given as much heart, soul, brain, and tongue to the game he loved—football."

Indeed, as a coach Yost was a wily tactician, a brilliant innovator, and an incredibly fierce competitor. He adapted to the times better than anyone in history, and he remains the winningest of all coaches whose careers spanned at least 25 years (having won 82.8 percent of his games).

Yost earned his nickname because on the practice field he was forever screaming at his players to "hurry up!" as fast play and conditioning were keys to his early, monstrous success.

His first Wolverine team went 11–0, won the first Rose Bowl game, and outscored the opposition 555–0. That made Yost an instant demigod in Ann Arbor. Make no mistake: Michigan football was Yost's baby now.

As Notre Dame would rue for generations to come.

Off the track

It was only a coincidence, and he had nothing to do with it, but the first major spat between Notre Dame and Michigan occurred one month after Yost became Michigan's head coach.

Like some of the feuds that would follow, this one was more than just Michigan against Notre Dame. It was really the Western Conference, led by Michigan, against the "small" colleges, led by Notre Dame. As usual, it got quite ugly. When all was said and done, Michigan and several other conference schools boycotted Notre Dame in all sports during the 1901–02 school year.

The tiff began in February 1901, when the governing body of the annual Western Conference track-and-field championships was restructured. Previously, the conference had entrusted alumni of member schools to run the meet, under the auspices of the Western Intercollegiate Athletic Association. The meet was open to all schools in the region, so it was really serving as the midwestern collegiate championships. Nonconference schools even had a voice in the way the meet was run, as each had a representative on the all-important eligibility committee.

But in the latest attempt to disempower alumni and place athletics under direct faculty control, the Western Conference—or "Big Nine," as it was now commonly called—decided to do away with the W.I.A.A. and its governing hierarchy. The new Intercollegiate Conference Athletic Association was to be run by an executive committee of faculty reps from conference schools. The old alumni executive was retained but only to look after the petty details of the meet. Significantly, the old eligibility committee was abolished entirely and replaced by a three-man panel of Big Nine reps, which alone would determine who could compete from conference and nonconference schools alike.

The small colleges went ballistic. They strenuously objected to no longer having a say on eligibility matters. To get it back, Notre Dame, Drake, and Nebraska went so far as to apply for admission into the conference as full-fledged members, only to be turned down.

The ringleader of the revolt was Notre Dame, and it let everyone know just how upset the small colleges were. Dan Murphy, Notre Dame's representative on the old eligibility committee, told the press: "We are willing to have the records of our athletes investigated by any committee, but we object to being discriminated against. It seems to me that the conference colleges are unjust to us here. According to the original resolutions of the conference, the eligibility of students in the Big Nine shall be determined by committees of their own institutions, but the nonconference colleges have no such privilege."

As a compromise, the Big Nine decreed that the new eligibility committee would work in concert with the faculty athletic boards of all participating schools, nonconference colleges included. The I.C.A.A. would retain the final say, however.

This wasn't enough of a concession to Notre Dame, which again went public with its discontent. The squeaky wheel, however, would get no more oil. The squeaky wheel, in fact, was becoming quite a nuisance to conference schools.

While the Big Nine officially announced it had "only the most friendly feeling" for the small schools, this sentiment certainly did not apply for Notre Dame. Athletic matters aside, faculty at these state-run universities in the Midwest had long looked down on denominational schools such as Notre Dame, deeming the educations they provided as purely second rate. Such academic elitists were the ones who ran the Western Conference, and it was they who continually rebuffed Notre Dame in its attempt to join their old-boys club. Thus, the earliest squabbles between the conference and Notre Dame were rooted in academic snobbery, and likely no small amount of anti-Catholic discrimination, too.

Up until the turn of the century, Notre Dame hadn't been much of a threat athletically, and the conference apparently had no problem with the Notre Damers as long as they were seen, beaten, and not heard. But with ND beginning to flex its muscles, and intent on becoming a major player in the West, Big Nine schools probably viewed the uppity Catholic college with not only disdain but distress.

The two most powerful conference members, athletically and politically, were Michigan and Chicago. Both would become the staunchest athletic foes of Notre Dame, perhaps because both had the most to lose by Notre Dame's ascension to athletic supremacy. Already, both had thrown up roadblocks in the path of ND. In 1898 Michigan had voted to deny Notre Dame admission into the W.I.A.A., on the grounds that Notre Dame's "amateur sentiment is not strong enough to ensure purity in their athletic dealings." And Amos Alonzo Stagg, the paragon of Chicago athletics, began a football boycott of Notre Dame in 1900 that died only when the sport did at the Midway school in 1939.

It was Michigan and Chicago who pushed through the track-and-field reform, and a few months later they saw to it that relations between the conference and Notre Dame eroded further. In June 1901 they orchestrated the conference's banning of Notre Dame from the initial I.C.A.A. track meet, after a Notre Dame athlete was disqualified at an eastern competitition over charges of professionalism. Notre Dame had been coming under attack again for suiting up less-than-pure athletes, and this scandal evidently was the last straw.

Accordingly, Michigan, Chicago, and several other conference schools severed all athletic relations with Notre Dame for the coming 1901–02 school year. It wasn't that they questioned Notre Dame's desire to play by the rules. Rather, they just believed Notre Dame wasn't doing nearly enough to catch all of its crooks. A prominent Michigan alumnus, Harry Bates, pointed this out in a letter to M.A. Quinlan, secretary of the ND Faculty Board of Control of Athletics:

> Notre Dame has certainly taken a long step forward. . . . Should you, or any member of your committee, certify that the Notre Dame contestants were eligible under the rules I should feel that you were absolutely sincere, and the only question in my mind would be as to whether you were sufficiently acquainted with the schemes often adopted by students to circumvent them.

In January 1902 the Notre Dame faculty set out to foil the schemers once and for all. Every conference regulation was adopted and every one was to be strictly enforced. Indeed, Notre Dame was now going "all the way" with the conference, in the name of clean athletics and in the hope that it could finally join the conference.

As a result, the Big Nine boycott was dropped almost immediately. By March, Michigan athletic director Charles Baird signed up Notre Dame for a fall meeting on the gridiron, ending the one-year hiatus.

But the undercurrents of ill will still flowed strong; the conference flatly denied Notre Dame admission, and Notre Dame was not happy about it.

VII. A most magnificent struggle, '02

Toledo? Why Toledo? Why would Michigan and Notre Dame play in, of all places, Toledo, Ohio?

The 1902 game was originally scheduled to be played in Ann Arbor on October 18. But sometime in the summer, officials of both schools decided to move it to the industrial city on the mouth of the Maumee River.

Turns out, the switch was made for the same reason the 1899 game was almost moved to Grand Rapids: to satisfy the local Michigan alumni, who were rabid athletic rooters, desperately wanted to play host to a big game, were promising that the townies would come out in droves to watch, and were vocal about their perceived neglect.

Back in June, these Toledo alums had successfully lobbied Michigan athletic director Charles Baird to bring the Michigan-Cornell baseball game there. About 3,000 people attended at $1.25 a head, so it was a financial boon.

Baird must have been convinced a fall football game would do at least as well. But which home game should Michigan move to Toledo? This city just south of the Michigan border was seemingly an appropriate place to play Ohio State. But Baird chose Notre Dame, perhaps because Toledo was a true neutral site—neither in Michigan nor Indiana—and perhaps because it contained about the same number of Notre Dame grads as Michigan grads. Anyway, ND officials agreed to the switch.

A week before the game, Notre Dame's team was in disarray. Wins over Michigan Agricultural College, 33–0, and Lake Forest, 28–0, were followed by a listless practice scrimmage against the South Bend Athletic Team that was termed "very discouraging" by *The Scholastic*. Worse, the ND line was in tatters and scrubs were quitting left and right. *The Scholastic* implored any and all able-bodied students to sacrifice themselves for dear old alma mater: "The Varsity needs plenty of practice during the coming week for the Michigan game, and it is up to you, fellows, to see that they get it." Old coach James McWeeney, now the South Bend chief of police, even helped out that week by lining up with the scrubs.

Michigan had no such manpower concerns. This was Fielding Yost's second Point-A-Minute team, and already it had posted four blowout victories: 88–0 over Albion, 48–6 over Case, 119–0 over Michigan Agricultural, and 60–0 over Indiana.

Notre Dame was supposed to be the fifth foe to lay over and die, but thanks largely to the brilliant play and leadership of fullback Louis (Red) Salmon, the Notre Damers knocked a huge fright into the Wolverines before finally succumbing 23–0 on the sawdust-covered, gummy clay at Armory Park.

Again, the heavens chose to rain down, rather than smile down, prior to a Michigan–Notre Dame game. But perhaps it was fitting that the Wolverines and Notre Damers made like mudhens in their lone visit to Toledo. End runs and speed plays were almost useless, thus both teams resorted almost exclusively to bucking between the tackles. The perpetual pounding made for a markedly rough game.

Typically, the Wolverines took a quick lead, mashing the ND line until tackle Joseph Maddock carried over for the score. That was five points in eight minutes—not quite worthy of Michigan's new nickname, but apparently an indication that another binge had begun for the Point-A-Minute team.

"The never-say-die spirit of Notre Dame, however, came to the rescue," *The Scholastic* reported, "and our fellows went into the fight determined to stave off defeat from their beloved colors until they dropped."

For the rest of the half, Salmon and Co. dazzled the 1,700 or so pigskin neophytes who braved the damp weather. Once the Notre Damers took possession at midfield, they smashed their way toward the Michigan goal. Salmon, who as a freshman in the 1900 game had clearly established his potential, was now a bona fide star. He was said to be the greatest plunging back in the West and was proving it on this drive. Only occasionally did he need to be spelled.

It was amazing, really, what Notre Dame was doing here. The ND linemen were short on size and experience, yet they were knocking the Michigan veterans off the line. And if there was no hole to be found, too bad—Salmon crashed ahead for positive gains anyway.

Push came to shove when Notre Dame advanced to the Michigan 10-yard line. Salmon bulled for four, then was stopped for no gain. On third down he slipped and was stacked up right there at the six-yard line. End of drive, Michigan's ball.

The Notre Damers kept fighting, though, and matched the Wolverines bruising block for bruising block, crushing tackle for crushing tackle. The ball seldom left Michigan's side of the field, and the shocked Wolverines had to content themselves with only a 5–0 lead at intermission.

As the second 25-minute half progressed, the Wolverines' talent, size advantage, superior conditioning, and experience began to take an ever-greater toll. Michigan's star halfbacks, Willie Heston and Al Herrnstein, also started ripping off huge gains. Heston, who possessed world-class speed and had elusive moves to boot, is considered one of the game's all-time great running backs. The NCAA credits him with having scored 71 touchdowns from 1901 to 1904, though some sources give him as many as 110. The first two-time All-America from the West, Heston claimed the correct figure was 92.

Earlier in the game, the great Heston had been largely offset by the great Salmon—Notre Dame's first All-American, albeit as a third-teamer. Salmon was as fierce a tackler as he was a runner, and he repeatedly stopped Heston's dashes as few defenders ever did. "When Red hit 'em, they stayed hit and were mighty slow getting up," remembered spectator Aaron B. Cohn 50 years later.

Still, Heston and Herrnstein avoided Salmon often enough to set up three Wolverine touchdowns in the second half—two more from Maddock and one from fullback Paul Jones.

On the other side of the ball, the Wolverines also gradually dismantled the ND attack. Salmon never got as close to the Michigan goal as he did on Notre Dame's memorable charge in the first half. But Salmon was utterly exhausted—and woozy. He was knocked out no less than four times during this game, so it's amazing he was able to accomplish all he did.

The 23–0 final score shocked the pundits and thrilled the ND supporters. McWeeney, the old coach, had been the most optimistic of Notre Dame prognosticators, believing the best the Notre Damers could do was hold the Wolverines to five touchdowns (30 points, if all converted). Most others had conceded that Notre Dame's only hope was to hold the score below 60.

The fact that Notre Dame almost made a touchdown was another great accomplishment. Scoring on Michigan was almost unheard of during the Point-A-Minute reign, considering the Wolverines shut out 50 of 55 opponents from 1901 to 1905, and that each of Michigan's 11 foes in 1901 failed even to advance the ball inside the Wolverines' 35-yard line, let alone score.

"Our plucky lads put up the grandest and most magnificent struggle that has ever taken place on any gridiron in the West," boasted *The Scholastic*. ". . . The memory of their glorious achievement shall live as long as the Gold and Blue floats across the gridiron at Notre Dame."

Yost also did not soon forget the "fight" in the "Irish," but for other reasons. He felt the Notre Damers had gone beyond the realm of good sportsmanship in their dogged efforts to conquer his Wolverines.

This was the fierce, if not irrational, competitor coming out in Yost. Two things particularly rankled him. First, he was legitimately upset over some defensive chicanery employed by ND. Secondly, he accused Notre Dame's players of slugging Michigan's on several occasions, although the only player ejected on that account was a Michigan man.

The first matter centered on the centers. Yost was perturbed that Don O'Malley, Notre Dame's defensive center (noseguard in today's terminology), was interfering with Dan Gregory's snap—that is, slapping the ball as Gregory passed it to the Michigan quarterback. It was an old ploy that was now strictly forbidden. Yost spotted the infraction four times in the first half and complained to the officials, and they proceeded to penalize Notre Dame twice in the second half before O'Malley stopped the illegal practice.

As for the second matter, punching—or "slugging" as the football-ists called it—had long since been outlawed. The game was brutal enough without fisticuffs.

To get an idea of just how horrific the sport was before 1906, when the forward pass was legalized, consider that several Americans every year actually died from head injuries sustained on the football field, and hundreds more were seriously injured. Secondly, games were up to 10 minutes longer. (The rules stipulated two 35-minute halves, but when both teams agreed the length could be shortened considerably.) What's more, players usually stayed on the field the entire game (they went both ways, and there were few substitutions), and play after punishing play consisted of a tightly massed offense crashing into a stacked-up defense. Today, it would be like the same 22 men taking turns playing goal-line offense, for the equivalent of up to nearly five quarters, with optional, flimsy leather helmets, optional rubber nose-guards, and padded clothing as the only protective equipment. Brutal, indeed.

By all accounts, this game was particularly rough. Not only was Salmon knocked groggy throughout, but among all the other casual-ties, Michigan's Herrnstein finished the game with deep gashes around his eyes and his face a bloody mess. The only player ejected for slug-ging in all the mayhem was Michigan left end Curtis Redden, after he was caught striking Notre Dame's Frank (Happy) Lonergan. Yost and Redden were especially unhappy that Happy was not found to be more at fault.

Reports conflict as to which team was the more savage. The *Detroit News* said Notre Dame "was repeatedly caught and penalized" for rough play. Conversely, Salmon offered this version to the *Toledo Blade:* "The game was fairly free from slugging, although Michigan offended in that respect once or twice. I do not think we were given any the best of the umpiring." Suffice to say, both sides were guilty to some extent.

While these incidents left the Wolverines coach embittered, the turnout was what left the Michigan athletic director bothered.

"The attendance was not as large as I had anticipated," Baird said. "It was thought the people of Toledo were anxious to see college football, and for that reason the game was played here. I am not able to state now whether we will bring a game here next season."

Michigan did not. And has not since.

A lasting first impression

Months later, Fielding Yost was no less upset about the events in Toledo. And that didn't bode well for future football relations between Michigan and Notre Dame.

Yost had the biggest say in who Michigan played, even though Charles Baird now enjoyed both tenure and renown as one of the leading athletic figures in the West. In Baird's early days he consulted prominent alumni on scheduling, while the football coach was basically just an employee answerable to Baird and the Board in Control. That all changed with Yost's arrival. So when it came time to draw up Michigan's 1903 schedule, Baird had to consult the coach.

That Michigan did not strike up negotiations with Notre Dame might seem to indicate a Yost edict had been issued, but this circumstance was not unusual. Heavyweights such as Michigan rarely pursued games against the lightweights, as Notre Dame was still regarded. If the challengers wanted a fight, they usually had to come begging. Every December and January, Michigan was being deluged with such requests.

But for some reason or other, Notre Dame was late in arranging its 1903 football schedule. Not until March 13 did Byrne M. Daly, manager of the Notre Dame Athletic Association, write Baird as to "the possibilities for meeting Michigan in the coming season." He indicated Notre Dame was "willing to accept the same agreements as last season"—namely, a guarantee of $400. By then, however, the only dates Michigan had left to fill on its 12-game slate were October 10 and 24. Daly was interested in securing either vacancy, so Baird sought Yost's approval for scheduling Notre Dame. He didn't get it, because in his next letter to Daly he cited Yost's concerns about ND's slugging and snap interference in the '02 game.

Daly then apparently requested a meeting to discuss the matter further, and in April he visited Albert Pattengill, chairman of Michigan's Board in Control. Pattengill outlined the specifics of Yost's complaints, and Daly left the meeting with the impression Notre Dame would be given scheduling consideration pending assurances that no such illegal practices would again take place.

Upon his return to Notre Dame, Daly launched an in-house investigation into the matter. On May 3 he finally wrote back to Baird, giving Notre Dame's viewpoint of the tangle while making a final request for a game:

Being away on a baseball trip, I was unable to write you before this, the outcome of my meeting with Mr. Pattengill, as promised. However, I trust it is not too late.

The most serious objection, I understand, was that of slugging. This matter I have taken with Salmon and he says that there was some during the game, but it was not Notre Dame men alone, and he recalled an attempt of one in the Michigan backfield to wrench his neck. I believe, Mr. Baird, that [your] Board was not fully informed, for I remember well that time in the game as I did not know whom we could play in Salmon's place.

Regarding other matter, I must acknowledge that one of our men was repeatedly guilty of that offense. But I feel assured that he will not commit same fault again.

I wish you would let me know what will be done in regard to [a] game, as I have held back scheduling until I come to a full understanding. Hoping to hear from you soon and thanking you for past favors, I remain,

Yours sincerely, Byrne M. Daly.

He was too late.

By April 6 Michigan had filled the October 10 date with Beloit, and on April 21—nearly two weeks before Daly wrote his final plea—the Michigan athletic board had approved Drake for the October 24 vacancy. Obviously, Michigan was not waiting with bated breath for Notre Dame's response.

Even had Daly written sooner, Michigan probably would not have scheduled Notre Dame. Daly's contention that Michigan was also guilty of foul play, although apparently quite true, would have cemented opposition from the self-righteous Yost.

The 1902 game was Yost's initial contact with Notre Dame. Based on his interpretation of both the events in Toledo and the scheduling impasse, he saw Notre Dame as an upstart school bent on winning, however unsavory the means.

It was a lasting first impression.

Best way out of a bad matter

The radical restructuring of college football in 1906 indirectly prompted Yost and Michigan to change their anti–Notre Dame stance.

The brutal nature of the game was meeting increased public outrage. The impetus for change came when President Theodore Roosevelt urged reforms that would open up the game and make it less violent. Accordingly, several drastic changes were enacted in 1906, the most significant of which were the legalization of the forward pass and the increase in yards needed for a first down to 10 from 5 (while keeping the number of downs at three).

More significant to this story, the Western Conference introduced a number of extreme administrative reforms that same year. Among the original proposals: (1) A mandatory one-year residency rule, which would effectively ban first-year players; (2) the reduction of an athlete's participation limit from four years to three, to be retroactive; (3) the elimination of the training table (team meals); (4) a severe reduction in the number of football games allowed, to five; and (5) a requirement that all coaches be regular members of the school's faculty.

Michigan reacted with great hostility to these proposals. It was alleged Amos Alonzo Stagg of Chicago was pushing through the coaching rule, as it would effectively bar his archrival Yost, who then devoted most of the year to his business ventures in the South (Yost resided in Ann Arbor only during the fall season and spring-practice sessions). What's more, Michigan was a strong advocate of both training tables and long schedules, and, worst of all, the retroactive feature of the three-year rule was seen as a means of dismantling Yost's Point-A-Minute machine, because it would deny several star Wolverines their fourth years.

The coaching rule was soon dropped, but the Big Nine passed all the other reforms. In 1906 Michigan ignored the retroactive feature of the three-year rule and, after the season, lobbied the conference to repeal this clause, on grounds that those who started their football careers before 1906 were entitled to four years. Michigan also tried to reinstate the training table and raise the schedule limit. By a narrow margin, however, Big Nine schools voted in favor of retaining all of these legislations. After another year of fighting in vain to repeal them, Michigan withdrew from the Western Conference on January 13, 1908. The Michigan faculty generally opposed the move, but students and alumni, likely spurred on by coach Yost, were decidedly in favor.

In the meantime, Michigan was being boycotted on the football field by conference schools for not subscribing to all league regulations. Only Illinois played the Wolverines in 1906, and as of spring 1907 Michigan had no Big Nine teams lined up for either that year or 1908. The Wolverines thus began to look east for big games, while nonconference schools in the Midwest—especially Notre Dame—suddenly became far more attractive opponents.

So it wasn't that Michigan wanted to resume relations with Notre Dame as much as it felt it had to. The Wolverine baseball team was even ending a seven-year break with Notre Dame for the same reason, as the *Ann Arbor Daily Times News* explained in retrospect in 1910: "The Wolverines had to do something for a game that would attract some interest, and the game with Notre Dame was scheduled as the best way out of a bad matter."

Though Michigan tentatively approved a football contest with Notre Dame for October 19, 1907, at Ann Arbor, it was never played. Nowhere in the athletic archives at both schools, and in all the relevant newspapers, can a definite explanation be found. It's likely, however, that Michigan dropped Notre Dame so it could play Wabash in Indianapolis on the same date, for an astounding $10,000 guarantee.

In 1908, Michigan negotiated and followed through with a game against Notre Dame, on October 17 at Ann Arbor.

VIII. Time was on Michigan's side, '08

After this game, it was clear a number of patterns had emerged in this series.

Notre Dame would be abundantly confident beforehand, match up surprisingly well, but would make ruinous mistakes and pay dearly for them. As well, controversy would swirl, the field would be a mess, and—oh, yes—Michigan would win.

The Wolverines escaped with a 12–6 victory this time, before about 4,000 fans at Michigan's two-year-old stadium on Ferry Field. Notre Dame dominated play, scoring the only touchdown while preventing Michigan from ever advancing past the ND 20-yard line. Man for man, Notre Dame was the superior team—except in the kicking department. The Notre Damers had no answer for Dave (Pig) Allerdice, whose marvelous right leg booted Michigan to its eighth straight win in this series.

Allerdice needed to boot only three field goals to tally the 12 points because the value of a field goal was four points (its value had dropped in 1904, and would drop again to three in 1909).

Also unique about this game is that the first forward passes in series history were thrown. Because of its makeshift lineup, Michigan attempted "only the simplest" passes in its arsenal, and, according to the *Detroit News-Tribune,* "the Catholics managed to spoil every one." Meanwhile, Notre Dame completed all three of its passes, but each went for less than 10 yards.

Notre Dame was enjoying one of its best seasons to date in 1908. Six starters returned from the undefeated '07 team, and the new talent was proving to be even better than the departed. ND didn't allow a touchdown all year, and this was its only loss. In fact this was Notre Dame's only defeat in a stretch of 27 games from 1906 to 1910.

That this Wolverines team pulled the trick was astonishing because it was one of Fielding Yost's worst at Michigan. It struggled desperately to go 5–2–1, and the two losses were ugly. The Point-A-Minute days were but a distant memory now. Already short on talent, the Wolverines lost two starters in the days leading up to the game, and a few hours before kickoff, captain Adolph (Germany) Schulz—renowned as the game's greatest center of the era—was ruled scholastically ineligible. Thus, three Wolverines made their first career starts, and several regular starters were switched to new positions. It's no wonder, then, that confidence was not radiating from Ann Arbor.

The play of the day actually occurred just before kickoff. Yost, knowing his team could not stay with the Notre Damers for the requisite 70 minutes, asked ND coach Victor Place if he'd be willing to play 25-minute halves instead of 35. Place, an All-American at Dartmouth in 1904, reluctantly agreed—a decision he would later regret.

Yost then must have served up one of his demonstrative pregame pleas, because the Wolverines came out in a fit of fury and got the early, crucial jump. On their first possession they smashed their way down to the ND 35-yard-line, where Allerdice dropped back and nailed a field goal from placement. With four minutes having elapsed, Michigan led 4–0.

Michigan kept pressing. Allerdice missed a field goal snapped from 40 yards out, but on Michigan's next possession he nailed one from 20. So with only 11 minutes gone, Michigan led 8–0.

The Notre Damers clearly were lethargic, either because they were over-confident (if you believe *The Michigan Daily*) or just plain nervous (according to *The Scholastic*). Whatever the reason, ND shook off the doldrums and played Michigan to a standstill the rest of the half.

After the intermission Notre Dame totally dominated play. Quarterback Don Hamilton, who called and played a masterful game, found the weak spot in the Michigan line, the right side, and continually attacked it.

With about 10 minutes remaining, Notre Dame left half Paul McDonald busted free around right end and dashed anywhere from 40 to 85 yards (reports vary) for a touchdown. But an official called it back, ruling that a footprint at the Michigan 30-yard line—only two inches out of bounds—belonged to McDonald. "But it was not McDonald who touched the sideline," halfback Harry (Red) Miller remembered. "It was I, who ran along with McDonald a little behind and between him and the sideline. He veered in without having crossed the line. The official was mistaken."

After gaining 10 yards down to the 20, Notre Dame went for a field goal, but Hamilton's attempt failed. With time running out, the Notre Damers were in danger of being shut out for the fifth straight time by the Wolverines. What did they have to do to ever score again on Michigan?

Precisely this.

After Hamilton returned an Allerdice punt to the Wolverine 50 (it was a 110-yard field in those days), Notre Dame fullback Pete Vaughan scooted around Michigan left end Bill Embs, juked several other tacklers, and burst downfield. At the 30 Vaughan was briefly brought to the turf by Michigan's Billy Wasmund and Allerdice, but Notre Dame's Miller, Sam (Rosey) Dolan, and quarterback Hamilton instantly jerked him to his feet. Some of the Wolverines stopped, thinking the play was dead, but Vaughan continued across the Michigan goal. Referee Ralph Hoagland ruled Vaughan's momentum had not been properly stopped (back then, tackling a ball carrier to the ground was not enough), and he allowed the touchdown. It was just as dazzling a run as Notre Dame's first and only other touchdown run against Michigan—Harry Jewett's landmark score in the first game of 1888.

Wasmund protested, as did Yost afterward, that Vaughan should have been whistled down, to no avail. Hamilton's conversion kick was perfect, and ND now trailed 8–6.

In the final minutes the Notre Damers continued to push the Wolverines around, but Michigan's saving grace—as it had been throughout the second half—was Allerdice. The fleet halfback was as brilliant a punter as he was a placekicker, and he continually booted ND back when drive after Michigan drive stalled.

Allerdice sealed the victory shortly after pinning the Notre Damers back to their 25. Fay Wood shanked a return punt only nine yards, and

Wolverine halfback Prentiss Douglas signaled for a "free" catch at the 34. There, Michigan had the option of beginning a drive or attempting a free placekick. With Allerdice on the field there was no deliberation. His field goal attempt was good, and Michigan led 12–6 with two minutes left. The Wolverines took the ensuing kickoff (scoring teams had the option of getting the ball back) and ran out the clock.

For the umpteenth time, Yost's reliance on the kicking game had paid off. Yost felt he could beat anyone with a great kicker, as he stole many a game from foes who had the edge in manpower. "I believe that I can trace the play-by-play of nearly every football game and show where the turning point may be found in some kicked ball," he once observed.

Place, the ND coach, was kicking himself afterward. Chopping 20 minutes off the length of the game had greatly aided the Wolverine cause. "We had the condition on Yost's men," he grumbled afterward, "and if I had insisted on 35-minute halves instead of giving in to Yost's request for 25-minute halves, we would have cleaned up on them. Allerdice should never have had the chance to win the game with his kicks. . . . Michigan hasn't any backfield—that's a cinch—and she hasn't any line. We should have beaten Michigan. Yost can consider himself lucky."

And that he did.

"I think that Michigan was mighty fortunate because when I learned that Schulz would be out of it, I confidently expected Notre Dame to win," Yost said. "But I am well satisfied with the showing the men made, considering the fact that the 11 players had never run through signal practice together before they appeared at Ferry Field today."

Any Notre Dame players hoping to exact revenge next year were lucky, too—lucky that Yost had no complaints about the play of the Notre Damers, as he did after the 1902 game. "My men unite with me in saying it was one of the cleanest battles they ever fought in," Yost said.

Thus, there was no reason for Michigan to not sign up Notre Dame for a return encounter in 1909.

Disintegration: 1909–10

IX. Red-letter day, '09

Eleven fighting Irishmen wrecked the Yost machine this afternoon. These sons of Erin, individually and collectively representing the University of Notre Dame, not only beat the Michigan team, but they dashed some of Michigan's fondest hopes and shattered Michigan's fairest dreams.

With that flowery lead, E.A. Batchelor of the *Detroit Free Press* popularized a moniker Notre Dame teams would later come to embrace—and aptly summed up the greatest athletic achievement to that point in Notre Dame history.

At long last, the "Fighting Irish" recorded their first victory over the Wolverines, by a score of 11–3 on November 6, 1909. The fact it came against one of Fielding Yost's greatest teams, and was a ruinous loss for him and Michigan, made it all the sweeter for Notre Dame.

For what must have seemed like forever, Notre Dame had the midwestern summit plainly within view, but eight previous swipes could not topple the well-perched Wolverines. This year, a direct hit was scored by these 11 fighting Irishmen: linemen Howard (Cap) Edwards, George Philbrook, Ed Lynch, Sam (Rosey) Dolan, and Ralph Dimmick; ends Lee Matthews and Joe Collins; halfbacks Harry (Red) Miller and Billy Ryan; fullback Pete Vaughan; and quarterback Don Hamilton.

Ironically, it took a former Wolverine to ensure the victor wasn't Mich-again. Frank (Shorty) Longman, a fullback on Yost's Point-A-Minute teams of 1903–05, was Notre Dame's new, roughneck coach. He knew how to beat the master. And he had the players to do it, as most of the previous year's squad returned.

For eight weeks Longman had been carefully preparing his players for this day. The Irish were 4–0 when they arrived in Ann Arbor, having defeated Olivet, Rose Poly, and Michigan Agricultural College before raising a lot of eyebrows back East a week earlier with a 6–0 win at Pittsburgh.

Michigan assistant coach Prentiss Douglass had scouted the Pitt game and came away impressed with Notre Dame, especially with its offense, but he still was of the opinion the Wolverines were two touchdowns better.

That's exactly what Longman was hoping for. He had tricked the Michigan scout by not using any of his pet pass plays—short ones over the line—and by virtually ignoring halfback Red Miller, upon whom he would depend so much against Michigan. Longman's deception didn't end there. He had sent out "bear stories" (ruses) all week about how battered and listless his players were in their preparations for Michigan, and he told the *South Bend Tribune* that Notre Dame didn't scrimmage once on account of player shortages.

Longman was just borrowing from the master's playbook here. He wanted to beat Michigan as badly as did any Notre Dame player, because none of Yost's Wolverines had ever come back to beat the old man as coach of another team. Dan McGugin at Vanderbilt and Al Herrnstein at Ohio State had come close, and many others who got their jobs at Yost's referral craved the opportunity. But Longman knew he had a great shot, and he pulled out all the stops to make history.

The master was not entirely fooled by the pupil's ruses, however. The Michigan varsity worked heavily on defensive play all week in preparation for the vaunted Irish offense. Yost had originally viewed Notre Dame as just a tough tune-up for Michigan's final two opponents, mighty Penn and eventual Western Conference champion Minnesota. But he was now wary of the Irish threat. "We've got to work as we have never worked before," he told the *Ann Arbor Daily Times News.* "Notre Dame is coming up here Saturday with a bunch of men that have had more football experience than any of the players on our team. They are almighty strong. Saturday's contest will be as hard as either the Pennsylvania or Minnesota games."

The Wolverines had beaten Case, Ohio State, and Marquette before traveling to Syracuse the day Notre Dame was in Pittsburgh. The Orangemen were supposed to have presented a stiff challenge, but Michigan surprised the eastern folk by crushing Syracuse 44–0. That spawned comparisons of these Wolverines to their Point-A-Minute predecessors.

Because of each team's showing thus far, this was the first Michigan–Notre Dame game to arouse national interest. Walter Eckersall of the *Chicago Tribune,* considered the leading expert on western football, rated the game as not only the day's most important in the West, but on equal footing nationally with the Dartmouth-Princeton clash. The fact legendary Walter Camp chose to attend—among several other prominent eastern experts—was proof positive Notre Dame–Michigan had truly arrived.

Among the 6,000 fans at Ferry Field, hundreds were rooting for the

Fighting Irish, even though an official excursion by Notre Dame students was canceled the day before. Back at Notre Dame, telegraph returns were read to the mass of pupils that had gathered on the campus gridiron.

Shortly after two o'clock, the teams rushed onto—get this—a dry, sun-swept field. Perhaps that old Ann Arbor jinx Notre Dame used to grumble about was actually secreted somewhere behind the rain clouds of autumn, because such was nowhere to be found on this beautiful day.

Early in the first half, though, Michigan again was raining on Notre Dame's parade.

After the Irish marched to the Michigan 20, Billy Ryan's 30-yard field goal attempt from placement was blocked, and Wolverine end Stan Borleske fell on the ball. Several possessions later, Michigan right halfback Dave Allerdice threw up the first of only two forward passes attempted by the Wolverines this day, and Ryan intercepted for Notre Dame—but right away he fumbled and Borleske recovered on the Notre Dame 20. One play later, Allerdice drilled a field goal from placement snapped from 20 yards out, and Michigan led 3–0 with 18 minutes having elapsed.

"Notre Dame was suffering from stage fright," wrote Harold Titus of the *Detroit News-Tribune.* "But it didn't take long for this scare to lose itself in the heat of the contest. Edwards, the big captain-tackle, pleaded. And his team responded."

Especially Red Miller.

The speedy halfback snared momentum for Notre Dame after fielding a Dave Allerdice punt. "Miller was racing along, right down the sidelines," wrote Titus. "A Michigan man dove and missed his flying legs. Another grabbed at his waist and was shaken off. But Borleske was coming. It was a long, sensational dive—over five yards—and his right shoulder crashed into the Notre Dame man's knees." Borleske, Michigan's sensational left end, made the tackle but did not get up. With the crowd shouting his name in unison, Borleske was eventually helped off the field, his collarbone broken and his season finished. Jamie (Okie) Rogers, a little-used sub, took Borleske's place at left end. The Irish correctly smelled a weak spot.

With about 10 minutes left in the first half, it was Miller time again. The redhead put on one of the most spectacular individual displays in series history by almost single-handedly marching the Irish from midfield down to the Michigan two-yard line. "Quarterback Hamilton had me carry the ball about 10 successive times," Miller remembered, "which almost exhausted me and forced me to beg him not to do it again."

Hamilton obliged and called on Pete Vaughan to finish off the drive. Two line smashes bent the Michigan forward wall ever so slightly, Vaughan bringing the ball to within inches of the Wolverine goal— with third and final down coming up. (They had three downs to gain 10 yards at that time.)

"Six thousand people were silent," Titus wrote. "Up in the bleachers, Hamilton's voice could be heard, snapping out the signals." Vaughan again got the call, and he charged toward the right wing before disappearing under a heap of bodies stacked around one of the goalposts. Did he make it? No one could immediately tell.

"Then the players disentangled themselves," Titus continued. "They stood up in a close circle and none but they could see where the ball had stopped. Referee [Ralph] Hoagland elbowed his way through the panting, padded players.

"A Notre Dame sub was holding Longman. The Notre Dame coach had thrown aside his coat. His hat, crumpled and broken, laid somewhere on the sidelines.

"Then the knot of players gave way. Yelling, dancing like madmen, the Notre Dame players ran down the field. [Vaughan] laid with his back on the goal line and hugged the ball to his chest. And the ball was across the chalk mark."

Touchdown!

Legends grow with time, and for years thereafter, Notre Dame freshmen were annually regaled with the story of how Pete Vaughan hit the Michigan line so hard, the goalpost left an imprint on his jersey. It wasn't long before it was the story of how Pete Vaughan not only knocked over the goalpost, but did so with his head. Day-after newspaper accounts mention nothing of the kind.

Ryan's conversion was off the mark, so Notre Dame led 5–3 with a few minutes left before half.

When Michigan finally secured possession again, it had time to run only two plays, the last of which was a lame pass from Allerdice that Lee Matthews intercepted.

The fired-up Irish stormed off the field, having completely dominated play. The short passes were befuddling the Wolverines, and the end runs were killing them. As near as can be deduced from newspaper play-by-play accounts, the Irish amassed almost 200 total yards to Michigan's 45. If it hadn't been for two missed field goals the Irish would have been comfortably ahead.

No one need guess what fiery orations Yost and Longman—perhaps the fiercest orators in football—peppered their players with at halftime. Titus's *Detroit News-Tribune* account provides the details:

Yost hurried his men to the field house and there, mounted on a bench, roared at them while [trainer] Keene Fitzpatrick went over their steaming bodies.

"Git 'em low, I tell you. Git 'em low! Fight, fight, FIGHT!," Yost roared, shouted, emphasizing his words with extravagant gestures. And out on the field Longman was talking to his men.

"You've got only 35 minutes more, boys!," the photographers heard him say. "You've got 'em beat. It's Michigan you're playin'—Michigan. Yost's team. Now be good boys and hold 'em. Think of it! The chance of a life-time! Yost—Fielding Yost, the man I played for. Can you understand?!"

They understood perfectly. According to one treasured tidbit of Notre Dame folklore, a player stood up and pleaded, "What's the matter with you guys? You're all Irish and you're not fighting worth a lick." Some writers eavesdropping along with the photographers jotted down the expression, and that's likely how E.A. Batchelor of the *Detroit Free Press* got the idea for the term "fighting Irishmen."

To be sure, the Irish would have to fight like hell to hold on to their 5–3 lead in the second half. Longman instructed quarterback Ham-ilton to play more conservatively, forgoing the passing game and limiting the number of end runs.

Meanwhile, Yost decided to utilize the great Allerdice to maximum effect. Throughout Yost's 25 years as Wolverine coach, he loved to employ his coveted "kicking game"—a strategy of patience, defense, and opportunism.

The idea was this: By punting the ball away immediately, and forc-ing the other team and its weaker punter to boot it back right away, Michigan would gradually gain yardage on the exchanges until the foe was pinned deep in its own end. The Wolverines would keep trading kicks until the opponent inevitably coughed up the ball (it was Yost's belief, and experience, that any team eventually buckles under the pressure of constantly playing in the shadow of its own goalposts). Then the Wolverines would discard the ultraconservative approach for the other extreme, uncorking a wide and wide-open variety of trick scoring plays. And because the Yostmen would have been conserving their offensive energy, they'd be fresher than their opponents and more likely to convert the miscue into points.

This "kicking game" was boring to watch but greatly effective through-out Yost's career. He ordered his quarterback, Billy Wasmund, to em-ploy it in the second half. (Sending in or signaling plays from the sideline was not allowed, so coaches relied entirely on their quarter-backs to carry out their plans).

Of course, the Yost strategy would fail if the Michigan defense could not stop the Irish. But in the second half the Wolverines, so thoroughly shredded in the first 35 minutes, stiffened. Notre Dame was able to pick up only the odd first down before punting. Michigan booted the ball back almost exclusively on first down, and gained a little better field position each time—exactly as designed.

Yost's strategy appeared to pay off with about six minutes remaining and Notre Dame still leading 5–3. After Red Miller returned Allerdice's 11th punt of the half to the Irish 25, Ryan fumbled a pitchout from quarterback Hamilton. Albert Benbrook, Michigan's towering All-America guard who played a magnificent game, recovered at the 15-yard line.

The Yostmen had their break.

On first down, left halfback Joe Magidsohn crashed off Philbrook for three. Then Magidsohn slashed for six. That brought up third and one on the six, the ball directly in front of the goalposts.

What to do: go for the first down, or attempt the go-ahead field goal now? The Notre Dame players appeared exhausted, having burned so much more energy in running off so many more offensive plays than Michigan—about 60 to Michigan's 20. A gain of one measly yard would give the Wolverines three cracks at a touchdown from within the five-yard line.

"The Michigan rooters saw victory," Titus wrote. "The big bleachers shook as thousands of feet stamped on the heavy planking. Down on the field, the Michigan men were holding a consultation."

Quarterback Wasmund was discussing options with Benbrook, Allerdice, and veteran tackle Bill Casey. Wasmund suggested they go for it by crashing Magidsohn into the line again. Benbrook and Casey were hesitant, not entirely sure they could whip the Irish linemen on this most crucial play. Allerdice then suggested they go for the sure field goal (he was accurate up to 45 yards). And that's what quarterback Wasmund called—much to the outrage of Yost and most of the spectators, as a converted touchdown would have given Michigan a 9–5 lead, instead of 6–5 with a field goal, and thereby forced Notre Dame to come back and score a touchdown to win.

"But Wasmund dropped back," Titus continued. "Carefully, he patted down the grass. The men on secondary defense poised themselves carefully."

Red Miller picks it up: "I was near the end of the line next to right tackle Ralph Dimmick. I glanced along our line. It was a thrilling tableau. There each man was set, like a tiger about to spring, his body taut, his face grim, his lips drawn back, his teeth flashing, a picture of power and determination. Confidence took possession of me. It was deadly quiet. Then suddenly it was broken. "We're going through!" someone called loudly in a hard, harsh voice I hardly recognized. It was my own."

Michigan's James Watkins, playing in his first and last game at center, snapped the ball back. It was low. Wasmund scrambled to place the ball down properly, while Allerdice swung his mighty right leg into the pigskin.

Thud! Half the Notre Dame line shot through and blocked the kick. The ball bounded all the way back to the Notre Dame 40, where Rosey Dolan fell on it for the Irish.

Just like that, all the fumbles, foibles, and follies that had so plagued Notre Dame in this series were suddenly thrown back in Michigan's face—with equal collective measure.

The Wolverines were dumbfounded. The Irish and their fans went berserk, as Notre Dame not only thwarted what might well have been the game-winning kick, but instantly had great field position with only five minutes left. Barring a turnover, there was little chance Michigan would again get so close to the Irish goal.

The Wolverines' next possession began at their 40 and, astonishingly, they did not open up their offensive arsenal. But Wasmund may have been under instruction not to use any trick pass plays, as Yost had wanted to save them for Penn and Minnesota, whose scouts were surely on hand. The one and only gamble Michigan tried backfired when Allerdice attempted an on-side punt (punts were live balls then, and this was a common means of gaining big chunks of yardage), because the ball was caught by Notre Dame's Billy Ryan, who returned it 18 yards to midfield.

Later, Ryan exorcized the last of the Wolverine demons, recovering a bouncing Notre Dame punt at the Michigan 30-yard line with only a minute or so remaining. On the next play, Ryan broke free around right end, eluded Joy Miller and two other Wolverines, and went the distance for a game-icing touchdown. Converting from placement was—who else?—Ryan.

Final score: Notre Dame 11, Michigan 3.

Kid brother had finally got the best of big brother.

While the disconsolate Michigan faithful sang along with the band as it played the school alma mater, "The Yellow and Blue," the Notre Dame partisans screamed with delight as the subs hoisted the 11 stalwart fighting Irishmen onto their shoulders and carried them off the field. Longman, Titus reported, was "bereft of his senses."

So was everybody back at Notre Dame. The students who gathered at Cartier Field went crazy when the last cable was received. They put on a huge bonfire that night, as school officials and students alike woke up the echoes.

There were plenty of heroes to honor in Notre Dame's titanic victory, including backs Billy Ryan and Pete Vaughan—and linemen Rosey Dolan, George Philbrook, and Ralph Dimmick. But the play of Red Miller was on another level. His was considered the greatest one-man performance on a Michigan football field since the days of Willie Heston. When Miller wasn't shaking off tacklers around end, or tearing through the line, or dashing upfield on punt returns, or leveling Michigan defenders with devastating blocks, he was a demon on defense. "There hardly was a play in the whole game in which he was not the central figure," Batchelor wrote.

The Irish certainly were deserving of victory, even though the Wolverines' strategy almost paid off. But even had Michigan elected to go for broke on the biggest down of all, Longman was of the opinion the Wolverines would not have made it. "I don't think they could have gained an inch," said the Notre Dame coach, adding with his best Yost imitation, "If they had been given 10 downs in which to make a first down, they couldn't have succeeded. They were outplayed and they should have little complaint to make."

The Wolverines themselves did not complain—in fact Red Miller said he had never seen better sportsmen—but Wolverine partisans sure did. Quarterback Wasmund was not exactly the most popular man in Ann Arbor afterward. Allerdice, the captain, had to release a statement the following day in order to explain that the decision to kick the field goal was ultimately his, not Wasmund's.

Yost was perplexed and angered by that decision. "I don't know what Benbrook and Casey could have meant by advising a placekick when we had such a short distance to go for a touchdown and we had just made two good gains."

The Michigan coach took the defeat hard. His ego hadn't been jolted like this since Michigan's 2–0 loss to Chicago in 1905, which ended the Point-A-Minute era.

"What makes me so dag-goned mad is that we might have won the game," Yost moaned. "Those are the worst kind of games to lose. They leave a worm in a man's heart to gnaw and gnaw. Oh, I don't know. I'm sick and tired of the whole business; it certainly is discouraging. Although we were outplayed we should have won. I take my hat off to the Irishmen."

No doubt after a forced gulp, Yost even praised Red Miller in post-game interviews. "Wish I had one like him and good-bye Penn and

Gophers," he said. "Some of the sting of defeat was taken away by the pleasure of seeing that Hibernian tear 'em up and shake 'em off."

The next day, coach Longman and Miller paid the master a visit. "When Shorty Longman introduced me to Mr. Yost, who had been my [idol] for years, I was thrilled beyond measure and my heart was beating fast," Miller recalled.

But the volcano that was Yost's wounded pride suddenly erupted.

"To my utter amazement and consternation, he greeted me by saying, 'Miller, you were guilty of the most unsportsmanlike conduct that I've ever seen in all my days.'"

The coach was upset with the way Miller had waited several times until the last possible moment before signaling for a fair catch of a Michigan punt. The Wolverines were penalized 15 yards each time for interference. The fair catches were perfectly legal, and Miller said the only reason he called for them was because the Michigan ends had been creaming him the instant he had caught Allerdice's high-sailing kicks.

Miller was astounded by Yost's charge.

"I couldn't believe my ears. I was shocked. I don't believe I had ever done an unsportsmanlike act in my life. I could not speak for a few minutes. . . . I finally blurted, 'I really don't know what you're talking about.'

"'You do, too.'"

After arguing to no avail, Miller simply walked away.

"I was deeply wounded. I often wondered if he could be right, however illogical it might be. Of every official and coach I met thereafter I made inquiry as to whether or not it was unsportsmanlike to signal for a fair catch at the last moment under the circumstances, and invariably the answer was an emphatic 'no.' . . . Later in the light of more mature years I know he was absolutely wrong."

But at the time, Miller was devastated. Yost's accusation "spoiled the victory for me," he recalled.

Soon the Michigan coach would go to far greater lengths to spoil the victory for all Notre Dame people.

Who's No. 1?—'09

This is the story of how the West was won. How Notre Dame won it, not Michigan. How Michigan won it, not Notre Dame.

Huh?

Exactly.

The mythical "Championship of the West" was never more hotly disputed than after the 1909 season. Some experts picked Michigan. Some chose Notre Dame. Others were utterly baffled. *Collier's*—the nation's most popular weekly news magazine—termed the situation "extremely complex."

It had all seemed quite simple after Notre Dame's landmark win over Michigan on November 6, but from there it just got progressively convoluted.

A day after the victorious Irish returned home from Ann Arbor, Walter Eckersall of the *Chicago Tribune* annointed Notre Dame and Minnesota—which was crushing everybody in the Western Conference—as the best in the West. The vanquished Wolverines weren't even in the picture anymore. Eckersall lobbied for a postseason matchup of the Irish and Golden Gophers: a dream game for the western championship, provided, of course, each team remained undefeated and untied.

Minnesota, having mauled its five previous opponents by the combined score of 118–6, still had two teams to play: the ever-powerful Wisconsin Badgers, in the game to determine the conference champion, and the Michigan Wolverines. (The Gophers had ignored the conference boycott and signed the renegade Wolverines to a two-game, home-and-home series beginning in 1909.)

Notre Dame, having thrashed its five opponents 152–14, would finish up with Miami of Ohio, Wabash, and Marquette. Only the latter was seen as having any kind of chance against the Irish.

The dream Irish-Gophers matchup was no less appealing a week later. Minnesota pounded Wisconsin 34–6 to win the "Big Eight" title hands down, while Notre Dame spanked Miami 46–0.

But suddenly entering the discussion of western honors again was Michigan. The Wolverines bolted upright from the Notre Dame leveling to post a shocking 12–6 upset of previously unbeaten Pennsylvania in Philadelphia. It marked the first time a western team had ever knocked off one of the "Big Four" of the East (Yale, Harvard, Princeton, and Penn). The trick plays Fielding Yost had saved for the Quakers worked, and one—a long-bomb pass off a fake placekick—set up a score. Michigan's victory went a long way toward wiping out the sting of the Notre Dame loss.

Now Eckersall lumped Michigan with Minnesota and Notre Dame as a threesome in a class of its own in the West, although he said the Wolverines were as "erratic" as they were dangerous. Next week's Gophers-Wolverines tilt was seen as the game that would determine the western champion. If Minnesota won, it would get the nod. If Michigan won, Notre Dame—by virtue of its win in Ann Arbor—

would be the logical pick, so long as the Irish's record remained unblemished.

Yost, too, was of the opinion the Michigan-Minnesota game would determine western honors, but his equation did not include Notre Dame. "I am confident that we will give (Minnesota) a terrific battle for the championship of the West," he predicted.

That the Wolverines did. Michigan left the Minneapolis gridiron with a convincing 15–6 upset, having ripped the lauded Gopher line on both sides of the ball, and having stopped in its tracks the vaunted Minnesota shift.

Yost was the toast of the West again. Eckersall reported the Michigan mentor had outfoxed Minnesota's respected coach, Dr. Henry Williams, "at every stage of the game." Yost's pride swelled to Point-A-Minute proportions. Accordingly, he did his best to downplay Michigan's earlier defeat to Notre Dame—its only blight on a 6–1 season—while he gloated to reporters in Minneapolis. In fact Yost concocted a new, if not outrageous, version of events to try to win over the press.

"Of course we are champions," he said. "What else did we come up here for but to carry away a title? It is well enough to put Notre Dame in as a claimant, but that doesn't get the Hoosiers anything. They don't approach [Michigan or Minnesota] in eligibility rules. We took on the Indiana team because we needed work, and we got it all right. But as for any championship claim of Notre Dame, that doesn't go at all. There are men on the Notre Dame team who have played years beyond the recognized limit in the West, so that bars them. They have a good team down there, but you must recognize the fact that we went into that game caring little whether we won or lost. Practice was what we wanted."

No one will ever know how many newspapers were flung in outrage in Indiana the next day, but suffice to say Notre Dame partisans reacted with absolute abhorrence. To suggest Michigan had suffered a "slump" the day it played Notre Dame—as many experts were now maintaining—was one thing. But to contend that the Wolverines cared little whether they won or lost was deemed to be one of the most appalling cases of sour grapes ever exhibited. Yost's claim that Notre Dame suited up ineligible players was no less galling to them.

Besides, to the Fighting Irish way of thinking, how could Michigan have crept back into title contention? Notre Dame had beaten Michigan soundly in Ann Arbor—case closed. What's more, Michigan's victory over Minnesota effectively eliminated the Gophers from championship consideration, and Notre Dame had just destroyed Wabash 38–0. A Thanksgiving Day win over Marquette in Milwaukee four days hence would nail down the title for Notre Dame.

Most western critics sided with the Irish.

"Notre Dame must be considered the logical champion," Eckersall wrote, "because the Hoosiers defeated Michigan earlier in the season and the Wolverines in turn trounced Minnesota, the champions of the Western Conference." Yet he qualified that remark. "Coach Yost's players were not at their best when they met Notre Dame, and if the two teams were to meet next Saturday, Michigan in all probability would be the winner. However, results count, and Notre Dame should be given full credit."

Even the eastern snobs were beginning to take notice of the Irish. There was talk that efforts were now being made to pit Notre Dame against the runaway eastern champion, Yale, in a postseason tilt to decide the national championship. The Bulldogs had razed the East, going undefeated, untied, and unscored upon.

Then everything was thrown upside down.

Marquette, a team Michigan edged 6–5, proved no turkey on Thanksgiving by tying Notre Dame 0–0. The Irish could not overcome the loss of three stars to injury: guard Rosey Dolan, halfback Billy Ryan, and fullback Pete Vaughan.

Football authorities suddenly were reevaluating their western rankings, because Notre Dame's final record was blemished (7–0–1). And Yost was seeing to it that Notre Dame's reputation became likewise, thereby planting more seeds of critical reflection. "They will have to do some juggling to make the Indiana bunch champions of the West," Yost said upon learning of Notre Dame's tie. "Let them fight it out in the newspapers, y'know. We are satisfied. The games that counted, Michigan won."

Yost successfully chopped the Irish reputation down yet another notch after excluding all Notre Dame players from his all-western team. He included no fewer than six Wolverines. "I have eliminated Notre Dame from consideration altogether, though that team has some fine players," he explained. "My reasons for so doing are that the Longman team has so many men who are ineligible under college rules as accepted by the leading teams, that it is not properly to be classed with the others who observe stricter regulations.

"To my certain knowledge, Dolan, Miller, Dimmick, and Philbrook would be ineligible to compete at any of the conference colleges or at the University of Michigan, and there may be others. One of the men I have mentioned has played nine years of college football."

Yost's accusations, though unsubstantiated, were beginning to hold significant weight among the critics in the West, and back East. That cloud of suspicion, coupled with Notre Dame's tie, prompted the majority of writers to change their minds and award the western championship to Michigan.

Walter Camp, perhaps the foremost expert in the country, sided with the Wolverines (a team the eastern paragon had largely downtrodden in the past). "Michigan's showing is superior to that of Notre Dame, taking the whole season and the schedules of both into consideration," Camp wired the *Detroit News-Tribune.* Michigan supporters viewed Camp's All-America selections as another slap at Notre Dame, because the only Irish player he included was Red Miller, on the third team. Camp named four Wolverines: Albert Benbrook to the first team, Joe Magidsohn and Dave Allerdice to the second, and Bill Casey to the third.

Many other prominent authorities picked Michigan over Notre Dame too, including *Baseball Magazine,* a misnomer for one of the nation's leading all-sports publications.

Yet some experts refused to take the honor away from the undefeated Irish. Still others were completely confounded by the whole affair, including *Collier's.*

In the hope the western champion could be properly appointed once and for all, E.C. Patterson—*Collier's* noted authority on western football—traveled to Notre Dame on December 3 to investigate the charges laid by Yost. The *Chicago Tribune* subsequently reserved its judgment "while the hold of the Notre Dame football ship is being searched for contraband cargo."

In the Christmas issue, Patterson announced his findings after completing a "thorough" examination of Notre Dame's athletic policies and of the playing histories of five Irish players: Rosey Dolan, George Philbrook, Ralph Dimmick, and, although he didn't name these two, presumably Red Miller and Lee Matthews—all of whose names were popping up in the speculative stories.

With regard to Notre Dame's policies, Patterson learned that the school no longer was complying with two of the major Western Conference reforms introduced in 1906: namely, the one-year residency rule and the three-year limit of participation. Notre Dame had stopped complying in 1907, after again being denied entrance into the conference. That snub was about all Notre Dame could take. What was the point in continuing to suck up to the conference when all it caused was grief and, by subscribing to all the strict codes, a greater likelihood of losing? Thus, beginning in 1907 Notre Dame again allowed freshmen and four-year men to play. That's why the Irish were now being boycotted by all conference members.

So Yost was correct in his assertion that Notre Dame's rules were more lenient, because Michigan—nearly two years removed from the conference ranks—was still complying with the one-year residency and three-year limit rules. Michigan, however, was sticking to its guns in opposing the retroactive feature of the three-year rule, and thus was still granting a fourth year to those who had begun their college careers before 1906. The only Wolverine starter who fell into that category in 1909 was Billy Wasmund, and he was properly held out of the Minnesota game.

But while Notre Dame's rules may not have been as strict as Michigan's and the conference's, they were no more relaxed than those of many other western colleges and of almost all the eastern schools—including Yale, Harvard, and the like. Thus, Patterson found no unfair advantage here.

As for the five players in question, Patterson was given full access to Notre Dame records. He learned that Miller and Dolan were the only players in their fourth years at the school. Dimmick, Philbrook, and Matthews were in their second years. Nobody else had been at Notre Dame for more than three seasons. So what of Yost's claim that Notre Dame had men who had played "years beyond the recognized limit in the West?" That could only be true if some had played elsewhere before coming to Notre Dame.

Thus, Patterson also sought the previous playing histories of the five players. He took signed statements from each and did some digging of his own—and found nothing to support Yost's assertion. Among his findings:

Dolan played at Oregon Agricultural College in 1905. But he was a prep student that year, and Notre Dame did not count any years a student played elsewhere while taking preparatory courses. Therefore, Dolan had no previous college experience under Notre Dame rules and was eligible. It was later suggested that Dolan was the "nine-year man" Yost had been referring to, though Patterson found nothing to prove that contention.

Dimmick and Philbrook had both played previously at Whitman College in Walla Walla, Washington—in 1905 and 1906 as prep students, and in 1907 as college students. As Notre Dame did not count the prep years, this was the third year of competition for Dimmick and Philbrook.

Thus, the *Collier's* correspondent left Notre Dame satisfied the school was hiding nothing and thus was being unfairly criticized by Yost and others. "In view of the foregoing facts, and in fairness to all concerned, to the Notre Dame team must be conceded the championship of the West," Patterson ruled. He even named Dolan and Philbrook to his all-western team.

Such prominent backing exonerated Notre Dame to a large extent, and it gave the school as much right to the western championship as the backing of Camp and the others gave Michigan.

So the great debate was now a partisan issue as much as anything.

On that score, the students and townspeople in Ann Arbor and South Bend had no doubts as to who was No. 1. To say they were taking seriously their team's stake to the western title was the football understatement of the young century.

After Michigan had walloped Minnesota, Ann Arbor erupted in celebration as never before. Hundreds of ecstatic students and fans paraded the streets, firing guns into the air and—after a rally—lighting the sky with fireworks. For the first time in years, the most popular Michigan song was *The Victors. The Michigan Daily* honored the huge win with a banner headline, CHAMPIONS OF THE WEST.

South Bend was no less festive the day the Irish returned from their tie at Milwaukee. The largest celebration ever accorded a Notre Dame athletic team ensued. Nearly the entire student body met the boys at the South Bend train station and literally carried them all the way back to campus. The priests later joined in to pay homage at a rousing rally.

But as much as both sides reveled in self-indulgence, they found almost as much enjoyment in poking fun at each other. Reports that Notre Dame backers were indignant about Michigan's claim to the title "caused considerable laughter around Ann Arbor," the *Detroit News-Tribune* reported. And among all the derisions of Michigan in *The Scholastic* of Notre Dame, one poem by student George J. Finnigan deserves mention. He summed up Notre Dame's viewpoint in "Yost's 'Practice Game'":

> Oh, sportsmen, have you heard the dope?
>> It surely is a jest,
> For "Hurry Up" says Michigan
>> Is Champion of the West.
> He says he conquered every team
>> Excepting Notre Dame,
> And then he only took her on
>> To get a "practice game."
>> Ha! Ha!

> "I didn't care a bit," says Yost,
>> "If N.D. lost or won."
> Of course he don't recall his words
>> When that hard-fought game was done;

"I'm tired and all discouraged, and
   I'm sick of it." His fame
Had got a little jolting from
   That "work-out" "practice game."
         Ha! Ha!

Of course he don't recall his words,
   "It makes me dog-gonned mad
To think we might have won from them,"
   And others we might add,
"A game like that's the worst to lose,
   It sets one's heart aflame,
It leaves a worm to gnaw and gnaw,"
   Expensive "practice game."
         Ha! Ha!

So, men of sport, what think you now?
   Such action's small at best,
N.D. alone can rightly hold
   The prestige of the West.
She struggled hard, her slate is clean,
   The just respect her claim,
And Mr. Yost should not forget
   That dear-bought "practice game."
         Ha! Ha!

Nobody got the last laugh, however. Not Notre Dame. Not Michigan. The debate in the newspapers continued into the new year without it ever being properly resolved.

On January 17, the *Chicago Tribune* finally washed its hands of the entire, exhausting matter: "We have awarded the championship to the [7–0–1] Missouri Aggies, as a mollifying and compromise position. We trust this will be satisfactory; also that the incident may be regarded as closed."

Mucker spirit

It was but a few hours after Notre Dame's first win over Michigan in 1909.

Fighting Irish coach Frank (Shorty) Longman had been soaking up all the glory, and that didn't sit well with at least one Notre Dame player, who allegedly gruffed to a reporter: "Here we've been playing nine years, learning this game, and around comes Longman and takes credit for what we learned."

Nine years, you say?

That single comment became the talk of Ann Arbor. It prompted Fielding Yost's attacks against Notre Dame after the 1909 season, and those attacks, in turn, spawned one of the most controversial off-field incidents in college football history: the last-minute cancellation of the 1910 Michigan–Notre Dame game.

It was Michigan that called it off, 24 hours before the scheduled kickoff on Saturday, November 5, at Ferry Field. The Wolverines contended that at least two Fighting Irish players were ineligible under the rules of the game contract, and when Notre Dame refused to sit them out Michigan pulled the plug on the contest, and, as it turned out, on the series for the next 32 years.

Just who was right and who was wrong is almost impossible to ascertain, because the status of the disputed players rested on the vague and variant eligibility rules of the day. That each side devised interpretations to suit its position, then steadfastly defended that position, should come as no surprise. Nor should the explosions that followed.

Actually, the game was destined for disaster right from the start.

Sure, Notre Dame was as keen as ever to play Michigan again. And the Wolverine players, to a man, desperately wanted the chance to make amends for 1909. But the Michigan athletic authorities (namely, the Board in Control, new athletic director Phil Bartelme, and coach Yost) were prepared to break off football relations, for the same reasons all of the Western Conference schools were snubbing Notre Dame: (1) It did not subscribe to the strict conference eligibility rules; and (2), as one conference official once remarked, "It is no glory to beat you, but it is a disgrace to be beaten by you."

Michigan leaders finally decided to risk another disgrace, solely to allow the players a chance for retribution. But the approval would be conditional. Michigan would agree to the game only if Notre Dame was willing to play on Michigan's terms. The 1909 contract had not prevented the Irish from playing their freshmen and four-year men, and Michigan—with backing, if not active urging, from coach Yost—would insist that such players be barred this time.

But right before negotiations began, the stone thrower suddenly saw its own house turn to glass. In late December 1909, Michigan discovered that starting end Joy Miller had registered in the Engineering Department for the fall term but had not enrolled in any classes, and that he had duped the Board in Control by signing a false statement. The Engineering Department took full blame, claiming that because Miller had been a student at Michigan since 1906 the depart-

ment assumed he was properly enrolled. Miller was eventually expelled, but Michigan athletic officials wasted no time in alerting the
media and sending letters of apology to all schools against whom
Miller played in 1909.

A few days later, the *Chicago Record-Herald* further rocked the
Michigan boat by claiming the Wolverines had played three other
ineligibles in 1909. Michigan authorities doubted the allegations but
launched investigations into the backgrounds of these men straight
away.

Although none of the *Record-Herald* charges stuck, they and the
Miller incident were the source of much embarrassment to Michigan.
Just one short month before, the Wolverines had been publicly pointing the accusatory finger at Notre Dame when they themselves were
no model of purity.

Yet Michigan officials were able to save face, to a large degree, by
the swift, open, and decisive manner in which they tackled these
scandals. That's why they were able to enter into discussions with
Notre Dame without hat in hand.

After the two sides agreed to the November 5 date at Ann Arbor,
Bartelme dropped the bombshell on Notre Dame in his January 10
letter to graduate manager Harry Curtis:

> I am herewith enclosing contracts for our football game of next year,
> and in explanation of the terms of that contract would say that our Board
> in Control has insisted that the rules of eligibility which govern candidates
> for our teams shall be made a part of this contract. In the belief that your
> eligibility rules are very much like ours, I trust that you will find the rules
> herein, made a part of our contract, entirely satisfactory.

Notre Dame, of course, was taken aback by Bartelme's demand. The
Board of Control discussed the issue on January 15. "It was decided to
send manager Curtis to Michigan to try to secure terms reasonable
and fair to us," the board minutes read. "It was argued that Michigan,
reversing her policy so suddenly and without warning to us, had
placed us at a serious disadvantage this year."

Not only would the four-year men be barred, but so would any Notre
Dame freshmen. And Michigan was probably well aware the Irish
would need to rely on incoming talent to replace several departing
stars.

Two days later, Curtis entrained for Ann Arbor intent on securing
more "reasonable terms." Curtis met with Bartelme and his assistant,
Frank Ritchie, but Curtis hit a stone wall. Bartelme would not budge.

What transpired next at the meeting would be hotly disputed by both sides come autumn. After some discussion as to whether Notre Dame's star linemen, George Philbrook and Ralph Dimmick, would be deemed eligible under the contract, Curtis finally expressed his opinion that they indeed were "all right," and later maintained that Bartelme gave him verbal assurance that Michigan would not protest either man. Bartelme later emphatically denied Curtis's claim, because not only was it out of his jurisdiction to issue such a promise, but he said the whole point of playing under Michigan's rules was to bar players such as Dimmick and Philbrook.

Whatever was discussed, the contract was not changed in any way and Curtis signed it. The final hurdle was cleared on January 27, when the Michigan Board in Control formally ratified the contract.

In the meantime, Shorty Longman was retained as Notre Dame's coach. The ex-Wolverine made his permanent home in Ann Arbor, where he co-owned an automobile dealership. He had been a well-liked Ann Arborite since attaining Point-A-Minute stardom, but he had recently been estranging many of the townies by wantonly gloating about Notre Dame's victory over the Wolverines. The late Doug Roby, who played at Michigan in the early 1920s, remembered an old grouse about Longman parading around town his pet bulldog that wore a tiny jacket advertising the annoying 11–3 score.

Come spring, Longman was determined to add another score to the dog's jacket because the locals were now returning the insults. "Every day I have it rubbed in on me what they will do to us next year," Longman wrote to a Notre Dame friend on April 7, "but I know that from President Cavanaugh to Brother Bonnie we're going after them, and by Heck you know the rest."

Other than back-and-forth jabs such as these, a football rivalry seldom sees the hatreds roused in spring or summer. That was the last thing the Notre Dame–Michigan rivalry needed this year, but that's exactly what it got on June 4.

It happened in Ann Arbor, at a Michigan–Notre Dame baseball game. An outstanding pitchers' duel lasted 18 innings, with Michigan finally winning 3–2.

The controversy occurred in the 11th. When umpire Charles (Chief) Zimmer ruled a Michigan runner safe at first, the Notre Dame outfielders rushed the infield and joined their outraged teammates in crowding around Zimmer, protesting the call. Zimmer listened to the arguments, shook his head, and began walking back to the plate. Then Notre Dame right fielder Don Hamilton, the football team's starting quarterback, voiced his displeasure in profane terms. Zimmer instantly rushed Hamilton and slugged him once before players from both sides broke it up. The *Detroit News-Tribune* said Hamilton got in one punch and had to be literally dragged back to his post in right. Both benches emptied but no other punches were thrown.

The next day, managing editor Lee A. White of *The Michigan Daily* wrote an editorial that is likely the most scathing broadside ever fired at Notre Dame athletics. It shows Yost wasn't the only one in Ann Arbor who now had it in for Notre Dame. Under the heading "'Brass-knuckle' Athletics," White wrote:

> It's time to call quits with Notre Dame. There is no reason for evasion. The plain, blunt fact is that there is a limit to the amount of rowdyism that even a freelance university such as Michigan has to stand. The disgraceful demonstration of the Indiana athletes during yesterday's game is the climax of a long series of questionable acts, and common decency demands no less drastic action than a complete severance of all athletic relations with them. . . .
>
> Wouldn't it be interesting if a varsity debater were to be incensed at the decision of a judge, and should thereupon proceed to seek him out, call him by foul names, and start a slugging match?
>
> Were this a single instance of the coarseness of Notre Dame's athletes there would be little enough to say, but it isn't. The close observer of the conduct of that school's teams could cite you any number of like incidents; one dates but a year back, on the local diamond. Why does Michigan continue to give that institution character and prestige by putting up with her mucker spirit?
>
> And the worst of it is we have absolutely nothing to gain by the association that we have built up. We have known all along that despite chicken-hearted "investigations" Notre Dame is universally a supporter of "ringsters" and ineligibles such that she has absolutely no standing in respectable company. . . .

If that wasn't enough harm, another controversy dogged Notre Dame the very same day, in Urbana, Illinois.

The Irish concluded their outstanding 1909–10 athletic year by becoming the first nonconference school to win the I.C.A.A. western championship track meet. The Irish finished with 29 points, well ahead of Stanford (with 17), Chicago (13), Illinois (12), and California (12).

The star of the meet was none other than George Philbrook, the disputed guard on the Notre Dame football team. Philbrook won the shot put and discus events and placed third in high jump. He amassed more points, 11, than any other athlete in the meet. His old friend and fellow disputed lineman, Ralph Dimmick, took second place in the hammer throw and added three points to the Irish cause. So Notre Dame's West Coast connection, Dimmick and Philbrook, together amassed more points, 14, than every other team but Stanford.

But before the competitions had even started, a protest was filed against Dimmick and Philbrook by the University of California. Someone connected with that team no doubt knew the two husky athletes had starred years before at Whitman College in Walla Walla, Washington. The managing committee of the meet then summoned Dimmick and Philbrook. In the end they were allowed to compete, based on their statements and the fact Cal had no proof to support its claim that Dimmick's and Philbrook's experience at Whitman should count against the three years of eligibility allowed under meet rules. The conference committee made it clear, however, that it reserved the right to further investigate the protest, and that the status of the Notre Dame athletes was contingent on those findings.

The Irish were irate after this all-fronts weekend barrage.

"For the hundredth time," *The Scholastic* wrote, Notre Dame's reputation had taken a vicious beating from Michigan. And no thanks to the Western Conference, another monumental Notre Dame athletic achievement was in danger of being discredited, or even revoked. It all just served to cement the belief that both Michigan and the conference were out to get Notre Dame.

The Irish could have had no idea they were about to get it even worse.

Indeed, when fall rolled around, Wolverine officials picked up on Cal's protest of Dimmick and Philbrook. What did the Californians know that had eluded the "chicken-hearted" investigation of *Collier's* E.C. Patterson in 1909?

Patterson had reported that Dimmick and Philbrook played at Whitman College as prep students in 1905 and 1906, and as freshmen in 1907. But had they played elsewhere before entering Whitman?

In 1909 Yost seemed to be implying that. Perhaps he had been told something to that effect by two of his former players who had coached against Dimmick and Philbrook out West. More likely, Yost's informant was a current Wolverine, Stan Borleske, who had actually played alongside Dimmick and Philbrook at Whitman in 1907. Borleske was a fellow freshman with Dimmick and Philbrook that year. But whatever Borleske knew about the pasts of Dimmick and Philbrook, he apparently had no definite information.

Michigan was determined to get to the bottom of it. And if what it found on Dimmick and Philbrook meant canceling the 1910 game, well, at least *The Michigan Daily* wouldn't object.

At the first fall meeting of the Michigan Board in Control on October 4, athletic director Bartelme was apparently commissioned to launch his own investigation into the playing careers of Dimmick, Philbrook, and a third Notre Dame football player whose past was under suspicion, Lee Matthews.

Here's how that search progressed, how each side argued the issues, and how the cancellation ultimately came about:

October 5

Bartelme writes Whitman College for the academic and athletic histories of Dimmick and Philbrook.

October 10

Bartelme writes Oregon Agricultural College, asking if Dimmick and Philbrook ever played there.

Bartelme writes the University of Washington, asking if Lee Matthews ever played there.

October 14

Bartelme writes conference arbiter Clarence A. Waldo for the status of Whitman College. Wolverine officials evidently realize an obscure conference rule might get Dimmick and Philbrook off the hook. The rule is this: Any athletic experience a student gains at a college, or colleges, not on the conference's "list" does not count against him. This list was devised after hundreds of small schools and obscure institutes took up football. At some, the level of play was so inferior, or the curriculum so laughable, the Western Conference decided that only where big-time ball was played, or where enrollment was large, or where academics were first-rate, should a player's experience count against him.

But the big problem with the list was this: Before 1907 it included few colleges outside the Midwest. Therefore, it could not always be used as the final determinant. Notre Dame had always been on the list, but Whitman wasn't before 1907. And that's what Bartelme asks Waldo to rule on: Whitman's status through 1906.

October 17

The Western Conference Board of Directors, which ran the I.C.A.A. track meet back in June, meets in Chicago to discuss Cal's protest. After a lengthy discussion, no determination is made.

October 18

The University of Washington answers Bartelme's query about Matthews: "The only Matthews that we have any record of . . . is Robert Lee Matthews, who entered here from the Berkeley [Calif.] High School in September 1907, and who played quarter on the Varsity football team for that season. He had also been in attendance at Vachon College, a military school in this state. . . . Matthews was never a prep here. . . . He is now at Notre Dame, and has been for some two or three years."

So with one year at Washington (1907) and two previous at Notre Dame (1908 and 1909), 1910 is Matthews's fourth year of varsity competition. All came after 1906, thus even under Michigan's retroactive rule he is ineligible to play.

October 19

Arbiter Waldo answers Bartelme's letter, confirming that the conference's "list of colleges" is not the final determinant of any school's status. Waldo indicates Whitman's pre-1907 status is currently under investigation by the conference, for the purpose of determining Cal's protest.

October 21

Bartelme wires Whitman and Oregon Agricultural College to please rush their responses.

Oregon A.C. later wires Bartelme that neither Dimmick nor Philbrook ever competed there.

Whitman responds with this wire, which reveals that Dimmick and Philbrook had indeed played elsewhere before arriving in Walla Walla, Washington: "George Philbrook, age twenty, and Ralph Dimmick, age twenty one, enter Whitman preparatory (third year) 1905, played varsity football 1905–6–7. Varsity track, Philbrook 1906–07–08, Dimmick 1906–07. . . . Competed for Pacific University before entering Whitman. Disqualified here four-year rule, June 1908."

So Philbrook and Dimmick are now in their seventh years of intercollegiate football, after one at Pacific, three at Whitman, and two at Notre Dame. Even under Michigan's rules, which allowed them four years instead of three because their careers had begun before 1906, they are ineligible—so long as Whitman is found to have been a college of sufficient standing before 1907.

Therefore, Waldo's ruling is now paramount to Michigan's case.

October 21–23

Bartelme either wires or writes Pacific University of Forest Grove, Oregon, for the playing histories of Dimmick and Philbrook.

October 24

Michigan sends Notre Dame its certified list of players, in accordance with a stipulation in the contract. Michigan requests Notre Dame now do likewise.

Bartelme writes the conference arbiter, Waldo, and informs him of Michigan's discovery that Dimmick and Philbrook apparently played at Pacific before entering Whitman. Bartelme requests that Waldo determine the past status of Whitman by November 1, four days before the Michigan–Notre Dame game.

October 26

James Hope, the new Notre Dame graduate manager, wires Bartelme to say shipment of Notre Dame's eligibility list is delayed while the director of studies is out of town.

October 29

Pacific University president W.N. Ferren sends Michigan this confirmation by wire: "Ralph Dimmick and George Philbrook competed on football team of Pacific University in fall of 1904."

October 30

Arbiter Waldo writes Bartelme about the status of Whitman, saying his verdict is being delayed until a final rebuttal from Notre Dame vice-president Rev. Thomas Crumley arrives. Crumley's contention, of course, is that Whitman was not on the conference's "college list" for two of the three years Dimmick and Philbrook attended it, so that experience should not count. The arbiter writes he will make his decision the next day.

Monday, October 31

Waldo does not wire Bartelme.

With the game only five days away, Hope finally sends Notre Dame's eligibility list by special delivery, and it arrives in Ann Arbor at about 10 P.M. Dimmick, Philbrook, and "R.E. Matthews" are on that list.

Tuesday, November 1

1:04 P.M., Waldo wires Bartelme: "Whitman was college athletically in 1905–06–07–08." Waldo bases his decision on several factors, among them that Whitman's scholarship standards had been "probably the very highest and best" in the Northwest, and that Whitman had been an athletic power in that part of the country since the late 1890s.

With its investigation now complete, and with Notre Dame's intention to play Dimmick, Philbrook, and Matthews confirmed, Michigan is ready to file an official protest to Notre Dame. Evans Holbrook, chairman of the Michigan Board in Control, cites excerpts from the Washington, Whitman, Pacific, and Waldo correspondences in a special-delivery letter addressed to William L. Benitz, chairman of Notre Dame's Faculty Board of Control: "Under the said agreement it is obvious from the facts in our possession that Messrs. Philbrook, Dimmick, and Matthews are ineligible to play in the Michigan–Notre Dame game of November 5th, 1910." Holbrook "assumed" Notre Dame now would not permit these men to play.

Wednesday, November 2

Michigan awaits Notre Dame's response. Notre Dame officials evidently mull over the facts as presented in Holbrook's letter, prepare a defense, but do not respond on this day.

Neither side goes public with the matter, except someone at Michigan leaks the story to the afternoon dailies. The *Detroit News,* the *Ann Arbor Daily Times News,* the *Chicago Tribune,* and the *South Bend Tribune* all carry sketchy stories of Michigan's protest of the three players.

Thursday, November 3

A Notre Dame official calls Bartelme by telephone in the morning. Bartelme is asked whether he assured Harry Curtis back in January that Michigan would not protest Dimmick and Philbrook. Bartelme says no, with much vehemence. At this point, the Notre Dame caller ends the discussion, promising to phone later. He does not.

Both teams continue to practice, although Michigan coach Fielding Yost is out of town. He is in Kalamazoo for the day to arrange a game for the Wolverine freshman team.

In late afternoon, the Western Conference acts on Waldo's report and announces it has upheld Cal's protest, thereby stripping Dimmick and Philbrook of the medals they won and the points they amassed at the I.C.A.A. track meet. Stanford is declared the proper meet champion.

In the evening, the Michigan Board in Control meets for three hours. An ultimatum is framed then wired to Notre Dame, citing the conference's decision regarding the track meet as further backing. The board empowers Chairman Holbrook to cancel the game if Notre Dame refuses to withhold Dimmick and Philbrook.

Strangely, the status of Lee Matthews is no longer of major concern to Michigan—although it appears Michigan has an airtight argument only in this case. One document, however, suggests Michigan was unable to find proof that Matthews played at Notre Dame in 1908. He did, but Notre Dame appears to have denied it.

When the Michigan board meeting concludes, this press release is issued: "No statement is made as to the proceedings of tonight's meeting, but the Board hopes and expects that Notre Dame will not play any men who are not eligible under their contract." Notre Dame authorities remain silent.

A special-delivery letter from Notre Dame arrives very late at Michigan. Notre Dame's defense is this: (1) That before coming to Notre Dame, Dimmick and Philbrook had taken only preparatory academics, hence their athletics should be considered preparatory as well. (2) To suddenly say now that Whitman should have been on the conference's "list" in 1905 and '06—thus revoking the eligibility of Dimmick and Philbrook halfway through their third seasons at Notre Dame—is totally unfair. (3) What bearing should a conference decision on its track meet—indeed, any conference decision—have on a football contract between two nonconference schools? (4) Why should Notre Dame obey a retroactive conference ruling (on Whitman's status) when Michigan would not obey one (the retroactive feature of the three-year rule)?

Friday, November 4

Michigan does not open its ticket office.

11:22 A.M., Notre Dame's Crumley wires Holbrook, asking if the special-delivery letter sent the previous night was received, indicating "it seems to explain why we have right to play Philbrook and Dimmick."

Holbrook immediately wires Crumley that the Michigan board's decision to cancel the game unless Dimmick and Philbrook are barred "is final." Michigan disputes Notre Dame's argument that the schools are not bound by a conference decision on eligibility, as Michigan— under whose rules the game was contracted—still abides by every conference eligibility rule and ruling, save the three-year retroactive clause. But as a compromise, Michigan offers not to play Fay Clark and Wheaton Cole, who are in their fourth years but who had begun their careers before 1906. Michigan's rules never specifically stated its interpretation of the three-year rule, and that ambiguity allowed Michigan the option of suddenly and magnanimously offering to bar these men. This concession submits to the Irish argument that Michigan was hypocritical for demanding that Notre Dame obey a retroactive conference rule while it did not.

At noon, Michigan tells the press that an announcement, one way or the other, is imminent.

A series of discussions between Holbrook and, presumably, Crumley are held via long-distance telephone. Finally, neither side backs down. Notre Dame refuses to withhold Dimmick and Philbrook, and Holbrook, in turn, cancels the game at about two o'clock.

Bartelme immediately wires all officials about the cancellation, promising they'll be paid anyway.

Both schools issue official press releases outlining their positions. Michigan also announces that all athletic relations with Notre Dame are severed.

Yost boards a train for Philadelphia, to scout Penn's game against Lafayette. Curiously, his name is barely associated with the entire fracas. Years later, he denied having any role whatsoever in the cancellation, but Bartelme remembered that Yost was consulted throughout. Yost's only statement at the time was in response to the charge that Michigan was afraid to play Notre Dame. His rebuttal was quintessential Yost: "If we were so timid that we would run from a second-rate team, we'd have a sweet chance to win from Pennsylvania and Minnesota, wouldn't we."

It has often been written that the Notre Dame team traveled by train as far as Niles, Michigan, before turning back. Not true. Original plans called for the team to leave the South Bend train station at 9:10 A.M. and arrive in Ann Arbor at 2:40 P.M. But with the game up in the air, the team would not have left. The next train didn't leave South Bend until 4:25, and by then it was all over.

Notre Dame fans and students who had taken the first train are likely none too happy upon arrival in Ann Arbor.

The afternoon papers get the full story.

In the evening, Bartelme decides to stage a free game Saturday between the Michigan varsity and the scrubs, in lieu of Notre Dame. All tickets to the Notre Dame game, which cost 50 cents each, will be refunded.

● ● ●

People in 1910 were no more clear as to who was right or wrong than we are today.

The newspapers went big with it. For almost a week thereafter, the midwestern dailies chronicled the charges and countercharges. Michigan's Holbrook and Bartelme slammed Notre Dame, while ND's Crumley and former grad manager Curtis shot back at Michigan—all of which added up to the ugliest off-field controversy of its generation.

The school newspapers, of course, best captured each side's militant point of view.

From *The Michigan Daily*:

Notre Dame and Michigan have played their last game together, and for this we are truly grateful. . . . A local paper bemoans the loss of the hotly contested Notre Dame games. But Michigan need not worry. When the field of fair and square colleges, capable of putting up a good fight against Michigan, runs below the number necessary to fill our schedule, we'll be ready to vote for the cessation of athletic competition.

From *The Scholastic*:

We are right—we are sure of that. The ruling which may possibly deprive us of two athletes will be a ruling on a technicality, and no sane man will consider that a fault. . . . We can win a football game or a track meet, but in the matter of post-factum technicalities we're outclassed.

Among the war of words, Michigan had many valid points, but Notre Dame had just as many. "Post-factum" research and analysis provide each side with even more fodder:

For Michigan:

• Athletic director Bartelme recalled 26 years later that Notre Dame's Crumley "assured me that the provisions of the contract would be lived up to, but in the last breath said they considered Filbrick [*sic*], Dimmick, and a third player whose name I do not recall, as eligible." That version is corroborated by the late Notre Dame historian Francis Wallace, who in 1949 wrote: "I recently came upon a story from a Notre Dame source which would support the Michigan position. According to this admittedly hazy recollection, Notre Dame had issued orders not to take the two disputed men to Ann Arbor, but those instructions were 'forgotten.'"

• When E.C. Patterson of *Collier's* magazine investigated Dimmick and Philbrook after the 1909 season, why wasn't he told about their having played at Pacific before enrolling at Whitman? And if the two players had hidden the fact from everyone, why were ND authorities still backing them when that information came to light?

• The eligibility list Notre Dame sent Michigan included several other players who were clearly ineligibile under Michigan's rules. Halfback Billy Ryan and guard John Duffy both were definitely in their fourth years at Notre Dame, while Thomas Foley and Frank Madden were in their first years at the school. There was probably no way for Michigan officials to have known this, however, and that's why they didn't try to bar them. Other obvious errors in Notre Dame's eligibility list suggest these four men may well have been included inadvertently, as the Notre Dame athletic department in 1910 was poorly organized.

• Foley, although in his first year at Notre Dame, was no "freshman," according to one true freshman on the team, Knute Rockne. He remembered: "I had sat at the feet of a learned tramp athlete whose name then was Foley, although he had played for many schools under aliases. He was typical of young men who roamed the country, overflowing with college spirit, regardless of the college."

• A letter in the archives at Notre Dame suggests at least one Irish football player had been lured to Notre Dame by the prospect of financial "assistance." Philbrook himself revealed this chicanery in a letter to graduate manager Hope on September 14: "I am after [Walter] Clinnen on all fours. He is very anxious to go back to ND but he can't see his way clear to leave his family, as they need some of his earnings. However, since he would be a very valuable man to have, I think we will be able to fix things for him here in [Chicago]." Clinnen became the starting left half for Notre Dame in 1910.

For Notre Dame:

• Stan Borleske, the teammate of Dimmick's and Philbrook's at Whitman in 1907, should never have been allowed to compete at Michigan. The reason he didn't return to Whitman in 1908 was because he was barred from amateur competition in the Northwest after having been caught playing pro baseball. Transient athletes of this era often lied about their pasts, so it's possible Michigan authorities were unaware of Borleske's. Still, it was a textbook example of Michigan hypocrisy—protesting Notre Dame's use of two ex-Whitman players, on arguable grounds, when Michigan itself was using a clearly ineligible ex-Whitman man. But Notre Dame didn't know of Borleske's West Coast banishment, otherwise it would surely have protested him.

• A letter from Coach Longman supports Harry Curtis's contention that Michigan athletic director Bartelme assured Curtis in their January meeting that Michigan would not protest Dimmick and Philbrook. Longman's letter is dated April 28, 1910, and is addressed to Curtis's interim successor, Ed (Copper) Lynch: "Just had a talk with Bartelme and he says they have talked it over with the Board and [influential trainer] Keene Fitzpatrick and decided to raise no question whatsoever as to Dimmick and Philbrook."

Bartelme's vehement denial of ever making such a statement is disputed by this letter. In postcancellation interviews, Notre Dame officials argued that Bartelme's apparent flip-flop rendered all of Michigan's subsequent investigations, charges, and ultimatums entirely moot.

• Eight years after Longman died in 1928, his widow, Edythe, blamed the cancellation on Yost: "After a man sent out by Mr. Yost returned to Ann Arbor to tell him the real strength of the Notre Dame team, Michigan withdrew from the agreement and the game was canceled."

• Yost's own recruiting tactics in these early days were, to say the least, highly questionable. "He completely disregarded rules in early talent searches," journalist Edwin Pope wrote.

• Notre Dame had ruled star quarterback and baseball player Don Hamilton ineligible after the summer of 1910, when he was accused of playing pro baseball. Evidently, the facts were not stacked overwhelmingly against Hamilton, but Notre Dame barred him anyway—hardly the action of the "rules renegade" Michigan made Notre Dame out to be.

• The timing of the conference's verdict on Cal's protest against Dimmick and Philbrook—it came less than 48 hours before Notre

Dame's football game against Michigan—certainly suggests the conference was in concert with the Wolverines on this case. The correspondences between conference arbiter Clarence Waldo and Bartelme would support that view. But why would the conference rush the decision to help Michigan, a former member currently on the outs with most conference schools? Perhaps it was a gesture to win over Michigan people and thus expedite the return of what had been the conference's most prestigious member. More likely, it was just a case of the conference and Michigan ganging up on their old mutual foe, Notre Dame.

🏈   🏈   🏈

The bottom line? Clearly, neither school was above reproach in those days.

Michigan was right in its contention that Dimmick and Philbrook had played more than anyone's fair share of intercollegiate football, and that Notre Dame's more lenient rules provided a tremendous recruiting advantage (why go to Michigan and sit out a year when you go to Notre Dame and play right away?). But it is equally clear that Michigan officials were in no position to be pointing a finger at anyone.

So why did they? Why did Michigan go to such great lengths to cast Notre Dame into disrepute? This question is the crux of the entire controversy.

We'll never know for sure, but this is the probable answer:

Michigan didn't like the fact that its commitment to pure athletics had been publicly questioned after the 1909 season, after the Joy Miller scandal and the *Chicago Record-Herald*'s charges. Although Michigan was not in the conference anymore, it cared deeply about how it was perceived by its former brethren. The last thing it wanted was to be classed with the common renegades of the West. After all, Michigan's differences with the conference lay in technicality, not wholesale policy. That's why Michigan officials in 1910 were intent on proving their athletics were indeed clean. One way was to bar all football players against whom there was even a hint of suspicion, which they made an effort to do. But perhaps the best way was to break off relations with Notre Dame (a school already blacklisted by the conference), and in so doing somehow show the conference that the Catholics were the real dregs of athletic society, not Michigan.

If this was Michigan's plan, it couldn't have worked out better, because the Wolverines' reputation was largely repaired—and Notre Dame was cast not only into disrepute, but into oblivion.

And Michigan accused Notre Dame of employing "mucker spirit"? Indeed.

"Do not favor Notre Dame game": 1911–17

This is precisely what football oblivion meant to Notre Dame: Ohio Northern, St. Viator, Butler, Loyola of Chicago, Pittsburgh, St. Bonaventure, Wabash, Marquette, Adrian, Morris Harvey, and St. Louis.

That's the sad roll call of Fighting Irish opponents in 1911 and '12. Only Pittsburgh, Marquette, and St. Louis were any good, and they were being shunned by all the major powers in their respective parts of the country. It was a fine crowd that Notre Dame was now associating with—renegades and rejects. So even though the Irish themselves were teeming with talent and didn't lose once in this two-year span, going 13–0–2, the conquests were hollow.

The cancellation of the game with Michigan in 1910 had, rightly or wrongly, erased the Irish's remaining marks of credibility in the West, and that's why reputable schools wanted nothing to do with them anymore, in any sport. This treatment only hardened Notre Dame's resolve to play under its own rules, which only worsened its predicament. Things had gotten so bad for the Irish that even Michigan Agricultural College was boycotting them.

But following the 1912 season the Notre Dame Faculty Board of Control suddenly said enough was enough—no more playing the rebel. The board made what remains the most crucial decision in the history of Notre Dame athletics: to once and for all embrace the highest of athletic ideals, including all of the Western Conference's eligibility rules. This newfound commitment to purity was to be sincere, vigorously implemented, and never again open to question. The importance of this decision cannot be overstated, for had Notre Dame continued down the path it was on, odds are the school's athletic prowess would be no more nationally renowned today than St. Viator's, Ohio Northern's, and Morris Harvey's.

The Irish sought one man to turn this turnabout into reality—someone who would, with tact and humility, open all the doors that had been so viciously slammed in their faces. Another graduate manager of athletics just wouldn't do, because the long-standing practice of appointing students to this position, and changing them every year, was largely an abysmal failure. For instance in 1910, when the job changed hands three times, the football schedule wound up a shambles and the year a financial disaster.

No, it was time to hire the school's first athletic director. The faculty board wasted no time in securing Jesse Harper.

Raised on a farm in Illinois, and a halfback under A.A. Stagg at Chicago, Harper had earned immense respect around the West in the way he ran athletics at both Alma College in Michigan, from 1906 to 1908, and since 1909 at Wabash College in Indiana. Harper was perfectly suited for Notre Dame's ambitious job. He was well organized, uncommonly but pleasantly frank, and, above all, a skillful diplomat. It didn't hurt that he was also one hell of a good coach, in football, baseball, and basketball.

"I realize I am tackling a big job [but] I know I can win out," Harper wrote just after being hired in early December 1912. "It will probably take me two or three years to get all the games just as I want them but I am sure I will, eventually."

The one football game Notre Dame really wanted was Michigan, as the Irish were prepared to bottle their residual bitterness from the 1910 blow-up. Was Michigan? Notre Dame faculty board member William E. Cotter thought so. When he suggested Harper "feel around" and try to resume relations with the Wolverines, he commented: "They want to play Notre Dame [but] they hate to approach us, as we have hated to approach them."

From a scheduling standpoint alone, the Wolverines had every reason to accept a Notre Dame approach, because they, too, were having difficulty lining up attractive games. After Michigan had defeated runaway conference champion Minnesota in 1909 and 1910, the league instituted what amounted to the "Michigan boycott rule." And the three perennial powers of the East—Harvard, Yale, and Princeton—were snubbing Michigan for the same reason many Western Conference schools had once avoided Notre Dame: because they had everything to lose and little to gain.

The strongest nonconference team in the West other than Michigan was Notre Dame, but the unbending Wolverines wouldn't even consider this as a scheduling option, so they looked east for all their big games. Thus Penn, Syracuse, and Cornell became Michigan's new archrivals.

Over the next five years, Harper mustered all his diplomacy to convince Michigan to rethink its anti–Notre Dame position.

One of the first things he did upon securing the Notre Dame job was write Phil Bartelme, who remained the Wolverine athletic director. Harper's few dealings with Bartelme in the past had been pleasant. In his December 11, 1912, letter, Harper exhibited the skills that would help him mend so many fences for Notre Dame:

By the time this letter reaches you, the news will be published that I have been elected athletic director at Notre Dame for next year. I am making out the football schedule for next fall and am writing you in regard to a game. If you should decide to schedule this game, I judge you would want it played at Ann Arbor. The same contract you had for the game in 1910 is satisfactory to me.

I believe, on account of the record [Notre Dame] made this year, you would find this game a very good drawing card. I would like to suggest the dates of Oct. 11th, or 18th, for the game should you decide to schedule it.

I am sorry the trouble came up in regard to the last game scheduled, and I can assure you nothing of the kind will come up in the future. . . .

Very truly yours, Jesse Harper.

Unfortunately, Bartelme's return letter has long since dissolved, but this is how Harper in turn responded on January 14:

Your very fine letter came some time ago. I want to thank you very much for the things you said. I certainly will try to live up to the things you have heard about me in the past. I hope to carry on athletics at Notre Dame in such a way that Michigan will be very glad to take up athletic relations again.

I am very sorry you could not think it best to schedule a game for next fall. If at any time you should find that your schedule is not working out to suit you, and that you could use the Notre Dame game, I would be very glad to hear from you and, if possible, I will do all I can to make arrangements for a game. . . .

Harper proceeded to knock on dozens of other doors—across the Midwest, along the East Coast, and even down South. He wound up arranging Notre Dame's most ambitious schedule ever for 1913. Trips were arranged to West Point, Penn State, St. Louis (to play the Christian Brothers), and Texas.

What happened in the Army game is now legend. Gus Dorais and Knute Rockne befuddled the Cadets with forward passes, and fullback Ray Eichenlaub ripped the Army line as the Fighting Irish shocked the country with a 35–13 win. This was Notre Dame's springboard to national prominence.

Suddenly more doors, bigger doors, began opening for Harper. He lined up Yale, Syracuse, and Carlisle for the 1914 season and was trying again to schedule Michigan. Harper also asked Bartelme to resume relations in other sports, especially baseball.

This time, the Michigan athletic director did not dismiss Harper's request hands down. On December 13, 1913, Bartelme took up the matter with the Michigan Board in Control. Following deliberation, the board instructed Bartelme to obtain specifics about Notre Dame's new rules. Six days later, the executive committee of the Michigan board met, and "after discussing the eligibility rules and conduct of athletics at Notre Dame, as presented by athletic director Harper, [the committee] authorized director Bartelme to schedule three games of baseball for the season of 1914 with Notre Dame."

This was a huge victory for Harper, even if the Wolverines weren't yet ready to resume relations in football. Consider that only three years earlier Michigan officials had been intent on never again playing Notre Dame in anything. But Harper had impressed them.

Not satisfied with his inch, Harper tried to take a yard the next year. On November 19, 1914, he made another football pitch to Bartelme, this time dangling a financial carrot:

> No doubt, you will start arranging your football schedule in a short time. If you decide to make any changes, especially of your heavy games, I would like very much to have you consider Notre Dame. How would you like to play a game in Chicago? Mr. C.A. Comiskey has kindly offered me his park for use at any time and at no expense. We had about an $11,000 crowd at the Carlisle game. I am very sure that the Michigan game would more than double this amount.
>
> As soon as you get started on your track and baseball schedules, I would [also] like to hear from you. . . .

Harper probably never knew it, but Michigan gave this football request careful consideration.

The three Michigan board members responsible for scheduling matters were director Bartelme and alumni James Murfin and James E. Duffy (the same Duffy who had played against Notre Dame in 1887 and '88). In December they were considering these schools to fill two October vacancies on the forthcoming 1915 schedule: Notre Dame, Michigan Agricultural College (later to be called Michigan State), Brown, Dartmouth, Nebraska, and South Dakota.

"It occurs to me," Murfin wrote Bartelme on December 21, "that we could not do much better than to again put Notre Dame on our schedule."

A day later, Duffy indicated to Bartelme that Notre Dame would be his second choice for the October 23 opening, behind Michigan Agricultural. "Each of these teams will attempt to fit themselves for the Michigan game, as this will probably be their most important game, while to us they will be somewhat incidental. It would seem to me, therefore, to be more advisable to take on only one of these teams, in which event, in view of our past policy, that one would naturally be M.A.C."

Don't get the wrong impression here. While these men had valuable input on scheduling, and were among the most powerful men on the Michigan board, they didn't *really* decide who Michigan played. Coach Fielding Yost still had the final say. His wish was their command, so they naturally sought his input on the Notre Dame discussion. The coach responded with this telegram:

> Do not favor Notre Dame game. It would be a hard game, not much money or prestige if we won. We have three hard games in Syracuse, Cornell, and Pennsylvania, which we must win. Would not consider game which compels us to get team ready early unless very important.

So here was Yost throwing another roadblock in front of a Michigan–Notre Dame football resumption. But others on the 11-member Michigan Board in Control shared his view. Even Bartelme, who was being so receptive to Harper, was not keen to see the football series resume, at least not in 1915. In a letter to Duffy, Bartelme cited additional reasons for not playing Notre Dame, reasons Bartelme said Yost agreed with:

> I feel that it would be very unfair to any college to take them on for a year and then drop them in order to take on a more important game. I also believe, as you do, that we should endeavor to bring our people more from year to year to a realization that the winning of our big games should be the prime consideration, and that less importance should be attached to the result of the earlier games of our schedule.

Although Notre Dame's teams were seemingly on par with Michigan's during the 1910s, Wolverine officials apparently still liked to view the Irish as secondary competition. Harper would have loved the opportunity to convince Michigan otherwise, but he never got it. This was the closest he ever came to resuming the football series.

Well, at least the varsity football series.

Before his final autumn at Notre Dame, in 1917, Harper convinced Bartelme to schedule a game between the Michigan and Notre Dame freshman football teams. (Michigan won it in convincing fashion, 19–3, on November 17 at Ann Arbor.) The only other consolation for Harper was that he was able to resume the Notre Dame–Michigan track series, too.

Had Harper been able to befriend Yost, he would have had a much better chance in football. But nowhere among Harper's vast and meticulously filed correspondences, circa 1912–18, exists a letter to or from Yost. Fact was, these men weren't friends at all—as a later letter would reveal.

Harper left Notre Dame in the spring of 1918 to help his father-in-law run a cattle ranch in Kansas. But the mark he left on Notre Dame athletics is indelible. Although the Irish were still fighting a bad reputation, Harper saw to it that the days of scrounging, scoundrels, and scatterbrained management were permanently left behind.

●   ●   ●

As the 1910s progressed, the most hated man on the Notre Dame campus continued to be one Fielding H. Yost.

Especially after the 1913 season.

Yost had infuriated ND students by placing three Wolverines on his All-America team and, once again, excluding all ND men. Typically, *The Scholastic* vented its anger in satire, chastising Yost's vanity and irrationality in a first-person piece by "Yielding Fost":

"This [All-America] team was picked by me," Fost explains. "Therefore it ought to be accepted throughout America. . . . I never brag about myself [but] I've produced the best team in the West this year. . . . I have utterly ignored that little runt of a school, Notre Dame, because they beat me four years ago. Besides, I hate that red-headed Harry Miller they produced in 1909."

Ah, grudges. Yost had his and the Notre Dame students had theirs—especially the seniors. This class of '14 had witnessed firsthand the 1910 cancellation as frosh; had endured two years of honorless banishment; and now had to swallow one last bitter pill, courtesy of the hated Yost.

One graduating football player carried his grudge forever. This pug-nosed end, who had confounded Army with his pass-catching ability, was garnering considerable postseason praise in 1913. Walter Camp even named him a third-team All-American, but, as a final slap, Yost snubbed him entirely.

The player's name? Knute Rockne.

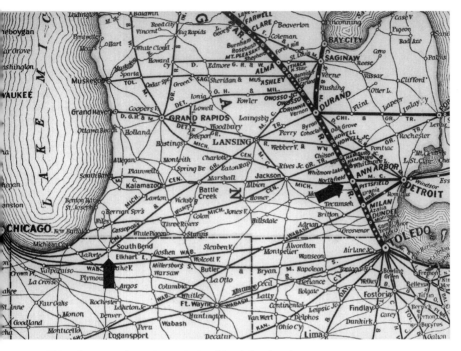

This railway map shows the proximity of South Bend, and
thus Notre Dame, to Ann Arbor. Bookended by metropolitan
centers Chicago and Detroit, the two universities are only
150 miles apart.

(Ann Arbor Railroad and Steamship Lines, 1890.)

The three men who arranged the first
Michigan–Notre Dame game: former
ND students George DeHaven and Billy
Harless of Michigan (above), and faculty
member Patrick Connors ("Brother Paul")
of Notre Dame.

The men who literally taught football to Notre Dame: the 1887 Michigan Wolverines.
Michigan won the abbreviated game 8–0 on November 23, 1887, at Notre Dame.
(Rentschler Studio Collection, Bentley Historical Library, University of Michigan.)

All but three players from Notre Dame's first team returned
in spring 1888—when this photo was taken—to play the
Wolverines again. Michigan won on successive days, 26–6
and 10–4.
(University of Notre Dame Archives.)

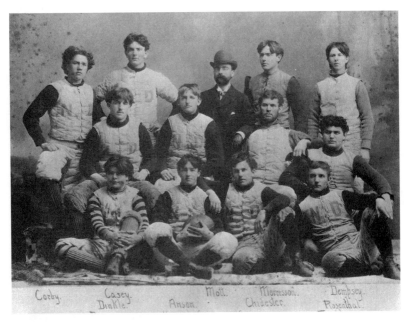

Corby. Casey. Mott. Morrison. Dempsey
Dinkle. Anson. Chidester. Rosenthal

In 1894 Michigan sent Notre Dame its first coach, former Wolverine James Laury Donaldson Morrison (back row, second from right). Morrison was paid $40 plus expenses for a two-week stint. "They want to smoke," Morrison lamented of his players, "and when I told them that they would have to run and get up some wind they thought I was rubbing it in on them."
(University of Notre Dame Archives.)

H.G. Hadden played at Michigan before becoming Notre Dame's second coach in 1895. Hadden later was an assistant coach at Michigan and, in 1900, served as umpire in the Notre Dame–Michigan game.
(Richard Wagner Collection, Bentley Historical Library, University of Michigan.)

"Sure — we won the Game! We outplayed them you know!" F.H. Yost.

One of the most successful coaches, and certainly the most boastful, of all time: Michigan's Fielding H. "Hurry Up" Yost. From 1901 to 1941, Yost was the central figure and leading instigator in the usually stormy Michigan–Notre Dame relationship.
(Fielding Harris Yost collection, Bentley Historical Library, University of Michigan.)

Michigan's Joseph Maddock (arrow) smashes across the Notre Dame goal line for the Wolverines' first touchdown in a 23–0 victory at Toledo in 1902.
(Russell Van Horn for the *Toledo Blade*, October 30, 1902.)

Charles Baird, Michigan's athletic director from 1894 to 1908, scheduled Notre Dame six times (1898, 1899, 1900, 1902, 1908, 1909).
(Rentschler Studio Collection, Bentley Historical Library, University of Michigan.)

Right guard Sam "Rosey" Dolan (facing camera without helmet) and his Notre Dame teammates get set to run a play in the 1908 game at Ann Arbor. Michigan won 12–6 to improve its series record to 8–0.
(*Michiganensian*, 1909.)

This 1905 Michigan team photo shows coach Yost, top right, and fullback Frank "Shorty" Longman, bottom left. Longman went on to coach Notre Dame in 1909 and 1910.
(Rentschler Studio Collection, Bentley Historical Library, University of Michigan.)

Harry "Red" Miller of Notre Dame (far left) breaks into open field in the monumental 1909 game at Ann Arbor. Miller led the way as Notre Dame beat Michigan for the first time in nine tries, 11–3.
(Detroit News-Tribune, November 7, 1909.)

In addition to Miller (holding dog), these "fighting Irishmen" conquered Michigan on November 6, 1909. Included are coach Longman (next to Miller, wearing his Michigan sweater) and disputed linemen Ralph Dimmick and George Philbrook (third row up, second and third from left). Twelve months later, Michigan canceled the game with Notre Dame 24 hours before kickoff because ND authorities refused to withhold Dimmick and Philbrook, who were ineligible according to Wolverine authorities. Michigan would not schedule Notre Dame again for 32 years.
(University of Notre Dame Archives.)

These men (listed from top left to bottom right) argued each school's position during the 1910 hostilities: Evans Holbrook, chairman of the Michigan Board in Control of Athletics (UM Faculty Portrait Collection, Bentley Historical Library, University of Michigan); Harry Curtis, ND's graduate manager of athletics in early 1910 (University of Notre Dame Archives); Rev. Thomas Crumley, ND vice president (University of Notre Dame Archives); James L. Hope, ND's graduate manager of athletics in late 1910 (University of Notre Dame Archives); and Phil Bartelme, Michigan's athletic director (Dept. of Intercollegiate Athletics Records, Bentley Historical Library, University of Michigan).

Jesse Harper was Notre Dame's first bona fide athletic director (1913–18). His smooth diplomacy wasn't enough to convince Michigan authorities—especially coach Yost—to resume the football series.
(University of Notre Dame Archives.)

The bitterest two-man feud
the game has ever known:
Fielding Yost vs. Knute
Rockne.

(Rockne, University of
Notre Dame Archives.)

Yost (left) at a dinner with the Big Ten's first commissioner,
Maj. John L. Griffith. The muck Yost and Rockne frequently
flung at one another often plopped first on the desk of Grif-
fith, a good friend of both.
(Dept. of Intercollegiate Athletics Records, Bentley Historical
Library, University of Michigan.)

Glenn Warner — Knute Rockne — Babe Ruth — Christy Walsh - T.A.D. Jones - F. H Yost
Christmas "Dinner
New York — Nov. 30th 1925

This is perhaps the only surviving photo with Yost (far right)
and Rockne (second from left) together. At the time, both men
wrote stories for Christy Walsh's newspaper syndicate.
(Fielding Harris Yost collection, Bentley Historical Library,
University of Michigan.)

Yost (right), chief proponent of the punt-formation offense, lobbied hard throughout the 1920s to outlaw Rockne's pet offense, the shift (below, Rockne pitching ball). The feud reached vicious proportions by the late '20s. (Bennie G. Oosterbaan collection, Bentley Historical Library, University of Michigan; University of Notre Dame Archives.)

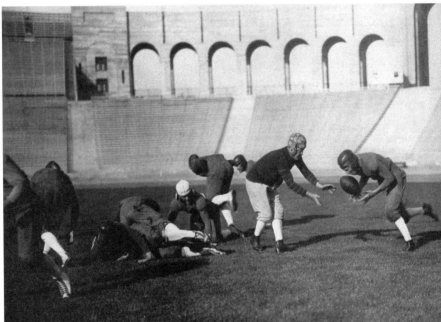

As these photos clearly show, Notre Dame Stadium (top) was a virtual clone of Michigan Stadium, which was built three years earlier in 1927 with an original capacity of only 72,000.
(University of Notre Dame Archives; Dept. of Intercollegiate Athletics Records, Bentley Historical Library, University of Michigan.)

In a stunning turnaround in the late 1930s, Yost made peace with Notre Dame. Elmer Layden, ND's young, diplomatic coach and athletic director, had a lot to do with it. Here Layden (right) welcomes Yost on a visit to Notre Dame in 1939. The two contracted a home-and-home series for 1942–43, thus ending the long hiatus.
(University of Notre Dame Archives.)

Ed Slezak, a Michigan grad, served as swimming instructor at Notre Dame in 1939 and '40. He was the middle man in negotiations between Yost and Layden.
(Ed Slezak personal collection.)

The hillbilly vs. the likeable fellow: 1918–31

Personal antagonism

Knute Rockne's self-described "first big thrill" in football was Fielding Yost's first colossal tragedy in football.

That about sums up the bitterest two-man feud the game has ever known, for Rockne and Yost were seemingly always at opposite ends of the football spectrum.

These intense men grew to detest one another. The back-stabbing became so vicious, and so frequent, it made for the darkest days of the Notre Dame–Michigan rivalry, eclipsing even the hostile 1910 era. Prospects for a game were never as bleak; in fact, there was even opposition in the Notre Dame athletic department—probably the only time in series history this has ever been the case.

Yost and Rockne must have been destined for enmity, judging by that symbolic, diametrical beginning.

Fade to Marshall Field in Chicago. The date: Thanksgiving Day, 1905. Amos Alonzo Stagg's greatest Chicago team shocked the nation with a 2–0 upset of mighty Michigan, ending the Point-A-Minute team's 56-game unbeaten streak. It was the first time any football team of Yost's was ever beaten out of a league championship, and he was duly crushed. But Rockne, then half Yost's age at 17, was delirious along with 27,000 others up in the stands. Having been raised in Chicago since his family emigrated from Norway 12 years earlier, Rockne was a fan of the hometown Maroons, and every Chicago partisan in those days despised Michigan and its cocky coach.

The chasm between Yost and Rockne only widened during the latter's college days at Notre Dame. "It was then," wrote Notre Dame historian Francis Wallace, a friend of Rockne's, "that this young man with the low boiling point, fierce loyalty, and blazing competitive spirit—and natural love of feuds—set up the personal antagonism he was always to carry against Yost."

And make no mistake, this antagonism was personal—and mutual.

The feud didn't fire up until almost halfway through Rockne's reign as head football coach and athletic director at Notre Dame (from 1918 to 1931). During the height of the hostilities, 1925–29, Rockne and Yost seemed intent on making life as miserable as possible for one another. In a sporting sense it was Al Capone vs. Eliot Ness, only each saw himself as the righteous Ness and the other as the evil Capone.

But before we walk into the figurative shootouts, a closer study of the two antagonists is in order.

Knute Rockne, of course, is a legend. America was never more in love with its heroes than in the '20s, and Rockne's celebrity was enormous—matched in the sporting world only by Babe Ruth's. "Rock" attained nationwide fame because his Fighting Irish teams were incredibly successful and because they were on display from coast to coast. They rambled from New York to Los Angeles, Minneapolis to Atlanta, thrashing foe after foe along the way and picking up national championships in 1919, 1924, 1929, and 1930. That's how the Fighting Irish went from being a midwestern outcast to America's team so quickly. The 1924 squad was probably Rockne's most celebrated. Led by the famed Four Horsemen backfield, these Irish went 10–0 and whipped Pop Warner's greatest Stanford team in the Rose Bowl. From that point on, Rockne was generally hailed as the wizard of the coaching fraternity.

But it was the sheer charm of his personality that really won over the masses. He was a positively riveting speaker whose endearing wit and demeanor melted audiences, and left even legendary humorist Will Rogers in awe. Rockne's tragic death at age 43 in an airplane crash over the plains of Kansas, on March 31, 1931, confirmed his legend, and prompted this comment from Rogers: "It takes a big calamity to shock this country all at once, but Knute, you did it. You died one of our national heroes."

No one has ever been quite as brilliant a coach as Rockne, which explains why he won 88.1 percent of his games, the best success rate of all time.

From a purely X's and O's standpoint, his modes of attack were revolutionary, his game-day strategies almost flawless. The crucial thrust of his approach was to emphasize brainpower over manpower, eschewing the "ox-knuckled players" with "bovine expressions" for the smaller, speedy, thinking player.

As a leader of young men, Rockne was in a league of his own, as Benny Friedman—ironically, Yost's greatest quarterback—so aptly explained in an article for *Liberty* magazine in 1934:

There have been, and there are, coaches who can teach fundamentals as well as Rockne did, but no other coach has ever had quite so much magic, so much dominating influence over his players. . . .

The [1920s] player was different from his ponderous predecessor. The old stuff worked no longer. Coaches could not ask the new crop to do or die for dear old Alma Mater. Players were not only lighter and faster but more sophisticated.

The brow-beating methods were passe; but some of the coaches did not realize it. . . . Rockne tossed away the lash and the spurs and resorted to psychology. He dealt in subtlety. He studied individuals, worked on them, played to their vanity, their weak spots. He used his magnetic personality to weld each player to him, to make him play for "Rock."

This "some need a kick in the ass, some need a pat on the back" approach has since become so universal it's now a cliché. But back then only Rockne and a handful of others were keen to such a subtle approach. Most long-tooths weren't.

One oldtimer who was, whose teams were as dominant as ever in the mid-1920s, was Michigan's Fielding H. Yost. He may have clung to the long-tooth's brand of football, but he was as successful as the moderns in varying his motivation methods from player to player, then emotionally binding them all on game day. In his own book printed in 1905, Yost had expanded on the notion that "the coach must divine early in the season the character and traits of the men." And as an example of his binding ability, Yost had his Wolverines so primed to beat Ohio State in the 1922 dedication of Ohio Stadium, he was unable to give a pregame pep talk—because "all of us were crying," he recalled. Michigan stormed out and beat the Buckeyes, 19–0.

Indeed, Yost wasn't always the hyper bumpkin. He was also a highly successful businessman (his mining and hydroelectric pursuits in the South made him probably the richest coach in the country), and in letters he actually came across as a man of class, control, polish, and persuasion. A former circuit court judge once wrote him, "as an advocate either orally or in writing you have no equal."

Thus, although subtlety wasn't Yost's middle name (as it was Rockne's), neither was it a word foreign to his dictionary.

This was just one intriguing aspect of Yost's and Rockne's "magnetic" personalities. Some of their respective traits were parallel, others north and south—but, always, they seemed to repel one another.

Among their other similarities, Rockne and Yost each possessed an intellect that approached genius; they were emotional men who had a remarkable enthusiasm for everything they cared about; they had humongous egos; their stares could sear holes through the back of your head; and, most of all, they had competitive streaks that surpassed vindictiveness and often reached viciousness.

Just as intriguing as these likenesses were their differences.

One trait Rockne and Yost didn't come close to sharing was humor. Yost took everything seriously; a joke was funny to him only if he was telling it and he was not the brunt of it—a by-product of his enormous vanity. But Rockne *preferred* to poke fun at himself with his clever, charming wit.

Never was this disparity on better display than at a banquet in New York following the 1925 football season. Yost and Rockne were among the featured speakers. Yost's Wolverines lost only once that year and were among the best teams in the country, while Rockne's Fighting Irish struggled to go 7–2–1 with the Four Horsemen having graduated.

Yost took the podium first and proceeded to praise his '25 team from one end of the earth to the other, calling it the finest he ever turned out, calling Benny Friedman the best quarterback there ever was, calling . . . well, you get the idea. Yost also argued that that era's greatest star, halfback Red Grange of Illinois, couldn't compare to Willie Heston of his Point-A-Minute teams. "Heston is beyond doubt the finest back that ever lived," Yost crowed. "Heston didn't make 50 or 60 points a season but 200. He would have made a million in the modern game."

Rockne, who despised the braggart in Yost more than anything, was probably ready to vomit at this point. When it finally was his turn to speak, he had little to say: "If anyone knows where there are four more Horsemen, I'll see him outside immediately."

It wasn't that Rockne's ego was so much smaller than Yost's; it wasn't. But Rockne knew how to harness his, realizing it didn't look good to brag in public. What's more, he knew people are, by nature, hesitant to pour more praise into the glass already full. By draining his own glass through self-disparagement, and leaving it bone dry, Rockne compelled others to pour away. This is one aspect of human nature Yost could never figure out, and it's one reason Rockne's fame remains overflowing while Yost's has all but drained away.

Considering all these jagged angles to their personalities, Yost and Rockne were destined to gash whenever they clashed. Each's long-fermenting disdain for the other's school only sharpened the points, increased the velocity of attack, and deepened the wounds.

So why has so little been written about all the cutting? Because it was not a subject either liked to discuss. Both were largely successful in keeping the feud off the sports pages, off the radio, and out of books, for each held immense sway over the media corps of the day. Rockne and Yost were far too smart to assault each other in public; it wouldn't have looked good on either of them, to say nothing of the grief and embarrassment it would have caused their respective institutions. But anyone associated with college football in the middle to late 1920s was fully aware of the hostilities.

The proof today is found in the reams and reams of letters Yost and Rockne wrote and received during their careers, which remain stored in the archives of their respective schools.

In a nutshell, here's what each came to think of the other from 1923 to 1931.

Rockne, then in his late 30s to early 40s, saw in Yost a "hillbilly" who was forever grinding the religious ax against Notre Dame, who was as crooked as a dog's hind leg, who was selfish and vain beyond comprehension, who was blindly jealous of Rockne's own success and ascension to national stardom, and who coached boring, neanderthal football. Publicly, Rockne made sure everyone knew Notre Dame had spiteful enemies, but seldom did he assess Yost this way outside of confidential letters and private conversations.

Yost, then in his middle to late 50s, saw in Rockne a coach who feared the regulatory confinement of a conference, who ran a renegade football factory at Notre Dame, who sought unfair advantages over his opponents, and who continually and deliberately broke football rules with his controversial offense. But Yost was sly in his public and private accusations. In fact, in the tens of thousands of Yost's correspondences that survive, covering 45 years, Yost slams Rockne on perhaps only one occasion, and mildly so. Asked by the University of California to assess the Notre Dame coach, Yost accused Rockne of seeking unfair advantages and of "fretting" Western Conference regulations. The worst thing Yost would call Rockne was "a likeable fellow." Even in public, Yost would only fire disguised missiles at Rockne—saying "Notre Dame" was doing this, or "Notre Dame" was not complying with that. Behind the scenes, however, Yost's actions were far more revealing than his words.

Yost and Rockne confronted each other only once in letters. These missives—which, luckily, survive—were prompted by the tumultuous event that put these men forever at odds: the hurdle-race episode of 1923.

The thread is slashed

Before June 2, 1923, Yost and Rockne had actually been cordial, if not close, acquaintances.

As football coaches and athletic directors of their institutions, they would bump into each other several times a year, most often at coaches' conferences and banquets. At one particular dinner in December 1922,

Yost and Rockne were the keynote speakers, and they engaged in friendly banter all night long.

Yost had even helped Northwestern in its aggressive but unsuccessful bid to hire "Rock" after the 1921 season. "I did all I could to show him that it was for his best interests in the long run to cast his lot with your institution," Yost later wrote O.F. Long of Northwestern.

Rockne, meanwhile, had twice directed young coaching aspirants toward Michigan, although each time Yost respectfully declined their services.

Yet despite their friendly association, Yost and Rockne were not matching wits on the gridiron. Rockne was willing to play, but Yost wasn't. The Michigan coach had opposed all attempts to resume the Notre Dame series ever since the bitter cancellation of the 1910 game. It didn't matter that Rockne, who happened to be a freshman reserve on that 1910 Notre Dame team, was getting along with Yost. It would have taken much more than a passing friendship to budge Yost on this matter.

Other Michigan athletic teams were playing Notre Dame in 1923, but recently Yost was having serious misgivings even on that score. You see, for Yost a loss to anyone in anything was ruinous, but a loss to a school holding the upper hand was criminal. And he was now of the firm mind that Notre Dame owned several unfair advantages over Big Ten schools.

Many circumstances led Yost to that conviction. To properly explain them, the policing of intercollegiate athletics in the 1920s must be addressed.

It was still an entirely different ball game, as compared to today. The infant NCAA didn't have the power to lay the law for all universities. Such a nationwide, uniform set of rules was a pipe dream. From school to school, there remained wide discrepancies in regulations covering many key matters—academic eligibility, transferring, recruiting, scholarships, length of playing season, and freshman team and "B-team" competition.

The Western Conference, which by the 1920s was commonly called the Big Ten, was still the most restrictive in these areas. Some midwestern independents continued to do pretty much as they saw fit, as did many eastern colleges.

Yost had always despised losing to teams with advantages, but this disgust had intensified during Michigan's time away from the conference, circa 1908–17. In this 10-year span, the Wolverines had compiled a dismal 11-13-3 record against its three principal archrivals: Penn, Syracuse, and Cornell. While Michigan had continued to adopt almost all of the evolving Big Ten guidelines, these eastern schools did not. And for Yost, who probably took football and its rules more seriously than anyone else in history, these numerous defeats rankled his very soul.

That's why, in spite of his earlier opposition, Yost was relieved when Michigan opted to return to the Big Ten in 1917. "We can and will fare better against conference teams than those outside," he wrote at the time. "This is due, primarily, to the fact that we have competed against at least two teams each year that have played freshmen and four-year men against us and who have had other advantages."

When Yost added the athletic director's portfolio to his coaching duties in 1921, he resolved for Michigan to pursue what he termed "equality of competition." It wasn't that he had become a reform zealot—far from it. He just could not stand to play anybody who could get away with more than he could. The way Yost saw it, if he had to abide by harsh constraints, so should everybody. By June 1923 he made it his goal to see every Big Ten member playing only those schools "hitched in the same kind of harness."

And in his eyes, Notre Dame was a wild stallion.

Yost was at least partially caught in a time warp here, still believing that Notre Dame was snubbing the strict Big Ten academic requirements and, worse, was suiting up anyone who could play. He was flat wrong on that assumption, as Notre Dame's eligibility rules in the 1920s were almost identical to the Big Ten's, and, for the most part, were strictly enforced.

But while Yost was usually vague in these eligibility condemnations, he was far more specific—and upset—about competitive advantages he saw at Notre Dame, ones that allowed its athletes to become more experienced. In the early '20s the Fighting Irish were playing 10 and 11 games a year, while Big Ten football teams were limited to seven. As well, Notre Dame was allowing freshmen and hall athletic teams to play outside games, when this was disallowed in the conference. These and other practices gave Notre Dame athletes opportunities to gain added playing experience, and Yost always stridently maintained that the more seasoned team owned a tremendous edge, especially in football.

With this view, it's surprising Yost was allowing any Wolverine teams to play the Fighting Irish. But until June 1923, Yost had held off from actually enforcing his master plan of college competition. Yost's modest friendship with Rockne was probably the only thread linking Michigan and Notre Dame athletically.

That last strand was shredded—dramatically and suddenly—on the weekend of the 1923 Big Ten outdoor track championships, held

June 1 and 2 in Ann Arbor. As always, this competition signaled the end of the busy Big Ten athletic season, and, as always, important scheduling and policy meetings were held in conjunction.

The setting for the pending drama was the University of Michigan's athletic complex, known then as Ferry Field.

Both the stars of our show were on hand. As A.D. of the host school, Yost had a vested interest in the smooth running of the events. Rockne was there because he was coach of the Irish track team (he had assumed that post in 1914, four years before becoming head football coach).

Yost played the role of instigator, firing the first shot at the Saturday morning meeting held exclusively for Big Ten athletic directors. He decided, at last, to launch his "fair field and no favors" campaign against Notre Dame and the other schools he deemed as outlaws. Those athletic directors close to Rockne were shocked by Yost's broadside, which apparently included a remark about Rockne being a Protestant holdout at a Catholic school.

That set the confrontational mood for the day, and it all reached a climax during the long-awaited track meet.

Michigan and Illinois, the defending champion, were the class of the field. Each was strong in every event, and each featured future Olympians. Notre Dame, one of four nonconference teams invited to participate, was shooting for third like everyone else.

The fateful race was the 120-yard high hurdles. Michigan's DeHart Hubbard—the first black ever to win a varsity track letter at Michigan— had convincingly won his heat on Friday in 15.0 seconds. Frank (Pitch) Johnson of Illinois finished second, two-fifths of a second behind. In Saturday's final, it was Johnson who reached the tape first, repeating his time of 15⅖ths. Hubbard placed a disappointing fifth after stumbling over the third hurdle.

Enter the controversy.

Almost immediately it was determined that the third hurdle in each runner's lane had inadvertently been placed out of position, and that each runner had been thrown off stride to some extent. Detroit papers reported the misplacement to have been five feet, while *The Daily Illini* later said the third row was but eight inches removed. Anyway, after a short deliberation, meet referee Charles A. Dean ordered the race run over. But Illinois, suspecting Yost's influence at work, refused to reenter Johnson. Coach Harry Gill even pulled his Fighting Illini from the field in protest. A few other schools—first Notre Dame, then Wisconsin, Purdue, and Minnesota—withdrew in support of Illinois. So with no compromise in sight, and the lid coming off Pandora's box, Dean decided to throw out the results and scrap the event entirely. The boycotting teams returned and the meet concluded.

Michigan barely won the championship, 57½ points to Illinois's 57; Notre Dame finished fifth with 14½ points. Had the 120 high hurdles results stood, Illinois would have prevailed, 62 points to Michigan's 58½. Gill, naturally, was fuming afterward and lodged a protest with the Big Ten board of directors.

Yost had watched the entire hurdle-race episode unfold from the infield. What outraged him most was Notre Dame's participation in the boycott. Yost felt Rockne had committed the ultimate act of betrayal, siding against his and Michigan's interests in a moment of crisis and instead backing Michigan's archrival. The fact that Notre Dame was the first school to back Illinois was all the more distressing.

During the height of the hurdles dispute, Yost had sought out Notre Dame captain Gus Desch on the infield and, through him, relayed some harsh words to Rockne, calling him a quitter and, according to one report, promising Rockne his "dirty Irish" would never again be allowed on Ferry Field.

This verbal salvo shot Rockne into orbit. He was already seething at Yost. Several of the conference athletic directors had just come to him with news of Yost's diatribe at the meeting that morning, in which he had implored the other Big Ten schools to shun the Irish in all sports. That caught Rockne completely off guard.

Although criticism of Notre Dame was nothing new to Rockne, the mere suggestion that Notre Dame was a rules renegade struck an exposed nerve. Even the weakest of jabs was sure to have him come out swinging with both fists. Thus, Rockne—every bit as combative and headstrong as Yost—would not let this attack go unanswered. He went hunting for the head Wolverine right after the track meet ended, but Yost had left immediately on a trip to Michigan's upper peninsula.

Rockne refused to let the matter die.

Two weeks later he initiated a series of blunt exchanges—each wrote the other twice—in which they staked out their positions on the track tangle and discussed the merits of Notre Dame's purported advantages. Any remaining fibers of mutual goodwill disintegrated after this run of correspondence.

On the hurdles dispute, Rockne told Yost he would overlook his comment to Desch as "having been made in heat of anger." Yost replied it was a statement he was "perfectly willing to repeat," and did:

When I saw you rushing up and down on the walkway in front of the South Stand, hat off, hurrying Desch out on the field to withdraw all of

Notre Dame's competitors [because the referee] did not decide something
to suit you, I said to him, "You can tell Rockne that if he withdraws his
team under these circumstances, so far as I am concerned, they would not
be invited back to Ferry Field for any other other competition."

As I look at it, Notre Dame was in this meet by invitation and those in
charge of the Notre Dame team should be willing to abide by the decision
or decisions of those in charge of the meet. *Certainly no objection to a
decision should merit the withdrawal of a team. On that principle we can
have no intercollegiate competition.* [Emphasis added.]

I have been told that you suggested to coach Gill, of Illinois, that if he
would withdraw his team you would withdraw your team.

Seeing that Yost had already had it in his mind to "get" Notre Dame
that weekend, it's entirely possible he used the track tangle just as an
excuse to make the final break. Yet three years earlier he had stated
his criteria for ending relations with a school, and they are consistent
with the reason he cited to Rockne, italicized above. In December
1920, Yost wrote: "If the time ever comes that we lose faith in the
honor and integrity of those in charge of our opponents, I for one will
consider it time for all relations to cease. I know that no good can
come from competition where confidence and goodwill does not exist."

Rockne answered Yost's 1923 letter with the intention of "clearing
up" some misunderstandings:

Regarding my threat to withdraw my team, this was just simply doing
what several of the Conference teams were doing. I was staying with them.
I had no man in the event and I was interested in a fair deal. Reports
came to us that [Dean's first decision] was influenced by you. Though you
were out meddling on the field, something no other Conference director
has ever done, I realize [this] report was untrue and I sincerely apologize.

Reports that I in any way influenced Harry Gill are untrue and Mr. Gill
will tell you so.

Illinois and several Conference teams were withdrawing from the meet
but you made no remarks to them such as you made to Mr. Desch. It is
true we were guests, and we appreciate the privilege very much, but we
were entitled to the same rights as the other competing teams.

I will say that the story of the way you knocked Notre Dame upset me
to the extent that I did what I might otherwise not have done.

Yost's reply to this letter refuted the claim that he was "meddling."
Gill's protest was later denied, and Yost cited to Rockne a paragraph
from the conference report that found no one connected in any way
with the University of Michigan had protested the 120-yard high hur-

dles. Yost concluded his last-ever letter to Rockne with this little parting shot about their roles in the hurdles dispute: "It is not so much where you are as what you do."

The bulk of discussion in these crucial four letters, however, addressed Notre Dame's alleged advantages. Rockne always believed Yost's accusations were just a smokescreen for his real motives— jealousy of Notre Dame's success and anti-Catholic prejudice. It was an era of rabid anti-Catholicism in America, when the Ku Klux Klan had a foothold even in the rural Midwest. Notre Dame, the bastion of Roman faith for many American Catholics, was forever the brunt of vicious prejudicial scorn.

Rockne could barely restrain his anger as he began his first letter:

A half a dozen of my friends among the [athletic] directors in the Conference came to me Saturday and told me that you had been haranging them all not to play Notre Dame in anything. I think this was very unfair of you. We live up to Conference *eligibility* rules as given in your code book, but not your *special* [competition] regulations, as we are not a member of the Western Conference. We belong to the Indiana Intercollegiate Conference, which allows our freshmen teams to play two games and our Varsity teams as many games as faculties will agree to. The same as Yale, Harvard and Princeton do.

Then Rockne lost it:

The Western Conference could put in a regulation that all coaches had to join the Ku-Klux-Klan, but that certainly will not apply to us any more than some of the other freak regulations they may have. We do have men down in their classes and not eligible, but we do *not* believe in *disgracing* loyal athletes to *exploit* the school. If the Conference will publish names of all students who flunk, we will do the same.

Now if you personally do not want to meet Notre Dame, that is your business, no holler from this end. If you do not feel that we are fair, we do not want to play either. But I do not think that it is fair for you to carry on a knocking campaign against us. I have always been a loyal booster and admirer of yours and I hope always to be. However, I am *no quitter*. . . . I will not sit by quietly and have my school knocked even though I am not of its faith. I play the game fairly and squarely and any time I don't I will resign from all athletics.

Assuring you of my hope of remaining friendly, even if we do not compete against each other, I am,

Sincerely yours, K.K. Rockne.

Yost's reply to this rocket revealed the more subtle side to his character. Yost knew Rockne would be expecting a vociferous counterattack, but, as a law graduate, Yost knew an argument presented unemotionally and rationally carries far greater weight. So he attempted to show up Rockne with a calm, collected approach—and, as a final dig, presented it formally and neatly typewritten under University of Michigan letterhead, because Rockne had chicken-scratched his letter on undersized hotel stationery:

Your letter of June 14th received. This I have read carefully.

Since I have been Director of Intercollegiate Athletics at the University of Michigan for the past two years, I have been a strong advocate of equality in competition. I mean by this that universities competing with each other should have common eligibility rules and *regulations* governing the number of games, practice periods, time away from the university, etc. No university should have or want advantages over its competitors.

In my opinion, if a university deems it advisable to play on Thanksgiving, has a 10- or 12-game football schedule, and has freshmen competition with other schools [all of which Notre Dame did], it should seek its competition with universities that have the same standards and privileges. This is true of your university or any other one.

In discussing this problem at directors meetings I have cited [these universities as] having more liberal rules of competition than the Conference: Notre Dame, Wabash, DePauw, University of Detroit, [Washington and Jefferson], West Virginia—my old university—and perhaps others.

Creed has nothing to do with it. Three out of the last four football captains at Michigan have been Catholic and many of my best friends are.

In your letter you state that a half dozen of your friends among the directors of the Conference told you that I have been "haranguing them" not to play Notre Dame in anything. I will admit that under the discussion of "equality in competition" in [eligibility] rules as well as in regulations governing competition, that this might easily be inferred by any director, for the Conference rules of competition are more strict in many ways than [Notre Dame's].

I do not believe that the Universities of the Conference should handicap their teams and men and put them in competition with any university that has many advantages that go toward the development of an athletic team with much added experience in competition. Even under these conditions, Michigan has competed with Notre Dame for years, and the past year had games with your institution in baseball, hockey, basketball and tennis. . . .

I have made you a frank statement of my position and my viewpoint and I want to assure you that nothing personal enters into this in any way. . . .

Very truly yours, Fielding H. Yost

Yost also told Rockne he was sending copies of their letters to all the other Big Ten athletic directors, since Rockne did not name those with whom he conferred.

Rockne responded immediately, this time with a typewritten letter under University of Notre Dame letterhead, and this time with less emotion (Score one for Yost). But Rockne was no less emphatic:

I wish to thank you for your frank letter which reached me today. I do not see where it changes my position in any way. . . .

I have your notes on the function of college athletics. I consider most of it very fine thought. However . . . I reiterate very strongly that we obey the same rules of eligibility as the Conference. Your statement to the contrary merely libels our entire faculty.

We do play a 10-game schedule in football and our hall and freshmen teams do play two games outside. We also travel a little more than you do. As we have to support a large department of physical education from football funds alone (we have no tax support from the state), we just now have to play 10 games. In a year or two we may be in a position to cut down to eight. As we believe in competition for as many as possible, our hall and freshman teams do play two games outside, as well as their games at home between themselves. I believe that we are entitled to our point of view and that it has merit.

As teams in our own class in [the] Middle-west will not play us in football, we have to go east and south for games suitable to our size. However we are not absent from school for any one game any longer than you are. . . .

Yale, Harvard, and Princeton have played 10-game schedules and maintain freshmen teams. Do you presume that they are undesirable competition for you? Furthermore, why should we have the onus without the bonus? Admit us to your Conference and we will obey every regulation besides your eligibility code.

I think you are unfair in sending a copy of my previous letter to the Conference directors without my permission. However, I will save you the trouble this time by sending copies myself [Score one for Rockne.] I think your position is unfair but I am relying on the fairness of the other Conference directors. However, should they decide not to play us I will accept their decision quietly and will try and carry on as best I can the work I am doing at Notre Dame.

I have personally in the last five years put out of college competition seven very good men on information gathered by ourselves. . . .

I believe in being fair and square in everything. If anyone can show otherwise I will resign my position here at once. As loyal Americans I feel that we are entitled to a square deal.

In conclusion, Rockne laid it on even thicker than Yost did for the eyes of the other conference A.D.s:

I have the highest respect for the University of Michigan and I am sorry that we will not compete with them. Whether or not they compete with us, I have the highest respect for the Western Conference. They have had a wonderful influence for good on our college athletics. As a body they have always preached and practiced the highest ethics, and they, as a body, have always been fair and square.

Very truly yours, K.K. Rockne

Yost's reply, the fourth and final letter in this series, covered only the track dispute.

Yost would never forgive Rockne for his desertion at the track meet.

Subsequently, the Michigan mentor followed through on his threat to boycott the Irish: The next time a Notre Dame athletic team received an invitation to play at Ferry Field was 1937.

Thus was launched this intense two-man war. The battle lines were drawn, the artillery moved to the front. On one side was Yost, with his old anti–Notre Dame passions reawoken. On the other was Rockne, with his old anti-Yost passions reawoken.

Muckraking

During the height of their hostilities, 1925–29, Yost and Rockne hurled huge gobs of muck at one another—usually over perceived rules transgressions, for the last thing these two ultracompetitive men could stand to see was the other skirt the rules.

Yost did most of the mudslinging, but Rockne flung back some big-sized chunks of his own.

Following the hurdle-race episode, Yost and Rockne were no longer on speaking or writing terms, so the muck usually went through a middle man. More often than not, it plopped on the desk of the Western Conference's first commissioner—Major John L. Griffith. Thus, Griffith probably knew better than anyone the animosity that existed between these fiery men.

To be sure, Griffith was caught square in the middle of this feud. Complicating his position was: (1) the fact he owed his very job to Yost, because Yost was the one who suggested the conference hire a commissioner in the first place; and (2) Griffith was a friend of Rockne's and annually relied on Rockne to place advertisements about his coaching school in Griffith's sidelight publication, *The Athletic Journal.*

So Griffith could never really take sides, even though he had many opportunities, on a variety of rules-related issues.

● ● ●

Yost was forever whining that Notre Dame was a lawless football factory, and he implored Griffith to sever the conference's relations with the school. (Rockne's arguments following the hurdle-race episode had not shaken Yost one iota from this stance.)

Notre Dame's looser competition regulations peeved Yost the most. By 1926, Notre Dame was still playing more games than conference schools were allowed (10 to 8). And hundreds of ND students played on intramural football teams, while the hall and freshman teams were still allowed outside games.

Yost saw it as no coincidence that, as of December 1926, Notre Dame had won its last 12 games against Big Ten schools over a six-year period. So he fired off this diatribe to Griffith:

. . . One can readily see how the Conference is helping Notre Dame, a freelance, to obtain all of the advantages of the Conference without any of its restrictions or regulations. . . .

It is just as I said—they are without restriction, they have competition for all their teams, hall teams, freshmen teams, and second teams—they can play as long as they like and can be absent from college two weeks, and so far as I know, never have a man ineligible scholastically that was a good varsity man.

In other words, we are furnishing all the funds and prestige to help maintain this institution athletically in the course it is pursuing.

Rockne always defended Notre Dame's competition rules, especially the one that allowed all students—not just the varsity—to play organized football. His point was that most students had little or no chance of making the varsity, anyway. "A thousand boys may take violin lessons but one only can become a Kreisler," Rockne maintained, "and a thousand boys may take piano lessons and one only become a Paderewski."

Yet on at least one other occasion, Rockne admitted that his multi-tiered football structure was indeed an advantage. Wrote Allison Danzig of the *New York Times* in 1929:

Rockne attributes, in part, the success of his teams [to] the system of mass athletics that he, as athletic director, has built up at South Bend, where a dozen dormitory teams play regular schedules with each other.

So Yost's "football factory" charge was not, in fact, empty.

But what of Yost's beef that Notre Dame's longer schedule was a competitive advantage? He claimed that the more opportunities any team has to fine-tune, the better it will undoubtedly become. Yost rationalized Rockne's monstrous success, in part, with this argument. Of course, the flip side of this argument is that the more times a team plays, the more opportunities it has to lose. But Rockne's teams seldom did.

Even if a longer schedule was an advantage, whether this or any other was an *unfair* advantage is another question entirely. Besides, as Rockne pointed out to Yost after the hurdle-race episode, Notre Dame had enough onuses—being a private school fighting an unwarranted reputation and anti-Catholic prejudice—that maybe it was entitled to a few bonuses.

What's more, by 1929 these advantages disappeared. Big Ten teams had begun intercollegiate competition for "B teams"—the equivalent of Notre Dame's hall teams—and Notre Dame reduced its schedule to nine games, the same number conference schools were now allowed.

So was Rockne correct, after all, in his belief that Yost concocted these competition-rule squawks just as a smoke screen for his more sinister, petty motives?

Most likely not.

To Yost, any advantage was an unfair advantage, period. And it has been conclusively shown that he held this view long before his run-ins with Rockne, and that Notre Dame wasn't the only school Yost ever boycotted for having more lenient rules. He refused to play Pop Warner's Carlisle and Pitt teams in the 1910s, in addition to all those schools he listed to Rockne following the hurdle-race episode, which included his very own alma mater, West Virginia.

So although Yost may have exaggerated these competition concerns, they genuinely riled him.

🏈   🏈   🏈

Occasionally, Rockne would get a letter from a fan or acquaintance asking if it were true Notre Dame did not follow the strict eligibility rules of the Western Conference. Each time, Rockne flatly denied the charge. To one inquirer he wrote:

This story about the eligibility of our football teams is one of Fielding H. Yost's which he is always peddling out of the University of Michigan. It is absolutely untrue.

We follow the Western Conference rules without exception on eligibility. . . .

In case you run up against more of this Michigan propaganda . . . I'd suggest that you have them name specific instances.

Indeed, Yost was forever "peddling out" these accusations. Rockne was so miffed in early 1927 that he publicly complained, although he didn't mention Yost by name or by school. "One of the Big Ten universities is going out of its way to question the athletic eligibility standards at Notre Dame," he said at a speech in Chicago.

Rockne's mentor, Jesse Harper, read about the remark in Wichita, Kansas. "I suppose you are referring to our mutual friend Yost," Harper wrote, indicating a lingering bitterness from his days at Notre Dame. "I am mighty glad you called him and did it [publicly]. He has needed calling for a good many years."

Yost usually qualified his sweeping, general indictments of Notre Dame's eligibility rules with his favorite crutch, "so far as I know." But on one occasion in 1928, anyway, Yost did indeed name specific instances.

The former president of the Notre Dame Alumni Association, lawyer F.H. Wurzer, demanded that Yost back up claims he had made at a speech in Detroit, because "we are, of course, both interested in getting at the real facts and the full truth for the general benefit of all football followers."

Yost obliged with a return letter, in which he reeled off in lawyer-like fashion two specific charges. One, as it turns out, was entirely baseless, but the other, according to the evidence in Yost's possession, appears genuine: that star center Bud Boeringer had played two years at St. Thomas College in Minnesota before playing two more at Notre Dame (one year too many). "If I am wrong in any of my above statements," Yost concluded, "I would be glad to have you correct me."

Wurzer replied merely to acknowledge receipt of Yost's letter.

Oh, how that must have made Yost's day! Believing he had won this "trial" hands down, Yost drafted copies of these letters and gave them the widest possible distrubution. Many uncirculated copies remain in his files.

Fact was, Notre Dame's eligibility rules were almost identical to those of the Western Conference. For the most part, they were strictly enforced. Yet Murray Sperber, author of the most accurate account of the Rockne years at Notre Dame, points out that Rockne often clashed with the Faculty Board of Control on cases of eligibility. On one occasion a star halfback flunked out, and Rockne vigorously lobbied to have him reinstated, to no avail. Rockne's record on eligibility, then, certainly was not clean.

But Yost's was no cleaner.

In early 1925, Rockne complained to Commissioner Griffith that Michigan's track captain, world-class pole vaulter James K. Brooker, was currently in his fourth year of varsity competition—after two previous at Michigan and one before that at Michigan Agricultural College. Rockne knew this because, as the Irish track coach in 1921, he had seen Brooker compete for M.A.C. against Notre Dame.

Griffith brought the allegation to Yost's attention on February 26, ever careful not to mention Rockne as the informant. The chairman of Michigan's Board in Control, Ralph Aigler, replied to Griffith on March 11 that Brooker claimed he had given only exhibition vaults for M.A.C. and had not actually competed.

Upon hearing this, Rockne sizzled. On March 17 he provided Griffith with details of Brooker's participation in the M.A.C.–Notre Dame meet, adding, "I believe Brooker himself realizes he is ineligible, as he made a remark to the other pole vaulters at the Illinois Relays the other night." In concluding his letter to Griffith, Rockne lost all control of his hair-trigger temper:

> I do not want to become involved in this thing because whenever any
> of my men are involved, I investigate the matter thoroughly myself, and
> I don't try to shield, to the best of my ability, any of my athletes about
> whom there is any question.
>
> However, of course, I have my own opinions regarding the people in
> charge of the athletics at Michigan, and I am very glad we are not compet-
> ing against them in any sport. Personally, I am inclined to think that Yost
> is not a bit more honest now than he was 20 years ago. Evidently, a leop-
> ard's spots do not change.

Michigan subsequently investigated Brooker's past and discovered that, indeed, he had participated in varsity competition for M.A.C. in 1921. "The question of whether he should have competed for M.A.C. or not, or whether he knew he was actually competing or giving an exhibition, is aside from the question," Yost wrote Griffith on April 28 in explaining the oversight. "He actually competed and the points were counted, so Brooker has been declared ineligible for further athletic competition at the University of Michigan."

Griffith later apologized to Yost for having to put the screws to him, but "some pressure was being exerted from another source."

The fact that Brooker was also a student member of Michigan's Board in Control was further embarrassment to Yost. Oh, how the "source"—one K.K. Rockne—must have loved that one!

Yost's record on eligibility is further sullied in the minutes of the

Michigan Board in Control, circa February 1924. The board was examining the academic status of Richard Vick, starting fullback on the '23 varsity football team. The "inescapable conclusion" was that Vick was negligent in his studies. A vote was taken and Vick was ruled ineligible. The sole faculty member who opposed the ruling was Fielding Yost.

●   ●   ●

Another of Yost's muck-raking concerns was Rockne's laissez-faire attitude toward keeping professionalism out of the college game.

Yost's disdain for pro football was exceeded only by that of his Purity League partner, Amos Alonzo Stagg. Remember, this was the era of Jim Thorpe's Olympic disgrace, when amateurism was the holiest of athletic ideals. By the 1920s, the Western Conference had embarked on a crusade to once and for all weed pros out of college sports, especially football. It passed legislation that banned any players, coaches, or game officials who took part in pro games. But college football players had, for years, been routinely earning money on the side on Sundays with club and town teams, and despite the Big Ten's crackdown the practice continued into the '20s.

The beginning of the end didn't come until November 27, 1921, when teams representing two Illinois towns squared off. Representing Taylorville were practically the entire starting 11 of the University of Illinois. Representing Carlinville were eight or nine Notre Dame starters. Taylorville won 16–0, and it was said that among all the townies present, some $35,000 changed hands. Word of the outrageous game quickly spread, and from that point on, Sunday games involving college players gradually died off, clearing the way for the ascent of the National Football League.

In fact it was a fledgling NFL team known as the Chicago Bears that was the center of a Yost-Rockne clash after the 1924 season. When Yost and Stagg discovered that Notre Dame assistant coach Hunk Anderson had been earning some money on the side with the Bears, they forced a confrontation with Rockne. The righteous twosome weren't there to debate the pros and cons; their point was that pros *were* cons. Anderson recalled his conversation with Rockne following the meeting:

"Yost and Stagg were over and they want me to get you to quit playing pro ball with the Bears," Rockne told me. "They insist that if you refuse, I am obligated to fire you. Yost says that you are giving college football a black eye and I can't repeat what Stagg says . . . not on an empty stomach."

I decided to fight back.

"Hell, Rock, you played and coached pro football when you were an assistant at Notre Dame," I reminded him.

"Times have changed, Hunk. Besides, what if you get hurt . . . you have kids to worry about."

"Oh yeah, you had kids to worry about, too. Come on Rock, you aren't going to let those guys dictate to you, are you?"

Rock shook his head and his face evinced exasperation and defeat.

"Okay, Hunk . . . you win. See you tomorrow."

This left Yost and Stagg, long the bitter foes of Notre Dame, with more fodder.

Similarly, Yost was indignant over the appointment of Dick Hanley as Northwestern's football coach in 1927. Seems Hanley had, before taking the job with the Wildcats, been playing pro ball on the side while coaching Haskell Institute in Oklahoma. Yost asked Commissioner Griffith to investigate, for the sake of amateurism and the conference's pristine slate thereon.

That's not the way Rockne saw it, however. He didn't think it a coincidence that he and Pop Warner—another old nemesis of Yost's—were good friends with Hanley. At a meeting of athletic directors, Yost shot salvos at Hanley, Warner, Rockne, and even Tad Jones of Yale. "It seems the old boy [Yost] is getting a little childish in his old age and can't stand to see anyone else get along," Rockne wrote Warner afterward. "My attitude is to ignore him entirely, and he did not get to first base in any way in his wild talk." In the end, Hanley's appointment was not revoked.

⬤   ⬤   ⬤

In all his attacks on Notre Dame regarding rules transgressions, Yost curiously never mentioned anything about the illegal recruitment or subsidization of athletes.

That's because, at least on this score, Yost knew he couldn't throw stones—for his glass house was more vulnerable than Rockne's. Indeed, it wasn't that these illegal practices weren't happening at Notre Dame. It's just that they weren't as widespread or as organized as at Michigan.

Subsidization of athletes hadn't been a contentious issue in college athletics since the 1890s. Weeding out tramps had been the main concern in the interim, and mission was accomplished in the '20s with the wide adoption of the one-year residency rule. Thus, "high school halfbacks from heaven" could no longer be wooed by the prospect of immediate playing time with little or easy study time. The only carrots left to be dangled were jobs and various forms of financial aid, such as scholarships—that is, get the kid a job on the side, or have the alumni "take care of him," and he'll go to your school. If that didn't work, alumni might establish slush funds or provide athletes with bogus, high-paying jobs.

No one denied such chicanery took place. Athletic department employees tried to absolve themselves of blame by claiming to have no control over what zealous alumni do. In fact, such chicanery became scandalous only when it was learned athletic department employees were involved. This was a liaison of the worst order termed "organized recruiting."

Nothing especially damning was revealed against either Michigan or Notre Dame until 1929, with the release of the "Carnegie Report," a blockbuster exposé of the cancers of college athletics.

The report was especially critical of Michigan. It cited Michigan as "among the least fortunate" of 100 or so schools surveyed in the manner in which both the university and its alumni clubs provided loans, jobs, and other forms of aid to athletes. Yost and his staff were also criticized for "vigorously" recruiting athletes. The source for all this information was the Michigan athletic department's very own correspondence files.

The report was far less critical of Notre Dame, but it cited the school and its alumni for making vague promises to "take care of" prospective athletes. The source, again, was athletic department letters.

Both Yost and Rockne vehemently denied the claims of the "Carnegie Report" about their respective schools.

At Michigan, Ralph Aigler, chairman of the athletic board, was especially outraged. First, he charged the Carnegie people with having a decided anti-Midwest and antiathletics bias. He also wondered why Michigan had been found so guilty when Iowa was given a virtual clean bill of health, despite the fact that Iowa had been suspended from the conference for a wide range of violations including direct loans to athletes totaling thousands of dollars. Finally, Aigler contended the Carnegie people unfairly strung together excerpts from the letters found in Michigan's files "in such a way as to make out the skeleton of a 'system.' . . . [And] the interesting and startling fact is that not one of the boys written about ever came to Michigan. If it is true that we have not only a system, but that it is subtle and intense, it is perfectly evident that there has been a gross lack of efficiency somewhere."

Following the release of the "Carnegie Report," Yost got a ringing endorsement from Commissioner Griffith. He informed Yost that he believed everything at Michigan was "on a sane and sound basis. . . . Our colleges and universities may well look at Michigan as an ideal." Later, Griffith indicated to Aigler that various confidential surveys of conference athletes revealed nary a single charge against Michigan regarding inducements. "My own conclusion," Griffith wrote, "is that Mr. Yost and his men are playing the game honestly and conscientiously. I do not believe there is any organized recruiting at Michigan."

Other evidence suggests otherwise, however.

After the Wolverines had stumbled to a 3–4 record in 1919, Yost whipped alumni and students into a recruiting frenzy. Yost suggested the campaign motto be "Michigan loyalty should be expressed in service." A year later, that service was so fervent that Yost himself was publicly cautioning alumni from "overindulging" in recruiting. But Yost's own letters reveal he was involved at every step of the way with the very man whose job it was to oversee this vigorous recruiting campaign—Robert (Bobcat) Clancy, the field secretary for the University of Michigan Club of Detroit. In addition to "fixing up" players through various means such as the "Detroit loan fund," Clancy was always telling Yost of his arduous efforts to ensure that all the star Wolverines remained scholastically eligible.

It would be naive to believe such practices were wiped out at Michigan by Yost's singular plea in 1920 for alumni to stop "overindulging."

In addition, in May 1927 Commissioner Griffith approached Yost with a story of how a certain lot of land in Detroit was being sold over and over again, with "real estate deals practically closed by Michigan men and then Michigan athletes calling in to get the credit for work they did not do." One Michigan alumnus whose name Griffith said was associated with the scam was Cy Huston, a good friend of Yost's.

Griffith's informant was, of course, Rockne, although the commissioner was very careful to conceal this fact from Yost.

But Rockne, like Yost on eligibility matters, was in no position to be throwing stones.

Wells Twombley, in his authorized biography of Frank Leahy, wrote that during Leahy's playing days at Notre Dame, 1927–30, illegal aid for players was available. "In order to be certain that Notre Dame continued to be the finest, fittest college football team in the nation, Catholic businessmen, as a point of pride, regularly subsidized players," Twombley wrote. "In fact, just before he left, Frank Leahy was told by Denny Lannon, a Notre Dame graduate from Winner, South Dakota, with a few dollars in his account, that if he did well and finances became tight there would be a place to go for comfort."

Rockne himself was actively involved in securing on- and off-campus jobs for star recruits. In fact, Leahy recalled in the early 1970s that "Rockne did things recruiting that would appall a modern coach." What's more, Rockne relied heavily on his alumni "bird dogs" to corral talented players and send them his way, although his system apparently was nowhere near as sophisticated as Yost's.

If it had been—if Notre Dame were getting away with more than Michigan—Yost surely would have known about it and surely would have howled about it, for he was meticulous in searching out and "whining about" the slightest of Notre Dame advantages. But he never mentioned anything about recruiting or subsidization scandals at Notre Dame.

◗   ◗   ◗

While most Notre Dame and Michigan books paint Rockne and Yost as paragons of virtue, it's clear that much of the muck they flung at one another stuck.

A shift of philosophies

On the field, the rage in college football in the '20s was an offensive system known as the shift. Its most valiant proponent was Rockne, who perfected and popularized it. Its most virulent opponent was Yost, who thought it illegal and grossly unethical.

So there they were again, at opposite ends of the ocean. Only this was the stormiest cesspool of them all.

While Yost enraged Rockne with all his mudslinging, and through his incessant lobbying of Big Ten schools to shun Notre Dame, nothing Yost ever did caused Rockne more angst, more soul-searing torment, than his ceaseless efforts to have the shift abolished. As the decade wore on, and the antishift faction grew in number and resolve, Rockne worried himself sick that his bread-and-butter offense was going to be sliced from existence.

It almost was.

About 20 years earlier, Stagg had been the first coach to shift players from one offensive alignment to another before the snap of the ball. By 1909, Minnesota coach Dr. Henry Williams was the first to implement the shift wholesale, not only shifting the backfield but rearranging all 11 players into strange and varied alignments, and with much success.

The shift didn't become a national rage until Rockne refined the shift attacks of his Notre Dame predecessors, Jack Marks and Jesse

Harper. His Fighting Irish attack wreaked havoc like few others ever had. Rockne had his four backfield men jump, in perfect sync, from the basic T into a box formation, staggered either left or right of center.

Critics contended the Rockne shift provided illegal momentum, as originally it occurred almost simultaneous with the snap of the ball. Although Rockne admitted on at least one occasion that, in the early years, momentum had indeed been a by-product, he always stridently maintained it was never a motive. "We aim for maximum deception," he explained. "Seeing our shift going to the right, the defense will go to its left, but the odds are the defense will shift too far, not far enough, or not quickly enough. No matter which, our offense has strategic points of attack opened up for it. In concentrating its strength to its left, the defense leaves its right greatly weakened, and before it has time to figure out where we're going, the ball has been snapped and the play is gone."

On another occasion Rockne said, "Our shift is all lateral. It's a matter of getting the blocking angle on the defensive players, getting them out of position. It's smart football."

Too smart to Yost's way of thinking.

His argument was that a legal shift should never bear any momentum, and under that constraint a shift is utterly useless. "I always wanted my boys to get where they're going in the shortest time. We never shift," he once explained.

Yost was still employing his beloved kicking game in the '20s. The press was now dubbing it the "punt, pass, and prayer" offense: punt away as early and as often as possible, pray you force a turnover, then unleash all your trick pass plays. This offense was run out of the "punt formation"—what we'd call the shotgun formation. One halfback stood about seven yards back of the center, while his backfield mates arrayed themselves closer to the line. The ball could be snapped to any one of them. "The best authorities on football have maintained through the years that the punt formation is the most valuable in football," wrote veteran *Detroit News* football expert H.G. Salsinger in 1926. "It is the one formation where the defense cannot possibly guess whether the ball will be kicked, thrown, or carried. No defense can accurately guard against it."

As Rockne was the leading advocate of the shift, Yost was the leading advocate of the punt formation. And as Yost detested the shift, Rockne detested the punt formation.

It is important to note that both men held these divergent football philosophies even before their feud heated up. Once personalities entered into it, though, Knute Rockne became the shift personified to Yost, and likewise Fielding Yost and the punt formation to Rockne.

Speaking of personalities, it's not a coincidence their tricky modes of attack perfectly reflected their personal traits, and also their tendencies as players. Rockne, a pudgy man at five-foot-eight, depended on quickness, on clever blocking angles, and the flashier the better. Yost, a comparative giant at a solid six feet, depended on in-your-face toughness, on dull but effective fundamentals, and on sudden sneak attacks.

Neither ever shifted from his position.

The first cries against Rockne's shift were heard after the 1919 season. Rockne's second team had hopped and run to a 9–0 record and a national title. The critics immediately piped up. They charged that shifting teams such as Rockne's practically got away with a running start, that the backs never seemed to come to a full stop before the snap and therefore had unfair momentum. Officials were as bewildered as defenders. All the rulebook stipulated was that when the ball was snapped, only one player could be in motion. The other 10 could conceivably be in motion until a hundredth of a second before the snap.

After Rockne's 1920 team also went 9–0, the rule was clarified, mandating that the feet of all offensive players had to be "stationary on the ground" after a shift.

Rockne, like any wily coach, continued to obey the letter of the new law. Both feet stationary on the ground? No problem. He had his backfield men stop their feet all right—but he didn't have them stop their upper bodies from swaying, and their momentum was largely retained.

Opponents of the shift were livid. Rockne was disobeying the spirit of the law, they charged, and his 1921 team continued to steamroll the opposition, going 10–1.

Yost was particularly incensed. To him, the football rulebook was as holy as the Bible itself. And although he himself was forever springing trick plays that brushed the fine line of legality, Yost was genuinely appalled by shifting teams such as Rockne's that, in his view, clearly crossed that line.

In a letter to rules icon Walter Camp, Yost let his venom fly:

[The current rule on shifts] is the cause of more disagreement and the source of more trouble than all the other rules in the book. . . . I do not think the official lives who can determine after a quick hop whether the feet of all the men hopping came to a full stop before the ball was put in play, with the body swaying and in motion at the same time.

Those coaches that do not train their men to come to a complete stop of the body and feet are attempting to beat the rules. If we are to have the flying wedge, let's have it. Then we will all do it. I am sure that there will be much better spirit in the game and much less friction if the rule is made so plain and definite that no coach can avoid it.

And that's what Yost spent the rest of the decade doing—lobbying long and hard for the rule to be made so plain and definite that no coach could avoid it. Not even Rockne.

The rule was clarified before the 1922 season to mandate a "complete" stop: "both feet stationary on the ground means that there is sufficient momentary pause for the official to be able to see that the play is legal and that the ball is not snapped while the man is in motion." But that was vague enough to allow Rockne's teams to continue swaying after they shifted, and his 1922–25 teams compiled a 34–4–2 record and won another national title, in 1924.

Surely, the critics reasoned, something had to be done to stop this. And something was done. Beginning in 1926, shifting teams had to come to an "absolute stop"—no swaying, no leaning. The penalty for not complying was five yards.

Rockne's answer? He had his 1926 team come to an absolute stop, all right. But it was a very brief absolute stop, so brief that Rockne's Irish continued that fall to confound opposing defenses and officials.

Yost couldn't understand how Rockne and the other shifters continued to get away with it. "I have gone to the Rules Committee several times before this, until the rule now is in very plain English and is very positive," Yost wrote Walter Eckersall of the *Chicago Tribune*. ". . . I say the shift has already been abolished if the rules are enforced. . . . It is now a question of enforcement by the officials."

Such enforcement took place on the afternoon of October 23, 1926. The events that day kicked off probably the most tumultuous six months of the Yost-Rockne feud.

Notre Dame was in Evanston to play Northwestern. The head linesman in that game, Meyer Morton, penalized Notre Dame all afternoon, especially for failing to bring its shift to an absolute stop. Rockne remembered that, by the end of the game, the Irish had been penalized 95 yards to the Wildcats' zero (although the *South Bend Tribune* reported the ratio to be 75–45).

In fact, Rockne would always say that "the only time in my life I ever got sore at an official" was at Morton in this game.

Meyer Morton, as Rockne well knew, was a conference man. Worse, a Michigan man. Still worse, a Yost man. Indeed, Morton was a prominent member of the University of Michigan Club of Chicago, and his correspondences with Yost and others dot the Michigan files of the '20s and '30s. In fact, the Michigan award for the most improved player following spring practice is today still named after Meyer Morton.

Rockne had virtually no say in Morton's selection as head linesman, as he undoubtedly lamented. Coaches usually had the last word on choosing officials, and they always tried to line up those who were sympathetic to their cause. But in a game involving a Big Ten school, a conference committee dictated to both teams who the officials were, even after the inevitable political wrangling. One of the committee members was Ralph Aigler, chairman of the Michigan Board in Control. This was a particular sore point with Rockne. "We are not playing Michigan, hence, I cannot see any reason why [Yost] is picking our officials," he wrote Commissioner Griffith in 1925.

Whether Yost—er, Aigler—picked Morton for Notre Dame–Northwestern is not known. But Rockne was absolutely livid with Morton during the game and let him know it, too. When Griffith later asked about it, Rockne replied, "The only thing I said to the head linesman was, 'It looks to me like a Big Ten suckhole.'"

In the future, Rockne went out of his way to warn his coaching friends not to use Morton in their games. "He is very much a Big Ten homer," Rockne alerted one coach.

But the Morton incident cracked open a whole new chasm of pain for Rockne in November 1926. Immediately there was talk in the papers that the precedent-setting conference was now mulling legislation to outlaw the shift entirely. Even Stagg, the shift's founder, regrettably and outwardly shared his concern with the tactic's current form.

All these incidents left Rockne at his wit's end. Griffith tried to calm him down in a letter on November 3:

> As a friend I want to say to you that in my judgment you are sitting pretty compared to most men that I know in athletics. It is true that you have a lot of petty annoyances which will wear you out and make you nervous if you let them. However, they are trivial and should not count. You are at the top of the football profession and are recognized throughout the country for your ability and character. In a few years, if you want to, you can go into some other business and be independent, and the fellows who yap at you now will then snarl at your successor. You cannot satisfy everybody but in my judgment you satisfy about 98 per cent of the people who know.

But Rockne wasn't alone in his distress. Minnesota and Purdue were also shifting teams, and battle lines within the conference were

being drawn. On the same day he wrote Rockne, Griffith also sent Yost
this plea for help:

> There is considerable evidence to support my belief that many animosi-
> ties and hostilities are developing in our athletics here in the Middlewest.
> If they are allowed to grow we will lose all the ground that we have gained
> in recent years. You more than any of the other directors have attempted
> to develop friendly relations in athletics in the Conference and I am writ-
> ing you about this to suggest that we give the matter serious thought and
> see if we cannot do something at our coming meeting to prevent trouble.

Prevent it? Hell, Yost was looking to make as much trouble as
possible.

With so much at stake, these 1926 Big Ten policy and scheduling
meetings—slated for Friday, November 26, and Saturday the 27th in
Chicago—were as monumental as they came. How crucial were they
to Rockne? So much so that it may have influenced his decision to
leave his team on the day of a game for the first time.

"It was Rockne's fear of what Mr. Yost might do to Notre Dame that
kept him away from his squad and back in Chicago at the Big Ten
meeting the day that Walter Steffen's Carnegie Tech squad slapped the
Irish into a 19–0 coma," recalled *Los Angeles Examiner* columnist
Mark Kelly, a good friend of Rockne's.

Yet the main reason Rockne was in Chicago was to fulfill a contractual obligation with the Christy Walsh syndicate to write a column
about the Army-Navy game.

What would Rockne have had to fear at the Big Ten meetings? Only
that Yost might orchestrate either a conference abolition of the shift,
or a conference boycott of Notre Dame. Or both.

Rockne had good reason to fear a conference boycott because he was
aware Yost had, in recent weeks, been pestering Griffith for details of
Notre Dame's competition rules. As well, rumors were rife that the
conference was going to demand that members play more games against
each other, thus leaving fewer scheduling opportunities for them to
play nonconference schools such as Notre Dame. Rockne's Fighting
Irish had played three Big Ten teams in 1926, the most since 1921, and
he went to the meetings determined to line up three more for 1927.

As the meetings got under way on Friday, Rockne must have been
relieved to learn that Yost was not, after all, going to bully conference
members into shunning Notre Dame. But the conference did mandate
that all member schools had to play at least four of their eight football
games against one another. Consequently, Rockne was able to schedule only two Big Ten opponents for '27: Indiana and Minnesota.

Far worse news for Rockne, however, was that his gravest fears with regard to the shift were realized. Yost and the other conference coaches passed a rule mandating a two-second delay between the end of the shift and the snap of the ball in all games involving member schools.

The death knell for the shift had sounded, experts across the country believed.

Yost and fellow shift-hater Bob Zuppke, the Illinois coach, had won the bruising fight against Minnesota coach Doc Spears and Purdue coach Jimmy Phelan, both good friends of Rockne's. In fact it was Yost who finally ramrodded the rule through by vowing to sever football relations with Minnesota if it didn't agree to the two-second delay. Spears and the Gophers finally opted to surrender their coveted offense rather than their most popular rival.

So the problem now facing the shifters was this: a shift with a two-second delay was totally ineffective. Not even Rockne would be able to fox his way out of that trap. Momentum aside, the shift's greatest asset, as Rockne maintained, was the way it confused the defense and took it out of position. By giving the defenders two seconds to readjust, however, any offensive advantage would be eliminated.

On December 4, 1926, after the Irish edged USC in Los Angeles, the beleaguered Rockne got away from it all and took his family on a month-long dream vacation to Hawaii.

Upon returning in January, his nightmare resumed. It was now believed the national rules committee would follow the lead of the Western Conference and adopt the two-second rule.

"If they eliminate the shift I guess we will all have to use punt formation or Warner formation, which ought to standardize the game enough for any of the thick heads," Rockne wrote his old college roommate, Gus Dorais, now coach of the University of Detroit.

Rockne was a man who would rather fight than pout, however, and he resolved to lobby hard for some sort of compromise. He recruited his shift disciples to assist him in thumping the cause on the dinner circuits. By the end of February he was convinced the shift would somehow be salvaged. "I have been making quite a few speeches around the country defending the shift," he wrote an acquaintance at West Point. "However, I don't believe the Rules Committee will do as much to the shift as some of our friends would have them. Mr. Yost is certainly very bitter against it, but for selfishness I think he takes the cake."

Finally, Rockne came up with a compromise. He got down on his figurative hands and knees and begged E.K. Hall, chairman of the national rules committee, to consider it:

I do not believe that the good gentlemen who have in their hands the destiny of the American game of football wish to abolish the shift. It is my personal opinion that a lot of the teams copying the shift, and executing it improperly, have been the cause of most of the outcry.

If you will pardon the suggestion—what do you think of a fifteen yard penalty for a shifting team which does not come to a stop? In my opinion, any team can come to a complete stop in a second at least, but a time element of stopping, such as the two-second stop, is purely ridiculous. A team either stops or it does not stop. A fifteen yard penalty on the shifting team that does not stop will immediately change their cadence and *will* stop.

I have always tried to coach the clever style of football, as I appreciate the fact that whenever, in the old days, Notre Dame outplayed some teams such as Michigan we were immediately called the "Dirty Irish" by the "Lily White" folks. . . . If you abolish the shift I am afraid we will have to go back to the rough football which the rest of the "Lily Whites" play and we will suffer as a result as we will be called harsh names. . . .

At a meeting in March 1927, Hall and the rules committee adopted Rockne's suggested 15-yard penalty, but proceeded to institute a time element on the stop—not two seconds but "approximately" one. It was suggested officials rapidly count "1–2–3–4" to determine the one second. The Western Conference subsequently relented from its harsh stance and adopted this one-second rule.

Rockne was elated. He even wrote one of his shift brethren that "all we need to do is spend two counts in position, the same as we used to spend one count, and the shift will be perfectly all right."

What followed, of course, is that Rockne's shifting teams continued to roll up victories during the next three years, winning another national title in 1929. The critics? They continued to howl, this time citing the ambiguity of the "approximate" one-second stop as the source of friction.

So the rule was clarified further in 1930 to read "at least" one second, and officials were now asked to rapidly count "1–2–3–4–5–6" to determine the one second.

Rockne was outraged, not so much at the passing of the new rule but at the manner in which it was passed. The rules committee comprised various coaches from around the country, and Rockne's beef was that although about a third of the coaches nationwide were employing the shift, none were on the committee, or even on any advisory committee. Rockne likened it to the Boston Tea Party: "Taxation without representation."

No matter, Rockne now drilled his backfield to stop for one and two-tenths seconds so as to eliminate any doubt whatsover about the legality of Notre Dame's shift. His exasperation overflowed in a 1930 newsreel clip from practice:

> Every year they want to slow the shift up slower and slower and slower, which in my opinion is absolutely ridiculous. Whether the referee counts six or whether he counts 20, the question simmers down to this: Is there any unfair advantage? And in my opinion, if a shifting team stops for one second, that's long enough for anybody except the stupid defensive team, and football wasn't made for any defensive team. . . .

That last comment might have been a swipe at the defensive-minded Yost. But his teams were hardly stupid. The Michigan coach liked to think he could devise a defense to beat any shifting team, and, as was usually the case with Yost's boasts, he could back it up. From 1920 to 1926 Minnesota's shifting teams failed ever to beat Michigan, and the Gophers had two chances in '26 (Yost's last official year as head coach). The 1925 Gopher shift was particularly quick and powerful, but Yost solved it, as explained in *Detroit Saturday Night* magazine:

> Yost was guilty of a species of low cunning. . . . Michigan played her defensive line a yard and a half back, so her momentum was forward instead of sideways. In other words, she had a running start on defense, just as Minnesota had on offense. Captain Bob Brown attended to the little matter of smashing the two guards, who are the key to the shift. The rest was easy.

Michigan won that game 35–0.

Stop and think for a moment what a colossal matchup it would have been: Rockne's shift versus Yost's defense. Imagine how much prep time Rockne and Yost would have put into it. Imagine how many variations and tricks they would have come up with. Imagine how much pressure the officials watching the shift would have been under. Staggering.

But back to reality. And the reality for Rockne was that much of the shift's usefulness was gone. With the rule made so plain and definite that no coach could avoid it, Yost and the antishift league appeared to have won the decade-long war.

Underline *appeared*.

Because although hamstrung like never before, Rockne's 1930 team— his last—continued to shift. It went undefeated and won the national championship.

"We couldn't satisfy some of our enemies if we'd stop five seconds,"

Rockne said that year, "because their objection is not to the shift, it's to us."

The next time the shift rule was modified was 1949.

Michigan Stadium, Jr.

Rockne didn't respect much about Yost, but he sure respected his architectural sense and business acumen. That's why Notre Dame Stadium came to be a virtual clone of Michigan Stadium, right down to its redwood bleachers.

In building Michigan Stadium, Jr., Rockne and Notre Dame borrowed the same basic design and employed the same architectural firm, a similar financing plan, and a similar parking scheme.

Although Yost and Rockne had no direct discussions on the matter, Yost did lend some assistance to Notre Dame's project, and Rockne did get crucial help from somebody else at Michigan.

That either of these now-legendary stadiums was ever built at all is a sole credit to the respective tenacity of Yost and Rockne.

Yost had mustered all his political power, from Ann Arbor to the state capitol, to gain approval for Michigan Stadium, which opened in October 1927. The University of Michigan's Board of Regents approved seating for only 72,000, but Yost got his wish to have the footings constructed so that the capacity could, in future years, be increased to at least 100,000. After four relatively simple renovations, Michigan Stadium currently seats 102,501. Michigan lore has it that the extra one is Yost's phantom seat.

Yost chose the site, the architect (Bernard L. Green of the Osborn Engineering Company of Cleveland), and the contractor (James Leck Company of Minneapolis), then oversaw every last detail of construction. It was his decision to model Michigan Stadium after the Yale Bowl and to nestle it into a hillside, like Stanford Stadium. (In fact, only the top rim is above ground, so today you can drive by the nation's largest football stadium and not even know it's there.)

Yost also helped devise the financing scheme. Michigan Stadium's price tag was almost a million dollars, so to cover that massive expense Yost sold tax-exempt bonds at $500 apiece through the athletic department. The bond-holder was guaranteed two tickets between the 30-yard lines for 10 years and could cash the bond—at 3 percent interest—at any time. By the time the stadium was two months old, $1.5 million in bonds had been sold.

Word of Michigan's enormous success quickly spread, and perhaps that's why in fall 1927 the push was on to construct a new stadium at

Notre Dame. Rockne had, for years, been begging the Notre Dame hierarchy to do so. Old, dilapidated Cartier Field could squeeze in only 27,000, hence Rockne's Fighting Irish were forced to play some of their biggest games at Chicago and New York. "Rockne felt that Notre Dame should now have a stadium worthy of the school's stature in intercollegiate football," recalled Hunk Anderson, Rockne's assistant.

Notre Dame resolved on December 18, 1927, to address the stadium question. Two committees were formed to investigate the plausibilities: one with regard to financing, the other with regard to design and construction.

A day later, the newly appointed chairman of the finance committee, Albert R. Erskine, wrote University of Michigan president Clarence Cook Little for details of Michigan Stadium's financing plan. "Frankly, I am more impressed with the practicability of your plan than any I have seen and it might be that Notre Dame could follow your example," offered Erskine.

His letter was referred to Yost.

Now, you might think Mr. Anti–Notre Dame would rather have adopted the shift than help Notre Dame with its stadium plans, but such was not the case. Erskine, probably unknowingly, had in his letter massaged Yost's ego, and when anyone—even a Notre Dame man—asked for more details about how great Yost was, well, Yost told him.

Accordingly, Yost's response was forthright and detailed, if not overly friendly. "After you have read this letter and looked over the enclosed printed matter, you might write me again for more specific information," Yost wrote. Erskine later thanked Yost for his assistance, which "will be found very useful to us."

As for the design and construction committee, the two members entrusted with the majority of the work were Rockne and Rev. Thomas Steiner, professor of engineering at Notre Dame. The committee member who likely held the most power was Rev. James Burns, a former Notre Dame president.

It was Burns who suggested Steiner and Rockne go to Ann Arbor and inspect Michigan Stadium, as its appearance and practical construction were just as appealing as its financing. But how in the world would Rockne ever get Yost's permission to do that?

Fact was, Rockne couldn't possibly go through Yost. So he called on Tad Wieman, the assistant athletic director and successor to Yost in 1927 as head football coach. Wieman and Rockne had struck a modest friendship the previous fall, when Rock had asked Wieman for tickets to the Michigan–Ohio State game. "I hate to bother a man as busy as you," Rockne wrote at the time, "but I didn't know to whom I should write." Wieman graciously obliged him with the tickets.

Actually, it appears Rockne could have written just about anybody besides Yost in the Michigan athletic department and been helped. Rockne had "no greater admirer anywhere" than business manager Harry Tillotson, according to *Detroit News* columnist H.G. Salsinger. As well, Philip Pack, the publicity manager and thus Yost's right-hand man, had perfunctory but friendly communications with Rockne.

But could Wieman come through on the imposing stadium request? To Rockne's undoubted relief, he could.

Wieman invited Rockne and Steiner to Ann Arbor on March 27, 1928. He led them on a tour of Michigan Stadium then allowed them free access to cost sheets, blueprints—everything.

Where was Yost? On a trip through the South, which had begun in early March and wouldn't end until mid-April. Did he know about Rockne's visit? Yost never once discussed it in any of the hundreds of letters in his files from March through June.

But odds are Wieman would not have dared do something as dastardly as invite Knute Rockne to Yost's offices without first having the old man's permission. Who knows, maybe Yost was even tickled that his archenemy would come groveling for assistance to copy Yost's own dream project.

Then again, a year later Yost fired Wieman and apparently was still embittered with him—for whatever reason—a decade later.

Anyway, Rockne and Steiner left Ann Arbor extremely impressed, with both what they had learned and the way they had been received. Two days later, Rockne sent this off to Wieman:

> Just a note expressing my sincere appreciation of all the kindnesses and courtesies which you showed us last Monday morning.
>
> Meeting a man like you makes one realize that perhaps this athletic game is worthwhile and I want to sincerely wish you everything good in getting your team in shape for the fall.

Steiner was equally laudatory of Wieman in his detailed report to Father Burns, concluding, "If we decide to build a sunken stadium, we could do no better than follow Michigan's plan."

The Notre Dame hierarchy finally decided, a month later, in April 1928, to go ahead with a new stadium. It would be patterned after Michigan's but would not be sunken. It would be designed by the same Bernard L. Green of the Osborn Engineering Company, but a local contractor would build it. Michigan's financing plan would be adopted in principle but modified to suit Notre Dame's fan base—fewer real alumni and more "subway" alumni. Similarly, Michigan's parking plan was studied but modified to suit Notre Dame's surroundings.

Notre Dame Stadium opened in October 1930. Like Michigan's it was a rectangular, single-deck stadium. Like Michigan's, the continuous, short wall separating the stands from the field comprised red bricks. Like Michigan's, the press box was centered atop the west-side stands. And, oh yes, Notre Dame too used redwood bleachers. About the only noticeable difference, at least inside, was that the players' entrance was located behind the goalposts at the northern end zone, while at Michigan it was centered along the eastern sideline.

Yost was invited by Notre Dame president Rev. Charles O'Donnell to attend dedication ceremonies on the October 10–11 weekend. "Your presence at the dinner on Friday evening is particularly requested," O'Donnell wrote.

The invitation, Yost replied, "is very much appreciated. I regret, however, that it will be impossible for me to attend these exercises."

Summing up

It would be comforting to report that Rockne and Yost shook hands and made up before Rockne's death. Unfortunately, that did not happen. Their relationship ended as strained as ever.

Rockne was always hoping teams such as Minnesota would "take Michigan with a big score" while Yost was "very anxious" for teams such as Southern Cal to whip Notre Dame.

Bedridden with phlebitis on New Year's Eve 1929, Rockne bit back at Yost like never before in response to yet another inquirer of Notre Dame's cleanliness. After likening Yost to an infamous anti-Catholic U.S. senator, Rockne wrote:

> We have exactly the same rules of eligibility as Michigan and he knows it. Our schedules with the finest teams and our fine relations with the best schools in America testify to that fact. . . .

> We have enough prejudice, hypocrisy, and bigotry in our politics without having this sort of negative influence enter our college athletics. The director of athletics of the University of Michigan would do the game a lot of good if he should resign and go into something else where his influence with young men would not be felt. He has lost all influence among all athletic men and, as far as this letter is concerned, I don't care to whom you show it or how you deal with it, as we are doing the best we can to do athletics right, and in no way say anything untrue or unfair about the University of Michigan, as it is a very fine institution in spite of the director of athletics.

If Yost had ever been so moved to bare his soul in letters, he surely would have assessed Rockne with similar disdain. Perhaps he eventually would have done so had the feud continued to ferment. But on March 31, 1931, it came to a sudden and shocking halt, when Rockne was killed in a plane crash in Kansas.

News of Rockne's death saddened the nation. Athletic men everywhere were asked to eulogize Rockne, and Yost was surprisingly praiseworthy—perhaps in an attempt to quell any thoughts a reporter might have had to raise the subject of his feud with Rockne.

"Football has lost its most colorful character and outstanding coach in Knute Rockne," Yost said in a release. "His has been a remarkable leadership in the division of modern football. A Rockne-coached team played clean, hard, fast, versatile football and was never beaten until the last whistle."

The *Detroit News* was apparently the only paper to reach Yost for additional comment, and in that interview he was even more laudatory. "Rockne has done more than any other single man to attract general interest to the game," Yost said.

Commissioner John L. Griffith sent flowers to the funeral in the names of all the Big Ten athletic directors; Yost sent nothing on his own. Of the reams of condolences sent to Mrs. Rockne by athletic men everywhere, nothing came from Yost. And among all the contributions from coaches around the country to the Knute Rockne Memorial Fund (donations ranging from $5 to $200), Yost sent $10.

Maybe it was just as well Yost did not overdo it, for had he shown up for the funeral, heaven knows what kind of riot might have ensued against the man who often made life hell for Rockne.

Did Rockne go to his grave hating Yost? Perhaps. But if his own fictional book about football is any indication, Rockne might not have taken all of Yost's badgering to heart.

The nemesis in Rockne's self-penned *The Four Winners* was clearly intended to be Yost. In the story, Rockne has the hero, "Elmer," describe this evil rival "Coach Smith" as "the greatest self-interest fellow I ever knew in my life. . . . All he thinks about is Smith, Smith, Smith. I think he is a detriment to the game, and I think it is men like him who cause some of our faculty men to lift their eyebrows whenever you mention the word football."

That was Rockne's real-life view of Yost to a T.

But toward the end of the story, Elmer takes a step backward. "He realized now that he no longer hated Coach Smith—the idea was absurd!—and that so far as average human beings go, Coach Smith, after all, was not such a bad fellow. He was a man with certain frailties—but no one is perfect."

Perhaps Rockne, too, took that step backward when exasperation got the best of him.

⬤   ⬤   ⬤

In the final analysis, there can be no mistaking that it was Yost who ignited this feud—on that infamous June 1923 weekend in Ann Arbor—and it was he who splashed the most fuel onto it. Rockne threw most of his Molotov cocktails in self-defense.

What were Yost's true motives for his continual attacks?

All the various rules differences at Notre Dame genuinely galled him. So did the Rockne shift. But there were other factors.

First, Rockne's charge that Yost was blindly jealous of his and Notre Dame's success seems valid, in light of Yost's immense vanity. For the record, Yost apparently was never quoted, or ever wrote in a letter, about having any such envy.

But for two decades Yost had been the midwestern coach that writers across the country raved about, whose coaching disciples were forever being sought by other schools. Then this Rockne guy comes along, implements a controversial offense, piles up the wins, steals away most of the accolades and coaching referrals, and becomes the most well-known coach the game has ever known. Thus, it probably wasn't a coincidence that Yost cut the cord with Rockne and Notre Dame at the precise time Rockne was becoming a national celebrity.

Another factor was anti-Catholic prejudice.

Rockne was certain Yost's "Kluxer mind" was his main motive. "Fielding H. Yost is a very capable business man in every sense of the word," he once wrote, "but he is a hill-billy . . . and hence very narrow on religion."

But remember the exact words Yost used in one of his letters to Rockne following the hurdle-race episode: "Creed has nothing to do with it. Three out of the last four football captains at Michigan have been Catholic and many of my best friends are."

Giving Yost the benefit of the doubt that he wasn't prejudiced against Catholic individuals, it does appear, however, that he was biased against Catholicism itself, and certainly against Catholic schools. Remember, Yost was raised by a devoutly Methodist family in West Virginia in the late 1800s, so he surely must have been exposed to a strong anti-Catholic sentiment.

In one of his letters, Yost's disdain for Catholic institutions was evident when he referred to them as "a rather independent lot." In fact, Yost got almost as much grief from Detroit-area football followers for refusing ever to play the University of Detroit, a Catholic school, as he did for not scheduling Notre Dame. Yost's alleged religious swipe at Rockne on the weekend of the hurdle-race episode—chastising Rockne for being a Protestant holdout at a Catholic school—was a typical anti-Catholic comment.

But Yost's religious feelings played a minor role in his feud with Rockne. Yost took football deathly serious, thus football issues—and competitive issues—mattered far more to him than religious ones.

Accordingly, Yost had one other competitive motive for feuding with Rockne. That is, Yost lost all respect for his Notre Dame counterpart during the hurdle-race episode. He never forgave Rockne for deserting him, and he left that weekend believing Rockne was a "quitter" who sought competitive shelter at Notre Dame.

Two years later, in assessing Rockne as a prospective candidate to run the athletics program at the University of California, Yost wrote:

> In my opinion, [Rockne] would "fret" under the administration and
> restrictions as exist in our [Western Conference]. Personally, I would not
> expect to secure Mr. Rockne as coach at our university, [as I do not] feel
> that he would be satisfied to co-operate in the program as it exists
> here. . . . I do not want to do Mr. Rockne any injustice. Personally he
> is a very likeable fellow.

Remember, it was Yost who had urged Rockne back in 1921 to jump to Northwestern. Perhaps Yost viewed Rockne's reluctance to take that job as a reluctance to be "hitched in the same kind of harness" with Big Ten teams.

But just because Rockne preferred the environment at Notre Dame does not mean he "fretted" leaving it for that of a Big Ten school. In fact Rockne indicated as much to Yost in one of his letters following the hurdle-race episode: "Admit us to your conference and we will obey every regulation besides your eligibility code." Indeed Yost, above all others, should have known that the last thing Rockne was was a coward.

And that is the most important point of all.

Yost's jealousy, prejudice, hatred of the shift, bitterness over Notre Dame's advantages, and loss of respect for Rockne indeed fueled the feud. But it wouldn't have become anywhere near as explosive had Rockne been a passive man. Unlike his predecessors and successors, Rockne steadfastly refused to "sit by quietly" while Yost took his potshots. Every time Yost dished it out, Rockne flung it back with equal venom and vigor. And back and forth it would go.

It was this one-upmanship that aroused every competitive fiber in these men; that exposed all the jagged angles of their clashing personalities; that magnified their divergent football philosophies; that inflamed Yost's jealousy and anti-Catholic sentiments. And all this, in turn, elevated the Yost-Rockne feud to the acerbic heights it so often reached.

No other anecdote better reveals the all-consuming, rabid competitiveness that was the staple of the Yost-Rockne relationship than this excerpt from *Many a Saturday Afternoon,* the book written by Mary Stuhldreyer, wife of Harry Stuhldreyer, one of the Four Horsemen:

> I remember the story Jay Wyatt told me.
>
> Jay was an official and also a salesman for A.G. Spalding's Sporting Goods Company. One spring day, he stopped at South Bend to see Rockne and get his equipment order. However, Rock said that he was overstocked with thigh guards, hip pads, pants, and jerseys. Even though Jay begged and pleaded for an order, he could not break down Rock's sales resistance.
>
> "How about footballs?" Jay said hopefully. "We've a new line which is a big improvement over what you've been using."
>
> "I've plenty of footballs," Rock said emphatically. "I can't use anymore."
>
> Another man might have taken the hint and given up on Rock. But not Jay. He died hard, and he was determined not to leave South Bend without some kind of order. "You can't?" he said. "Well, that's a shame. I just came from Ann Arbor and Yost was so pleased with our new line that he said he'd take three dozen."
>
> "He did?" Rock snapped. "Then I'll take three dozen and a half."

Smoothing out the frictions: 1931–41

Sometimes, in rare scenarios, real life transcends even the most out-landish of Hollywood scripts.

If you don't accept that premise, you won't believe what happened with Fielding Yost in the 1930s. For in the irony of all ironies, Yost gradually transformed from the single greatest opponent of a Michigan–Notre Dame game to the single greatest proponent.

And they all lived happily ever after, right?

Believe it. This is no fairy tale.

Of course, it didn't happen overnight. It wasn't as though Yost was visited by the ghosts of Notre Dame past, present, and future. But his transformation in attitude was as wholesale as Ebenezer Scrooge's on Christmas morning.

This is one of the most incredible stories in the 107-year history of the Notre Dame–Michigan rivalry.

A series of events thawed Yost's icy heart.

The first may have occurred less than two months after Knute Rockne died. John Nicholson, the Fighting Irish track coach, wrote Yost because "we feel at Notre Dame that our system of awarding varsity letters in track is not quite satisfactory, and believe that of the Western Conference is better. Can you give us the system by which you award varsity letters . . . ?"

Perhaps sensing a release of pent-up frustration in his Notre Dame correspondent, Yost not only replied but was amazingly helpful. "After you have read our rules, and there is any other additional information you desire, I shall be pleased to have you write me," Yost indicated.

The first significant step occurred after the 1932 football season. Yost allowed Harry Kipke, head coach of that year's undefeated Wolverines, to accept an invitation to attend Notre Dame's football banquet on January 16, 1933.

Both Kipke and Rockne's successor as Notre Dame coach, Hunk Anderson, had been stars at their respective schools in the early '20s (Kipke was one of the greatest halfbacks and punters of the era, Anderson one of the greatest linemen). They shared a solid friendship, thus it was probably Anderson who invited Kipke to this function.

"Some of you fellows haven't seen a Michigan man since 1909," began toastmaster Jimmy Crowley as he introduced Kipke to one of the warmest receptions ever accorded a visiting coach. Kipke then prompted an avalanche of gossip by saying he looked forward to more frequent appearances at Notre Dame.

This ray of hope gave the best indication of just how badly the public had been craving a resumption of this rivalry. The story topped sports sections across the Midwest over the next two days, with headlines such as, KIPKE "PERSONALLY" FAVORS GAME BETWEEN MICHIGAN AND NOTRE DAME, and WOLVERINE-IRISH FOOTBALL GAME RUMORS AFLOAT.

Kipke probably had no idea his modest comment would have sparked such a response. Reporters scurried to track down the perceived principals—the coach and athletic director—at each school.

Notre Dame's position was made clear by Coach Anderson and athletic director Jesse Harper (who had returned after Rockne's death). "We are ready to play Michigan any time they want to meet us," Anderson said. "It's a natural. That game would pack either stadium. It would be the big game of the year and can you imagine the backing a contest like this would get?" Said Harper: "Play Michigan! We're ready to play that game any time. But for further information you had better see Mr. Fielding H. Yost."

When reached, Yost at least was not violent. Evasive? Belligerent? You bet.

Question 1: Is Michigan planning to play Notre Dame? Yost: "I don't know anything about such a game being planned."

Question 2: Are you in favor of such a game? Yost: "I don't know anything about it."

Question 3: Are you in favor of resuming relations with Notre Dame? Yost: "I don't know anything about it and have nothing to say."

End of interview.

It didn't matter that Kipke was saying he "personally would favor the game." Yost still called all shots on scheduling, and four days after the Notre Dame banquet he shot down all ideas of a resumption when he hauled in Kipke and the coaching staff to discuss future scheduling. Two hours after the meeting, it was announced Michigan had no opportunities to play Notre Dame within the next few years, and if a vacancy should suddenly appear, the University of Detroit would get the first crack.

End of speculation.

The Detroit-area papers generally let Yost off the hook, but three years later he was finally called publicly on his anti–Notre Dame stance—by, of all reporters, a dogged college kid.

Fred DeLano was the junior sports editor of *The Michigan Daily.* He grew up in Dowagiac, a small town in the extreme lower-west portion of Michigan only 22 miles north of Notre Dame. DeLano desperately wanted to see his alma mater–in–waiting play his backyard power, and he believed Yost wasn't providing good enough excuses for balking at the game.

So DeLano did what no Detroit-area writers of that, or any earlier, era had the gumption to do: He publicly challenged Yost on his contentions.

DeLano wrote two columns on this subject in *The Michigan Daily*. The first, on January 12, 1936, addressed the need for a resumption:

> It seems illogical that another great institution should exist barely 150 miles from Ann Arbor, in the heart of the Midwest, and yet due to alleged differences between the athletic administrations of the two schools, they do not meet on the athletic field. . . .
>
> We would (and don't think that thousands of others wouldn't also) appreciate seeing the differences ironed out and friendly relationships established between Michigan and Notre Dame. Certainly Michigan has no fear of meeting Notre Dame. Or has it?

DeLano next addressed the reasons for the hiatus. He lined up an interview with Yost and asked him pointblank why Michigan refused to play Notre Dame. Yost offered the same standard reply he had been giving out for three decades—that Notre Dame's eligibility and competition regulations differed "considerably" with the Big Ten's (although Yost admitted he hadn't checked Notre Dame's rules lately).

But this DeLano kid wouldn't leave well enough alone. Next, he wrote Elmer Layden, who had taken over in 1934 as both football coach and athletic director at Notre Dame, and asked for a copy of ND's rules. Layden most happily obliged DeLano, adding, "The attitude of Notre Dame toward Michigan is most friendly." But Layden, one of the era's greatest diplomats, suggested the matter ought to remain a private one between the two schools.

DeLano wasn't about to pull back now, though. In his follow-up column on January 19 he wrote:

> I have in my possession a copy of Notre Dame's intercollegiate athletic rules, if Mr. Yost is interested, and have carefully checked them against Western Conference rules, a copy of which I also have. Mr. Yost is free to do the same. . . .

DeLano addressed Yost's concerns, one by one, and concluded Notre Dame's eligibility and competition rules were as close as could be to the conference's. In fact, president Rev. John O'Hara had already initiated the Notre Dame tradition—that continues to this day—of remaining one step *ahead* of the conference with regard to entrance and eligiblity rules.

In summary, DeLano wrote:

> Recalling that Mr. Yost stated he would not object to renewing relationships with Notre Dame if their rules did not differ with Big Ten rules (and he had not checked them to see if they did or not), what is there standing in the way of a Michigan–Notre Dame series? Also recalling coach Layden's statement that Notre Dame's attitude toward Michigan is most friendly, the logical answer is nothing. And so, directors Yost and Layden, why not give the fans what they want (they're really paying your salaries, you know) and arrange for the greatest rivalry in athletics?

Midwestern scribes, suddenly awoken like hungover drunks by buckets of ice-cold water, kicked their feet off their desks, grabbed their pencils and pads, and went scurrying off to Ann Arbor and Notre Dame.

Notre Dame's athletic authorities—vice president Rev. J. Hugh O'Donnell and Layden—said they were willing to schedule a game but, as Jesse Harper had insisted three years earlier, Michigan would have to make the first move.

Yost couldn't be reached for comment because he had just left for Nashville to attend the funeral of his closest friend and brother-in-law, Dan McGugin.

The story stayed red-hot for days, again topping the sports pages. But without comment from Yost the matter remained on hold. In the interim, the papers resolved to partake in some journalistic archaeology, unearthing the events of 1909 and 1910 and rehashing them for the modern generation. Barely a word was written about the Yost-Rockne feud, however.

While out of town, Yost was kept fully informed of all the stories by his secretary, Andrew Baker. When Yost was finally reached on January 30, he had no comment.

The other prominent man in Michigan athletics did have something to say, however. Ralph Aigler, the longtime chairman of the Board in Control, absolved the coach somewhat. "Mr. Yost is not the only one connected with the University of Michigan . . . that is not in favor of a resumption of athletic relations with Notre Dame," Aigler said. "The whole agitation is in bad taste."

Other prominent Michigan people agreed. "I think the large majority of Michigan alumni and the friends of the university would prefer to see Michigan continue along the line of the present, rather than to be driven into athletic activities with Notre Dame," wrote Andrew Reid, a lawyer who had officiated football games in the Midwest for some 30 years. "I very sincerely believe that Michigan has nothing to gain by athletic allegiance with Notre Dame."

Such was the anti–Notre Dame monster Yost had created after 26 years. And such was the anti-Catholic prejudice of the day.

But as 1936 progressed, it seems Yost gave serious thought to the "agitation" started by DeLano. Should Yost reevaluate his anti–Notre Dame stance? After all, the high tensions of the Rockne feud were now well behind him; the Depression was forcing schools everywhere to reestablish old rivalries for the purpose of much-needed gate bonanzas; and there was even said to be political pressure being exerted within Michigan for Yost to resume relations with Notre Dame.

More significantly, Yost himself was softening. He was now in his mid-60s, and Father Time had transformed his steely, black-eyed stare into a receptive, gentle glare—more likely to warm your soul than ice your heart.

In October 1936, Yost did something that, for him, would have been unthinkable 10 years earlier.

A friend of his, Bernard Weadock, had previously gone through Yost's best friend, Dan McGugin, to get tickets each year to the Army–Notre Dame game in New York. Weadock was now asking Yost to secure the ducats. We'll never know how much hand-wringing and nervous pacing preceded his decision, but Yost resolved to take up the matter with Notre Dame's Elmer Layden. Yost had long since forgotten how to be friendly to a Notre Dame football man, which was painfully obvious by his overly apologetic letter to Layden:

> This is something I rarely do, and that is try to secure football tickets for friends other than thru the regular channels. However, I have a very intimate friend who lives in New York. . . . Can you refer me to the best source to secure these tickets? If it is too much bother, let it go.
>
> Most sincerely yours, Fielding H. Yost

Layden, then only in his mid-30s, had helped Notre Dame reestablish relations with other long-standing enemies in the Big Ten, and he jumped at this opportunity to begin a friendship with Yost:

> I shall be happy to provide you with the tickets. . . .
> I am glad to see your team came back so nicely on Saturday and wish you the greatest success for the remainder of the season.
>
> Yours sincerely, Elmer F. Layden

Layden was more than willing to suck up to Yost if that's what was needed to resume competition with Michigan. Unaccustomed to receiving such a kind gesture of goodwill from a Notre Dame athletic man, Yost was duly impressed. "I appreciate the courtesy and the spirit of [your] letter," he replied to Layden.

Yost's next conciliatory move came in February 1937 when he allowed his head coach, Kipke, to hire Hunk Anderson as line coach. Hunk had been coaching North Carolina State in relative anonymity since being fired by Notre Dame after the '33 season. Michigan's outdated "punt, pass, and prayer" offense was fizzling out by this time, and Yost had allowed Kipke to bring in whoever he thought could help him most. Yost probably had no idea Kipke would pick a Notre Dame man— indeed the very coach he and Stagg had wanted banned back in the 1920s for playing pro football—but he offered no resistance.

Actually, it was an outstanding move for Yost politically because it "removes the suspicion of Notre Dame boycott," wrote veteran *Detroit News* columnist H.G. Salsinger, in a confidential letter to Ralph Aigler. Salsinger probably had a better feel for the pulse of the Michigan sports community than anyone. The letter continued:

> In Detroit there are more than 200,000 Catholics and many of them have felt, for several years, that Michigan is the bitter enemy of Notre Dame. By hiring Anderson, a former head coach of Notre Dame, Michigan contradicts the set belief. Many people who have been bitterly opposed to Michigan football will be favorable now.
>
> Fielding H. Yost, who has been the target of much Catholic ire, issued a public statement that should absolve him. He pronounced Anderson the best line coach in the country. . . . Fielding won over a lot of good Irish hearts by his attitude and public utterance.

Yost's own heart, meanwhile, was being increasingly won over by Layden in early 1937. The two were now seen engaging in friendly conversation at Big Ten functions. After meetings held in Ann Arbor in May, Layden congratulated Yost on his "splendid handling of tedious arrangements," adding that he enjoyed playing the university golf course (notwithstanding "that trap I bought"), and appreciated Yost's "kind hospitality."

Come fall 1937, Yost asked "The Thin Man," as he and others called Layden, to again secure Army tickets for Bernard Weadock. This time Yost wished Layden "good luck and best wishes in the remainder of your games." Layden indicated it would "be a pleasure" to help Yost again, and did.

Layden was charming Yost's socks off. His youthful diplomacy was the key element in being able to befriend such athletic directors as Yost who were twice his age. In fact, Layden recalled that his greatest asset was something his parents had taught him—"be polite and considerate of your elders." While he didn't approach such athletic elders "as a boy with hat in hand," Layden made sure they got the impression he respected their experience and position. This approach especially worked wonders with Yost.

By the end of November, Yost was completely won over. He decided, at long last, to end his 14-year athletic boycott of Notre Dame.

A day after breaking the good news to Layden by telephone, Yost announced the resumption of relations between Michigan and Notre Dame on December 1, 1937. Contests were immediately scheduled in golf, wrestling, and track. "Although football schedules of both schools have been arranged through 1940," the Michigan press release stated, "it is understood there is nothing to preclude a meeting in that sport after that date."

The midwestern dailies were as shocked as they were pleased.

"M" SEEKING IRISH GAME screamed the main headline atop the very front page of the next day's *Detroit Free Press*. ND, MICHIGAN MAY RENEW RELATIONS thundered the *South Bend Tribune*. "Fielding H. Yost and Notre Dame have buried the proverbial hatchet—and not in each other's back," quipped *The Michigan Daily*.

Within days of the announcement, however, Yost suddenly had more pressing concerns at home.

Kipke was sacked as Michigan head coach after his fourth straight nonwinning season, and the search was on for a replacement. After much political in-fighting, Yost lost the battle with Chairman Aigler and the Board in Control to have his choice hired, former Navy coach Tom Hamilton. Aigler's choice—Princeton head coach and athletic director Fritz Crisler—was endorsed instead.

Crisler also became Michigan's assistant athletic director, with the understanding that when Yost retired in June 1941, he would lose the "assistant" tag and—more significantly—would assume Aigler's role as chairman of the Board in Control, while Aigler would be reduced to secretary. This was the pivotal concession Crisler had held out for.

Thus, the fact Crisler soon would be running Michigan athletics instantly made Yost a lame-duck athletic director, and this must have been a jolt to the man who had had the last word on Michigan football for the past 38 years. Yost may have been preoccupied with interior politics throughout 1938, placing such outside matters as scheduling Notre Dame in football on the back burner.

By early 1939, Layden may have realized another healthy dose of diplomacy was needed to rekindle Yost's interest in resuscitating the football series. So on April 29 he sent Yost a most eloquent birthday telegram. Bedridden with sickness, Yost was genuinely touched. "It was mighty kind of you to remember me on this occasion," Yost replied. "I hope the future years furnish us a real opportunity to know each other better."

Rekindled Yost was. With the end of his career now in sight, Yost decided indeed to get to know Layden better.

Over the summer of 1939 he mulled the idea of traveling to Notre Dame to watch the Fighting Irish in action, as a personal guest of Layden himself. Michigan alumni living in South Bend were thrilled by the prospect. Although still in fragile health, Yost decided at the last minute to make the trip and see Layden's squad play Purdue on September 30—Yost's first visit to Notre Dame, it was said, in 30 years. He watched the game from the press box and afterward attended a party at Layden's house. A week later, Yost was said to be still raving about Layden's hospitality.

That was the clincher. Yost was now absolutely determined to ink a Michigan–Notre Dame football contract before he retired.

But it wasn't simply a matter of Yost and Layden signing on the dotted line. There remained daunting obstacles.

H.G. Salsinger wrote that some powerful alumni of both schools opposed a Notre Dame–Michigan game, a residue of the bitter broth that had been simmering for decades. More significantly, though, there appears to have been men in high places at both schools who opposed the football resumption. Exactly who is not clear, but they were probably men who were susceptible to alumni pressure.

Yost and Layden were so wary of these dissenting elements, they struck up football negotiations in abject secrecy through a middle man—Ed Slezak, a Michigan grad who at the time was Notre Dame's swim coach and assistant director of the newly opened Rockne Memorial Building.

Slezak had befriended Yost during his undergraduate days at Michigan in the late '30s. Both were experts on Custer's Last Stand, and they often met at the Michigan Union to challenge each other's knowledge. During one debate, Yost mentioned his desire to resume the Notre Dame football series. Come January 1939, Slezak stopped working on his master's degree at Michigan to take the double-pronged job at Notre Dame.

By mid-1939 Slezak got to know Layden well. It was then that he began passing messages back and forth between the two athletic directors. Slezak would see Yost at swim meets in Ann Arbor, then rendezvous with Layden at various places on the Notre Dame campus. "I was the liaison man," Slezak recalled. "The contact was a natural one, because here was a Michigan man at Notre Dame."

The big scheduling break came in December 1939, when the University of Chicago announced it was dropping its already deemphasized football program. Suddenly, Michigan was left with open dates in 1940, 1941, and 1942. "That's when it began to warm up very, very fast," Slezak said.

As 1940 began, Chairman Aigler made it clear whose responsibility it was at Michigan to fill these vacancies. "Schedule-making is left entirely in the hands of Coach Crisler and Fielding Yost," Aigler announced before departing on a semester-long sabbatical.

That year's vacancy had to be quickly filled and was. Michigan arranged to play Cal at Berkeley, and would become one of the first college football teams to travel by air.

That left the 1941 and '42 dates to fill. What followed during the early months of 1940 was an extraordinary amount of political arm-bending, clandestine negotiations, and internal jostling.

Crisler wrote confidentially that "terrific pressure" was being applied by Michigan's Board of Regents to schedule the University of Detroit, a Catholic school Yost had been boycotting for an eternity and one Crisler apparently didn't care to schedule, either. In addition, politicians in Lansing were still anxious for Michigan to play Notre Dame and were turning screws to that end.

The biggest power struggle of all apparently occurred in the Michigan athletic offices, between Crisler and Yost.

Yost wanted to play Notre Dame. Crisler wanted to play Pittsburgh, and in fact was negotiating with Pitt athletic director Jim Hagan to fill the 1941 and '42 vacancies. But Yost still had more authority than Crisler, and the Michigan board members had for decades been rubber-stamping any schedules Yost brought to them. What's more, Crisler's key ally on the board—Chairman Aigler—was out of town all spring, and second in command was secretary Yost.

At the April 20 board meeting, Yost initiated perhaps the final significant power play of his career. He addressed the scheduling situation and indicated "that information had come to him that Notre Dame is interested in getting a football game with Michigan." Yost mentioned other interested schools, but not Pitt. Crisler was present at this meeting, but his input on scheduling, if he indeed had any, was not recorded in the board minutes.

A couple of weeks later, on May 8, 1940, the Notre Dame Board of Control also discussed scheduling. Layden, the diplomatic taskmaster for the university's hierarchy, did not even attend. According to the minutes, Layden was instructed to "explore the probability of a series of football games with the University of Michigan."

By this edict, it's obvious the new Notre Dame leaders—president Rev. J. Hugh O'Donnell and vice president Rev. John J. Cavanaugh—wanted to be informed about how the Michigan negotiations proceeded. But Layden wrapped up his talks with Yost in private.

"I was more or less under an oath to keep my mouth shut," Slezak recalled. Why? "Because some of the higher-ups at Notre Dame did not want the game," he said emphatically.

Back at Michigan, at the May 18 board meeting, Yost seconded a motion that he and Crisler be authorized to begin football negotiations with Notre Dame. The motion passed. But of course, thanks in part to Slezak, negotiations were already complete.

Within the next few days, Yost and Crisler worked out a compromise. Pitt would be signed to a one-shot deal in 1941, but Notre Dame would get a home-and-home series, in 1942 at Notre Dame and in 1943 at Ann Arbor. The news was announced at the Big Ten scheduling meetings on May 25.

After 33 years, the Fighting Irish and Wolverines would again meet on the gridiron.

Layden later called this resumption his "biggest triumph" as athletic director. Yost, too, was elated. On May 28 he thanked Slezak for his role in the negotiations. "You really did help," he wrote.

The powers that be at Notre Dame, however, were not pleased that Layden had exceeded his authority by announcing the resumption with Michigan before the board could approve it. Remember, Layden had been instructed only to "explore the possibilities" with Yost. Thus, Vice President Cavanaugh released a short statement to the press indicating the faculty board had "not yet acted officially" regarding the resumption. It wasn't until the next meeting on June 1 that the ND board ratified the games against Michigan.

What's more, Slezak said word of the secret negotiations, and his role in them, somehow leaked to the Golden Dome. He and Layden were hauled into President O'Donnell's office to explain themselves. Slezak said he caught so much flak it led to his resignation a month later. The secret talks also contributed to Layden's souring relationship with O'Donnell and Cavanaugh.

Yet no matter who at both schools, besides alumni, opposed the resumption, there was nothing anybody could do after Yost and Layden announced it publicly. Maybe that's why the two of them acted so secretively and so quickly after getting the go-aheads from their respective boards.

Football fans were generally ecstatic, and the newspapers—even though they had been half-expecting such an announcement since December 1937—gave the story banner headline treatment.

Most of the credit properly went to Yost. "He wanted the game very badly," Slezak recalled. "He was the one who pushed, pushed, pushed for it." Indeed Yost, now 69, had finally made amends with Notre Dame.

He had even made peace with Knute Rockne.

Journalist and Notre Dame historian Francis Wallace revealed this publicly in December 1940 at the Heisman Trophy presentation dinner. Yost was there to see Wolverines halfback Tom Harmon get the coveted award. When it was Wallace's turn to speak, he recounted what had happened when Yost, on his visit to Notre Dame back in September 1939, toured the Rockne Memorial for the first time:

There's a bust of Rockne there, a grim and fearsome bronze, a wide miss on his personality, but the face he had probably always turned to Yost. Yost just stood and looked for quite a while. Rock glared back. [Those of us present] said nothing. This was drama of a sort.

Wallace then told the audience that he thought he had witnessed the "end of the feud between two of football's toughest and greatest men." Wallace later recalled that to say this was "a bit on the delicate, daring side, since I had never cozied up to Yost and did not know how he would react."

But after the dinner, Wallace said Yost "sought me out and thanked me for saying what I had."

Two months later, in February 1941, it was announced that Elmer Layden was leaving Notre Dame to become commissioner of the National Football League. Yost was retiring in June of that year.

"It is an odd coincidence," Layden wrote Yost, "that we should be winding up our collegiate careers together. However, I am happy that we could arrange the relationship between two fine institutions. I am sorry that I will not be here to coach the teams that will play, but maybe we can get together to witness a game or games in the future."

Sure enough, Yost and Layden watched the 1942 game together from the Notre Dame press box.

Although Yost had also planned to spend some time with Ed Slezak in the stands, he didn't make it down. Later, he sent this note to the young man who had helped arrange the game:

I hope that the results of our efforts will develop into a very satisfactory relationship with both institutions. There's no reason in the world why it shouldn't. It will be up to you and the other boys to carry on. May there be many more fine contests between Michigan and Notre Dame.

To another "M" man, Homer Hattendorf, Yost was a bit more revealing:

This clears up a very controversial situation, and I hope that from now on we [Michigan and Notre Dame] will develop a regular football schedule. Notre Dame is a natural in many ways, and I see no reason why these two great institutions should not be keen but friendly rivals.

Yost died on August 20, 1946. An acute gallbladder attack took him at his Ann Arbor home. He was 75.

⬮   ⬮   ⬮

How does one explain the 46-year merry-go-round that was Yost's relationship with Notre Dame? Thirty-six years of bitterness, pettiness, and vindictiveness followed by a decade of increasingly sincere goodwill.

On the surface, the complete turnaround might seem unbelievable. But look a little deeper and it appears to make sense.

Yost became reflective in his old age, and he obviously didn't like everything he saw in his past. Thus, he genuinely sought to right the wrongs of his life, as Michigan alumnus Louis B. Hyde aptly summed up in September 1940:

It can be said that the life of Fielding H. Yost is a saga of success. He has accomplished much, influenced many, and yet lives to reap his reward.

Strong and aggressive men who by their very force and power are bound to create feuds, often show real greatness by smoothing out the frictions of younger days as they reach the shadows of life. Time is the great leveller.

It seems to me that Fielding H. Yost, in these mellow days of his tenor of office at Ann Arbor, is reaching the end in peace. There is tranquility for himself. No harsh situations now exist in the university's athletic relationships. He thus is making apparent the more gentle side of his nature.

The bruising power of his first five Ann Arbor years, the enthusiastic urge to win, the drive of his personality in those Point-A-Minute days, very naturally created jealousies and enmities. The world generally is against the champion. "Crush Yost" became the battle cry across the land. But the Yost record grew to terrifying proportions.

Came in time, therefore, the feud with [Amos Alonzo] Stagg; the overwhelming opposition of other Western Conference coaches; the major fight

with that organization and Michigan's withdrawal; the lean years; the Notre Dame episode . . . struggle, retaliation, hard feelings, worry.

The Yost personality paid a price. . . .

[But] the broad vision became the fait accompli. The hot passions of
youth became the generous impulses of wise leadership. The last of the
feuds is erased. . . . Notre Dame [is] scheduled in football. . . .

Yost an institution, then Yost a tradition.

Wartime blitzes: 1942–43

10

H.O. (Fritz) Crisler

Herbert Orin Crisler was as shrewdly powerful as any man in college football in his time.

As Michigan's athletic director, Crisler's influence in the Western Conference was virtually unrivaled from 1941 to 1968. And because the conference's might both on the field and off was never greater than during this time, it follows that Crisler was one of the most influential men within the increasingly powerful NCAA. Crisler also held various official posts of national importance: During the Second World War he was chairman of a physical education and public health committee; he was a leading officer of the American Football Coaches Association; and, most significantly, he became chairman of the NCAA football rules committee in the 1950s.

One would never guess that such a successful power broker grew up on a farm in rural north-central Illinois—in fact, fewer than 10 miles from where Jesse Harper was raised. Crisler attended the University of Chicago from 1918 to 1921 and became one of the school's greatest all-around athletes, winning nine letters in three sports and earning all-Western recognition in football as an end in 1921. It was during these years that coach Amos Alonzo Stagg nicknamed him "Fritz," after the famed violinist of the day, Fritz Kreisler. Crisler remained at Chicago for the rest of the decade as a loyal assistant coach under Stagg, absorbing all the old man's old-fashioned virtues in the process.

Crisler cut the cord in 1930 when he took the head coaching job at Minnesota. After quickly turning around the Golden Gophers' fortunes, Crisler became Princeton's first nonalumnus head coach, and from 1932 to 1937 he fully restored the roar to the Tigers. Then the Wolverines came calling. He probably wanted the Michigan job desperately but held out for that huge concession from the Board in Control: upon Fielding Yost's retirement, Crisler not only became athletic director but chairman of the board. Thus, Crisler assumed absolute athletic power.

This was typical of Crisler's astute bargaining style. When he held the upper hand, his counterpart generally didn't have a prayer.

Crisler the athletic director was also frugal, conservative, and ardently loyal to Michigan coaches of all sports; he never fired anybody.

Crisler the football coach was among the most successful of his generation. At Michigan, from 1938 to 1947, he won at an .805 clip. His offense was a razzle-dazzle combination of the Rockne shift and Pop Warner's single wing, featuring everything from fullback spinners to buck-laterals. As one of the most innovative coaches of all time, Crisler also devised the concept of using entirely different units for offense and defense: two-platoon football.

As with everything, Crisler approached the game with a cool, calculating rationality. His formula was to be as scientific and as unemotional as possible: break the game down to its simplest elements for his players, have them perfect it all gradually through mechanical repetition, then, on game day, appeal to their "higher sensibilities" rather than arouse them with a tear-jerking sermon—because "the fellow who isn't ready will not be helped any," he reasoned.

When faced with controversy, Crisler took this coolness to a higher level. He could be coy, reticent . . . in a nutshell, about as politically correct as imaginable. He forever said the right things about, and to, the right people. Whenever he did open up publicly, which was rare, it was probably to some desired effect. Even in letters he seldom let his guard down.

Thus, few people were ever sure what Crisler's true feelings were on any controversy that involved him.

Such as his pending relationship with Notre Dame.

Frank Leahy

In December 1930, when Knute Rockne was holed up at the Mayo Clinic in Minnesota for a leg operation, the new coach of the Minnesota Golden Gophers—Fritz Crisler—paid Rockne a visit.

It was then that Crisler first learned of the coaching potential of one Francis William Leahy. A senior guard who hadn't played that fall because of an injured knee, Leahy was also being treated at the Mayo Clinic. Rockne introduced Crisler to Leahy, then later predicted, "Fritz, that boy Leahy is going to make a great coach some day."

And a great one Leahy became.

As position coach, he molded the famed Seven Blocks of Granite forward wall at Fordham in the '30s, then moved up to head coach at Boston College in 1939 and '40, where he went 20–2. In 1941 his dream was fulfilled when Notre Dame summoned him to replace Elmer Layden as head coach and athletic director.

This tough, deeply religious Catholic from—appropriately—a town called Winner, South Dakota, woke up the echoes of the Knute Rockne era. Indeed, the successes Leahy compiled from 1941 to 1943, and 1946 1953, are positively staggering. His overall winning percentage of .864 is second all-time, behind only Rockne's .881. (Leahy was .855 at Notre Dame.) He won national championships in 1943, 1946, 1947, and 1949 and produced four Heisman Trophy winners.

Leahy was not so much an innovator as a perfectionist. He borrowed his concepts from others, including his famed T-formation offense—the first system to feature a throwing quarterback who took the snap from under center. But through the blood, sweat, and tears of his players, his coaches, and especially himself, Leahy produced the ultimate versions.

Absolute perfection was what Frank Leahy continually craved, and it could be argued that he came as close to achieving it as any coach of any era.

But, oh, how he paid the price.

X. Michigan runs amok, '42

Few games in college football history to this point were as eagerly anticipated as the one played at Notre Dame Stadium on November 14, 1942.

Notre Dame publicity director Joe Petritz was so swamped with media inquiries, he had begun cutting off credentials in September. The game was broacast by 10 separate radio crews (including NBC and CBS), smashing the previous college football record of seven. And among the crowd of 57,011—the largest in the 13-year history of Notre Dame Stadium—were political dignitaries and national celebrities, including Bob Hope.

All this is quite astonishing considering the Second World War, for Americans, was in its early, tenuous phase—only 11 months after Pearl Harbor. Seldom did war news take a backseat to sport, but it certainly did this weekend in the Upper Midwest. That Notre Dame Stadium was jam-packed is, perhaps, the greatest testament to the interest surrounding the game. Wartime travel restrictions prevented fans from getting to South Bend by train—still a highly popular and necessary mode—and long-distance automobile trips were nearly impossible due to wartime gas rationing. Even so, the traffic jams in and around South Bend were unprecedented.

That neither team was undefeated took away nothing from the

hoopla, since experts realized each's schedule was among the toughest in the country.

Michigan, 5–2 and ranked sixth in the Associated Press poll, was an offensive wrecking crew. Leading the way was the Wolverines' famed Seven Oak Posts line, anchored by tackle Albert (Ox) Wistert and guard Julius Franks. It was one of the most revered lines of the era. In Crisler's single-wing offense, the quarterback was mainly a blocker, and captain George Ceithaml (pronounced SY-ham-ul) also helped open holes for Michigan's three tough, speedy runners—fullback Bob Wiese, wingback Paul White, and tailback Tom Kuzma. The most talented back, Kuzma, had been slowed all season by knee and ankle injuries.

To indicate how much the game meant to Crisler, he locked out all reporters from his practices that week—the first time he had done so all season—and introduced a wave of new defensive schemes.

Notre Dame, meanwhile, came into the game 5–1–1 and ranked fourth in the AP poll (having lost only to No. 2 Georgia Tech). This was the first year for Leahy's T-formation, and the growing pains had been evident in recent weeks. The aerial game just wasn't clicking, even with quarterback Angelo Bertelli—one of the greatest passers of the decade—at the helm. What's more, the Fighting Irish were coming off a costly 13–0 win over Army. Halfback Fred (Dippy) Evans was out and backfield mate Pete Ashbaugh had an assortment of leg injuries. As well, center Wally Ziemba was slowed by a sore knee. Among the healthy, halfback Creighton Miller—Red's son—and end Bob Dove were as dynamic as any in the country at their positions. And the Fighting Irish line was gigantic for that time, averaging slightly more than 200 pounds.

To indicate how much the game meant to Leahy, he took his entire team to the grave of Knute Rockne two hours before kickoff. "Leahy dedicated the game to Rockne," remembered line coach Ed (Moose) Krause, "and said a little prayer."

Those prayers went unanswered, however, as the blue-jerseyed Wolverines ran amok over the green-clad Fighting Irish and won 32–20 on a brisk, sunny day.

Such a score appears modestly high by today's standards, but it was as wild as anything ever seen in the first half of this century. In fact, it was only the second time either school had ever been involved in a game in which one team scored as many as 30 points and the other at least 20. "I've looked at football everywhere under any conditions for years and years," Fielding Yost said afterward, "but there never was one like this for action."

The offensive maelstrom prompted one old scribe in the press box to say: "It was worth waiting 33 years to see a game like this."

Notre Dame jumped out to a 7–0 lead in the first quarter when, on third and goal from the Michigan seven, Bertelli hit a wide-open Dove in the back of the end zone—the first touchdown pass in series history.

Michigan coaches had warned the Wolverines that when the Irish got ahead, they "give you a lot of lip," remembered Ceithaml. "And they did."

At least one did. Guard Harry Wright—as feisty a talker as he was a blocker and tackler—snickered, "Where's that great Michigan line I've heard so much about?"

He found out in a hurry.

The Wolverines answered with a 53-yard touchdown drive all on the ground, Ceithaml capping it with his first collegiate score on a one-yard quarterback sneak. Michigan 7, Notre Dame 7.

After recovering a botched Notre Dame lateral pass in the second quarter, Michigan scored again—with the help of some Crisler trickery. A successful fake punt kept the drive alive, and on fourth down from the Notre Dame three-yard line the Wolverines scored on a fake field goal, holder Don Robinson picking up the ball and scooting untouched around left end. The extra point was missed, and Michigan led 13–7.

Just before halftime, Michigan's Kuzma fumbled away a punt on the Wolverine 12. Three plays later, Miller blasted over from two yards out to give Notre Dame a 14–13 halftime lead.

As the Wolverines started jogging off the field, they were generally content with their play thus far. When they reached the tunnel, however, some of their tempers flared. Remembered Ox Wistert: "The fans above us kept shouting, 'That's all, Michigan, better wait till next year,' or 'Too bad, Michigan, too bad.' That doesn't sound like much but it made us pretty mad."

That and Harry Wright's comment had the Wolverines sizzling with determination and confidence as they rested up in the locker room. Thus, when Crisler told Captain Ceithaml that Michigan would elect to kick off to start the half, the senior was unable to mask his disappointment. Backfield coach Earl Martineau picked up on it, and asked Ceithaml if he would rather Michigan receive. Ceithaml said yes. A few minutes later, as Ceithaml made his way out of the locker room and up the tunnel for the second half, Crisler pulled him aside. "Would you rather receive?" Crisler asked him. "Yes," answered Ceithaml. "Okay," was all Crisler said.

Seldom did Crisler ever change his mind about anything, so Ceithaml wasn't the only elated Wolverine. "We thought we could ram the ball down the field against Notre Dame," Wistert recalled. "We let out a yell and charged onto the field."

The Wolverines took the kickoff and promptly smashed their way through, over, and around the Irish defenders until they had gone 58 yards for the score. Paul White went over from two yards out, and Michigan led 20–14.

Creighton Miller fumbled the ensuing kickoff, and Bob Kolesar recovered for Michigan at the ND 25. Seven plays later, Kuzma bulled in from three yards out to give the Wolverines a 26–14 lead.

Michigan then forced an immediate Notre Dame punt, and Kuzma returned it 34 yards to the ND 36. The Wolverines moved to the three before the drive stalled. But on Notre Dame's second ensuing play, Bertelli threw an unwise, off-balance pass from his end zone that White picked off at the ND 24. Five plays later, on the last play of the third quarter, Kuzma darted over from one yard out.

Three touchdowns in eight minutes had given the Wolverines a 32–14 lead.

In the fourth quarter, the Wolverines continued to run roughshod. The Fighting Irish, however, refused to be blown out and scored on a 14-yard run by Miller, off the Statue of Liberty play—a Yost invention.

Final score: Michigan 32, Notre Dame 20.

"We were so revved, we could have played two more quarters," Ceithaml recalled with all sincerity. "The coaches never had to say a word to get us jacked up. We're Michigan. And the personal pride—the pride of beating Notre Dame—was intense."

In scoring the most points against Notre Dame since 1905, the Wolverines hogged the ball for an incredible 90 plays, only nine of which were passes. They rolled up 319 yards on the ground—114 by fullback Wiese, 90 by tailback Kuzma, and 61 by wingback White. Quarterback Ceithaml called a great game, continually attacking Notre Dame's weaker right flank.

"It was certainly the greatest display of offense in my entire coaching career," Crisler said afterward. "My team has never fought like it did today."

Michigan's Seven Oak Posts deservedly received much of the praise. "Never have I seen a line charge so hard and fast as that Michigan line did with almost no substitutions," Leahy said. Center Merv Pregulman and Julius Franks did yeoman work inside, but Ox Wistert was the true star. He was carried off the field by appreciative teammates afterward, and was later named team MVP and All-American.

Today, the 1942 win against ND stands as one of the most cherished in Michigan history. Even then, the players sensed its importance. "This was more than just a game to us," Ceithaml recalled. "The renewal meant an awful lot. It placed ourselves as individuals, as a team, and as a school, on the line."

Thus began the tradition of Michigan storming back in the second half at Notre Dame Stadium.

● ● ●

Michigan actually rang up two wins over Notre Dame in 1942.

In the weeks leading up to the game, the schools couldn't agree on the all-time series record. Michigan records indicated it was 7–1 in the Wolverines' favor, but Notre Dame records showed it was 8–1.

Turns out, the second game in 1888—the Wolverines' narrow 10–4 win—never did make its way into Michigan's record books.

Fred DeLano, the Michigan student who had lobbied for a resumption of this series back in the '30s, was now Michigan sports publicity director. After snooping around some more, DeLano wrote his Notre Dame counterpart, Joe Petritz, to this effect: "I have talked with two members of the 1888 teams, one of whom says there was only one game and the other says there 'might have been' a second. Needless to say, if it was played, we are willing to accept credit for the victory."

So Michigan's overall record in football jumped from 353–101–21 to 355–101–21. Notre Dame's fell to 328–71–26.

XI. Miller time again, '43

Like father, like son.

The last time a Notre Dame team played at Michigan, in 1909, everyone went home raving about Miller, the ND running back. His fleet feet, elusive moves, and all-around outstanding play helped Notre Dame to its greatest win of the era—and handed Michigan a devastating loss, its only one of the season.

This exact scenario was replayed thirty-four years later. Only this time, it was Red Miller's son, Creighton, who drew the raves. And this time, Notre Dame's domination was absolute. The green-clad Fighting Irish avenged the 1942 loss with a 35–12 shellacking of the Wolverines on October 9 at Michigan Stadium.

These 1943 squads barely resembled their 1942 predecessors. Graduation had taken its usual toll, but mass enlistments into the armed services also gutted their rosters. The Irish returned only two starters (Miller and quarterback Angelo Bertelli), the Wolverines only three (lineman Merv Pregulman and running backs Bob Wiese and Paul White).

But no one was shedding a tear for either school, because Notre Dame and Michigan were among the fortunate four institutions in the Midwest recently awarded navy and marine training programs (Northwestern and Purdue were the others). Star athletes from other schools were now being recruited and assigned to these "lend-lease" universities, where young men could continue playing sports while training to become officers.

Michigan, with only three backups returning, relied heavily on these transfers, as well as on incoming sophomores and freshmen (the latter of whom were made eligible for the duration of the war). Four transfers were especially talented and became instant starters: from Minnesota, bruising fullback Bill Daley; and from Wisconsin, shifty halfback Elroy (Crazy Legs) Hirsch and linemen Robert Hanzlik and Fred Negus. Even though the line appeared weaker than the Seven Oak Posts, the press oozed over Michigan's conglomeration of talent, especially the dream backfield of Daley, Hirsch, Wiese, and White.

Notre Dame, meanwhile, had plenty of material with which to build around Miller and Bertelli. In fact so many quality backups returned that only one transfer cracked the starting lineup, standout halfback Julie Rykovich from Illinois. Rykovich, Bertelli, Miller, and fullback Jim Mello comprised a backfield at least as dreamy as Michigan's. But more importantly, the entire second-string line from 1942 returned intact. Led by tackles Jim White and Zygmont (Ziggy) Czarobski, this was a devastating unit.

Notre Dame came into the game 2–0 and ranked No. 1 in the Associated Press poll, while Michigan was 3–0 and ranked No. 2. It was the first time the top two teams in the AP poll had ever played each other, so of course the buildup was again immense. Press-box seats were as difficult to come by as tickets. Indeed, although wartime travel constraints were still in effect, and although the Office of Defense Transportation was requesting that Michigan officials sell tickets only in a "local" area, a record crowd of 86,688 jammed Michigan Stadium.

In some locales Notre Dame was a 6–5 favorite, but the odds were generally even. Michigan might even have been a slight favorite had tailback Hirsch been healthy. The week before, against Northwestern, he had strained a knee ligament and was doubtful to play against Notre Dame.

Crisler's biggest fear, however, was that his patchwork offensive line would be no match for Leahy's bulldozers. "I have been aware that our line was weak from the start," a glum Crisler wrote confidentially the day before the game. "It didn't show in the first two games because neither team hit there. Northwestern found a weakness in the middle [and] made considerable ground. . . . We are not in very good shape for tomorrow."

After the three o'clock kickoff, Notre Dame's line indeed mashed Michigan's to smithereens, allowing the star-studded Irish backfield—and thus Leahy's T-formation—to shine like never before. Quarterback Bertelli was brilliant, executing play-action passes to perfection. Fullback Mello continually ripped through the gut of the Wolverine defense. And Miller had the game of his life, with his proud father watching from the stands.

"We were all emotionally charged, that's for sure," Miller remembered. "Leahy gave us an emotional speech before the game."

But contrary to what has often been written, revenge was not primary on the Notre Dame players' minds. "We were nervous, to tell you the truth," Miller said. "Having been licked the year before definitely was a factor, but rather than a matter of us being cocky or vengeful, I think it just turned out that they were flat and we were at the top of our game."

Only 5:15 into the first quarter, Miller displayed his sprinter's speed and deadly faking ability. On the first play after a short punt, Miller shot through the right side of the line, badly faked out Michigan halfback Don Lund, then dashed to the end zone for a 66-yard score and a 7–0 Notre Dame lead.

Years later, Lund and Miller—like many Michigan and Notre Dame players from this generation—became golfing buddies. Lund would always tell Miller, "If you come to our stadium, and you look closely at Michigan's 45-yard line, you'll find a jockstrap there. That's mine."

The Wolverines fought back to score a touchdown of their own early in the second quarter, on a four-yard plunge by Michigan's one-man wrecking crew, Bill Daley, the fullback from Minnesota. Seldom did Daley have holes to run through on this day, so he simply churned his tree-trunk legs and dragged Notre Dame tacklers as far as he could. He had set up his own touchdown by intercepting a Bertelli pass and returning it to near midfield. The extra point was missed, so the Irish led 7–6.

From that moment on, it was all Notre Dame.

A minute and a half later, Bertelli hit freshman halfback Fred Earley for a long-bomb, 70-yard touchdown. On ND's next possession, Miller tore through the line and galloped 58 yards for another apparent score, but a clipping penalty nullified it. No matter, Notre Dame got the ball back and scored on another lightning-bolt drive—36 yards in two plays, capped by Mello's two-yard smash.

Halftime score: Notre Dame 21, Michigan 6.

Notre Dame's buzz-saw offense continued to shred Michigan in the third quarter. Julie Rykovich returned a punt 31 yards to the Michigan 30, and four plays later Bertelli's two-yard quarterback sneak gave Notre Dame a 28–6 lead. Miller set up the score with a 17-yard burst up the middle.

Soon, it was Miller time again. He dashed for gains of 10 and 28 yards as Notre Dame drove to the Michigan 16. From there, Miller grabbed a short Bertelli pass, eluded three Wolverine tacklers, and pranced over for his second score of the game.

According to the game clock, it was now late in the third quarter. The Irish couldn't figure out why they were all so tired. "We all figured we were out of shape," recalled Miller.

But in reality, it was midway through the fourth. Michigan Stadium's electronic clock malfunctioned, and about 23 minutes of game time elapsed in the third quarter before the officials finally stopped play and mulled what to do. After discussions with both Leahy and Crisler, they shortened the fourth quarter to seven minutes.

Up 35–6, Leahy played both the second and third strings in the abbreviated final quarter. Michigan kept fighting to the bitter end, though, and scored on the final play of the game when Paul White took a pass from Hirsch—who had hobbled into the game in the second quarter—and carried tacklers into the end zone for a 13-yard TD. With no time left on the screwy clock, Merv Pregulman missed his second extra point.

Final score: Notre Dame 35, Michigan 12.

Miller finished with 159 yards rushing on only 10 carries. Throw in his 58-yard touchdown run that was called back and he would have had, statistically, the greatest rushing game in series history. "I would say that game was the highlight of my career," Miller remembered. "I don't think it was so much that I did anything special. The whole team clicked. Where you'd usually get three or four yards on a play, we'd get 15 or 20."

One new play that was especially effective was called 48-blind. Because defenders keyed so much on the T-formation quarterback's movements, Leahy put in this play in which Bertelli, without turning around, blindly lateraled back to Miller, who would cut back to the weak side. It was a big gainer every time because the fooled Wolverines figured Bertelli still had the ball.

Bertelli properly drew raves of his own afterward. He had accounted for three of the touchdowns and completed five of eight passes for 138 yards. He went on to play three more outstanding games before going off to war with the marines. Despite missing the last month of the season, Bertelli won the Heisman Trophy (Miller finished fourth in the balloting, Daley seventh).

Just as impressive as Notre Dame's offensive play, though, was its defense. Leahy had preached defense all week to his starting 11. After the 1942 loss to Michigan, former ND and Michigan coach Hunk Anderson had told Leahy that "the T-formation didn't lose that game. You did! You had the team in the wrong defense, and you should have known it. Fritz Crisler did." So in 1943, Leahy and line coach Moose Krause devised a simple scheme to counter all the faking done in the Michigan backfield. "We had a tackle look for one of the faking backs, and he'd hit the hell out of him whether that back had the ball or not," remembered Krause. While Michigan gained 299 total yards on the day, 135 were battered out by the unceasing Daley—who, two weeks later, was shipped off to war by the navy.

The sporting press was genuinely astonished by Notre Dame's blow-out victory, but no more so than the Fighting Irish themselves. "Our scouts told us they had a great team, and it was," Miller recalled. "We were just hoping to win."

Said Leahy: "Gosh, I never thought we could beat a great Michigan team by 23 points."

But Crisler was not surprised by the score. "We didn't have the stuff up front," he privately lamented after suffering what would stand as the most lopsided loss of his coaching career. "The newspapers were blinded by our imposing array of backs and couldn't see the weakness in our line. . . . I was sure hell would break loose when Notre Dame came here."

Crisler gushed over Leahy's squad to reporters, calling it "the greatest Notre Dame football team I've ever seen," and maybe one of the greatest in college football history.

Indeed, the Fighting Irish beat every college team they played that year by at least 19 points. The only close games were against two wartime service teams both laden with pro players. One, Great Lakes, eked out a 19–14 victory. That didn't prevent the AP writers from awarding Notre Dame its first national championship since 1930.

Miller recalled that the Michigan victory was vindication for Leahy's T-formation and "the impetus for the whole season."

Thus began Notre Dame's winning tradition at Michigan Stadium.

The Crisler dodge: 1943–68

11

On hold again

Charles Wattles, an active Michigan alumnus living in South Bend, had long been a champion of the Notre Dame–Michigan football rivalry. He had pestered Fielding Yost to play Notre Dame in the '20s, had probably helped Yost mend broken bridges in the '30s, and was now doing all he could in the early '40s to see good relations continue.

But Wattles was among the first to learn Crisler did not care to extend the series past 1943.

Following Michigan's win in '42, Notre Dame had gone through Wattles to invite Crisler to the postseason Fighting Irish football banquet. Crisler personally declined the invitation, sending assistant coach Art Valpey in his place. "I know you will express to the Notre Dame group my deep disappointment in not being able to attend," Crisler wrote Wattles, with the ominous disclaimer, "No one, other than you, need to know that I have my tongue in my cheek when I say that."

Crisler had also instructed Wattles to give Valpey "some good sound advice on what to say and what not to say," but Valpey didn't recall any such instruction being given. Luckily for Valpey, Northwestern coach Pappy Waldorf tipped him off that he was going to be asked to address the future of the Michigan–Notre Dame series. "I ducked the issue completely," Valpey said, "concentrating on flowery remarks about the present series. Later, I caught Fritz and told him what happened. Asking what would have happened if I had said, say, 'It's a great series. We're looking forward to more of the same,' Fritz's reply was, 'I would back you in public for any quotes and then chew you out in private for going beyond your authority.'"

And beyond Crisler's intentions.

Unlike Crisler, though, Notre Dame athletic officials were as eager as ever to see the series continue. In February 1943, Notre Dame's executive vice president, Rev. John J. Cavanaugh, informed Frank Leahy that the one school heading the list of those "we should attempt to schedule" was Michigan. And after Notre Dame's win in Ann Arbor in October 1943, Cavanaugh wrote Crisler to praise him and all Michigan people for exhibiting such "fine American sportsmanship . . . under the circumstances." Cavanaugh also told Crisler the following:

I hope very sincerely that you and Frank Leahy may find it possible to continue this excellent relationship. If, in any way, I can be of assistance, I know you will feel free to call upon me.

The football-mad public and the press generally were all for a continuation, too. But following Notre Dame's win in Ann Arbor, there had been no official announcement either way from either school. The press properly reported that Notre Dame was keen. Was Michigan?

At a postseason football banquet in Detroit on December 17, 1943, the public got its answer.

Crisler and Leahy were both guest speakers at this function, and, of course, they were seen chatting together. Afterward, the reporters zoomed in. "Frank asked me if perhaps this wasn't the time to begin talking about playing again," explained Crisler to the Associated Press, "but we agreed that maybe we'd better wait until we know more about what football will be like in the next few years."

With the Second World War in full swing, nobody knew for sure what schools would continue even to play football, so it's true that no one could afford to look much past the upcoming season. But couldn't something tentative have been worked out for future years? Was Crisler balking for other reasons?

Midwestern scribes speculated.

Dale Stafford of the *Detroit Free Press* suggested Michigan officials didn't like that the recent Notre Dame games had suddenly assumed so much importance among Michigan fans. After all, in 1942 Michigan had lost the Western Conference title by losing to Ohio State, but few seemed to care because Michigan had beaten Notre Dame. Conversely, in 1943 Michigan had beaten Ohio State and won the Western Conference title, but still few cared because Michigan this time had lost to Notre Dame. Worse, Michigan crowds plummeted in '43 following the Notre Dame defeat. "In plain English," Stafford wrote, "Michigan is at a point where she must decide whether it is wise to subordinate the Western Conference season, with all its tradition and years of building, to one sure-fire sellout affair every year with Notre Dame."

Among all the hypothesizing, though, the reasons cited by *Grand Rapids Press* columnist Roscoe D. Bennett were the only ones privately endorsed by Crisler and the Michigan Board in Control. Bennett was spoon-fed his information by George C. (Bots) Thompson, a prominent Michigan alumnus and member of the Board in Control. Accordingly, Bennett wrote that Notre Dame was not high on Michigan's scheduling priority list:

Michigan State, Ohio State, and Minnesota will not be disturbed in any way. That is final, no matter what pressure is brought to bear. Further, all obligations to the Conference will be fulfilled and that is final. Finally, old friends who stood by in the lean years [various eastern schools] will not be forgotten and that also is final. So, if all of these obligations can be filled satisfactorily and Notre Dame can be worked in, it will be—but not before.

Bots Thompson asked Crisler to send Bennett a thank-you note, which he did:

. . . Of course you know a lot of people treat football emotionally, and to me it is very comforting to see you treat it rationally. There are many who do not realize all the angles having to do with this football relationship, but look at it only from the point of view of popular appeal. If Michigan were not a member of the Conference I think there would be no doubt about a Notre Dame–Michigan relationship. However, since Michigan is a part of the Conference and has a fine football tradition in the East, there are things that complicate our position which are not problems with Notre Dame.

So the series was on hold again.

Over the next few years, Leahy often asked Crisler for a game but was given the polite brush-off. Gradually, the Notre Dame coach realized Crisler had absolutely no intention of resuming the series.

In October 1946, Chairman Crisler and the Board in Control etched in stone that intention. They devised an official policy that, after "deliberate and careful consideration," effectively—and with no public fanfare at all—eliminated any chance of a Michigan–Notre Dame game for the foreseeable future. By conference rule, only three of Michigan's nine games could be played against nonleague opponents. And by a "definite" new policy of the Michigan board, Michigan State (not yet a conference member) would annually get one spot, while the other two would be filled by one eastern opponent and one from the Near or Far West. Thus, there was no place for a midwestern independent such as Notre Dame.

In some aspects, the Wolverines' new policy was merely putting precedent to paper. Michigan had played Michigan State virtually every year since 1910, and since 1925 Michigan had annually been playing at least one game against an eastern squad. The high concentration of Michigan alumni on the East and West coasts was also a legitimate motive for devising this policy.

But was Notre Dame merely an innocent victim of Michigan policy, or a specific target?

A letter in Crisler's scant correspondence files reveals he harbored a considerable resentment toward Notre Dame—one hauntingly similar to that which Yost held some 20 years earlier, and one that would stew inside Crisler for decades. In fact this feeling ran so deep, Crisler—unlike Yost—would never come around to scheduling Notre Dame.

In March 1944, Crisler wrote this to conference commissioner John L. Griffith:

> I have been a bit disturbed about Notre Dame being identified so closely with the Conference in recent meetings. Their representatives haven't contributed much and I do know that they use this association in promoting the idea that Notre Dame conforms entirely with Conference regulations. So far as the public is concerned, I think it is felt that they have the blessing of the Conference in whatever they do. I do happen to know that they are not going along all the way with the Conference.

Baring his soul in correspondence was rare for Crisler. Even more rare, though, was Crisler baring his soul on the subject of Notre Dame. In the ensuing years, he would cite a variety of reasons for shunning the Fighting Irish, including this decade's favorite, "just can't fit 'em into the schedule." But never, ever did Crisler publicly indict Notre Dame's integrity, as he did in this confidential letter.

In fact, Crisler was so uncomfortable about having come clean to Griffith on this occasion, he closed with the following astonishing request:

> These remarks are for your eyes only and I suggest you destroy this letter.

Who's No. 1?—'47

Almost every year, the college football season ends in controversy about who's No. 1.

But there was never more hot debate, or more coast-to-coast clamoring for a one-game national-title playoff, than there was in 1947.

Quite simply, this was the year that produced the deepest, most powerful teams in the long, storied histories of Michigan and Notre Dame football. In the years following the Second World War, these schools were the clear-cut kings of college football. From mid-1946 to mid-1949 neither lost a single game. Notre Dame was the consensus national champion in '46 and '49, Michigan in '48. They were in a league of their own.

In 1947, however, they were on a planet of their own. No other teams on earth could compare. The quality and depth of the talent amassed at Notre Dame and Michigan were staggering.

To this day, each school claims the 1947 national championship as its own. Officially, Notre Dame gets the honor, as it finished first in the official determinant of the day—the final regular-season Associated Press writers poll. (The coaches' poll had not yet begun.) But after Michigan crushed Southern Cal 49–0 in the Rose Bowl, the first-ever post-bowl AP poll was conducted, and it gave Michigan top spot over Notre Dame by a 2–1 margin. It was an unofficial tabulation, however. Subsequently, Michigan was voted No. 1 by *College Football Illustrated,* the Dunkel System, the Litkenhous System, and by the National Championship Foundation. Notre Dame garnered additional backing from a special post-bowl United Press poll, and from the Williamson System. The Helms Foundation split the honor.

Had the debate been settled on the field, college football records for attendance, scalping, wagering, hype, and partisan zealousness could have been obliterated.

There were several reasons both teams were so fabulously loaded. You have to go back to 1946 to gain the proper perspective. Freshmen had become eligible during the war, so at both schools there was an abnormally large number of experienced teenage football players. But more importantly, scores of veterans returning from smoldering Europe and the quieted seas of the South Pacific were anxious to resume their interrupted college careers.

It's not clear precisely why so many of these wisened, toughened young men flocked to Notre Dame and Michigan, but that they did—to the extent that Michigan coach Fritz Crisler had 125 standout varsity candidates from which to choose his 50-man squad in 1946; to the extent that Notre Dame's roster would soon include an incredible 42 players who would go on to play pro football.

A year of polishing later, the Michigan and Notre Dame juggernauts were primed to wreak supreme havoc in 1947.

Notre Dame, the defending national champion, was widely acclaimed as the team to beat. By now, Frank Leahy had laboriously worked out every last kink from his formidable T-formation offense. And in 1947 Notre Dame was especially loaded at the key position in the T: quarterback. Johnny Lujack, Angelo Bertelli's backup in '43, was now the superstar starter. Leahy would call Lujack "the greatest all-around football player it has been my privilege to coach," for Lujack was an outstanding passer, a shifty runner, a brilliant defender, and the team's punter to boot. His understudy was Frank Tripucka, a future star in his own right. The running backs included the likes of Terry Brennan,

Emil (Red) Sitko, and John Panelli. The veteran line was rock solid and perhaps the most destructive component of all. Thus, preseason magazines and newspapers quite properly reported that Leahy was on the verge of realizing his long-sought-after dream: perfection.

Michigan wasn't exactly undervalued by the prognosticators. The Wolverines had decisively won their last four games in 1946, and, as with Leahy's T-formation, Crisler's single-wing offense was at its zenith. This dizzying, rapid-fire series of fake handoffs, spins, reverses, pitches, and passes could involve every man in the backfield, as well as the ends. By year's end, tailback Bob Chappuis, quarterback Howard Yerges, fullback Jack Weisenburger, and halfback Bump Elliott would master it all and become known as the Mad Magicians.

Michigan's immense depth also afforded Crisler the luxury of employing football's first true version of the platoon system. Each time the Michigan offense punted the ball away, only Bump Elliott remained on the field. Ten players better suited to play defense then leapt off the bench and joined him. Two years earlier, Crisler had been the first coach to dabble with offensive and defensive platoons against Army, but now he was expanding the idea to have at his disposal a squad of collective, interchangeable parts: the first-string offense was the second-team defense, and vice versa.

There was no preseason AP poll in those days, but Notre Dame was voted No. 1 when the first tabulation came out on October 6. The Irish had crushed Pittsburgh 40–6 in their opener. Michigan was No. 2 after having whipped Michigan State 55–0 and Stanford 49–13.

The Fighting Irish and Wolverines proceeded to flip-flop atop the poll as the season continued. It's sad to note that, even then, AP voters were influenced far more by size of score than quality of opponent, for this mentality was reflected in each of the switches:

October 13

Notre Dame downs Purdue 22–7 while Michigan annihilates Pittsburgh 69–0. Michigan becomes the new No. 1, receiving 93 first-place votes to Notre Dame's 23.

October 20

Michigan dumps Northwestern 49–21, while Notre Dame mauls Nebraska 31–0. Michigan stays on top.

October 27

Michigan trails early but comes back to edge Minnesota 13–6, while Notre Dame blanks Iowa 21–0. Notre Dame regains the No. 1 ranking.

November 3

Notre Dame shuts out its third straight opponent, Navy, 27–0, while Michigan slips past Illinois 14–7. Notre Dame remains No. 1.

November 10

Notre Dame blasts Army 27–7, while Michigan beats Indiana 35–0. No change to the poll.

November 17

Notre Dame wards off Northwestern 26–19, while Michigan destroys Wisconsin 40–6. Michigan reclaims top spot with 140 first-place votes.

November 24

Michigan concludes its regular season with a 21–0 blanking of traditional foe Ohio State, while Notre Dame bombs Tulane 59–6. Notre Dame vaults in front again, taking 97 first-place votes to Michigan's 81.

December 1

An off week for Notre Dame, yet its top ranking becomes more tenuous. The Irish take 58½ first-place votes to Michigan's 54½. With one poll to go, the official national championship comes down to how Notre Dame fares in its season finale in Los Angeles against unbeaten traditional foe Southern Cal.

December 8

Notre Dame destroys USC 38–7, prompting Frank Leahy to comment, "I have never seen a better intercollegiate team than my boys who beat Southern Cal."

The Irish won the final AP poll in a landslide, grabbing 107 first-place votes to Michigan's 25.

There was a feeling among some Michigan people, however, that Notre Dame had a big advantage in any nationwide poll. Michigan alumnus Jimmy Baird pointed out to Crisler that "every Southern and Southwestern AP voter objects to color." That is, black players. The color barrier had yet to be broken at Notre Dame, but three star Wolverines—halfback Gene Derricotte and ends Bob Mann and Lenny Ford—were black. The big schools down South had always closed their doors to blacks, and in fact refused even to schedule any team that played blacks. This prejudice among southern writers "is greater than you might think," Baird indicated to Crisler.

With the regular season having ended, it didn't take long for the individual honors to start pouring in to Notre Dame and Ann Arbor. Lujack of Notre Dame and Chappuis of Michigan blew away the field in balloting for the Heisman Trophy. Lujack won it with 742 first-place votes to Chappuis's 555. (Doak Walker of Southern Methodist was third with 196.) As well, Michigan and Notre Dame were well represented on the various All-America teams, while Crisler beat out Leahy for the national coach-of-the-year award.

All these honors only fanned the flames of the Notre Dame–Michigan debate. It was now *the* sports story around the country. Who was better, the Wolverines or the Fighting Irish? Seemingly everyone had an opinion.

Michigan had one last chance to win over the masses, as the Wolverines were heading west to play Southern Cal in the Rose Bowl on New Year's Day. The Trojans had proved no match for Leahy's Irish, so this game was seen as the yardstick for comparison.

Before a crowd of 93,000 in Pasadena, the Wolverines amassed nearly 500 yards of offense in handing the Trojans their worst loss in school history, 49–0. Crisler said afterward that the '47 Wolverines were the greatest team he had ever coached.

Immediately the debate was stoked around the nation, reaching a white-hot intensity. A headline in the *Atlanta Journal* screamed "Irish-Wolverine Super Bowl Would Settle Individual Brawls."

Movers and shakers around the country had already been organizing bids for just such a Super Bowl.

As far back as October, the Cleveland chapter of the Knights of Columbus planned to stage a Great Lakes Bowl game and desperately wanted Michigan and Notre Dame as the adversaries.

In November, someone in Pensacola, Florida, wanted President Harry Truman to actually order a match between the two teams in Chicago, to benefit the March of Dimes. "I feel sure that . . . every seat in Soldier Field would be filled at $10.00 per ticket [a very high price for the day], and that almost everyone who owns a radio would be glad to contribute at least $1.00 by mail. . . . I don't see how either team could refuse if the President would ask them to play for a worthy cause."

Someone wrote Crisler that a game held at Philadelphia's Municipal Stadium could produce a $1 million gate. Another suggested Soldier Field in Chicago but with the cheapest seats going for no less than $20.

Perhaps the most impressive offer came on January 5. A group of wealthy citizens in Miami was prepared to underwrite a charity game at the Orange Bowl for $500,000. Fuller Warren, a wealthy Jacksonville businessman, proposed a late-January date with all the proceeds going to the Damon Runyon Cancer Foundation.

Of course, there was no chance that any such Super Bowl could ever take place. Postseason games were strictly against Notre Dame policy, and only one Big Nine team could play after Thanksgiving—the conference champion in the Rose Bowl.

So the debate raged on.

The Associated Press wouldn't drop the issue. Acting on the request of *Detroit Free Press* sports editor Lyall Smith, AP decided to conduct an unprecedented post-bowl poll of sports editors of all member papers nationwide. The poll was simple: Pick Michigan or Notre Dame and forget about everybody else.

While college football fans waited anxiously for the recount, AP commissioned Smith and his counterpart for the *South Bend Tribune,* Jim Costin, to write dueling columns that would be universally distributed.

Smith wrote that all the statistics favored 10–0 Michigan: comparative scores of the Pittsburgh, Northwestern, and Southern Cal games; average scores for and against (Michigan 39.4 to 5.3, Notre Dame 32.3 to 5.8); and opponents' records (Michigan's 42–46–5, Notre Dame's 30–45–6). In fact, Smith pointed out that only three of Notre Dame's nine opponents won even five games, while Michigan played six such teams. Thus, Smith wrote that the poll in December that put Notre Dame on top now looked "more out of place than a parade of bathing beauties through an icy Detroit park."

Costin wrote that 9–0 Notre Dame had been more impressive in its win against Southern Cal, despite the comparative scores. He said Notre Dame did not throw a single pass in the second half against USC, used nary a trick play, and removed its starters early in the fourth quarter as "coach Leahy had no desire to humiliate an old friend." Meanwhile, Crisler left in his first strings against USC and continued to pass like mad until the 49th point had been rung up late in the game. What's more, Costin pointed out that USC coach Jeff Cravath gave the nod to Notre Dame when queried after the Rose Bowl game. "I think Notre Dame is a better team than Michigan, and can beat the Wolverines," Cravath said. Finally, Costin wrote that if Michigan ever wanted to prove its superiority, all it had to do was schedule a very willing Notre Dame.

AP announced the result of the special, unofficial poll on January 6. Michigan won it handily, taking 226 first-place votes to Notre Dame's 119. The Wolverines drew their heaviest backing from the Midwest, even taking half of the votes in Indiana. Support was more or less split on both coasts, while the Irish were the overwhelming pick in the South.

"The men who voted couldn't have made a mistake if they had picked either team," was Crisler's diplomatic response. "Coach Leahy is a superb coach and both teams are fine. I am very humble, and happy for my kids about it all."

Leahy, too, was especially praiseworthy of his rival coach and school. "I am thoroughly convinced that the 1947 Michigan team will go down in football history as one of the greatest intercollegiate squads ever assembled. I have a very healthy respect for coach Crisler; there is no better coach in the business."

United Press, three years before initiating its weekly coaches' poll, decided to survey the 22 USC Trojans who had played against both teams. They voted 17–5 in favor of Notre Dame.

Who would have won the greatest game never played? Experts agreed Michigan owned a significant edge in team speed and, in the Mad Magicians, the more dynamic backfield. But experts were just as sure Notre Dame's grizzled, heftier linemen were far superior to Michigan's.

Irish partisans believed the Notre Dame forward wall would have devoured Michigan's much smaller yet speedier offensive and defensive lines, and thus controlled the game. Yet Wolverine partisans believed the Mad Magicians—hailed as the greatest backfield since the Four Horsemen—would have run circles around the slower Fighting Irish.

All the speculating apparently got on Crisler's nerves. "It isn't the function of an educational institution to win football games," Crisler remarked, "nor would victory [against Notre Dame] have any bearing on the degree the player gets."

Leahy, though, would have welcomed such a game. In a positively stunning moment back in October, when Michigan had displaced Notre Dame atop the AP poll, a reporter asked Leahy at a press gathering just how badly Michigan would beat Notre Dame. Leahy instantly shot back: "I just wish we had the opportunity to beat Michigan. We'd be happy to play them any time, on any Saturday, during any fall." The reporters' jaws dropped straight to the ground, as they had been trying literally for years to goad anything approaching a boastful reaction out of Leahy.

"It is really a shame that our two teams didn't get to meet in 1947," he said after the AP recount. "Not that the result would have been so important, but such a game would have given 85,000 football fans a great exhibition of the modern game of football as played by two fine teams."

Personal antagonism II

Great football coaches have at least one thing in common: They all have huge egos. The unassuming and the unsure don't stand a chance in this profession.

Self-confidence is essential. The coach who possesses great ability and conviction must make sure his players know it, and thus must believe in himself with every fiber of his being. He can respect rival coaches but must firmly believe each and every one is his inferior.

It is this timeless mentality that is entwined into every coaching feud. That was the case with Fielding Yost and Knute Rockne. And that was the case with Fritz Crisler and Frank Leahy.

Their strained relationship was hardly unique, for Leahy had few friends in the coaching fraternity. That Notre Dame was whipping everyone in the late '40s had plenty to do with it. So did repeated charges, probably unjust, that Leahy taught his boys to play dirty, that he took hard hitting past the point of good sportsmanship.

Leahy's woeful social skills also did him in, as he was forever rubbing others the wrong way. He wasn't one to spin yarns and trade good-natured fibs at cocktail parties. He was basically a loner who cared only about gladitorial combat, not glad-handing. Whenever he did take to buttering someone up, it came across as so blatantly phony that all he did was irk his rivals even more. "Rockne could beat them and make them like it," Notre Dame football historian Francis Wallace so aptly pointed out. "Leahy beats them and they wind up hating his guts."

Crisler was certainly perplexed by Leahy, summing up the commonly held view of the Notre Dame coach in an astonishingly frank interview with the *Detroit Times* in 1948:

> I don't know why I don't like Frank Leahy. I don't know why I do like Frank Leahy. He's a total enigma. One morning you see him and he's full of fun, full of life. The next morning you see him, he's morose and gloomy. One day you think he's going to fight fair. The next day he's telling you how he's going to destroy you. Some say his teams play rough but don't play dirty. I'm never sure what Leahy thinks is the difference between rough and dirty. I just don't know what to make of the man.

By the late 1940s, prominent schools were dropping Notre Dame from their football schedules. Illinois and Northwestern ended their respective annual engagements, and Army brought a close to its wildly popular rivalry with Notre Dame after 1947. It was believed Leahy's tense relationship with Army coach Red Blaik was a major factor.

Leahy wasn't exactly Mr. Popular among the press corps, either. His penchant for painting ultra-gloomy scenarios week after week in the late '40s, when Notre Dame was steamrolling everybody week after week, had become tiresome, especially when it was universally known that Leahy was as fierce and as confident a competitor as ever existed.

Football legend Red Grange was asked for his opinion of Leahy, and, unexpectedly, he gave the embattled coach an unrestrained, ringing endorsement:

You know why Notre Dame is the best college team in the country? It's because Frank Leahy is the greatest college football coach who ever lived. He's greater than Knute Rockne ever thought of being and I'm not knocking old Rock. But Leahy is just the best. . . .

They complain and say that he teaches dirty football and all that silly talk. The reason they complain is that Leahy is superior and he wins. They stay clear of Notre Dame for one reason: Frank Leahy. They don't want to get beat.

Leahy thought this was Crisler's reason for shunning Notre Dame, as he recalled in an interview shortly before his death in 1973:

In 1944 I asked [Crisler] directly if we could resume the series. He looked me straight in the eyes and said that Michigan was willing to meet Notre Dame any place, any time, and any Saturday. I believed him. I repeatedly asked him for a date that we could meet and he never could make room on his schedule for Notre Dame. Ooooh, they grew afraid of us in those post-war years. Notre Dame had the players, by far the best there were.

Publicly, Crisler continually cited Michigan's nonconference scheduling policy—of playing Michigan State and appeasing coastal alumni—as the only reason Notre Dame could not be scheduled. "We couldn't fit Notre Dame in," Crisler said in 1948, "and I might say we don't have a particularly large number of alumni in South Bend, Indiana."

That Michigan could have satisfied its East Coast alumni by playing Notre Dame at, say, Yankee Stadium shot holes through that line of reasoning. But the hiatus continued, and the Leahy-Crisler feud silently simmered.

By the time the 1940s had given way to the '50s, each man's role at his school had changed appreciably.

Leahy gave up the title of Notre Dame athletic director in 1949 but remained head football coach. The new AD was Ed (Moose) Krause—a star football and basketball player for the Fighting Irish in the early '30s and Leahy's line coach in the '40s. Krause was a smoothy all the way, and that likely had a lot to do with his promotion, for Notre Dame hadn't required this much athletic fence-mending since Jesse Harper was first hired in 1913.

At Michigan, Crisler handed over the coaching reins to Bennie Oosterbaan following the climactic 1947 season. This allowed Crisler to devote more time to his athletic directorship, to become a bigger wheel within the conference, and to expand his role on the NCAA football rules committee. Crisler became chairman of that committee in 1950, and it was in this function that he had his severest run-ins with Leahy.

The first incident occurred in 1952, when Leahy employed a common bit of trickery against Southern Cal. Notre Dame had the ball third and three on the USC nine and lined up in its familiar T-formation. Instead of snapping the ball, though, the Irish shifted, and USC jumped offside. The Irish got a first down, scored a touchdown, and won 9–0.

"It was a standard procedure and USC was aware of it," Leahy recalled. "The school made no complaint, probably because the athletic department realized that their coach would have done the same thing to Notre Dame under the circumstances."

A howl went up across the country, however. The "Notre Dame sucker shift" earned Leahy a ton of bad press, even though other schools performed such shifts and never fielded any adverse publicity. In fact, Leahy said Pittsburgh and Iowa had each sucker-shifted Notre Dame numerous times that very year, but only he and the Irish were being held to the higher standard.

After the season, the NCAA rules committee publicly censured Leahy for the unsportsmanlike shift. Leahy seethed, for he charged, as did many football experts, that the "original genius at the sucker shift" was none other than the chairman of the NCAA rules committee— one Fritz Crisler. Crisler had used a variation of the tactic while at Princeton in the mid '30s.

In 1953, Leahy was censured by the rules committee again—not once but twice.

In the summer of '53 he had illegally tried out prospective recipients of scholarships. Leahy's wrists were privately slapped by university officials, but the rules committee did so publicly.

"It is ironic," commented Notre Dame executive vice president Rev. Edmund Joyce, "to be subjected to public opprobrium for a minor offense which was decisively handled on the university level. There are many areas of really serious abuses . . . toward which the NCAA could have much more profitably turned its attention."

Joyce was probably referring to the slush funds and recruiting transgressions that pervaded college athletics.

But the tryouts and even the sucker shift paled in comparison to the furor over a tactic Leahy used twice against Iowa in November 1953. A fake injury by a Notre Dame player at the end of each half stopped the clock long enough for the Irish to score their touchdowns in a 14–14 tie with the Iowa Hawkeyes. Leahy admitted afterward that both times he had instructed the player to fake an injury.

Controversy exploded around Leahy like never before. He was attacked from coast to coast. Some snickering writers labeled his team the Fainting Irish. The Boston papers, long his staunch allies, were distancing themselves. Even many Notre Dame alumni were outraged. The consensus was that Notre Dame had avoided defeat by cheating—pure, plain, and simple.

But Leahy, with seemingly the whole world closing in on him, did not back down.

"Feigned injuries have been part of football since Walter Camp invented the first down more than 70 years ago," Leahy later argued. "Other coaches have told their players the same thing. Just ask any coach or player you know, at the college, high-school, or even the grade-school level. Yet you probably never heard about a feigned injury until our Iowa game [because] the extra seconds gained [almost always] avail a team little or nothing.

"It seems to me that the feigned-injury controversy was caused not by *what was done,* but by *who did it* and *how successfully.*"

Leahy's most vocal backer not connected to Notre Dame was his brother, Gene, who was appalled by the scorn heaped on his younger sibling. What especially galled Gene Leahy was Crisler's comment that the subject of feigned injuries "may" come up at the January 1954 rules committee meeting. Gene fired off this caustic letter to Crisler:

You KNOW [the subject] will come up, because NOTRE DAME profited by taking advantage of the injury—feigned or real. Had IOWA profited by it, nothing would ever come of it. That and the so-called sucker shift become a CRIME only when Notre Dame uses them.

What you anti–Notre Dame people failed to tell the public was that the shift was first introduced last year when Pittsburgh used it AGAINST Notre Dame. . . .

Why don't all of you, Mr. Crisler, who hate to see Notre Dame win,

make a New Year's resolution to be FAIR WITH NOTRE DAME, in the
interests of true sportsmanship. . . .

Crisler answered these allegations in a return letter. He sent a copy
to Frank Leahy:

When you make the charge that I am anti–Notre Dame and that I am
one who hates to see Notre Dame win, your indictment is so unfair and
slanted that I even hesitate to make any response to your letter.

With regard to the sucker shift last year and the incident in the Iowa–
Notre Dame game this year, I refrained from any comment on the ethics
of Frank Leahy of Notre Dame. It would be only natural that I do this
since I did not witness any of the incidents nor was I acquainted with any
of the facts surrounding them. Whatever remarks I did make were in
answer to questions put to me about football rules.

The matter of feinting injuries will come before the rules committee at
its meeting in January. If it is any source of comfort to you, please be
authoritatively informed that I, personally, will not raise the question or
make that request of anyone else.

On January 13, 1954, the rules committee released a statement
outlining its position on the "serious problem" of feigned injuries.
The committee was unanimous in terming the ploy "dishonest, unsportsmanlike, and contrary to the spirit of the rules," and it appealed
to the integrity of coaches and players alike to eliminate the practice.

This was generally seen as an indictment of Leahy.

The criticism surrounding him intensified, and it was taking its
toll. Leahy was only 45 but his health was in tatters. He had blacked
out at halftime of the 1953 Georgia Tech game due to a severe intesti-
nal spasm and was thought near dead. Doctors were now telling him
to retire or he would be playing Russian roulette with his health.

So that January, Leahy did indeed step down as Notre Dame's coach.
But the torment of the feigned injury episode would dog Leahy the
rest of his life, according to his official biographer.

Two months after retiring, Leahy finally bit back at all his foes in an
article for *Look* magazine. He addressed the contentious incidents of
the previous two years and drew this conclusion:

I will emphasize here my conviction that the NCAA's public censuring
of Notre Dame was inspired principally by some of the representatives
from a block of the more affluent members of the Western Conference.
These righteous personalities frequently commit football sins more
grievous by far than tryouts. Yet, they have sought to steer the policies not

only of their own Conference but of the NCAA, and have in considerable measure succeeded. They have long resented Notre Dame's dominant position in football.

It clearly was a shot at Crisler, among others.

Gene Leahy also got in a shot, in a second letter to Crisler, but, as in the previous case, he was slightly more direct than his brother:

I KNEW you could do it, as you did a year ago, point the finger of accusation at Notre Dame. . . . Mr. Crisler, because of his position, aimed another foul blow at NOTRE DAME. YOU, of all people, crying about not being able to legislate ethics, when YOU do not know the meaning of the word. It is like Russia accusing this nation of being war mongers. . . .

If you had a spark of sportsmanship in you, Mr. Crisler, you would schedule Notre Dame, and try to beat them LEGITIMATELY on the gridiron, rather than with subterfuge worthy of Russia's Molotov. HE don't care who he maligns just so it is THE UNITED STATES, and YOU don't care who YOU malign just so it is NOTRE DAME.

YOU have not had the GUTS to play Notre Dame since 1943, when they humiliated your DREAM TEAM, and have resorted to every foul trick within your reach to discredit them ever since. Why not have the CHARLIE HORSE between your eyes treated, and resolve to be a better sportsman, thereby giving your brain a vacation from prejudice? . . .

If YOU are a shining example of sportsmanship and lily-white ethics in sports, then STALIN should have become POPE. And even YOU must realize how impossible THAT was.

P.S. It was gratifying to learn that Frank has resigned his position as coach of Notre Dame. . . . Assuming that he is through with football now, he will be better off in this respect. He will never again have to breathe the POLLUTED air at meetings which would include YOU, *Crisler the prejudiced.* That blessing, more than anything else, should improve his health. . . .

This time, Crisler did not dignify Gene Leahy's charges with a response.

Whether any of Crisler's actions on the rules committee were indeed intended to malign Leahy and Notre Dame, we'll probably never know. Both Leahys were sure of it, but Crisler denied it, and there's no proof anywhere among Crisler's surviving files that he acted on spite.

Gene Leahy was right, however, that Crisler had a specific ax to grind against Notre Dame. Religion was on the cutting edge.

At cross-purposes

When Frank Leahy was long gone from Notre Dame, Fritz Crisler was as opposed as ever to scheduling the Fighting Irish. So their personal feud could not have been the sole reason for the continuing hiatus.

Crisler remained Michigan athletic director until June 1968, upon reaching the mandatory retirement age of 70. He never bent one iota from his anti–Notre Dame stance. In fact, Rev. Edmund Joyce, Notre Dame's executive vice president from 1952 to 1987, said he never had a single conversation with Crisler, which is amazing considering he and Crisler were concurrently the respective heads of these nearby athletic powers for 16 years.

Crisler did allow Michigan to play Notre Dame in low-profile sports—gymnastics, track and field, baseball, tennis, and golf—but he simply would not permit Notre Dame to be scheduled in the money-makers, football and basketball.

For 20 years, Notre Dame athletic director Moose Krause tried to convince Crisler otherwise. "I'd call him up and congratulate him on winning some big game, or something," remembered Krause. "We got very friendly. Very friendly. . . . Each time I'd go to a convention I'd talk to him about getting a series going with Michigan."

But each time, Crisler politely put him off.

In 1978, Krause told *Sports Illustrated,* "I think he didn't want to play us because we were a power in his own backyard. If Michigan lost to Army, well, they were back East. We were too close."

Theories, theories.

Exactly why did Crisler refuse to play Notre Dame all those years? Since he died in 1982, we are left with only the various opinions of those who knew him best, and those who worked at both schools during his era.

The commonly held perception among Michigan people today is twofold:

1. That Crisler thought Notre Dame was too much of a distraction for a school whose sole purpose in football life should be to win the Big Ten championship and go to the Rose Bowl.

2. That Crisler thought playing Notre Dame would split Michigan's fans along religious lines. That is, Michigan's Catholic fans and students would all root for Notre Dame instead.

The first theory is essentially true: Notre Dame is a distracting game, simply because it will always be a huge game on anybody's schedule, including Michigan's. Most of those who worked in the Michigan athletic department under Crisler cite this as his main reason.

But a writer who was close to the Michigan football scene in the '50s and '60s, Pete Waldmeir of the *Detroit News,* trashed the Big-Ten-comes-first theory. "That's the party-line bullshit," Waldmeir said. "It wasn't that at all. Fritz didn't give a damn about the Big Ten. I'll tell you what, he ran the Big Ten. And you can quote me on that. He told them what to do on football. . . . He had his people placed all around the Big Ten."

The second theory, about splitting the Michigan family, is endorsed by almost everybody who was close to Crisler—athletic department employees and reporters alike.

In 1956, Waldmeir may have been the first to write about it. "Fritz just said, 'You know, it's tough. Every Saturday morning, from every pulpit in town, they're praying for Notre Dame in Ann Arbor,'" Waldmeir remembered.

Don Canham, Michigan's track coach from 1949 to 1968, properly pointed out that times were different before John F. Kennedy was elected president in 1960, when the Catholic-Protestant division in America was very real. "Fritz didn't have a deep-seated hate of Catholics, or anything like that," remembered Canham, himself a Protestant who married a Catholic. "But, you know, in those days they figured if a Catholic ran for public office he couldn't win. The country was that divided. And in those days, blacks couldn't play on a team if they went south. I mean, it was a different world. And that's what you have to realize when you look at it with today's perspective."

Bump Elliott, Michigan's head football coach from 1959 to 1968, also said the concern about splitting fans along religious lines was genuine. Before coming to Michigan, Elliott was an assistant coach at Iowa in the mid 1950s, when the Hawkeyes annually closed their season against Notre Dame. Elliott remembered Catholic alumni of Iowa telling him, "We're going to root for you on eight Saturdays this year, but on that ninth one we're going to have to root for Notre Dame."

Notre Dame's athletic leaders, however, would positively scoff at the "split the Michigan family" theory. Father Joyce said the only two schools that ever cited this reason for not playing Notre Dame in his 35-year tenure were Michigan and Ohio State.

"I always thought the two of them were together on this," Joyce recalled. "I never believed it.

"Michigan State kept bragging that they had more Catholics on their team than we did. And a lot of the teams we played had Catholic chaplains. When we played Rice [in 1988], that coach had 40 Houston priests sitting on the bench to root for Rice. So that's why I take that argument with a grain of salt."

Krause was equally indignant.

"That's a bunch of bunk. Those Catholic boys would rather beat Notre Dame than anybody. . . . Don't ever bring religion into it."

"Ultimately," Joyce said, "Woody Hayes was a little more honest about it. He said he didn't want to play Notre Dame because the Michigan game was the only big game on their schedule, and they geared everything to beat Michigan, whereas if they played Notre Dame it would detract from the Michigan game. Now there may be some truth to that. In other words, what he was saying is they don't like to lose. . . . Those guys all had great egos and they didn't want to lose."

Waldmeir said there is validity to this theory. "I wouldn't be a bit surprised if Crisler thought that if he played them, they'd spoil his record," Waldmeir surmised.

Crisler did prefer to load up Michigan's schedule with as many home games as possible, as many as seven in a nine-game season. Before 1958, there was no Big Ten rule that mandated home-and-home contracts, and the shrewd Crisler was able to get some conference teams to come to Ann Arbor almost every year. From 1943 to 1958 Michigan played Indiana 15 times, all in Ann Arbor. And from 1945 to 1957 Michigan played Michigan State 13 times, 11 in Ann Arbor. Although Michigan State detested this arrangement, Indiana apparently didn't mind because back then visiting teams always got 50 percent of the gate, and by 1956 Michigan Stadium could house 101,001.

"He'd buy wins. I mean, for [these schools] to try to beat Michigan at home . . ." Waldmeir said incredulously. "And what the hell did he want to go to Indiana for, anyway? They had a 24,000-seat stadium. Even if they half-filled Michigan Stadium it was twice the size of a sellout down in Indiana, where he was splitting the gate with them."

Crisler wasn't able to work out such a cozy arrangement with every conference school, though. Ohio State and Illinois would never agree to anything but a home-and-home series, no matter how lucrative it would have been otherwise.

The point of all this is that Crisler wouldn't have been able to strike such a lopsided deal with Notre Dame, either. So why play Notre Dame when you can play six or seven home games a year against easier opposition? "He didn't like to lose," Waldmeir said, "and I think that's part of why he didn't play Notre Dame."

Elliott more or less agreed: "I think [Crisler] felt our schedule was tough enough without playing Notre Dame as well. Throughout the 10 years I coached at Michigan, every Big Ten school went to the Rose Bowl but Northwestern."

But if protecting Michigan's record was Crisler's main reason, why did he go out of his way to try to convince other conference schools—as Yost had done—to shun Notre Dame? What would Crisler have cared if other members lost to Notre Dame?

One reason was that since Rockne's time, Notre Dame annually stole much of the midwestern football spotlight away from the Big Ten. That didn't sit well with the conference hierarchy in the 1920s, and it didn't sit well with Crisler in his era.

And as Waldmeir maintained, Crisler held enormous sway in the Big Ten. The following ex-Wolverines were conference athletic directors in the late '50s or early '60s: Ivan Williamson at Wisconsin, Bill Orwig at Indiana, and Forest Evashevski at Iowa. And Biggie Munn at Michigan State had played for Crisler at Minnesota and had been an assistant coach for Crisler at Michigan in the early '40s. What's more, a Michigan grad, Bill Reed, was assistant commissioner of the conference from 1951 to 1961 and commissioner from 1961 to 1971. Waldmeir said Crisler "could get anything done that he wanted done."

Including, apparently, a boycott of Notre Dame.

"There was sort of this unofficial blackball," Father Joyce recalled. "Michigan and Ohio State were trying to keep other Big Ten teams from playing us.

"I feel sorry for the Big Ten teams that would have loved to have played us but weren't able to. Yet back in those years, they were influenced by Michigan and Ohio State. But Purdue just thumbed their noses at Crisler. They told him just to go to hell. This is where we'd hear that he was trying to do this. Purdue has been a wonderful friend of ours, and Michigan State, too. . . . They would die for us."

Perhaps the most logical explanation for Crisler's action toward Notre Dame all those years was provided by his son, Scott Crisler, who directly broached the subject with his father more than once.

Scott maintained his father shunned the Fighting Irish not because they were a distraction from the Big Ten season, and not because Crisler was afraid to play Notre Dame ("He played Army when Michigan had just freshmen and Army was loaded," Scott said. "I don't think he was afraid to play anybody.")

The main reason, Scott said, did indeed involve religion, but it was something Crisler apparently told no one else—and it came wrapped in a familiar package.

"He felt that it was unfair recruiting that Notre Dame had because they went national and used religion as the basis of their recruiting," Scott Crisler said. "A Big Ten school, or any other school, more or less had to go on their reputation in the state, or a little bit out of state. . . .

He felt Notre Dame should be no better or no worse than any other school, but he felt that they *were* better because of religion.

"It was the idea that they have a commmon thread in recruiting which he felt was unfair. Any good Catholic football player was supposed to go to Notre Dame. I mean, that was across the country."

If recruiting advantages indeed annoyed Crisler, he must have been especially peeved in the '40s and early '50s, when Notre Dame was awarding full athletic scholarships to players—as many as 32 per year—while Big Ten teams could offer only a few scholarships per year based on a player's scholastic aptitude. But Notre Dame was only following NCAA regulations, which just happened to be more lax than the conference's. It wasn't until 1957 that the Big Ten approved of athletic scholarships, but with a constrictive qualifier: "based on need." In other words, if a player couldn't prove he needed financial aid to attend university, he didn't get the scholarship.

When Crisler wrote commissioner John L. Griffith back in 1944 about Notre Dame "not going all the way" with the conference, he might also have been referring to Leahy's aggressive, off-campus recruiting campaigns—because the conference rule on recruiting hadn't changed since 1927: no making the first contact with athletes. But again, Notre Dame was only following NCAA rules.

Because recruiting had become the name of the game, Notre Dame's tendering of athletic scholarships and off-campus contact by coaches could be construed as advantages. The "every good Catholic should go to Notre Dame" mentality undoubtedly also helped attract talent.

Crisler was every bit like Yost in that he perceived any such advantages as grossly unfair. Thus, the Crisler dodge appears to have boiled down to the timeless Michigan mentality in this rivalry: Michigan wouldn't play Notre Dame because Michigan thought Notre Dame had unfair advantages. But again, whether these advantages were unfair is highly debatable.

And it must be pointed out that conference schools later confessed to having breached their strict pre-1957 scholarship and recruiting limitations—by actively enticing athletes with various forms of covert, illegal subsidization. "Notre Dame kept all the rules, which [conference schools] didn't do, frankly," Father Joyce recalled. So once again, the Big Ten was guilty of preaching purity to others when it, in fact, was not holier than thou.

But Crisler was a man of high scruples when it came to recruiting and subsidization. If anyone was responsible for holding the Big Ten back in this area, it was probably Crisler. He, like his mentor Amos Alonzo Stagg, positively despised recruiting. In fact, Crisler listed that as the main reason he got out of coaching in 1947. Crisler also detested that college football was more and more becoming a slave to the almighty dollar. The main reason he, as chairman of the rules committee, struck down two-platoon football in 1953—the tactic he himself had popularized—was because he could foresee the day when the game would grow out of control, when massive rosters would lead to massive athletic department budgets, which in turn would lead to massive recruiting and subsidization scandals. On that forecast, he most certainly was correct.

In addition to recruiting advantages, Scott Crisler said his dad also disliked the fact that Notre Dame "made a religious war" out of sports contests.

"He wanted to get it away from the religious content," Scott said. "He wanted to keep football as an athletic event, rather than some kind of expanded crusade. . . . He said, 'You know, before the game they march them all off to church and they say their Hail Marys and they come in and they make a religious campaign out of it.'"

Thus, the split-the-Michigan-family reasoning was probably just Crisler's way of offering for public consumption a more digestible version of his private antireligion stance, which would have been considered far more controversial.

Crisler's philosophy on religion and how it pertained to football was 180-degrees different than that of Frank Leahy, a devout Catholic. The crux of Leahy's coaching philosophy at Notre Dame was that every lap run, every touchdown scored, was a sacrament to the Virgin Mary. "All right, lads," he once said in a pregame speech, "in four and a half minutes, you will be out there defending the honor of Our Lady. . . . I don't think we can win it in the first half. But I know you can pull it out in the fourth period. I know that, lads! I believe in you, lads! Our Lady believes in you!"

Perhaps this clash of philosophies was also at the very root of the Leahy-Crisler tiffs. If it was, Leahy probably was never aware of it, for Crisler never spoke publicly about his antireligion feelings until long after Leahy had left Notre Dame.

Everyone interviewed who knew Crisler stated emphatically that he wasn't anti-Catholic in the traditional vein. What he was was antireligion, period. "He was not a churchgoing man of any denomination," Scott Crisler recalled. In fact Scott could only surmise that his dad was "probably Presbyterian" by baptism.

Thus, in the final analysis, Crisler was simply a man at cross-purposes with just about everything Notre Dame stood for—religiously and athletically.

Crisler felt that boycotting Notre Dame was the easiest way to voice his concerns. And by recruiting other members of the influential conference to join his boycott, Crisler successfully overturned the notion that had so irked him in 1944: Notre Dame no longer "had the blessing of the Conference in whatever it does."

● ● ●

Crisler's views must have made him wildly popular among those Michigan alumni who did possess the traditional Protestant prejudice toward Catholics. After all, Michigan generally turns out conservative, Republican alumni. One graduate in 1940 assured Crisler he could always count on "a public opinion sufficiently non-Democratic and non-Catholic."

There were probably far more Michigan alumni, however, who wanted to see the Wolverines play the Fighting Irish during Crisler's reign. In the late '40s, especially, Crisler took considerable heat from within the Michigan "family." "Hell, man, what are you afraid of from Notre Dame?" asked alumnus Robert Stierwalt. "With teams like we have we can beat them. Are you a man or a mouse?"

But by the mid-1950s, demand for a Michigan–Notre Dame game dropped off as dramatically as each school's football fortunes. From 1954 to 1963, Notre Dame went 51–48–0 under coaches Terry Brennan, Joe Kuharich, and Huge Devore; Michigan went 47–39–4 under Oosterbaan and Elliott. One could cite any number of reasons for the dual fall from preeminence, perhaps including a deemphasis on football at the schools, weaker coaching, outmoded attacks, a lingering hesitance to recruit blacks, and toned-down recruiting and subsidization efforts.

By the time Fritz Crisler stepped down as Michigan athletic director in June 1968, public desire for a Michigan–Notre Dame game was in abject hibernation. It had been 25 years since the last game. By the late '60s, college football fans had learned to get along fine without a Notre Dame–Michigan matchup, and Notre Dame had learned to get along fabulously without Michigan. "We were not going to beg for a game," recalled Joyce. "Not when we've got 50 people lined up wanting to play us. So we didn't need Michigan."

Ironically, Crisler's successor figured he needed Notre Dame.

Utmost respect: 1968–77

At a time when red ink was leaking all over college athletics, Michigan picked a man acutely familiar with both dollars and sports sense to be its new athletic director.

A native of Oak Park, Illinois, Don Canham had been an outstanding track coach at Michigan since 1948. A former NCAA high jump champion, Canham guided the Wolverines to 12 Big Ten championships.

But what best prepared Canham for his new job was his command of ledgers, not athletes. In 1954, Canham had started a modest sports-instructional-film company on the side, and it grew into a million-dollar enterprise selling both athletic equipment and teaching aids. He had also demonstrated his business acumen on the college scene, organizing the first NCAA indoor track and field meets in the mid-1960s and making them profitable.

So naturally, when Canham became Michigan A.D. in July 1968, he darted straight to the financial books. It was un ugly read. Michigan was projecting a $139,000 deficit for the coming 1968–69 athletic year.

Michigan's balance sheet was typical of the times, as the late '60s represented the dawning of the age of severe financial hardship in college athletics. The return to two-platoon football earlier in the decade had indeed shot expenses through the roof, as Fritz Crisler had warned.

Canham, though, surmised that Michigan's salvation lay in filling massive Michigan Stadium for every home football game.

The Wolverines had been drawing poorly, a result of their mediocre exploits over the previous decade. When the 1968 season ended, the average home attendance was only 67,000—some 34,000 short of a sellout.

Canham the businessman knew how to fill it up: by marketing the product and improving the product.

He devised extreme means to achieve these ends, comparatively as radical as anything else occurring on the Michigan campus in 1968—and that meant radical, man. This bold, self-sure 49-year-old wasn't just going to nudge Michigan football out of hibernation, he was going to jolt it out of bed upright with sirens blaring.

To market the product, Canham mailed out one million ticket applications, and placed ads in *Sports Illustrated, Time,* and *Fortune.*

Ads in magazines!

Didn't Canham know this was staid, old Michigan? What would Fielding Yost have said? What would Fritz Crisler *say*? Canham didn't care, just as Yost and Crisler hadn't cared what anybody thought of their actions.

To improve the product, Canham did three crucial things. The first was to hire a fiery young football coach by the name of Bo Schembechler after the 1968 season. (Bump Elliott was bumped upstairs to associate athletic director.) The second was to alternate, by year, the Michigan State and Ohio State home games, so as to entice more season-ticket holders on an annual basis. The third was to bring in higher-profile competition.

And that's how the modern-day Michigan–Notre Dame series came to be.

Canham simply turned his back on some seven decades of Michigan contempt and connivance and forged a friendly, enduring relationship with Notre Dame. If it weren't for Canham, this series might have remained on the shelf indefinitely.

"I can't take credit for being an emancipator or anything like that," Canham recalled. "I mean it was strictly a financial decision. I had one hell of a headache trying to balance the budget, and the first thing I did was try to beef up the schedule so we drew some people."

But Canham didn't think of signing up Notre Dame right off the bat. Moose Krause, the Notre Dame athletic director, was the one who suggested it. Krause and Canham had developed a solid friendship over the previous two decades, when Michigan and Notre Dame often competed in track and field.

Coincidentally, Krause's first move to resume the series took place at an identical setting to where Fritz Crisler had pulled the plug in 1943—at a football banquet in Detroit.

It was the annual postseason event put on by Chevrolet in December 1968, and prominent athletic men from across the country were present at the Book Cadillac Hotel. Future scheduling was on Canham's mind because, among other complications, Colorado had just canceled some dates down the road.

At one point during the evening Canham told Walter Byers, NCAA executive director, that Michigan Stadium would eventually be filled for every home game. Krause was within earshot, and he jumped right into the conversation.

"Doggone, I know how you can sell out a game," Krause interrupted.

"Yes, I know, by playing Notre Dame," Canham responded. "All right, Moose, let's do it. Let's look at our schedules."

They shook hands, and that was it. The agreement in principle came about that quickly.

When Krause returned to Notre Dame he immediately informed Rev. Edmund Joyce, the executive vice president, that Michigan wanted a game. "Really?!" Joyce answered incredulously.

Joyce and Krause, of course, were all in favor of a resumption of the long-dormant Michigan series, as was football coach Ara Parseghian. "We'd been butting our heads up against a wall," Joyce recalled. "We didn't have any hard feelings. I always felt it was a personal thing between Crisler and Leahy, but we're not going to hold it against the institution. . . . It was such a natural to play Michigan, and we like to play the best. That's been our policy."

So a meeting was held a month later, in January 1969, during the annual NCAA convention in Los Angeles. Canham brought along his assistant, Dave Strack, for a sit-down with Joyce and Krause in a hotel room. "Moose had his schedules and Don had his," Joyce recalled. "We hammered out the dates right there."

These dates—only four of them, initially—were a long way away: 1978–81. Why the delay? Because both schools had scheduled up to 15 years in advance, and because then, as now, Michigan's Big Ten scheduling commitments meant each year there were only a few dates in September the two sides could bat around. "They'd have an open date or two, but we didn't have it," Canham recalled. "That was the problem."

A few weeks later, Canham, Strack, and Elliott drove down to Notre Dame to talk contract. But not the usual split-the-gate contract. Joyce, the man who handled all financial negotiations involving Notre Dame athletics, and Canham revolutionized the way college football business was done. They agreed to let the host school essentially keep the entire gate.

It might appear as though Michigan—with the much larger stadium (then 101,001 to Notre Dame's 59,075)—would make a killing under this scenario, but that wasn't the case. Notre Dame had higher ticket prices and far fewer students (who got in cheaper), so the finances came close to evening out. Any deficiency would be more than made up by the fact that Notre Dame would get half of any TV revenue, while Michigan would have to share its half equally among the 10 conference schools.

So why the home-take-all feature? Simple. Canham and Joyce, both of them ingenious businessmen, knew this contract would set a major precedent: soon they would be able to draw up all of their home-and-home contracts this way. And that was important because some schools were coming into Notre Dame and Michigan and leaving with pockets full, having taken 50 percent of the gate, when the return trip would never wind up as lucrative for the Fighting Irish or Wolverines.

"Up until that contract was drawn, everybody just shared the gate," said Canham. "Now conferences all over the country are following the contract that Michigan and Notre Dame originated. Not keep your own gate 100 percent, but just give the visitor a flat guarantee."

In fact, Canham and Joyce wrote in a small guarantee for the visitor into their contract—$100,000—to cover various expenses. But, as Joyce pointed out, it was really insignificant because both sides would simply exchange checks every year.

There were other unique features to the contract: a disaster clause; a national emergency clause; and a clause that revealed the remarkable foresight of these men—one covering pay and cable TV rights.

Canham and Joyce were as firm-minded as they were forward-thinking, however, and that was borne out in these negotiations. "I remember we had some hot discussions," Joyce said. "But it was all in fun and games."

The hot discussions had to do with radio rights—specifically, Notre Dame's national Mutual football network. Normally, the host school retained all radio rights. "But when we went to Ann Arbor, we had to insist that we have the right to have our network carry the game," Joyce recalled. "It was very important to us. If they said no, well, we just wouldn't have played Michigan. They finally said, 'Okay, but give us some money.'"

Joyce pointed out to Canham, however, that Notre Dame wasn't making any money off Mutual back then. "It was absolutely insignificant," Joyce said. That was hard for Canham to believe, as it was for other Notre Dame opponents, Joyce said.

Strack recalled sitting back and getting a kick out of watching Canham and Joyce go back and forth on the radio issue. "Two bright people—and two strong-minded people," Strack said. "But then it all ended up amicably." Canham eventually believed Joyce's claim and backed off. "I enjoyed negotiating with Don," Joyce said. "He was just a lively, vigorous kind of guy."

The agreement that Michigan and Notre Dame would resume their football rivalry was announced to the press on September 23, 1969—nine years to the day before the series would again resume. The *Detroit News* screamed the story across the top of its sports section that evening.

"I was very proud of Don Canham," Joyce recalled. "It took a lot of courage on Don's part to come to us right away. I was surprised that he could take over like he did without any reference to Fritz or anybody else. But obviously he was his own athletic director."

Indeed, what was Crisler's reaction? Not what you might think.

"He certainly didn't disagree with me when I told him," Canham remembered. "He said, 'Well, you're the director now, and things change.' He didn't say, 'What the hell did you do that for?' or anything like that."

And the Michigan alumni's reaction? Whether they were for or against, Canham couldn't have cared less. "I didn't pay any attention to alumni pressure," he said emphatically. Besides, by the end of the '60s, anti-Catholic prejudice was not nearly as pronounced as it was in previous decades.

The contract for the double home-and-home series wasn't signed until Thursday, October 1, 1970, when Parseghian brought his Fighting Irish squad to Ann Arbor.

Canham and Schembechler had allowed Parseghian's team to work out on Michigan Stadium's artificial playing surface, to get a feel for it two days before playing a game on that surface for the first time up at Michigan State. After the Irish arrived in Ann Arbor, coaches Parseghian and Schembechler and ADs Krause and Canham met at the local Holiday Inn and signed the contracts.

Schembechler had been an assistant for two years under Parseghian at Northwestern in the late 1950s, and the two Miami of Ohio graduates remained close friends. Schembechler remembered saying something like this to Parseghian: "Ara, I can't wait till I get your ass." But Parseghian replied, "You will never have that opportunity." Even then, Parseghian had no plans to be around in 1978, and did in fact retire after the 1974 season. "But it would have been fun competing against Bo," Parseghian recalled. "He was a great competitor. They played clean, solid, fundamental football."

Bo and Ara almost had the opportunity to play late in 1970, because Joyce and Canham had flirted with the idea of arranging a postseason game.

Back in January 1970, the NCAA had passed legislation to allow an 11th regular-season game, raising the previous limit by one. Neither Michigan nor Notre Dame, though, had scheduled an 11th opponent for 1970, and by mid-November both schools were near the top of the polls with perfect records. That's when Father Joyce came up with the intriguing idea of pitting Notre Dame against Michigan at the end of the regular season, in a legal game under NCAA guidelines for the national championship.

Canham and Strack were all for it, and may even have bounced the idea off the Big Ten. But it didn't matter, because 9–0 Michigan lost its regular-season finale at Ohio State and 9–0 Notre Dame lost its at Southern Cal.

There were, however, Michigan–Notre Dame football games of a different sort played during the nine-year wait. Parseghian and Schembechler arranged for their freshman teams, and later their junior varsity teams, to square off against each other. The schools split a 10-game series played between 1969 and 1975. (See Appendix I for scores.) "There were a certain number of kids that didn't get a chance to play in varsity games," Parseghian remembered. "So we would set up games on a Friday, or a Monday. We had a pretty decent little schedule for them, and it gave them something to look forward to."

These games were indicative of the warm relations that now existed between Michigan and Notre Dame—as warm as they've ever been.

At the center of it was Canham, who more than 20 years later retained the utmost respect for Notre Dame. "You have to give Notre Dame credit," he said. "Any sport you want to name, Notre Dame goes after the best competition they can get. Look at the basketball schedule they play. It's murder. Murder! And the same in football. They'll play anybody—they don't care. And, you know, that's why Notre Dame is Notre Dame."

But an important point about Canham needs to be made.

As friendly as he was toward Notre Dame, his relationship with Big Ten Conference schools always came first. This was best exemplified in an incident that occurred at a Big Ten meeting in 1971.

Moose Krause had sounded out athletic directors George King of Purdue and Biggie Munn of Michigan State as to their interest in immediately adopting the home-take-all feature in their respective contracts. In no way was it an attempt to break the existing contract; Krause, a prankster, may even have just been trying to get a rise out of his old pals.

King and Munn took it seriously, however, for they wanted to squeeze every last penny from the 50–50 contracts with Notre Dame. They complained to Canham, who darted straight over to Krause. Canham recalled their conversation:

"I said, 'If you do that, I'll break our contract.' And Moose said, 'You wouldn't do that.' I said, 'You watch me.' And I would have."

🏈 🏈 🏈

By 1975 Canham indeed was filling Michigan Stadium for every home game (there hasn't been a crowd of less than 100,000 since). Canham also devised innovative marketing approaches, such as selling any kind of souvenir colored maize and blue or stamped with a block M. Such ventures proved so lucrative, Canham was constantly being consulted by athletic directors from across the country, including Krause. Canham retired as Michigan athletic director in 1988.

His counterparts at Notre Dame guided the Fighting Irish for almost as long; Krause remained athletic director until 1980 and Joyce executive vice president until 1987.

The mutual respect shared between these three men never subsided. Soon after arranging the 1978–81 contract, they extended the series all the way to 1990, but scheduling complications would force a two-year hiatus in 1983 and '84. Just before the series resumed in 1978, Canham and Krause extended it to 2000 by handshake agreement. A few years later this was confirmed through letter agreement, although Michigan agreed to drop the 1995 and '96 dates so Notre Dame could play a home-and-home series with Ohio State.

So what Canham, Joyce, and Krause did was make the Notre Dame–Michigan game an annual affair, thereby containing all hostilities between the schools to the gridiron.

The next generation: Coaching rivals
Frank Leahy of Notre Dame (above right,
with Moose Krause) and H.O. "Fritz"
Crisler of Michigan (right).
(University of Notre Dame Archives; Dept. of
Intercollegiate Athletics Records, Bentley
Historical Library, University of Michigan.)

MICHIGAN 32
NOTRE DAME 20

LINE OF
SCRIMMAGE

Holder Don Robinson (#46)
scoots around left end (above)
and scores (right) on a fake
field-goal attempt in Michigan's 32–20 win at Notre
Dame in 1942.
(*Michiganensian*, 1943; 1942 UM
vs. Iowa Football Program, Dept.
of Intercollegiate Athletics Records,
Bentley Historical Library, University of Michigan.)

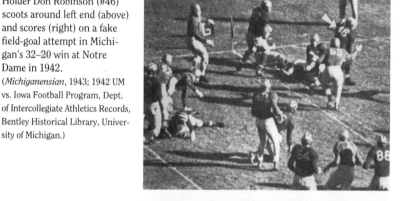

Like father, like son. Creighton Miller—son of Red
Miller, ND's hero against Michigan in 1909—breaks into
open field past Wolverine Merv Pregulman (#67) in Notre
Dame's commanding 35–12 romp at Ann Arbor in 1943.
(*Michiganensian*, 1944.)

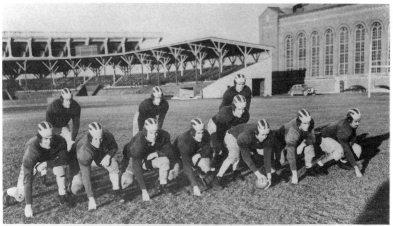

The 1947 National Champions—Linemen (left to right): Dick Rifenburg, Bill Pritula, Joe Soboleski, Dom Tomasi, J. T. White, Captain Bruce Hilkene, and Bob Mann. The backs are Bump Elliott, Jack Weisenburger, Howard Yerges (behind center), and Bob Chappuis.

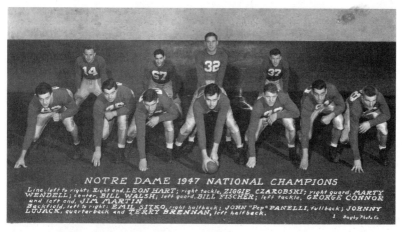

NOTRE DAME 1947 NATIONAL CHAMPIONS

Line, left to right: Right end, LEON HART; right tackle, ZIGGIE CZAROBSKI; right guard, MARTY WENDELL; center, BILL WALSH; left guard, BILL FISCHER; left tackle, GEORGE CONNOR and left end, JIM MARTIN
Backfield, left to right: EMIL SITKO, right halfback; JOHN "Pep" PANELLI, fullback; JOHNNY LUJACK, quarterback and TERRY BRENNAN, left halfback.

The greatest game never played: Michigan (top) vs. Notre Dame in 1947. These were arguably the deepest, most devastating teams in each school's long, storied history. Each school still claims the 1947 national championship as its own.
(*1993 Football Media Guide*, Dept. of Intercollegiate Athletics Records, Bentley Historical Library, University of Michigan; University of Notre Dame Archives.)

The Leahy-Crisler feud silently simmered in the 1940s. They are pictured here following the 1942 game. (Herbert Orin Crisler collection, Bentley Historical Library, University of Michigan.)

The feud boiled over in 1953 and '54. The NCAA football rules committee, chaired by Crisler (above), in effect criticized Leahy three times, and harshly so. The beleaguered Leahy, whose health was a shambles (right), stepped down as ND coach shortly afterward.
(University of Notre Dame Archives; Herbert Orin Crisler collection, Bentley Historical Library, University of Michigan.)

Crisler, pictured here in 1967, stonewalled all attempts by Notre Dame to resume the football series from 1943 until his retirement as Michigan athletic director in 1968.
(Herbert Orin Crisler collection, Bentley Historical Library, University of Michigan.)

The three men who, in 1969, arranged the modern-day series (left to right):
athletic director Ed "Moose" Krause and vice president Rev. Edmund Joyce
of Notre Dame, and new Michigan athletic director Don Canham.
(University of Notre Dame Archives; Donald B. Canham Papers, Bentley Historical
Library, University of Michigan.)

QB Rick Leach rolls out to throw during
Michigan's 28–14 win in 1978. Leach threw
three touchdown passes and ran for a score.
(John Heafield for Bob Kalmbach.)

Chuck Male kicks one of his school-record four field goals in Notre Dame's 12–10 victory in 1979.
(Bob Kalmbach.)

Craig Dunaway hauls in a deflected Wangler pass in the end zone, giving Michigan a 27–26 lead with 41 seconds left in the 1980 game.
(Dept. of Intercollegiate Athletics Records, Bentley Historical Library, University of Michigan.)

Michigan head coach Bo Schembechler (middle) counsels QB John Wangler, who twice came off the bench to vault the Wolverines ahead in the 1980 game.
(Dept. of Intercollegiate Athletics Records, Bentley Historical Library, University of Michigan.)

Probably the most dramatic play in series history: Harry Oliver boots a 51-yard field goal as both time and wind expire, giving the Fighting Irish the 29–27 win in the classic 1980 game.
(University of Notre Dame Archives.)

Schembechler and new ND head coach Gerry Faust chat prior to the 1981 game.
(Lewis Kryk.)

ND head coach Dan Devine was 2–1 vs. Michigan.
(University of Notre Dame Archives.)

Although John Krimm of Notre Dame would intercept this pass, Anthony Carter and Michigan rolled 25–7 in 1981.
(Lewis Kryk.)

In 1982, QB Blair Kiel and the Irish slammed Michigan 23–17 in the first night game played at Notre Dame Stadium.
(University of Notre Dame Archives.)

QB Jim Harbaugh celebrates his go-ahead touchdown in Michigan's 20–12 win in 1985. (Per Kjeldsen.)

Fiery Notre Dame head coach Lou Holtz quickly restored the fight in the Irish, beginning in 1986. (Jason Kryk.)

Holder Dan Sorenson and kicker John Carney, moments after Carney missed a potential game-winning 45-yard field-goal attempt in 1986. Michigan hung on to win 24–23.
(Steve Havratil for Notre Dame.)

Tim Brown outleaps Michigan's Allen Bishop and Erik Campbell to snare a TD pass in Notre Dame's 26–7 runaway victory in 1987.
(University of Notre Dame Archives.)

Unorthodox, diminutive placekicker Reggie Ho put the boot to the Wolverines in 1988, making all four of his field-goal attempts in a 19–17 ND victory.
(Cheryl A. Ertelt for Notre Dame.)

Notre Dame's Raghib "Rocket" Ismail blasted off into stardom in 1989, returning two kickoffs for touchdowns in a 24–19 Irish victory.
(Ed Ballotts for the *South Bend Tribune*.)

QB Rick Mirer, here pictured in the 1991 game, had a smashing debut in 1990, leading Notre Dame to its fourth straight win, 28–24.
(Jason Kryk.)

Gary Moeller succeeded Schembechler as Michigan head coach in 1990 and nearly upset the top-ranked Irish in his first game.
(Jason Kryk.)

After scoring on an end-around in the first half (top), Desmond Howard celebrated "The Catch"—a long, fourth-and-inches pass from Elvis Grbac, which nailed down a 24–14 Michigan victory in 1991. (Jason Kryk.)

Reggie Brooks twists away from diving Wolverine Tony Henderson (#79) en route to his spectacular 20-yard TD run in 1992, the year of the only tie in series history, 17–17.
(Jason Kryk.)

After a treacherous week, Lou Holtz had good reason to smile following Notre Dame's huge 27–23 upset of Michigan in 1993.
(Jason Kryk.)

The Notre Dame (right) and Michigan bands are almost as famous as the legendary fight songs they regularly play. (Jason Kryk.)

Bernie Kirk was one of several "Michi-Damers"—those who played for both schools. Kirk was a star end for Knute Rockne and, later, for Fielding Yost. (*Michiganensian*, 1923.)

ND quarterback Joe Montana is pressured in the 1978 game by Michigan's Mike Trgovac, who 15 years later gave a thunderous pregame pep talk . . . to the Fighting Irish. Trgovac had become the Irish defensive line coach in 1992. (John Heafield for Bob Kalmbach.)

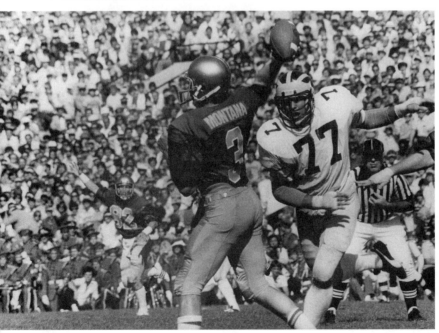

Bo Schembechler was on the verge of pulling the plug on the modern-day series when he retired in 1990.
(John Kryk.)

Schembechler's successor as Michigan athletic director, Jack Weidenbach (right), struck a firm friendship with his ND counterpart, Dick Rosenthal. Before Weidenbach retired in February 1994 he arranged with Rosenthal to extend the series to 2011.
(Dept. of Intercollegiate Athletics Records, Bentley Historical Library, University of Michigan; University of Notre Dame Archives.)

Modern classics: 1978–93

XII. The Guts and Glue, '78

No Michigan player was more anxious to play Notre Dame on September 23, 1978, than senior quarterback Rick Leach.

"I'd been dreaming about that game since I was a freshman," Leach recalled. "I knew we were going to play Notre Dame that year, my senior year, and I couldn't wait."

Nationally, the buildup for the first Michigan–Notre Dame game in 35 years was not nearly as immense as it had been in 1942 and '43. ABC-TV broadcast it only to a regional audience.

Leach, a starter since 1975, had guided the Wolverines to a 29–6–2 record heading into the game. But despite having won two of three Big Ten title showdowns against Ohio State, Leach and company had lost three straight bowl games and couldn't shake the tag of being unable to win the big one.

So when Leach severely sprained his right ankle in practice on the Monday before the ND game, he was properly devastated. So was his coach, Bo Schembechler, who scrambled to prepare Leach's backup, B.J. Dickey. "We were going into that game and, I mean, Leach was *out,*" Schembechler recalled.

During the critical Tuesday and Wednesday scrimmages, Leach hobbled on crutches. That's when Bob Ufer went to work on him.

Ufer, the radio play-by-play voice of the Wolverines since the 1940s, was also Michigan's most boisterous backer, and he proceeded to pump up the player he dubbed "The Guts and Glue of the Maize and Blue."

"He told me, 'This is going to be the first game in a great series. You'll have 60 minutes of football but a lifetime to remember it,'" recalled Leach. "Bob Ufer loved Michigan like nobody I've been around. He taught me a lot about its tradition."

Ufer's pep talks shot Leach into the outer atmosphere. "I was an excitable player," Leach explained. There was no way he could miss this game, regardless of the how much the ankle hurt.

So Leach indeed made the trip on Friday, gingerly took part in workouts at Notre Dame Stadium that afternoon, then tried to assure his skeptical coach he would be able to play. Schembechler had never allowed any player to start who had missed that week's Tuesday and Wednesday scrimmages. "But this was one time he bent the rules," Leach said.

Leach did start. And after a shaky first half that saw Notre Dame leave the field with a 14–7 lead, Leach and the Wolverines totally dominated play and walked away with a 28–14 victory.

Three times in the second half, Leach, an option specialist, surprised Notre Dame with play-action passes that went for touchdowns—two to tight end Doug Marsh and a bomb to wide receiver Ralph Clayton. Leach also ran for a score in the first half.

Wolverine defensive tackle Curtis Greer sealed the win in the final two minutes with an end-zone sack of Irish quarterback Joe Montana. Montana and Leach both went into the game as serious Heisman Trophy candidates, but only Leach emerged as one.

"Performance-wise, that wasn't his greatest game," Schembechler remembered. "Guts-wise? Oh yeah."

XIII. The can't-miss kid, '79

When freshman kicker Chuck Male left Western Michigan University after the 1975 season to enroll at Notre Dame and perhaps try his luck as a walk-on, WMU head coach Elliot Uzelac thought Male was making the biggest mistake of his young life.

"He said, 'Son, you're not going to play football ever again if you do this,'" Male recalled. "He was just being honest, because he probably thought Notre Dame had too many good kickers for me to ever play there."

Notre Dame had never had a kicker boot four field goals in a game, though. Male was the first to do it, on September 15, 1979, to give the Fighting Irish a 12–10 win over the Wolverines at Michigan Stadium.

A year earlier, Male had become Notre Dame's first-string place-kicker and was having a great season until tearing a thigh muscle on a kickoff against Georgia Tech. "I was back to square one," he recalled.

So going into the 1979 opener at Ann Arbor, Male wanted desperately to prove himself again—especially to Uzelac, a former Michigan assistant.

Male felt confident after the pregame warm-up, although he had a nagging concern. "I felt powerful," he said. "It felt like an explosion as I kicked through the ball each time. But I had that same feeling before Georgia Tech, so I was a little worried."

In the first quarter, after Michigan freshman flash Anthony Carter fumbled a punt, Male got his opportunity. He drilled a 40-yarder high into the netting to tie the game 3–3. "It felt so good," he said, "I'm sure I had it in my mind, at that point, that I couldn't miss a single field goal all day."

And he didn't. Male nailed a 44-yarder in the second quarter, a 22-yarder early in the third, and the game-winning 39-yarder late in the third to earn himself a place in Notre Dame lore.

Male probably wouldn't have had the chance to be the star had Notre Dame's offense not been so awful. The Irish finished with only seven first downs, zero pass completions in the second half, and 179 yards of total offense. Halfback Vagas Ferguson basically *was* the offense, amassing 118 yards on 35 tough carries. No other Irish running back had more than one carry.

The Wolverines scored all their points on their first two drives, but thereafter were shut down by the young Irish defense.

In the final two minutes, backup quarterback John Wangler came in and passed Michigan to near field-goal range.

With seven seconds left, Michigan's Bryan Virgil strode forward to attempt a game-winning, 42-yard field goal. Virgil was nowhere near the kicker Male was, however, and he got the ball barely five feet off the ground. It smacked square into the left hip of Irish linebacker Bob Crable, who had leapt up after stepping onto the back of Michigan center Mike Trgovac.

"But it had no chance. None," Bo Schembechler recalled. "It was a shot in the dark."

So the difference in this game was that Notre Dame got its kicks and Michigan didn't.

XIV. The game of the century, '80

What makes a game for the ages?

The requisites are debatable. Some of the most ballyhooed games in college football history are remembered more for what was at stake, or for who was playing, than for what actually unfolded on the field. Others are remembered for a fantastic finish alone, regardless of how ordinary the rest of the battle was.

But when the argument ultimately arises in 1999 as to which was the true game of the century, 1980 Notre Dame–Michigan ought to be mentioned prominently. Because for pure, heart-pounding excitement, this game has few equals. The finish alone is already one of the most memorable of all time: Notre Dame's Harry Oliver, a seldom-used junior, booting a desperation 51-yard field goal into a suddenly quieted wind, with the ball sneaking over the crossbar to give the Fighting Irish a 29–27 victory.

The late Vince Doyle, an old Notre Dame grad who did Michigan games on radio station WWJ in Detroit, said on the air: "This is the most thrilling football game I have ever seen in 31 years of broadcasting."

Outside of Michigan and Notre Dame followers, however, few people are aware of this game's greatness. That's mainly because it remains the only contest since the 1978 resumption not televised by a national network. Yet a lack of exposure should not preclude membership to the pantheon, especially considering the most-hyped sports events often are the dullest to watch.

The only thing dull about this game was the aching pain felt by many of the combatants. Oliver's field goal was just the exclamation mark. The preceding 59:56 of play was punctuated by three other lead changes, as well as a wide assortment of unlikely plays: a fake field goal, a quick-kick punt on third down, a long kickoff return, ill-timed fumbles, back-breaking interceptions (one returned 49 yards for a score), missed placekicks, pulverizing tackles, breathtaking runs, an end-around pass play, controversial calls, and, penultimately, a tipped-pass catch for a touchdown with only 41 seconds left that appeared to give Michigan a 27–26 victory. All of these plays were crushers, momentum-busters.

Ah, momentum.

That's really what made this game so special. ABC football announcer Keith Jackson often labels exciting seesaw contests as "emotional grinders." Well, in this game the momentum swung so swiftly and so severely so many times, that afterward the nerves of both participants and observers were ground into smithereens.

Every time it looked as though one side had it wrapped up, the other came roaring back. It was as if each was continually saying to the other, "Okay, beat that!" And then the other would reach still deeper down, into the nether regions of its proud football soul, and pull out an even greater play and bark back, "Okay, beat *that*!" And as time was running out, this one-upmanship became ever more frequent, producing ever-greater plays.

It all reached a stunning climax in the final three minutes.

At no other time, in no other place, in no other circumstance, did Michigan and Notre Dame ever embody all the excellence, all the pride, all the competitive drive of their football traditions, as they did in this game—which really stands as a metaphor for the entire rivalry.

Indeed, if ever the ghosts of DeHaven and Jewett, Heston and Salmon, Yost and Rockne, and Crisler and Leahy battled alongside their modern-day successors, this was the game.

That's why it warrants a detailed account.

● ● ●

Both the Fighting Irish and Wolverines had a game under their belts when they bolted onto the field at Notre Dame Stadium on September 20, 1980.

Two weeks earlier Notre Dame had walloped a good Purdue team 31–10 on national television (ABC opted to show that game instead of Notre Dame–Michigan). On September 13, Michigan had eked out a 17–10 victory over lowly Northwestern in the pouring rain at Ann Arbor. Astonishingly, it took a late end-zone interception to seal the Wolverines' victory. That played a big part in Michigan falling to 14th in the AP poll, and in No. 8 Notre Dame being made a four-point favorite.

The Irish and Wolverines seldom seem to endure quarterbacking controversies, but this year both teams were unsettled at that position.

Who Notre Dame would start against Purdue was a mystery right up until kickoff. Mike Courey—a receiver in 1978 and a third-string quarterback in 1979—got the call and played splendidly. But freshman Blair Kiel, who doubled as the Fighting Irish punter, owned the much stronger arm. In practice before the Michigan game, Irish coaches worked with only Kiel on an offense they were thinking of springing on the Wolverines—the shotgun. In this still relatively rare scheme, the quarterback normally stood about five yards behind, rather than under, the center and received the snap there. Notre Dame's version, however, was more of a short punt formation than a shotgun, as Kiel would stand 10 yards behind center.

The Wolverines had started sophomore option specialist Rich Hewlett against Northwestern. John Wangler, a pure passer, was the fan favorite but was listed No. 2 on the depth chart and had taken only a few token snaps against the Wildcats. Wangler had shown signs of brilliance late in 1979, replacing B.J. Dickey as the starter and throwing for 203 yards in the first half of the Gator Bowl before blowing out a knee on a tackle by North Carolina linebacker Lawrence Taylor, the future NFL great. Originally it was thought Wangler would have no chance of playing in 1980, but he attended therapy religiously and, eight months of toil and sweat later, was in uniform when Michigan's fall practice began. Still, Coach Bo Schembechler kept a red shirt on Wangler in practice (meaning he was not to be hit) right up until this game.

September 20 dawned overcast and rainy at Notre Dame. Late in the morning the sun burned through the clouds, and the day remained bright thereafter. That and the lingering humidity made it feel much hotter than the 78-degree game-time temperature. A strong wind, 15 miles an hour, blew out of the south.

The usual crowd of 59,075 packed Notre Dame Stadium for the 1:35 kickoff. Notre Dame, clad in green, chose to receive. Michigan, in its traditional road whites, took the south goal.

Games in this series usually begin with a bang, but only the hiss of the long, burning wick was audible during the first quarter.

Both Courey for Notre Dame and Hewlett for Michigan—the two number 2s—got the nod to start. Neither would finish.

And neither could engineer a first down on his team's first possession. Notre Dame's first three plays were stopped by Wolverine tackle Mike Trgovac, who would become the Irish's defensive line coach in 1992.

After this exchange of punts, Notre Dame again went three and out. Then Michigan took the first punch. The Wolverines drove from their 33 to the Irish 29, keyed by Hewlett's 16-yard option run. Notre Dame held, and Ali Haji-Shiekh's 47-yard field goal try was wide left.

Then came the counterpunch. And the flury.

The Irish pushed the ball 70 yards in 16 plays, mainly on the legs of shifty halfback Phil Carter. Carter darted over for the final six yards to give Notre Dame a 7–0 lead early in the second quarter.

After the kickoff, Notre Dame's fired-up defense stifled Hewlett's option and forced an immediate punt. Dave Duerson returned Don Bracken's short kick to the Irish 49, where Courey, Carter, and company went to work again.

This time a slick mixture of running and passing did the trick. Carter found his creases, and Courey found his big receivers: six-foot-four tight end Dean Masztak, six-foot-five split end Tony Hunter, and six-foot-five flanker Pete Holohan. Eleven plays later, Courey rolled out and hit Holohan with a 10-yard touchdown pass, and Notre Dame was in complete control, offensively and defensively, with a 14–0 lead.

The crowd was going crazy.

It was obvious Michigan had to do something drastic to wrestle away the momentum. Otherwise, this was going to be a blowout.

Recalled Schembechler in his book, *Bo:*

Damn, this was frustrating. Here we were with Anthony Carter, the most feared receiver in the Big Ten, and we're running an offense that can't utilize him. I looked down the sidelines at Johnny Wangs. He knew what I was thinking.

"Can you go, Wangs?"

"I can go, coach."

"All right . . . I'm putting you in there," I said, almost choking on the words. "I need you to throw, you got it? Throw. Just throw!"

"I'll do it."

I then gathered the offensive line. "Now listen to me! Wangs is going in this game and damn it, I don't want anybody to touch him! Nobody! You don't let those Notre Dame guys get a finger on him, because he can barely move, and when he goes back to pass that's where he's staying! There will be no scrambling here! If any Notre Dame defender touches Wangs, I'm blaming you! Understood?"

I didn't have to say any more. You could see the look in their eyes. They loved Johnny Wangs, I mean, absolutely adored him. They would have blocked a tank if necessary. Wangs went into that game and led one of the gutsiest comebacks I have ever witnessed.

Only 4:53 remained in the half. On Michigan's second play after the kickoff Wangler heeded his coach's instructions . . . he threw—eight yards to tight end Norm Betts for the Wolverines' first first down since the Notre Dame onslaught began. Two plays later tailback Lawrence Ricks burst up the middle on a draw play that covered 28 yards to the Notre Dame 26. "They broke that long one and I guess they gained the momentum," Bob Crable, Notre Dame's outstanding middle linebacker, said afterward.

On second down, Wangler threaded the needle to Anthony Carter for 17 yards to the eight. On the next play, Wangler hit Ricks on a swing pass for the touchdown, cutting Notre Dame's lead to 14–7 with 1:45 left in the half.

The revitalized Wolverines didn't stop there.

Irish head coach Dan Devine wasn't content to run out the clock—something he regretted later. Courey misfired on his first-down throw, incomplete. On second and 10 he heaved a long wobbler toward Phil Carter, but Michigan's Marion Body picked it off and returned it 20 yards to the Irish 27, with 1:30 remaining.

The Wolverines then moved only six yards in three plays, and Haji-Shiekh set up for a 38-yard field goal attempt. But it was a fake. Hewlett, the holder, rolled left and threw complete to fullback Stan Edwards down to the nine-yard line. The normally ultraconservative Schembechler then crossed up Notre Dame again by calling another first-down pass inside the 10 (run-oriented Michigan did that about as often as throwing on fourth and one). Wangler was right on target again, hitting his tight end, Betts, cutting across at the two, and Betts dove in for the touchdown with 31 seconds left.

Momentum was all Michigan's at halftime after Courey, on Notre Dame's very next play, lobbed another duck that Body again intercepted.

Now it was the Irish who had to regroup in the locker room.

But the Wolverines only turned up the heat as the third quarter began. Anthony Carter took Mike Johnston's kickoff and dipsied, doodled, and darted his way 67 yards to the Irish 32. Three running plays gained 15 yards, then Wangler hit Edwards for 11 more to set up first and goal at the six. Ricks bulled for four before Edwards dove over to give Michigan a 21–14 lead. The Wolverines were unstoppable, it appeared, with Wangler at the helm.

Notre Dame clipped on the ensuing kickoff and started at its 11. If that wasn't bad enough, three plays netted only two yards as the Michigan defense thwarted the Irish running attack for the first time since the first quarter. Michigan stood to gain outstanding field position with Kiel set to punt from his own end zone. Schembechler was licking his chops, sensing Wangler and company were ready to deal the Irish the knockout punch.

Not so fast.

Kiel boomed a rocket out to midfield. Anthony Carter failed to grab it, and the ball took a rifle-shot bounce all the way down to the Michigan 18, where Carter finally fielded it and returned it eight yards. Schembechler later called this one of the key turning points in the game. Indeed, this was the first sign that momentum was beginning to change colors again.

Michigan tried to hammer the Irish line, but Crable and company were digging in. One first down later, Bracken punted.

Again the Irish couldn't move. Two plays netted minus-six yards against the swarming Michigan defenders, who at this point were dominating the game. Schembechler was always respected for the way his coaches made midgame adjustments, and whatever tinkering they had done with the defense was working splendidly now.

But Dan Devine and his assistants were no less coy. On third and 16 from the Irish 15, Kiel suddenly replaced Courey at quarterback. The Irish set up in their deep shotgun formation. "Quick kick!" the Michigan coaches screamed at their free safety, Keith Bostic, but he didn't hear them. Kiel indeed proceeded to punt—way over Bostic's head. This time the ball rolled 59 yards to the Michigan 26, where Bostic was smothered immediately upon scooping it up.

Notre Dame had dodged another potential field-position bullet, and the pendulum swung a little more in its direction.

Michigan picked up a quick first down before Wangler was sacked for a seven-yard loss (the Wolverine linemen couldn't hold off the Irish rushers *all* day). Then tackle Don Kidd stopped Ricks for only a one-yard gain. On third down Wangler dropped back to throw, ostensibly to Anthony Carter. The Irish had two men draped all over him but Wangler threw anyway.

Intercepted!

Cornerback John Krimm leapt in front of Carter and, thanks to a great block by Crable, scooted 49 yards into the Michigan end zone.

Pow! In one fell swoop the momentum was sent crashing back to the Irish. "Carter started to curl but read the coverage and broke to the outside," said Krimm afterward. "The quarterback got a strong rush and didn't read Carter's break."

The saving grace for the Wolverines was that Notre Dame kicker Harry Oliver, a left-footed sidewinder, hooked the extra point wide— "I didn't point my toe," he lamented later—so Michigan clung to a 21–20 lead with a minute left in the third quarter.

By now it was clear to players and coaches on both sides that the loser of this game was going to be emotionally destroyed. Already, both teams had practically emptied their guts to get themselves back into the ball game. Helmet straps on both sides were retightened.

After the kickoff, with the crowd instantly ecstatic again, Schembechler benched Wangler for Hewlett, feeling Notre Dame now had a bead on Wangler's passing attack and a switch back to the option might mix them up.

It did not mix them up. Three plays gained three yards and, amid a thundering roar, Bracken punted from his goal line. Duerson returned to the Michigan 44, and now it was the Irish who seemed poised to deliver the knockout blow. But Michigan was all over the Courey-led offense once again, shoving Notre Dame back three yards before Kiel shanked a punt dead at the Michigan 26. A great opportunity had been squandered by the Irish, and the pendulum began swinging again.

It was now early in the fourth quarter, and the defenses were taking over. Notre Dame again stuffed Hewlett and the Wolverine offense, and Michigan in turn stuffed Courey and the Irish offense. In fairness to Hewlett, the starting Michigan tailback, Ricks, had left the game with bruised ribs, and Anthony Carter was now playing sparingly after suffering rib and leg injuries (the hitting was positively ferocious on both sides).

The Wolverines gained 20 yards on this latest exchange of punts, taking over at their 46 with 11:37 left in the game. Here Schembechler decided to reinsert John Wangler. He would not go back to Hewlett for the rest of the season, except in mop-up situations.

On third and four from the Irish 48, Wangler hit fullback Jerald Ingram for just enough ground to move the chains and give the momentum wholly back to Michigan.

Tailback Butch Woolfolk, the regular starter who hadn't been playing because of a sore back, ripped off 12 yards in two plays to breathe additional life into the drive.

A six-yard screen pass from Wangler to Ingram set up a crucial third and one from the Irish 24. Less than eight minutes remained. Wangler pitched out to Woolfolk, who cut up the right side for the first down and more until—wham!—a blistering belt by Crable separated Woolfolk from the ball. It was Crable's 19th tackle. Duerson recovered for Notre Dame at the 26, and bedlam returned to the stands.

"We had a chance to put the game away there," said Schembechler afterward, "[but] I don't want to be too criticial on a hit like that."

Notre Dame just couldn't let this break evaporate along with the others. Michigan still led 21–20, and the Irish offense hadn't picked up a first down—nor had Courey completed a pass—since midway through the second quarter. Devine had to shake things up, somehow. He opted not to turn to Kiel in this situation. Rather, he turned to the crumpled piece of paper he was carrying to remind himself of the three trick plays he wanted to spring. Two hadn't worked.

This one did.

Hunter took a pitchout on an end around, jogged right, stopped, and threw deep to Holohan, the flanker, who caught it 31 yards down the right sideline at the Michigan 43. It was Hunter's first collegiate pass.

Now momentum was all Notre Dame's. It was the jump start Courey and the Irish offense needed. Courey passed to Masztak for 10 yards to pick up another first down, and then the running backs took over. From the 32, with their partisans howling in delight, the Irish rammed the ball down the Wolverines' throats. Phil Carter slashed for nine. Backup fullback Pete Buchanon lugged for three. Carter then gained 13 on three carries before backup halfback Jim Stone twice pounded for two. On third and goal from the four, Carter dove off left tackle to score the go-ahead touchdown with only 3:03 left.

The Wolverine defenders were stunned. What happened? They had completely shut down the Notre Dame offense for almost two quarters, then they allow one big play and—bang—they can't stop anything.

Such is momentum.

With Notre Dame ahead now 26–21, Devine decided to go for the two-point conversion so Michigan could not win with seven points. But Courey's pass for Holohan was incomplete.

That hardly mattered to the partisan crowd. The place was a deafening madhouse now.

But while the celebrations had already begun up in the stands, on the Michigan sideline the Wolverine offense was more focused than ever—especially Woolfolk.

Wangler's first pass after the kickoff was incomplete to Betts, and the crowd went evermore crazy. But Notre Dame was called for pass interference. Then the howls really picked up. The Irish fans, as always, were trying to drown out the visiting team's signals—*"Ah-o-o-o-o-o-o-o-o-o-o-oh!"*—and for the next few plays referee Gene Calhoun, of the Big Ten, repeatedly allowed Wangler to wait until the crowd had quieted ever so slightly before starting the play.

Two downs later, Wangler hit Woolfolk on a swing pass good for 12 yards up to the Michigan 41. Two minutes, 35 seconds remained. Wangler then was sacked for a two-yard loss before Woolfolk busted free up the middle on a draw play. Suddenly he was hit—fumble! A mad scramble ensued, but guard John Powers recovered at the Irish 40, thereby saving the day for Michigan and ensuring that Harold Woolfolk's nickname remained Butch, not Goat.

The tension was almost unbearable.

With 1:37 left, Wangler overthrew sophomore tight end Craig Dunaway. On second down Wangler threw to Carter at the 25, but the acrobatic receiver couldn't quite hold on to this rope.

That brought up third and 10 from the Irish 40, and 1:16 on the clock. Schembechler did not delay in sending in the make-or-break play: a draw. "Nobody wanted to call it but me," he said later.

Wangler dropped back and handed off to Woolfolk. Guards Kurt Becker and Powers, along with center George Lilja, ploughed open a gaping hole and Woolfolk, a nationally ranked sprinter, was gone. He dashed untouched to the 25, where he cut, slipped between two tacklers, and continued off balance before free safety Tom Gibbons tripped him up at the four.

Whump!

The Michigan team and its smattering of fans went berserk. Everybody else watched in silent disbelief.

"We just got fooled," Devine said. "We simply weren't looking for the draw on that play. [Tackle] Don Kidd had just come out of the lineup and we weren't really settled."

The draw was always Schembechler's pet play on third down, but it had never worked better. "The four-man rush dictated that we use a lot of them," he said.

Woolfolk, suddenly the hero, was actually stomping mad because he hadn't made it all the way to pay dirt.

Michigan called its first timeout right after the play, with 1:06 left. That gave everybody in the stadium time to collect his composure—and take a breath.

Thousands of Wolverines fans, as usual, were cemented to their radios while Bob Ufer announced the game over the Michigan Football Network in his patented colorful, horn-honking, highly partisan style. He was beside himself: "Oh, Fielding H. Yost—if you ever smiled down on your successor, Bo (George Patton) Schembechler, you better do it now! But Knute Rockne's digging in on defense!"

And so were the Notre Dame fans. Now they really turned up the volume, especially the students.

On first and goal Woolfolk pounded for two yards, and Michigan called its second timeout. With 56 seconds left, Woolfolk took a pitch right and gained another yard down to the one before half the Irish defense shoved him back. Again, Michigan called timeout. Forty-nine seconds remained. The Wolverines later would lament their hair-trigger clock management, as they might well have been able to use up all of the remaining time.

As the teams took their positions again, Notre Dame suddenly called its second timeout.

"I didn't think Crable looked right out there," Devine explained. "He looked exhausted. As important a game as this was, it was more important for me to check Crable, and I sent a doctor out to look at him."

Crable caught his breath and stayed in.

After another crowd-noise delay—Irish fans were screaming for their lives—Michigan was set to run the most important play of the game, indeed one of the most dramatic plays in recent school history. It was third and goal on the one, from the right hash mark. Schembechler again tossed a curve, calling a pass play with the option of hitting either the tight end, Dunaway, or halfback, Woolfolk.

Wangler dropped back. The crowd instantly quieted. Immediately there was pressure, so Wangler faded right. Just before stepping out of bounds he improvised, lofting a high pass toward the well-covered Woolfolk. The pass was too high, and Woolfolk was able only to get the ends of his fingertips on the ball, and it deflected up into the air behind him.

But there, by chance, was Dunaway—six inches inside the back of the end zone—to haul in his first collegiate catch.

Touchdown!

The Michigan offense mobbed Dunaway as their teammates, coaches, and supporters went crazy along the eastern sideline.

"When I saw it thrown I knew it wasn't for me," Dunaway said, "but the catch was easy. Anybody could have had it."

Up 27–26 with 0:41 left, Michigan went for two—to force the Irish to go for the touchdown instead of the field goal in the highly unlikely event they got into position to win. Wangler's pass to Dunaway this time was off the mark, but what Wolverine player or fan cared at this point? It was their turn to start celebrating.

The Irish defense, as well as almost everybody else in the stadium, was crushed. "I came off the field, sat on the bench, buried my head in my hands, and prayed," recalled Crable.

What happened next, however, can be attributed as much to Devine intervention as divine intervention.

Just before Michigan scored, Devine and assistant coach Jim Gruden had told Kiel he was going in at quarterback, and that they'd implement the shotgun offense he had been working on all week. "(They) told me to relax and get ready," Kiel said.

Haji-Shiekh's kickoff sailed through the end zone, so Kiel and the Irish had 80 yards in front of them, one timeout left, and only 41 seconds on the clock. The mission: to get into the field-goal range of Harry Oliver. And Oliver had kicked only one field goal in his career, a 36-yarder against Purdue two weeks earlier. He had never kicked one longer than 38 yards in competition in his life. So the Irish seemingly had to advance to the Michigan 20 to give Oliver a decent chance.

"The players didn't say much in the huddle," Kiel said. "We all knew we had work to do."

Notre Dame needed a break of some kind and got one on the very first play. Kiel took the long snap from Bill Siewe and threw deep to Hunter—"a duck," Hunter later said. Marion Body came charging in and broke it up at the Michigan 48, just in front of the Wolverine bench.

Out came the yellow laundry.

Body was flagged for interference, and Schembechler exploded. "Absolutely ridiculous," he recalled. Absolutely warranted, Hunter maintained afterward, as he said Body indeed hit him in the side before the ball arrived.

The clock stopped on the penalty at 0:31. "Hang onto your hats, this ball game's not over," Ufer warned his Wolverine listeners. "The green bandannas may prevail after all."

On first down from the 48, Kiel lofted a pass to Holohan in the right flat. Wolverine strong safety Jeff Reeves darted in front of Holohan, in perfect position to intercept, but he bobbled the ball and dropped it. Had Reeves hung on, he might have run it back all the way for the game-clinching touchdown.

With 25 seconds left Kiel threw to Masztak over the middle, but he couldn't hold on.

On third down from the Michigan 48, and only 20 seconds left, Kiel threw complete to Phil Carter over the middle for a gain of nine. Michigan linebacker Andy Cannavino brought Carter down in bounds, so the Irish called their last timeout with 11 seconds left.

It was fourth and one from the 39—too far for a field goal as it would have been a 56-yarder, seemingly well out of Oliver's range. Had Steve Cichy, the regular kickoff man and long field-goal specialist, not been injured, perhaps Devine would have tried the kick right there.

So what to call? If the Irish didn't pick up the first down, the game was over. They had no timeouts left, so they couldn't run up the middle or the clock would expire. Similarly, any pass over the middle, however short, would end the ball game.

Devine called for a sideline pass to Hunter, out of regular formation this time, not the shotgun. Kiel dropped back and hit Hunter backing into the Notre Dame sideline, for a five-yard gain and the first down with four seconds left. Several Wolverines protested to no avail that Hunter had straddled the sideline as he came down, so the pass should have been ruled incomplete.

That set up the play of all plays.

The sun was still burning brightly, and the wind still blowing strong, when Harry Oliver sized up his 51-yarder at 4:33 P.M. It was purely a desperation attempt, but Irish assistant coach Brian Boulac was optimistic in light of Oliver's strong showing in pregame warm-ups.

Oliver might not have even been the man Devine sent out had Cichy not been injured. But here was the little-used junior ready to attempt a 51-yarder into a 15-mile-per-hour wind. To beat Michigan. To become a legend.

The crowd was softly buzzing. Nobody moved on either bench. Heaven was inundated with prayers, from both sidelines.

Michigan sent all 11 men to block the kick, as there was little worry about a fake now. The snap from Siewe was good, the hold by reserve quarterback Tim Koegel was good, and Oliver got all of the ball.

Michigan cornerback Brian Carpenter, coming around the corner, was milliseconds late in his diving attempt to slap it down.

The kick was true, but did it have the distance? Oliver had hit it low and hard to pierce the prevailing wind. Finally, dramatically, the ball sneaked over the crossbar by a matter of inches.

Good!

Final score: Notre Dame 29, Michigan 27.

Pandemonium ensued. Within seconds, Oliver was lost under a green mountain of jubilant teammates and fans alike. Notre Dame Stadium erupted like it had never erupted before. Everyone present knew they had just witnessed once-in-a-lifetime drama. Indeed, it was one of the grandest moments in Notre Dame's storied football history. A miracle field goal to cap a miraculous comeback. To beat Michigan. At fabled Notre Dame Stadium. With Touchdown Jesus signaling the kick good on the library mural that overlooks the north end zone. With the Fighting Irish band belting out *The Victory March*.

It was the quintessence of Notre Dame football.

"This could only happen here," summed up Notre Dame defensive tackle Pat Kramer.

Luck of the Irish? The ghosts of Rockne and Gipp? Help from above? Indeed, something mystical had happened on that last play, according to the holder. "As I placed the ball down, the wind died down. Almost stopped," Koegel beamed afterward. "I knew then we'd make it."

The Wolverines, meanwhile, had suffered a colossal blow. After all they had gone through, twice battling back to take the lead when all seemed lost, behind the spirited play of their gutty, gimpy quarterback—only to have their hearts torn out on the final play.

Suffice to say, this was the sweetest of games to win, the bitterest of games to lose. Tears flowed in both locker rooms afterward.

In Notre Dame's, Dan Devine called over all the misty-eyed players into a huddle after Captain Crable had handed Oliver the game ball. "I knew we weren't ever going to give up," Devine said. "There ain't a quitter in this room.

"I have to tell you what I believe. I believe Our Lady gave us a special blessing. And I don't care how late you stay out tonight!"

School president Rev. Theodore Hesburgh said, "I told you in practice that you're part of the ongoing history here. Today, you wrote a great chapter. You did what everybody said was impossible."

Oliver, understandably, was the center of attention when all the reporters entered. They asked him what he was thinking right before the biggest moment of his life.

"I just prayed a lot," he said, "and told myself, 'plant your toe into it.'"

Devine was typically modest with the press. "I didn't do much right today. This was a game of decisions—on both sides—and like I said, I didn't do anything right.

"The only thing that went right with that [last] series was the kick."

As the handshakes, high-fives, and hilarity continued in the Notre Dame locker room, the Michigan players did their best to wipe away the tears and compose themselves. Schembechler told them they had nothing to be ashamed of. About the last drive he gruffed to the press: "There were so many circumstances where we could have won the game. If they don't get the pass interference, they're not going to score. If we catch the interception they are not going to score. And finally, if we keep their out-cut in bounds, they're not going to score."

But Bo did not seem bitter.

"It was one of the most physical games I have ever seen. . . . We played our hearts out. I hated to lose that game in the worst way.

"It was the type of game that you win 20 times and lose 21 times. That's just the way this kind of battle is. That's what you expect when two great schools get together."

When Schembechler saw the film the next day, however, he was furious, believing Hunter indeed had one foot out and one foot in when he caught that fourth-down pass before Oliver's kick. (A video replay is inconclusive—the call could have gone either way.)

Eleven years later, Schembechler was still outraged.

"I have a right to be bitter over that one. That was a lousy, rotten deal," he bluntly stated.

"That game we won. I don't care what anybody says. We won that game. The officials just took it away from us. That was absolute robbery. Absolute robbery. My guys are over there yelling, 'No! No! No!' and the guy runs over and marks the ball. And that gives them the play to kick."

Schembechler insisted it should have been ruled an incomplete pass.

"Then it's over. It's our ball. You go down on one knee and it's over. That's what should have happened."

News of the purported blown call made the loss all the more ruinous for the Wolverines. The destruction was so total, so enveloping, that the entire team was emotionally numb for days. So were the coaches.

"The worst coaching job I ever did was the following week," Schembechler admitted. "That Notre Dame loss was so devastating, South Carolina beat us (17–14) at Michigan Stadium. That was my loss."

● ● ●

Before the season, Dan Devine had announced that 1980 would be his final year as Notre Dame coach. He had tired of the pressures of the position, and he wanted to spend more time with his ailing wife, Jo.

Enter Gerry Faust, who had amassed a phenomenal string of victories as head coach of Moeller High School in Cincinnati. It was hoped the enthusiastic, endearing, crackly voiced coach could transfer that success to the collegiate level.

Faust had already nurtured several of Notre Dame's current heroes. One was Harry Oliver—who provided the golden footnote to perhaps the greatest one-game chapter in college football history.

XV. Up to the challenge, '81

The Wolverines were emotionally ruined.

They had been the unanimous No. 1 preseason pick in 1981 but had promptly lost their opener at Wisconsin, 21–14. So here they were the next day in the team meeting room, awaiting their coach—and wondering how to regroup with the new No. 1 team in the country, Notre Dame, coming to Ann Arbor in six days.

What did Bo Schembechler do to try to revive his demoralized squad? He walked into the room, wrote "Ed Muransky" and "Stan Edwards" on the chalkboard, barked out, "The rest of you are quitters. I want nothing more to do with you," and left.

"That sent the message," recalled Muransky, a senior offensive tackle who stood six-foot-seven and weighed 275 pounds.

In Schembechler's opinion, Muransky and fullback Edwards were the only Wolverines who played with any intensity against Wisconsin. And Bo called on those two players to pull together the immensely talented offense, which included one of the greatest receivers in college football history, Anthony Carter; two future NFLers at running back, Butch Woolfolk and Edwards; a mutlithreat quarterback with blazing speed and a rifle arm, Steve Smith; and an entire line of future All-Americans (Muransky, Bubba Paris, and Kurt Becker in '81, Stefan Humphries and Tom Dixon in '83).

Schembechler wanted the Wolverines prepared to play a physical brand of football against Notre Dame, and Muransky recalled "there had to have been 10 fights in practice." Schembechler also challenged the offensive line: Michigan's first five plays would be scripted running plays, all with man-on-man blocking.

Muransky issued an additional challenge to the offense on Friday night. "I looked at everyone and said, 'If we continue to play as great individuals, we'll continue to lose. If we start playing as a great team, we'll start winning.'"

And the next day, on September 19, the Wolverines started playing as a great team—and smashed the Fighting Irish, 25–7.

On the first play of the game, quarterback Smith darted 26 yards on an option run. Then Woolfolk ripped off gains of 8, 1, and 13 yards before Smith rolled around left end for 8 more. "I think Notre Dame knew what was ahead after those first five plays," Muransky said.

Michigan led only 7–0 at the half—Smith had thrown a 71-yard TD bomb to Carter—but the Wolverines were dominant after the intermission. Smith hooked up with Carter again, and the Michigan running attack amassed 304 yards by game's end.

The Wolverines couldn't have played much better. Perhaps that's why Bo didn't get too upset when Muransky was quoted after the game as saying, "We kicked their ass."

This was also the game that burst the bubble of optimism surrounding Gerry Faust's first year as ND head coach. And it foreshadowed Faust's ineffectiveness at the major-college level.

Indeed, Schembechler and his staff had dissected the game film of every 1980 Moeller High game. Did Faust bring the same razzle-dazzle high school offense to Notre Dame in 1981? "Yup," Schembechler said. "That's why it was so ineffective."

XVI. Redemption at night, '82

Blair Kiel's confidence was practically shot after the 1981 season.

Even though as a freshman in 1980 he had quarterbacked Notre Dame to the Sugar Bowl and a shot at the national title, Gerry Faust came along in 1981 and alternated Kiel with Tim Koegel in Faust's Wing-T offense. How high-schoolish was this attack? "We didn't even have an audible system," Kiel recalled. "It was the dumbest thing I'd ever seen."

One of the smartest things Faust ever did, though, was bring in Ron Hudson in 1982 to coach the quarterbacks and to help develop a new pro-style offensive attack. Almost immediately, Hudson made Kiel—a strong-armed pocket passer—the unquestioned starter. "Confidence is more than half the battle," Kiel said, "and coach Hudson helped me a lot that way."

By the time No. 10 Michigan arrived on September 18 to open Notre Dame's season, Kiel was ready for redemption. So was the entire Fighting Irish team, coming off a disastrous 5–6 season.

If that wasn't enough motivation, this was the first night game at Notre Dame Stadium, and ABC was showing it live to the nation.

"We worked out under the lights on Thursday night," Kiel remembered. "It was just awesome the way the stadium looked, the way our gold helmets reflected the light. From that point on, everybody was really excited."

The Fighting Irish carried that excitement to another level on opening night and utterly destroyed the Wolverines, although this was not reflected in the final score, 23–17. On both sides of the ball, the Notre Dame lines ravaged Michigan's.

On defense, the Irish held the Wolverines to their lowest rushing total in 12 years (41 yards) and sacked quarterback Steve Smith seven times. Michigan's touchdowns were flukes. The first came on a dazzling 72-yard punt return by Anthony Carter, the second on what *Sports Illustrated* referred to as the "true immaculate reception." In the fourth quarter, Smith's deep pass to Gilvanni Johnson was broken up on a wicked tandem hit by Stacey Toran and Dave Duerson, but the ball lay perched on the back of Toran's shoulder pads for two full seconds. Toran and Duerson stood frozen, unsure where it was. Michigan tailback Rick Rogers saw the ball, darted up, snared it off Toran's back, and ran untouched into the end zone.

Notre Dame had led 13–0 and 23–10 before those unlikely plays, and Kiel said "some of us had thoughts of 'Here we go again.'" But after Michigan had driven to the Irish 35 with 2:14 left, Duerson saved the day when he ripped the ball out of the hands of Wolverine receiver Vince Bean for a game-icing interception.

On offense, Notre Dame battered out 278 yards on the ground, 116 by strong-legged fullback Larry Moriarty, who scored once. As for Kiel, he was virtually flawless in directing the new ND attack, completing 15 of 22 passes for 141 yards.

"That game was a big deal for me," recalled Kiel, who 10 years after his night of redemption was still playing pro football.

XVII. The crossroads, '85

Never was a Notre Dame–Michigan game more pivotal for both teams than the one played at Michigan Stadium on September 14, 1985.

Michigan was coming off its worst season in 17 years, 6–6, and its fourth straight with fewer than 10 wins. Some critics were suggesting the game had passed Coach Bo Schembechler by.

Notre Dame was coming off another mediocre campaign, 7–5, and Coach Gerry Faust was entering the final year of a five-year contract.

It was believed Faust had to take the Fighting Irish to a major bowl game to have any chance of staying.

Thus, for both teams, for both coaches, this game *was* the crossroads. The winner would spring toward the path of rejuvenation, the loser would turn back and battle the same old demons for yet another season.

A week before, things looked mighty hellish at Michigan.

The first-string Wolverine defense had mauled the starting offense in the final preseason scrimmage, picking off two of quarterback Jim Harbaugh's passes. "The offense couldn't do anything right," remembered Harbaugh. "We got a major chewing out from Bo. He ripped me in particular, and threatened to start Chris Zurbrugg instead."

But Schembechler did not bench Harbaugh in favor of Zurbrugg, the quarterback in Michigan's final five games of 1984 after Harbaugh had gone down with a broken arm. Schembechler's threat was probably just a ploy to motivate Harbaugh and the offense.

"The coaches got really serious," Harbaugh remembered, "and everybody on the team was really uptight."

Uptight and unsure.

"We didn't know what was going to happen against Notre Dame," Harbaugh said. "You have to do something well to have confidence, and we didn't have a lot of confidence going in."

And that's precisely the way the Michigan offense played in the first half—tentative and unsure. Notre Dame went to the locker room up 9–3 and might have had a commanding lead had the Wolverine defense not stiffened twice after lengthy Irish drives, forcing a pair of field goals.

But on the second-half kickoff, destiny appeared at the crossroads and sent each team on its way.

Notre Dame's Alonzo Jefferson ran up to catch Rick Sutkiewicz's kickoff, but the ball slipped through Jefferson's hands, bounced off his knee, and dribbled into the cradling arms of diving Wolverine Dieter Heren at the Irish 14. Three plays later, from the 10, Harbaugh dropped back to throw but promptly darted up the middle on a quarterback draw for a touchdown.

That was the burst of confidence Harbaugh and the Michigan offense apparently had been waiting for. On their next two possessions, the Wolverines drove 80 yards for another touchdown and 74 yards for a field goal.

The tenacious Michigan defense also stepped it up a notch, sacking Irish quarterback Steve Beuerlein four times and picking off his desperation, last-minute pass at the Wolverine 11.

Final score: Michigan 20, Demons 12.

XVIII. Michigan . . . barely, '86

Bo Schembechler generally knew what type of offense Lou Holtz would implement in his debut as Notre Dame's head coach. "He came from Minnesota," Schembechler recalled. "We had Holtz down cold."

Well, not exactly.

"They knew certain things I liked to do," Holtz later agreed, "but they did not know what we liked to do with the personnel that was available at Notre Dame. So we had an advantage."

And Holtz milked every drop out of that advantage on September 13, 1986, at Notre Dame Stadium.

He devised a wide-open game plan for his unranked, unrespected Fighting Irish. From a myriad of formations—single-back, three-receiver, wishbone—Holtz employed screen passes, option runs, deep curl-ins, draws, reverses . . . anything to keep the mighty, third-ranked Wolverines guessing.

For the most part, this strategy worked to perfection. The Irish marched up and down the field all game long, amassing 27 first downs and 455 total yards, and never punted once. Quarterback Steve Beuerlein hit on 21 of 33 passes for 263 yards, and the breathtaking Tim Brown—a wide receiver—took enough handoffs to lead the Irish in rushing with 65 yards.

Nonetheless, a combination of Irish miscues and Wolverine fortitude allowed Michigan to sneak out with a 24–23 victory in one of the most thrilling games in series history.

The killers for Notre Dame were two fumbles and an interception all inside the Wolverine 20. "We did self-destruct," Holtz said. "But Michigan didn't lose its poise. We had them on the ropes all day long, but they hung in there and did the things they had to."

The Michigan offense was outstanding, too. Quarterback Jim Harbaugh kept drive after Wolverine drive alive with elusive maneuvering in the pocket and pinpoint passing. Tailback Jamie Morris became the first Wolverine since the turn of the century to score three TDs against Notre Dame—two on runs and the other on a 27-yard pass out of the wishbone, a formation Schembechler hadn't sprung since 1978.

Late in the game Notre Dame appeared to have taken the lead on a third-down pass play to tight end Joel Williams at the back of the end zone. But back judge Ted DeFilippo ruled Williams's right foot had come down on the back line: incomplete.

With 2:36 to go, and Michigan up 24–23, Harbaugh might have secured the victory for the Wolverines when he hit wideout John Kolesar on a third-and-six bomb, good for 38 yards down to the Irish

40. But a fumble with 1:33 left gave Notre Dame one last chance, and Beuerlein moved the Irish into field-goal range.

John Carney, who had broken the NCAA record for most consecutive field goals from 40 to 49 yards (12), badly hooked his 45-yard attempt to the left. "I knew Carney would miss. This was my turn," Schembechler said afterward, in reference to 1980.

Holtz and the Fighting Irish were roundly praised. The next AP poll placed them 20th—the first and only time a team has ever moved into the top twenty after losing a game.

But Holtz would have none of it, a portent of glories to come. "Notre Dame doesn't have moral victories," he insisted.

XIX. Carefully played, '87

Exactly 100 years after being carefully taught football by Michigan in 1887, Notre Dame turned the tables and gave Michigan a refresher course on how to carefully play football.

"We went up there to not make many mistakes," Holtz recalled of the September 12 game at Michigan Stadium. "Being away from home, we wanted to play more conservatively than the year before."

Notre Dame's talent also dictated that it play this way. Although strong-armed passer Steve Beuerlein and a bevy of good receivers had departed, the 1987 returnees better suited Holtz's offensive ideal—an unstoppable, smash-mouth running game complemented occasionally by a big-play passing attack. Senior Terry Andrysiak was the ideal quarterback, because he was more adept at play-action and bootlegs than pure drop-back passing. Fleet wide receiver Tim Brown was the star, a game breaker who kept defenses honest.

And in Notre Dame's moment of truth—the opener at Ann Arbor—the Irish battered out 199 yards on the ground, threw only 15 times in 74 plays, controlled the ball for nearly 40 minutes, and committed only one harmless turnover (an interception 12 seconds before half-time) in beating the Wolverines authoritatively, 26–7.

In losing its first home opener in 19 years, Michigan was as generous as the Notre Dame hosts had been in 1887, only the Wolverines' big-heartedness came in the form of seven turnovers. Notre Dame scored all but three of its points off Wolverine cough-ups. "We never really did stop Michigan that day," Holtz recalled. "This time it was Michigan that self-destructed."

The first two Michigan miscues set the tone for the day.

After the Wolverines had driven down to the Irish 24, quarterback Demetrius Brown—making his first career start—was hit as he threw, and ND linebacker Cedric Figaro intercepted the errant pass. Andrysiak then piloted the Irish 44 yards in 11 plays to set up Ted Gradel's 44-yard field goal.

Then, after Jamie Morris lost a fumble on Michigan's next snap from scrimmage, Holtz summoned his offense's big-play capability.

On first down from the Michigan 34, Andrysiak hit Tim Brown for 24. Then Brown lined up at running back and lost a yard. On second down from the Wolverine 11, Andrysiak dropped back and looked again for Brown but couldn't spot him. Andrysiak shuffled his feet. Then shuffled again. Eventually he spotted Brown darting right-to-left across the front of the end zone. Andrysiak shuffled yet again, then went to throw but only pumped. Finally, Andrysiak set his feet, recocked, and threw to Brown deep in the left corner. In stride, the 6-foot-2 Brown outleapt two 5-foot-10 Michigan defensive backs, Erik Campbell and Allen Bishop, snared the perfectly thrown ball, and got a foot down before all three went crashing to the turf out of bounds.

Where were Michigan's pass rushers? "The protection on that pattern was rather incredible," Holtz explained.

Notre Dame went up 10–0 and could afford to stick to its conservative game plan, while Michigan was left to open it up with a rifle-armed quarterback prone to being scattershot.

Here endeth the lesson.

XX. Razor close, '88

The 1988 game—played on the evening of September 10 at Notre Dame Stadium—featured gruesome blocking, wicked tackling, and outstanding athleticism, as both Notre Dame and Michigan were loaded with college superstars and future NFLers.

So, of course, the game came down to the field-goal kickers. In fact, all the scoring was produced either directly or indirectly by special teams.

The game's unlikely hero was Notre Dame's Reggie Ho, a five-foot-five walk-on from Kaneohe, Hawaii, with probably the most unorthodox place-kicking motion the game has ever seen. Ho took the soccer-style kicker's tendency to keep the head down on the follow-through to its most exaggerated extreme. Ho kept his head buried in his abdomen until practically kneeing himself in the chops with his long, lunging follow-through.

How did his strange style develop? "I guess just by practicing with my dad," recalled Ho, a premed student who had walked on in early 1986. "It was my way of keeping eye contact on the ball."

Ho refined his accuracy with diligent practice. Even in the dead of winter, he would clear patches of snow from the Notre Dame practice field and kick, while his roommate, Kevin Thomas—who didn't even play football—held. "He was from California and I was from Hawaii, so we didn't get to go home much during the winters," Ho explained.

In 1988 Ho, a senior, became Notre Dame's designated kicker from within 40 yards because he seldom missed in practice. And in the opener against Michigan, Ho was perfect on all four of his attempts— from 31, 38, 26, and 26 yards. The last one gave Notre Dame a 19–17 lead with 1:13 remaining. "I can't take any credit for this," the bashful Ho insisted, "without thanking my snapper, Tim Grunhard, and holder Pete Graham. They always made it easy for me."

Bedlam erupted at Notre Dame Stadium after Ho's fourth kick. "It looked like we had the game won," Lou Holtz recalled.

But in four plays Michigan was at the Irish 32, with 18 seconds remaining. That's when Bo Schembechler clearly showed his own senior placekicker, Mike Gillette, how much confidence he had in him. Rather than try to pass the ball closer to the goalposts, Schembechler called for a running play up the gut—then let the clock wind down to 0:03 before calling timeout. Schembechler had long admired the cocky spirit in Gillette, who grew up in nearby St. Joseph, Michigan.

As Gillette set up for the last-play, win-or-lose, 48-yard field goal, Holtz called timeout and told his players: "Don't rough the kicker. I don't think he's going to make it." Even though Gillette had made a 49-yarder earlier in the fourth quarter, Holtz's theory was that "it's a lot tougher than you think with the game on the line."

After Notre Dame's second timeout, Gillette calmly jogged back into position, awaited the snap, then promptly nailed the ball.

"When he hit it, I thought it was good," Holtz recalled. "It looked long enough. Then I saw our players jumping up and down."

Gillette was razor close, missing wide right by about a yard.

XXI. Rocket blasts off, '89

Lou Holtz and Bo Schembechler had not only revitalized their respective programs by 1989, they had taken them to the top.

Notre Dame, the defending national champion, was ranked No. 1 and had a 13-game winning streak. Michigan, the defending Rose Bowl champion, was ranked No. 2 and had a 10-game unbeaten streak.

As loaded as both teams had been the year before, their 1989 lineups were even more star-studded. Michigan had the likes of Leroy Hoard, Greg McMurtry, and Greg Skrepanek on offense, and Tripp Welborne and Erick Anderson on defense. Notre Dame had Tony Rice, Derek Brown, and Ricky Watters on offense, and Chris Zorich and Todd Lyght on defense.

The biggest star on September 16 at Michigan Stadium, though, was Raghib (Rocket) Ismail. In what will forever remain one of the most outstanding individual performances in series history, Ismail blasted off into stardom by returning two kickoffs for touchdowns in the second half, and Notre Dame hung on for a 24–19 victory on a dark, rainy afternoon.

"After Tim Brown left [in 1987], everybody said, 'Well, there won't be another Tim Brown,'" Holtz recalled. "Rocket wasn't ready as a freshman to be another Tim Brown. But now Rocket was a sophomore, and we felt Rocket was really going to be something special. Nobody else did."

Including the Michigan coaching staff. After all, nobody had returned a kickoff for a TD against Michigan in 32 years.

So with Notre Dame ahead 7–6, Michigan's J.D. Carlson booted the second-half kickoff right to the 5-foot-10, 175-pound Ismail at the Irish 12. The Rocket exploded into the wedge, burst through the gap created by Rodney Culver, cut to the right sideline, and was gone. Touchdown.

Early in the fourth quarter, after the Wolverines had cut the Notre Dame lead to 17–12, Ismail was "shocked" to see Michigan boot the ball right to him again. "I just said, 'Okay. I guess they didn't learn anything,'" Ismail said afterward. And the Rocket promptly took off from the Irish eight, again hit the wedge, again found a hole blown open by Culver, cut to the left sideline this time, and was gone. Touchdown.

"I really thought we were going to be pretty good in covering kicks . . . until today," Schembechler told reporters. "That kid [Ismail] is the fastest I've ever seen. He's faster than the speed of sound. We just couldn't tackle him."

Ismail's heroics meant Holtz didn't have to open up his offense in such slick conditions. "We played it rather conservatively," Holtz recalled. *Rather* conservatively? Quarterback Tony Rice threw two passes all day. In fact, Rice completed a total of only four passes in his victories over the Wolverines in 1988 and '89.

Notre Dame's defense, like Ismail, was outstanding. For two and a half quarters it was nearly impregnable. Not until freshman quarterback Elvis Grbac (pronounced GUR-back) replaced the injured Michael Taylor did Michigan move with authority, but it was too little too late.

Schembechler retired after the season. This marked the only time in 21 years at Michigan he had lost to a school three straight years.

XXII. Smashing debuts, '90

"All his life he was a Michigan fan," Bo Schembechler recalled of Rick Mirer. "He had Michigan stuff on his car. He was Michigan all the way, but he got away. I was surprised."

Mirer grew up in Michigan, but he played his high school football near Notre Dame, in Goshen, Indiana. Schembechler assumed Mirer would go to Michigan so he didn't recruit him hard. Notre Dame showed far more interest, and Mirer went there.

So Mirer of course made his first career start against Michigan. Notre Dame was ranked No. 1, visiting Michigan was No. 4, and CBS was televising the September 15 game to a national, prime-time audience. If that wasn't enough pressure, the media made a big deal out of the fact that Mirer wore the same number (3) as legendary Joe Montana did in his days at Notre Dame. It was expected Mirer would wake up similar echoes during his reign.

So how did Mirer respond? By scoring a touchdown and leading the Fighting Irish to a 14–3 first-quarter lead, and by piloting Notre Dame 76 yards in the closing minutes for the game-winning touchdown in a thrilling, come-from-behind 28–24 victory. Mirer completed his last five passes on that drive, including the 18-yard winner to Adrian Jarrell with 1:40 remaining.

"I wasn't really nervous, even though I had a lot on my mind," Mirer said afterward. "I grew up a fan of Michigan, and it was sweet to get my first victory against them."

Bittersweet was the word to describe Gary Moeller's debut.

Schembechler's successor as Michigan's head coach had put everything into this game, desperately wanting to set the tone for his era with an upset of the top-ranked Irish. "That was a hard loss to take," Moeller recalled.

Yet Moeller's coaching was impressive. Showing a no-huddle look for the first time, the Wolverine offense was virtually unstoppable—rushing for 253 yards, passing for 190, and averaging a whopping 6.3 yards per play. "We never moved the ball like that in such a big game," Moeller said.

Michigan tailback Jon Vaughn also had a smashing debut, dashing for 201 yards in his first career start, the best single-game rushing performance in series history. And wide receiver Desmond Howard, in his first start, snared two touchdown passes.

The Wolverines had command of the game midway through the third quarter, up 24–14. But things started to unravel. A 43-yard drive went for naught when J.D. Carlson missed a 36-yard field goal. Then Mirer's desperation bomb on third-and-15, from his own 15, deflected off the fingertips of Rocket Ismail and into the hands of freshman Lake Dawson, who was finally tackled at the Wolverine 40. Notre Dame scored 10 plays later to cut the deficit to 24–21.

The real backbreaker for Michigan, though, came after the Wolverines smashed their way 71 yards, all on the ground, to the Irish 11 with 10 minutes remaining. "We just wanted to come up with a change of pace with a short pass to the fullback or tight end," Moeller recalled. But quarterback Elvis Grbac audibled and threw to wideout Derrick Alexander in the end zone. Notre Dame linebacker Mike Stonebreaker dropped back and picked it off.

A short while later, Mirer woke up his first echoes.

XXIII. The Catch, '91

It is permanently etched in Michigan lore as The Catch. *Sports Illustrated* said later in 1991 that it "may have been the most memorable college football play in many seasons."

Anyone who saw it live on September 14—either in person at Michigan Stadium or on TV—will certainly never forget it.

Here was Michigan, with 9:02 left, trying desperately to hammer the final nail into the Notre Dame coffin. The Fighting Irish had trailed 17–0 in the second quarter but had closed the gap to 17–14. Not a single Wolverine had ever tasted victory against Notre Dame, and the Irish were seemingly poised for another miraculous, last-minute rally to extend their series winning streak to five.

On Michigan's previous possession, Notre Dame had stuffed a fourth-down run, and this time the Wolverines faced fourth and a foot from the Irish 25. Surely Michigan would run.

But Wolverine quarterback Elvis Grbac dropped back and tossed a high, floating pass toward the far right corner of the end zone. Michigan wide receiver Desmond (Magic) Howard streaked past two Notre Dame defensive backs and, although he didn't appear to have a chance to get to the pass, stretched full-out in the air and barely snared the ball before quickly tucking it away and crashing to the end-zone turf. Touchdown.

Michigan tailback Ricky Powers later salted the game away with three dogged runs on third down that allowed Michigan to run out the remaining 6:30. Final score: Michigan 24, Notre Dame 14.

The Catch more or less locked up the Heisman Trophy for Howard, and it not only ended Notre Dame's series winning streak, but it gutted the Fighting Irish's national-title hopes.

It's widely believed this play was an audible called at the line by Grbac, who completed 20 of 22 passes on the day. But that's not entirely true. During the preceding timeout, Coach Gary Moeller called a quick hitch-pass in the right flat to Howard, a similar play to the one he scored on against Notre Dame in 1990.

"Desmond was just going to go down, hook, and turn in," Moeller recalled. "But the play converts, if the defender is close, for Desmond to just break it to the outside and take off.

"When the play started, Desmond thought the Notre Dame guy was going to roll up on him, and Elvis went to throw it and Desmond just took off. So Elvis had to bring it back down and throw it deep, which is a part of the play. I told Desmond later that no one in the world thought he was going to catch that ball."

ND coach Lou Holtz said it took outstanding execution on the part of Grbac and Howard, because Notre Dame fully expected Michigan would throw. "It was a play I'll live over the rest of my life," Holtz recalled. "We faked the blitz but we double-covered Desmond Howard. Boy, you wouldn't want to be in a better defense. We were going to concede the first down if they ran.

"I firmly believe that if they don't make it, we take the ball and go back the other way and score."

But the luck of the Irish wasn't with Notre Dame on this day. Quipped ABC play-by-play man Brent Musburger: "Just one time, you've gotta believe in the luck of the Wolverines."

XXIV. Fit to be tied, '92

It was shaping up to be another fantastic finish.

With 1:10 to go, the score was deadlocked at 17–17. Just a few minutes before, Notre Dame had wiped out a 10-point Michigan lead and appeared to have corralled all the momentum. But senior Michigan quarterback Elvis Grbac had just marched the Wolverines 50 yards, down to the Irish 30.

No quarterback in series history had ever started three straight years, but both Grbac and Mirer were this year. With one win apiece, they had alternately been avoiding blitzes and threading needles in the clutch in this rubber match.

So could Grbac pull off another game-clinching, miraculous play to cap an outstanding four-year career against Notre Dame?

Nope.

On Michigan's next play, Grbac dropped back to pass and, under heavy pressure, made the awful decision to throw the ball away deep down the middle, where he knew there wasn't a Michigan receiver within 20 yards. Problem was, ND defensive back Jeff Burris *was* there and intercepted at the Irish 12, with 1:05 left. "It was just a very stupid mistake on my part," Grbac said.

So could Mirer now pull off another nail-biting, last-minute, home-field win over Michigan?

Nope. He never really got the chance.

On first down, slashing fullback Jerome Bettis burst up the middle for seven yards. The clock kept running (. . . 0:50 . . .), Notre Dame huddled (. . . 0:40 . . .), then went to run a handoff to tailback Reggie Brooks (. . . 0:35 . . .), who had scored on a dazzling 20-yard touchdown run in the first half. But the play was whistled down. Illegal procedure, Notre Dame, with 0:30 left.

Why had Holtz wasted 35 valuable seconds with running plays? Because, he later explained, the last thing he wanted to do in this situation was punt, for Notre Dame's first- and second-string snappers were out with injuries. And he had no desire to kick the ball back to Michigan anyway. If Holtz had opened it up and Mirer threw three incomplete passes, the Irish would have had to punt with about 40 seconds to go. Or worse, Michigan could have intercepted and kicked the winning field goal.

"It's easier when you're behind," Mirer said afterward. "Then you just go for it and you have nothing to lose."

The crowd, though, was getting restless, especially when the clock began moving again after the penalty was marched off (. . . 0:20 . . . 0:15 . . .). Mirer finally took the snap and threw a deep pass that Lake Dawson caught out of bounds, incomplete. Seven seconds remained. The Irish called timeout, as second-guessers up in the stands and across the country howled.

Finally, Mirer's last-play, desperation pass was broken up by Wolverine Corwin Brown, at which point the crowd fell virtually silent, and players from both sides milled off the field, unsure how to feel about the 17–17 tie.

It had been such a great game—rife with momentum swings and outstanding plays. Then nothing.

"It was a crazy game that has left me with an empty feeling," Holtz told reporters.

XXV. All but written off, '93

Why was Michigan made a nine-point favorite to beat Notre Dame on September 11, 1993—the biggest point spread in modern series history?

Because the No. 11 Fighting Irish had looked awful in slipping past Northwestern the week before, while the third-ranked Wolverines appeared all-powerful in smashing Washington State.

But the main reason Notre Dame was all but written off—most experts figured the Irish were headed for a blowout loss at Michigan Stadium—was that a hurricane of controversy was surrounding coach Lou Holtz and Notre Dame.

The book *Under the Tarnished Dome: How Notre Dame Betrayed Its Ideals for Football Glory* had just been released and was the talk of the sports world. ABC's popular "Nightline" news show aired all the charges: that Holtz physically abused players, made players play hurt, and encouraged steroid use—while the school took hypocrisy, arrogance, and greed to new levels.

This was the fifth straight season Holtz had to endure some sort of preseason controversy involving himself or a player, but nothing had ever been as damning as this. How could Holtz possibly keep himself and his team focused on the daunting task of beating mighty Michigan? And how could the players possibly bounce back from such a sluggish game?

"Nothing is as good as it seems and nothing is as bad as it seems," Holtz said prophetically a few days before the game, during the height of the controversy. "Somewhere in between there, reality falls."

And the reality was, Michigan wasn't nearly as good as it seemed, nor Notre Dame nearly as bad as it seemed. And before the largest regular-season crowd in NCAA history—106,851—the Fighting Irish dominated play from the opening kickoff and shocked a national television audience with a 27–23 victory.

Little-regarded quarterback Kevin McDougal, who had warmed the bench for three years, was the offensive star for Notre Dame. Three minutes into the first quarter, McDougal kept on an option run around left end and darted 43 yards for a touchdown—setting the tone for the game.

By halftime, McDougal had rushed for 72 yards and two touchdowns and had passed for 137 yards in staking the Irish out to a 24–10 lead.

Holtz threw a restraining jacket around the offense in the second half and allowed his fast, furious defense to dominate. Michigan quarterback Todd Collins was picked off twice by free safety Jeff Burris and once by cornerback Bobby Taylor. Yet the high-powered Wolverine offense kept battling and scored two fourth-quarter touchdowns to make the score close.

The wide-smiling Holtz was given a victory ride as the clock ran out.

Holtz deviated from his usual doom-and-gloom protocol with reporters afterward, giving them all a shot for having written off Notre Dame. "I couldn't believe, after one game, you had us buried," he said.

The moral of any book on Holtz is you never count him out.

Postgames report

Notre Dame is quickly catching up to Michigan's once commanding series lead. ND's 8–5–1 record from 1978 to 1993 has narrowed the Wolverines' all-time lead to 14–10–1.

Coach Lou Holtz is the biggest reason for that. Under him, the Fighting Irish are 5–2–1 against the Wolverines (2–1–1 at Notre Dame, 3–1 at Michigan Stadium). If the Irish keep making ground at this rate, Michigan will lose its distinction of being the only active school with a winning record over the Irish (minimum two games).

Other interesting trends have occurred since 1978.

Without exception, all the last-minute thrillers have been played at Notre Dame Stadium, while all the authoritative drubbings have occurred at Michigan Stadium. And neither school has been intimidated when playing on the road.

Here's the script when the scene is Notre Dame Stadium: The Fighting Irish storm out and appear to be on the verge of winning in a walk, before the Wolverines roar back in the third quarter and invariably take the lead—setting up a wild, heart-stopping fourth quarter.

Indeed, in the seven games played at Notre Dame since 1978, Michigan has never held a lead at any point during any first half. Yet five times the Wolverines have wrestled away the lead by the end of the third quarter. The Wolverines went on to win two of those games, and held the lead at some point in the final two minutes on the other three occasions. Only in 1982 did Notre Dame hold the lead throughout the final two minutes—and even in that one, Michigan threatened to wipe out Notre Dame's six-point lead.

Conversely, here's the script when the scene is Michigan Stadium: A team takes the lead and doesn't surrender it. There has never been a single lead change in the final quarter of all seven games played in Ann Arbor since '79. Only twice has the team that took the lead there ever given it up.

Like the Wolverines at Notre Dame, the Irish have been formidable at Ann Arbor.

●   ●   ●

More stats and stuff, throwing in the 1942 and '43 games:

• Notre Dame holds a 9–6–1 series record since 1942 but only a 330–328 lead in total points scored.

• At Notre Dame Stadium, Notre Dame holds a 4–3–1 record but has been outscored 188–173 by Michigan, including 88–22 in the third quarter. Also, Michigan is 3–1–1 in afternoon games at Notre Dame Stadium.

• At Michigan Stadium, Notre Dame holds a 5–3 record and has outscored Michigan 157–140, including 57–33 in the third quarter.

• Notre Dame has gone into the game ranked No. 1 four times and has won three, including two victories over No. 2 Michigan at Michigan Stadium.

• 1992 was the only year these teams have ever been tied at any juncture of any fourth quarter, except for the first five seconds of the final frame in 1978.

Extra points

14

Who's No. 1?—Fight songs

Ask any American sports fan to hum the two most famous college fight songs, and you'll probably hear "The Victory March" of Notre Dame, and "The Victors" of Michigan.

Fight-song expert Bill Studwell confirmed the popular appeal of these songs in 1990, ranking the top 13 college tunes of the more than 100 written. Studwell placed "The Victory March" first, "The Victors" second. "These are clearly the top two," he later said.

● ● ●

"The Victors" was written first, in 1898, by Michigan junior music student Louis Elbel—an aspiring classical pianist, an accomplished sprinter, and, in his own words, Michigan's most enthusiastic fan.

Elbel's inspiration was Michigan's 12–11 victory over Amos Alonzo Stagg's Maroons in Chicago on Thanksgiving Day, 1898. Events of this day have been exaggerated in Michigan annals over the years. One account had Wolverine halfback Charles (Chuck) Widman, a little-used reserve, dashing 92 yards in the waning seconds for the winning touchdown.

But the speedy Widman not only started this game, he was one of the star Wolverines that year. And he dashed 65 yards for the winning score, his second TD of the game. The true circumstances of that run are far more astounding than the common exaggerations. Widman was merely trying to buck the line when a group of Chicago tacklers began pushing him backward. But Widman twisted away, broke outside, and sprinted down the sideline, with Chicago right end Ralph Hammil in hot pursuit, just a few feet behind. Two Maroons tacklers had the angle on Widman and tried crowding him out of bounds but couldn't. Finally, Hammil dived and tripped up Widman just a few yards short of the goal. But back then, ball carriers were not deemed tackled until held down, so Widman proceeded to crawl across the goal and touch the ball down for the go-ahead score.

What's more, Widman's touchdown did not come late enough in the second half to prevent Chicago from later marching back to kick a (then five-point) field goal, cutting the 12–6 Wolverine lead to 12–11.

Yet no matter how it all happened, it was a thrilling victory that
gave the Wolverines a 10–0 season as well as their first Western
Conference football title. Recalled Elbel:

Out of a student body of 3,500, 1,200 of us were in Chicago for the
game that day. When the fierce contest was finished we were literally
crazed over the result. We formed a procession and, yelling and shouting
and dancing the serpentine, we paraded around the old Chicago university
behind the little U of M band to the tune of "There'll Be a Hot Time in
The Old Town Tonight". . . .
Suddenly it occurred to me that such an epic victory as ours ought to
be dignified by something more elevating in music. We were all feeling
that exaltation of spirit that comes only to youth in moments of conquest.
That night, when I was alone, I found the strains of "The Victors" running
through my mind and gradually the entire march took form.

Elbel finished all the parts of the composition on the train ride back
to Ann Arbor, and published the work in early 1899.

The entire piece—referred to by Michigan band members as "'The
Victors' as written"—follows the standard construction of a military
march: a two-bar introduction, an opening eight-bar strain repeated
once, a second eight-bar strain repeated once, then the 16-bar chorus—
or "trio"—played three times but bridged by an eight-bar interlude.

The famous chorus consists of a simple, repeating musical phrase.
The lyrics:

> Hail to the victors valiant!
> Hail to the conq'ring heroes!
> Hail! Hail to Michigan
> The leaders and best!
>
> Hail to the victors valiant!
> Hail to the conq'ring heroes!
> Hail! Hail to Michigan
> The champions of the West!

Since at least 1930, the universally reported story is that John Philip
Sousa—the revered "March King" who wrote "Stars and Stripes Forever" and "The Washington Post"—performed the first public rendition of "The Victors," in Ann Arbor on April 8, 1899.

Not true.

Sousa and his famous band did indeed perform "The Victors" that
day. But three days earlier, on April 5, 1899, Elbel himself directed a
student orchestra's playing of "The Victors" during the on-campus
performance of an undergraduate musical, *A Night Off.* The audience,

comprised of both students and faculty, "greatly appreciated" Elbel's latest composition, *The Michigan Daily* reported, "and an encore was called for after its rendition."

In later years, "The Victors" was played by the French and German military bands during the First World War; was played by the American 125th infantry band as Michigan troops marched into captured Germany in 1918; was once heard in front of Buckingham Palace at the changing of the guard; and was played in 31 countries by the Michigan Marching Band on a world tour in 1961.

Studwell, the fight-song expert, said "The Victors" "has no peer in style. The purpose of a fight song is to inspire emotion, and 'The Victors' is a proud, stirring song. If you've ever heard a hundred thousand people at Michigan Stadium sing it, well, it leaves you breathless."

The song's greatest endorsement, though, was an assessment Sousa himself reportedly made on at least one occasion. Michigan alumnus Charles D. Kountz said Sousa told him in 1905 that "The Victors" was "one of the nation's finest military marches and the best original college song he had ever heard."

Elbel, meanwhile, graduated from Michigan in 1900 and studied classical piano in Germany for several years before touring Europe and America as a soloist with various orchestras. He annually returned to Ann Arbor for homecoming to lead the Michigan band in "The Victors," right up until his death in 1959.

One last thing about Louis Elbel. He was born, raised, and lived most of his adult life in South Bend, Indiana.

🏈   🏈   🏈

"The Victory March" was written in 1908 by then-recent Notre Dame graduates Michael J. Shea ('04) and his younger brother, John F. Shea ('06).

Michael was the gifted musician who composed the tune, while John was credited with having written the lyrics. Author Murray Sperber, however, has supplied strong evidence to indicate it was probably Michael, a graduate student at Notre Dame at the time, who also wrote most of the lyrics, and that John probably suggested word changes.

The song was largely inspired by Notre Dame's 12–6 loss to—who else?—Michigan on October 17, 1908.

The Sheas had been in attendance at Ferry Field that day, and no doubt had sat despondently while the Michigan band blared out "The Victors" and other school fight songs. Notre Dame lacked any such composition of its own.

A few days later back at Notre Dame, Michael put to piano "a tune that had been running through my head." A day after that, so the story goes, he and John completed both tune and lyrics—and together they performed the first rendition of "The Victory March" on an organ at Sacred Heart Church on campus.

"The Victory March" does not follow the usual military march progression. It opens with a four-bar introduction (taken from the chorus's conclusion), is followed by a 16-bar opening strain that repeats once, and concludes with the rousing 16-measure chorus that repeats once without interlude.

The world-famous lyrics come from the first two verses of the chorus:

> Cheer, cheer for old Notre Dame,
> Wake up the echoes cheering her name,
> Send a volley cheer on high,
> Shake down the thunder from the sky.
>
> What though the odds be great or small,
> Old Notre Dame will win over all,
> While her loyal sons are marching,
> Onward to victory.

In the 1920s, Notre Dame band director Joseph Casasanta rearranged the tempo of the song, around the same time the Fighting Irish became "America's team." Accordingly, "The Victory March" became not only the most famous college fight song, but one of the most identifiable songs of any kind in America.

Its popularity doesn't end there.

One Notre Dame alumnus heard it played on Chinese violins in Tientsin during the Second World War. Most revealing of its popularity, though, is the fact that at least one group of American POWs in Vietnam sang "The Victory March" daily as a morale builder. The Viet Cong guards generally wouldn't let the prisoners sing patriotic anthems, but the guards didn't fully understand the lyrics to "The Victory March." The prisoners picked this tune because one later pointed out that "it was the one song we all knew."

Studwell said "The Victory March" is, by far, the most copied and the most widely played college fight song. "It's an incredibly inspirational song," he said. "It just keeps you going and going."

Michael Shea, meanwhile, went on to become an organist at Saint Patrick's Cathedral in New York. Shortly before his death in 1940, he indicated his surprise over the mass appeal of his song, deeming it "very amateurish."

● ● ●

What's most amazing about these two songs is that they weren't written by grizzled march kings or Broadway composers. Louis Elbel was a 21-year-old music student, Michael Shea a graduate student who became a priest.

Neither ever again composed anything remotely as memorable. Years later, Elbel knew why:

> I have always been interested in the psychology of composing, but have never been able to explain just how a melody originates spontaneously under the stress of emotion. It is easy enough to make tunes. Anyone with the knack of it can compose a dozen songs a day. An improvisitore will sit at the piano and play unwritten tunes by the hour, composing as he goes along. But sweeping, inspiring strains are rarely made to order—they flash unawares.

That's why these fight songs are the single greatest testaments to "Michigan spirit" and "Notre Dame mystique."

Who's No. 1?—Marching bands

Tradition-laden. Proud. Competitive. Arrogant.

These descriptions apply as much to the Notre Dame and Michigan bands as they do to the respective football teams.

• At the 1993 game, some Notre Dame band members could be overheard mocking various Michigan fight songs—on cue shouting "High school cheer!" instead of "Let's Go Blue" at the end of each refrain of Michigan's other famous, original tune.

• In casual conversations in 1990, several Michigan band members rolled their eyes when asked to assess their Notre Dame counterparts. "Second rate," was one comment. "They think having that song makes them a great band. Hardly."

What else would you expect from the students who die the hardest for their football teams?

● ● ●

Notre Dame had the first organized college band in America.

It formed in 1846 and almost immediately took an active posture. In the early 1860s it gave rousing send-offs to students leaving to fight in the Civil War. In 1871 it played a benefit concert for victims of the Chicago Fire. In 1887 it performed at the very first Notre Dame–Michigan football game.

Joseph Casasanta, director from 1919 to 1942, pioneered many of the band's traditions and composed the other famous Notre Dame songs: "When Irish Backs Go Marching By"; "Hike, Notre Dame"; and "Down the Line."

Notre Dame's was among the first bands to include pageantry and picture formations, and also pioneered the use of walkie-talkies and amplified instruments.

In 1976 the Band of the Fighting Irish was declared a landmark of American music.

Today, under the direction of Luther Snavely, the band remains as famous as ever. Its rendition of The *1812* Overture, with all the students in rhythm pointing their arms forward and back, has become a staple on NBC's broadcasts of Notre Dame football games. The band also continues to form the word "Irish" as it performs "The Victory March."

🏈   🏈   🏈

Michigan's early band history is inauspicious by comparison.

"Prior to 1913," an untitled report in the Michigan athletic archives recalled, "there had been no organized effort to foster or maintain a university band. Various individuals filled with love of our Alma Mater and a desire for service, had each morning on the day of a football game recruited as best they could a motley array of musicians [who] swiftly disbanded after each game or, perchance, during a game."

These ad hoc bands first started showing up at Wolverine football games in the 1880s, but not regularly until 1897, and not in uniform until 1898. Organization became a prime concern beginning in 1913, about the time other popular Michigan songs were written, such as "Varsity" and "The Yellow and Blue." But it wasn't until the late 1930s, after William D. Revelli had taken over as conductor, that more than a handful of members annually majored in music.

From 1935 to 1971, Revelli turned the Michigan band into one of the most respected, innovative, and traveled in America. Under Revelli, Michigan became the first college band to perform its entire routine from original manuscript score, the first to use the public address system as an integral part of its program, and became famous for its high-stepping, toe-heel marching style.

In 1983, the John Philip Sousa Foundation awarded the Michigan band the first-ever Louis Sudler Trophy, based on sustained excellence, innovation, and achievement.

Conductor Gary Lewis continues the rich tradition begun by Re-velli, including the floating block-M formation as the band plays "The Victors."

Michi-Damers

Research for this book turned up a number of "Michi-Damers"—players who, at one time or another, suited up for both Michigan and Notre Dame.

It would be impossible to devise a definitive list, for two reasons. First, each school's all-time roster does not include every player who ever suited up—only those who won letters (Michigan) or monograms (Notre Dame). The second reason is that up until about 1910, tramps often changed their names when they changed schools, and Michigan and Notre Dame each had its share of vagabond football players.

One such tramp who apparently played at both schools was Frank Morse. According to a withering, unidentified clipping in the Notre Dame sports information department's files, a tackle named Frank Morse on the 1894 Notre Dame team had played the year before at Michigan. But Michigan's long list of 1893 lettermen includes no one by the name of Frank Morse. So did he not win a letter at Michigan? Did he use a phony name at Michigan? Was Frank Morse his pseud-onym at Notre Dame? Or was the report wrong? Who knows.

Two other Michi-Damers suited up for Notre Dame in 1894.

Notre Dame's first coach, ex-Wolverine tackle James L.D. Morrison, apparently returned to ND after his brief coaching stint with Hillsdale College—but as a player, not a coach. A "Morrison" played tackle for Notre Dame against Wabash on November 15, and Notre Dame records now identify this Morrison as James.

Jacob (Rosy) Rosenthal—described as "that big lump of guts" by Morrison in his initial progress report to Michigan's Charles Baird—began a three-year stint at Notre Dame in 1894. He had played for the Michigan freshman team in 1893.

There was at least one other Michi-Damer from this era. Tom Joyce had been a backup halfback for Notre Dame in 1905, and two years later he tried out at tackle for Michigan. But as of September 26, 1907, he was "still enduring conditioning work," according to the *Detroit News.* Joyce apparently did not make the squad.

◉   ◉   ◉

After Michigan's disastrous 3–4 season in 1919, in which the Wolver-ines were largely bereft of talent, Michigan alumni went on a vigorous search-and-distract mission. They looked high and low for the first-rate, state-bred boys who had gone elsewhere to play college ball, then tried wooing them to Ann Arbor.

One star athlete from Laurium, a mining town in Michigan's upper peninsula, was playing only 150 miles away—at the University of Notre Dame. His name was George Gipp, more commonly known after his death as the Gipper.

Gipp was as hearty a partier and a gambler as he was a halfback, and he often cut classes. By March 8, 1920, the school called his bluff and expelled him. Although Gipp was fully reinstated less than two months later, on April 29, he was reportedly flooded with offers to take his football talents elsewhere during his banishment.

One coach who was said to have wanted Gipp's services badly was Michigan's Fielding H. Yost. One account said Gipp had actually accepted an offer from Michigan and moved to Ann Arbor, but, according to this report, two weeks later Gipp realized he didn't want to play for Yost and went back to Notre Dame.

This story is shot down by the fact that Yost's own correspondences reveal he was never in Michigan between March 8 and April 29, 1920. Before 1921 Yost lived in Ann Arbor only during football season and spring practice, and that year Yost didn't leave his Nashville home until May 1.

The story about Gipp being induced to go to Michigan, though, makes perfect sense, given the alumni's zealous recruiting efforts at the time.

Gipp went on to have another brilliant season for Notre Dame in 1920. But, tragically, he died on December 14 of a severe strep throat infection. He learned of his selection to Walter Camp's All-American squad on his deathbed.

Eight years later, at halftime against Army, coach Knute Rockne made his famous "win one for the Gipper" speech.

◗   ◗   ◗

Gipp had been an outstanding passer as well as a runner, and his favorite receiver at Notre Dame in 1918 and '19 was Bernie Kirk, an end. Thus, Gipp must have been disappointed when Kirk transferred to Michigan in the summer of 1920.

Kirk was born and raised next door to Ann Arbor, in Ypsilanti, and his father was a Michigan grad, so the transfer was a natural in many ways.

Yet Notre Dame students howled. Rumor was, Kirk had been offered "big inducements" to go to Michigan. That can now be essentially confirmed in a letter from the man who was in charge of Michigan's stepped-up alumni recruiting campaign, Bob (Bobcat) Clancy of the University of Michigan Club of Detroit. On August 20, 1920, Clancy wrote Yost that "we are putting the work on [Kirk] and he will without much doubt come to Michigan."

Kirk, as a transfer, had to sit out his first school year, 1920–21. During that time, he didn't make nearly as many friends as he had at Notre Dame, and for a while it appeared as though he would transfer back. "I am having a very anxious time with Kirk," Clancy wrote Yost on January 28, 1921. "It will break my heart to lose him after all the blood I have sweated in landing him, and all the abuse I took [from] the newspapers."

But Kirk stayed and, in the 1921 and '22 seasons he was every bit as outstanding as he had been at Notre Dame. In fact, Yost told *Detroit News* columnist H.G. Salsinger in November 1922 that Kirk was an "expert on catching passes, the best I ever saw."

In a tragic coincidence, however, Bernie Kirk died under shockingly similar circumstances to those that surrounded the death of his friend, George Gipp, two years earlier. Kirk, too, died unexpectedly after his final season. Kirk, too, battled to stay alive for days after being hospitalized. And Kirk, too, was told of his selection to Walter Camp's All-America team on his deathbed.

But Kirk's cause of death was far different. He had suffered a fractured skull in a car crash on December 17, 1922, and died six days later after meningitis had set in. The details of the car crash weren't printed at the time, but one of Kirk's teammates and best friends at Michigan, Doug Roby, recalled them:

Christmas vacation had started. In those days, Prohibition was in. Things were dry. But the fellows would go once in a while to a Blind Pig—a saloon that sold liquor at a high price—in Ecorse [a city downriver from Detroit]. It's right across from Canada. There was a lot of rum-running going across the Detroit River in those days.

Bernie and a couple friends had gone to a Blind Pig in Ecorse that night, and they, of course, got a little boozed up. They smashed up the car on the way back.

Kirk was apparently the only man ever to have played for both Fielding Yost and Knute Rockne.

The stories he could have told. . . .

●　　●　　●

Other Michi-Damers include:

• Tom Roach, a tackle for Michigan in 1929 who played at Notre Dame in 1932 and '33.

- End Bob Van Summern and halfback Oswald Clark, both of whom played at Notre Dame in 1945 and at Michigan in 1948 and '49. (Clark also played at Michigan in 1950.)
- Don Dufek was a freshman at Notre Dame in 1947 but became a star halfback at Michigan from 1948 to 1950.

● ● ●

Some coaches have also had ties to both schools, including:
- James L.D. Morrison (player at Michigan in 1893, player and head coach at Notre Dame in 1894).
- H.G. Hadden (player at Michigan in 1894, player and head coach at Notre Dame in 1895, assistant coach at Michigan in 1899).
- Bert Maris (assistant trainer at Michigan in 1906, head trainer at Notre Dame beginning in 1907). Around the turn of the century, trainers were as important as any assistant coaches.
- Frank (Shorty) Longman (player at Michigan from 1903 to 1905, head coach at Notre Dame in 1909 and 1910).
- Hunk Anderson (player at Notre Dame from 1918 to 1921, line coach at Notre Dame from 1924 to 1927 and 1930, head coach at Notre Dame from 1931 to 1933, and line coach at Michigan in 1937).
- Chuck Heater (player at Michigan from 1972 to 1974, assistant coach at Notre Dame from 1988 to 1990).
- Mike Trgovac (player at Michigan from 1977 to 1980, assistant coach at Notre Dame from 1992 to present).

Trgovac is the only such coach who ever played in a Michigan–Notre Dame game. He started on the defensive line three times for the Wolverines, and his last game ended with Harry Oliver's miracle field goal in 1980, reducing the heartbroken Trgovac to tears.

It was with this unique perspective that Trgovac gave a thunderous pregame speech to the Fighting Irish in 1993, before they stormed out and roughed up the Wolverines at Michigan Stadium. "I was never so emotionally charged for a game," said Notre Dame linebacker Pete Bercich. "I came out pumped, with tears in my eyes and everything."

What did Trgovac tell the Irish?

"I just told them a little bit about the history of the game. It got me fired up."

Lou Holtz was so impressed, he said, "Knute Rockne's speech on the Gipper is now No. 2 on the all-time list behind Mike Trgovac's locker-room speech up at Ann Arbor."

Nearly uprooted:
Today and tomorrow

Believe it or not, Bo Schembechler grew up a huge fan of Frank Leahy's Notre Dame teams.

A half century later, Bo could still rattle off the starting 1942 lineup: "Rymkus, McBride, Ziemba, Wright, Neff, Murphy, Bertelli, Ashbaugh . . . I used to know all those teams. I'd listen to them on the radio. I was a great Notre Dame fan."

By 1989 he was not.

In fact, if Schembechler had not retired as Michigan athletic director on January 2, 1990, the Notre Dame–Michigan series would probably be skidding to a halt right now. Schembechler was on the verge of breaking it off. The reason? He felt the ND game was becoming too important, and he felt Notre Dame was—play it again, Sam—seeking an unfair advantage over Michigan.

"I got a little resentful over the way the thing was going," Schembechler said in an interview for this book in 1991. "In my judgment, they were trying to create an advantage for themselves."

The "unfair advantage" this time pertained to scheduling. From 1985 to 1990 the game was each school's season opener (except in 1989 when Notre Dame opened against Virginia in the Kickoff Classic). But sometime during the 1980s, Notre Dame had arranged to open against a weaker team the Saturday before the Michigan game from 1991 to 1994 (Indiana in 1991, and Northwestern from 1992 through 1994). This evidently caught Schembechler by surprise in the late '80s, as Michigan had made no such arrangements. And this was important to Schembechler because it was always his belief—a belief shared by other coaches, such as Lou Holtz—that a football team makes its greatest improvement between its first and second games. Schembechler did not view Notre Dame's action in this area as a coincidence. "Notre Dame put a game in front so they could be better prepared to play against us," he charged.

Schembechler was further irritated by the placement of the game on future Michigan schedules. Before Bo retired, Notre Dame was slated to be Michigan's third game from 1997 to 1999—immediately preceding the eight-game conference slate. "I didn't want to play Notre Dame there," Schembechler said. "I don't want anything to get in the way right before the Big Ten schedule starts." In 1989 Schembechler publicly indicated his displeasure with this arrangement, preferring that the Michigan–Notre Dame game again become each team's opener.

Yet no matter where it was fitted, Schembecher felt the Notre Dame game had become too big a distraction for the Wolverines.

"I don't know whether it's in the best interests of Michigan, because Michigan should be pointing to Iowa, or Michigan State, or Ohio State," he said. "Those games are much more important—have to be, otherwise drop out of the conference. And that was always my theory, and I don't care whether people liked it or not. We're in the Big Ten Conference to win that championship and go to the Rose Bowl. . . . What if you beat Notre Dame and lose the conference title? What have you done? You sit at home, or you go down to some second-rate bowl game.

"It had just gotten to the point where if I had remained there as athletic director, and Notre Dame continued to manipulate the position of the game, and to do some of the things they were doing, I'd have dropped Notre Dame."

Schembechler found it difficult to get his Wolverines to downplay Notre Dame. "When you're setting your goals in your first meeting prior to the start of the season, Notre Dame always pops into the picture," he recalled.

And if the players wanted to make it a red-letter game?

"Then you've got to say, 'Okay, men, we're going to shoot for Notre Dame, but I'm going to tell you something: Notre Dame is a *nonconference game,* and we'll always play it as that.' . . . There are only so many games where you can really get your team up to a fever pitch. And you've got two right off the bat—Michigan State and Ohio State. Those two are primary, I mean they are *primary.*"

For the record, from 1978 to 1989 Schembechler compiled winning records against Michigan State (9–3) and Ohio State (7–5) but went 4–6 against Notre Dame.

🏈　🏈　🏈

Jack Weidenbach, Michigan's athletic director from 1990 to February 1994, didn't grumble about Notre Dame opening a week earlier than Michigan. He did something about it.

"What Bo didn't realize is we can do the same thing with our schedules," Weidenbach said. "We can move games around, too."

During his four-year term, Weidenbach was largely successful in moving Michigan's nonconference opponent on the Saturday after the Notre Dame game to the Saturday before—for no other reason than to eliminate any disadvantage of opening against an Irish team with a game under its belt. Weidenbach made the switch in 1991 with Boston College, in 1993 with Washington State, and, in late fall 1993, he got Boston College to switch for the 1994 season. Houston could not accommodate in 1992.

What's more, Weidenbach didn't come close to sharing his predecessor's attitude toward Notre Dame. Weidenbach and ND athletic director Dick Rosenthal struck a firm friendship almost immediately, and by September 1990 they had contracted a Michigan–Notre Dame basketball series.

"From my viewpoint, it's good to have Notre Dame on the schedules," Weidenbach said in 1992. "Notre Dame draws people and interest. And I like them. They're nice people to work with down there. . . . And they're so close. You're not on the road long and don't miss any class time. It's an ideal situation."

So ideal, in fact, that Weidenbach felt compelled before he retired to extend the Michigan–Notre Dame football series far into the next century.

In summer 1993, Weidenbach invited Rosenthal to Ann Arbor. Together they drew up a "scheduling agreement"—essentially, a long-term contract—that will see Michigan and Notre Dame play every year from 1994 to 2011, except for 1995–96 (so Notre Dame can play Ohio State) and 2000–01 (because Michigan has other scheduling commitments).

Except for those two brief hiatuses, Weidenbach and Rosenthal resolved, in a handshake agreement, to make this game a permanent fixture on each school's schedule.

It took only a hundred-plus years.

🏈　🏈　🏈

Will this series indeed continue indefinitely?

Notre Dame leaders certainly have as much desire to play Michigan as ever. In fact, Rosenthal said in 1992 that Notre Dame's relations with Michigan couldn't be better.

"The most gracious people in the world are in the Michigan athletic department," Rosenthal beamed. "They have made it very clear that they would like to continue the series, and we feel the same way about it. . . . Like Southern Cal, we'll just keep playing them."

Rosenthal, in a diplomatic response to the concerns first raised by Schembechler, even moved up the dates of the 1998–99 games, from the third game of the year to the first. Rosenthal was unable to make the same switch for 1997.

As for Irish coach Lou Holtz, he said it's not his place to say whether Notre Dame should continue to play Michigan. "I'm not responsible for who we play," he said, "I'm only responsible for how we play." And against Michigan, his Notre Dame teams have played exceptionally well—even though Holtz downplays the game's significance.

But make no mistake, the Michigan game has assumed huge importance at Notre Dame. Clearly, it is Notre Dame's make-or-break contest. Dating back to 1985, each time Notre Dame has beaten Michigan it has remained in the national-title hunt at least into November. The years Notre Dame hasn't beaten Michigan, its title hopes evaporated almost immediately.

The greatest Notre Dame endorsement of this game, though, came from the man widely known as "Mr. Notre Dame," Moose Krause. Two years before his death in December 1992, Krause said in an interview for this book that Michigan had bumped Southern Cal as Notre Dame's top rival. "Michigan is our No. 1 game," Krause said. "I think the best way to explain it is that Michigan is a national school, like Notre Dame. It's got alumni all over. Consequently, there's no question in my mind right now that Michigan is *the* game."

But the past 107 years have shown that Notre Dame's desire to play Michigan has little bearing on whether these teams actually lock horns on the gridiron. Rather, it has always depended on the leaning of the one man in the Michigan athletic department with the last word on football scheduling. From Charles Baird, to Fielding Yost, to Fritz Crisler, to Don Canham, to Bo Schembechler, to Jack Weidenbach . . . those inclined to schedule Notre Dame did, those opposed didn't.

It's unclear which way the current Michigan regime is leaning. Joe Roberson has just settled into the job of athletic director, succeeding the retired Weidenbach in February 1994.

As head coach Gary Moeller sees it, there are both positives and negatives about the Notre Dame game.

"The good thing is playing it at the beginning of the season," he said. "It makes us have good early fall practices, as I'm sure it does for them. The kids work a little harder knowing they've got a great game right off the top.

"The other plus is a kid gets to go to South Bend to play, or gets to play Notre Dame at our stadium. . . . It's a fun thing to experience, and it'll continue to be that way. I have to say I like to play it. But, I also have to say truthfully, my job would be easier if I didn't play it."

Moeller agrees with his mentor, Bo Schembechler, that Michigan State and Ohio State should always be regarded as Michigan's top two rivals. But Moeller appears to be allowing his players to gear up for

Notre Dame a little more than Schembechler did, probably because he lets them focus seriously on winning a national championship—something Schembechler forbade.

Among the negatives, Moeller said, is that Notre Dame is a distraction from Michigan's Big Ten title/Rose Bowl objective. "I think it takes away from that because we have to prepare so well for them."

Looking ahead, there are two, more legitimate threats to the future of this series.

One is the addition of Penn State to the Big Ten. Moeller said the Penn State game will rapidly become one of Michigan's most important, because "we have a lot of alumni in the East" and because Penn State has a great tradition. "We've got enough good teams in our league to get enough big games now," Moeller said. "And when you throw Notre Dame on top of that, it'll get to the point where it's going to be tough."

The second threat would be the implementation of a Division I-A playoff. Who would qualify? The teams with the best records. Notre Dame and Michigan would both desperately want to qualify, so it's possible they might try to make their schedules less difficult. If Michigan were to drop a tough annual game, the first to go would probably be Notre Dame.

Wolverine players would hate to see that ever happen. They get as jacked up for Notre Dame as they do for anybody—Michigan State, Penn State, and Ohio State included (sorry, Mo and Bo). In 1991, quarterback Elvis Grbac said if the Wolverines were to go 1–10 that year, he would want the one victory to come against Notre Dame.

Michigan players have long held this view. George Ceithaml, who captained Michigan to its 32–20 win over Notre Dame in 1942, wrote Fritz Crisler some 27 years later to the effect that "Conference championships come and go, but beating Notre Dame stays forever!"

As this series grows with time, sprouting new branches of tradition each year, it will become increasingly difficult for anyone to uproot it. Since 1978, the Notre Dame–Michigan game has skyrocketed from a reunion novelty to the most important, most watched game every September. Consider:

• *Sports Illustrated* has made this game its cover story five times—in 1979, 1986, 1989, 1990, and 1991—and has given it feature-story treatment most other years (1978, 1981, 1982, 1985, 1987, and 1993)—even though it annually competes for position with the final weekend of the U.S. Open tennis tournament.

• This is the only rivalry whose games have been shown to a national network TV audience every year since 1981.

• In 1993, *The Sporting News* rated it the top rivalry in the Midwest—ahead of Michigan–Ohio State and Michigan–Michigan State.

That's why Don Canham predicted these September Super Bowls are bound to continue.

"People can say what they want, and coaches can say what they want," Canham said. "But Notre Dame–Michigan is a very, very important game, because the television audience is one of the biggest, and one of us is a preseason pick to be something. So I think the series will go on and on, even though the coaches may not really want it to. It's too lucrative and too prestigious a game now."

Former president Gerald Ford, an ex-Wolverine player himself, was a strong proponent of the modern-day resumption. In the late 1970s, he spotted Moose Krause at a golf tournament and singled him out, in front of a mob of dignitaries, to thank him for his role in resuming the series. "It's good for Michigan, it's good for Notre Dame," Ford told Krause, "and it's good for college football."

🏈   🏈   🏈

Perhaps Notre Dame defensive tackle Chris Zorich best summed up the rivalry. He had this to say about the fierce competitiveness that has punctuated relations between these natural enemies since 1887:

Michigan has a lot of tradition and so do we. Every year, we put that pride and tradition on our shoulders. Obviously, we feel ours is better, and every year we have to go out and prove that.

Appendix
Game results and summaries

All-time head-to-head record

Year	Date	Winner	Score	Site
1887	November 23	Michigan	8–0	Notre Dame
1888	April 20	Michigan	26–6	South Bend
1888	April 21	Michigan	10–4	Notre Dame
1898	October 22	Michigan	23–0	Ann Arbor
1899	October 18	Michigan	12–0	Ann Arbor
1900	November 17	Michigan	7–0	Ann Arbor
1902	October 18	Michigan	23–0	Toledo
1908	October 17	Michigan	12–6	Ann Arbor
1909	November 6	Notre Dame	11–3	Ann Arbor
1942	November 14	Michigan	32–20	Notre Dame
1943	October 9	Notre Dame	35–12	Ann Arbor
1978	September 23	Michigan	28–14	Notre Dame
1979	September 15	Notre Dame	12–10	Ann Arbor
1980	September 20	Notre Dame	29–27	Notre Dame
1981	September 19	Michigan	25–7	Ann Arbor
1982	September 18	Notre Dame	23–17	Notre Dame
1985	September 14	Michigan	20–12	Ann Arbor
1986	September 13	Michigan	24–23	Notre Dame
1987	September 12	Notre Dame	26–7	Ann Arbor
1988	September 10	Notre Dame	19–17	Notre Dame
1989	September 16	Notre Dame	24–19	Ann Arbor
1990	September 15	Notre Dame	28–24	Notre Dame
1991	September 14	Michigan	24–14	Ann Arbor
1992	September 12	Tied	17–17	Notre Dame
1993	September 11	Notre Dame	27–23	Ann Arbor

Michigan 14 wins, Notre Dame 10 wins, 1 tie.

Future games

1994	September 10	Notre Dame
1997	September 27	Ann Arbor
1998	September 5	Notre Dame
1999	September 4	Ann Arbor
2002	September 14	Notre Dame
2003	September 13	Ann Arbor
2004	September 11	Notre Dame
2005	September 10	Ann Arbor
2006	September 16	Notre Dame
2007	September 15	Ann Arbor
2008	September 13	Notre Dame
2009	September 12	Ann Arbor
2010	September 11	Notre Dame
2011	September 10	Ann Arbor

All-time head-to-head record, freshman/junior varsity teams

Year	Winner	Score	Site
1917	Michigan	19–3	Ann Arbor
1969	Notre Dame	17–7	Notre Dame
1970	Michigan	20–0	Ann Arbor
1971	Michigan	20–6	Notre Dame
1972	Notre Dame	17–7	Notre Dame
	Michigan	14–10	Ann Arbor
1973	Notre Dame	10–3	Notre Dame
	Notre Dame	20–3	Ann Arbor
1974	Michigan	31–12	Notre Dame
	Michigan	14–6	Ann Arbor
1975	Notre Dame	28–0	Notre Dame

Michigan 6 wins, Notre Dame 5 wins

Game summaries

For the games 1887–1909, details were culled from various newspaper play-by-play accounts. Crowd sizes and times of scores weren't always given, so estimates are provided.

Players are listed by position and full name. Second-string players are indicated by "-2" after position abbreviation, third-string by "-3" (e.g., FB-2 Lawrence Reid means he is second-string fullback).

1887

(Touchdowns worth 4 points, conversions 2 points, field goals 5.)

Michigan   8
Notre Dame   0

Just who scored the Michigan touchdowns was never recorded.
Length of halves: 30 minutes (only one half was played).
Attendance at Notre Dame's senior field: estimated 500–600.

1888 (1)

Michigan   20   6   26
Notre Dame   0   6   6

1st half

M: HB James Duffy TD. John Duffy missed conversion.
M: QB William Ball TD. John Duffy converted.
M: Lineman J.H. Duffie TD. John Duffy missed conversion.
M: HB James Duffy TD. John Duffy converted.

2nd half

M: QB William Ball TD. John Duffy converted.
ND: HB Harry Jewett TD. Ed Prudhomme converted.

Length of halves: 35 minutes.
Attendance at Green Stocking Ball Park in South Bend: estimated 300–
400.

1888 (2)

Michigan   6   4   10
Notre Dame   4   0   4

1st half

ND: Safety touch by Michigan C Billy Harless.
ND: Safety touch by Michigan HB John Duffy.
M: Lineman Ernest Sprague TD. John Duffy converted.

2nd half

M: C Billy Harless TD. John Duffy missed conversion.

Length of halves: 35 minutes, presumably.
Attendance at Notre Dame's campus field: estimated 500–600.

1898

(Touchdowns now worth 5 points, conversions 1 point. Field goals still
worth 5.)

Notre Dame   0   0   0
Michigan   11   12   23

1st half

M: LG William Caley, 2-yard plunge. Neil Snow missed conversion. 14:40 remaining.

M: LG William Caley, 1-yard plunge. Neil Snow converted. 1:00.

2nd half

M: LHB Clifford Barabee, 1-yard run. Neil Snow converted. 17:45.

M: LG William Caley, TD run. Neil Snow converted. 2:15.

Length of halves: 20 minutes. (The Wolverines had probably asked that each half be reduced from the standard 35 minutes because they had played Case Institute of Technology just three days before.)

Attendance at Regents' Field in Ann Arbor: 1,500.

1899

Notre Dame	0	0	0
Michigan	6	6	12

1st half

M: FB Leo Keena, 5-yard burst. Neil Snow converted. 20:00 remaining.

2nd half

M: LHB John McLean, TD run. Neil Snow converted. 15:00 (estimate).

Length of halves: 25 and 20 minutes. (This was a Wednesday game, so both teams probably desired a shorter game.)

Attendance at Regents' Field in Ann Arbor: nearly 2,000.

1900

Notre Dame	0	0	0
Michigan	7	0	7

1st half

M: LHB Arthur Redner, 1-yard buck. Arthur Webber missed conversion. 22:00 remaining.

M: Safety touch by Notre Dame FB Louis (Red) Salmon, who fell on an errant punt snap by C Charles Gillen. 1:00 (estimated).

2nd half

No scoring.

Length of halves: 25 and 20 minutes.

Attendance at Regents' Field in Ann Arbor: rough estimate, 500.

1902

Michigan	5	18	23
Notre Dame	0	0	0

1st half

M: RT Joseph Maddock, 7-yard smash. William Cole missed conversion. 17:00 remaining.

2nd half

M: RT Joseph Maddock, short-yardage plunge (exact length not reported). William Cole converted. 17:30.

M: RT Joseph Maddock, 5-yard buck. William Cole converted. 10:30.

M: FB Paul Jones, 5-yard run. William Cole converted. 3:45.

Length of halves: 25 minutes.

Attendance at Armory Park in Toledo: 1,700.

1908

(Field goals now worth 4 points.)

Notre Dame	0	6	6
Michigan	8	4	12

1st half

M: RHB Dave Allerdice, field goal snapped from 35. 21:00 remaining.

M: RHB Dave Allerdice, field goal snapped from 20. 14:00.

2nd half

ND: FB Pete Vaughan, 50-yard run. 5:00 (estimated).

M: RHB Dave Allerdice, field goal snapped from 34. 2:00.

Length of halves: 25 minutes.

Attendance at Ferry Field in Ann Arbor: rough estimate 4,000.

1909

(Field goals now worth 3 points.)

Notre Dame	5	6	11
Michigan	3	0	3

1st half

M: RHB Dave Allerdice, field goal snapped from 20. 17:00 remaining.

ND: FB Pete Vaughan, 1-yard plunge. RH Billy Ryan missed conversion. 7:00.

2nd half

ND: RHB Billy Ryan, 30-yard run. Ryan converted. 1:00 (estimated).

Length of halves: 35 minutes.

Attendance at Ferry Field in Ann Arbor: 6,000.

1942

(Touchdowns now worth 6 points, conversion 1. Field goals still worth 3.)

Michigan	7	6	19	0	32
Notre Dame	7	7	0	6	20

1st quarter

ND: LE Bob Dove, 7-yard pass from QB Angelo Bertelli. Bertelli converted. 7:30 remaining.

M: QB George Ceithaml, 1-yard sneak. Jim Brieske converted. 2:30.

2nd quarter

M: Holder Don Robinson, on fake field goal, jogs around left end for 3 yards. Jim Brieske's conversion blocked. 12:00.

ND: LHB Creighton Miller, 2-yard plunge. Angelo Bertelli converted. 7:00.

3rd quarter

M: WB Paul White, 2-yard run. Jim Brieske converted. 11:55.

M: TB Tom Kuzma, 3-yard plunge. Jim Brieske missed conversion. 7:15.

M: TB Tom Kuzma, 1-yard run. Jim Brieske missed conversion. 0:00.

4th quarter

ND: LHB Creighton Miller, 14-yard run on Statue of Liberty play. Angelo Bertelli's conversion blocked. 12:00 (estimated).

Attendance at Notre Dame Stadium: 57,011.

Individual statistics

RUSHING—Michigan: FB Bob Wiese 26–114, TB Tom Kuzma 22–90, WB Paul White 13–61, TB-2 Don Robinson 6–36. Notre Dame: LHB Creighton Miller 13–77, FB Cornie Clatt 11–40, RHB Bob Livingstone 3–21, LHB-2 Dick Creevy 3–14, FB-2 Gerry Cowhig 2–4.

PASSING—Michigan: TB Tom Kuzma 3/9, 1 int, 0 TD, 43 yards. Notre Dame: QB Angelo Bertelli, 6/14, 3 int, 1 TD, 78 yards.

RECEIVING—Michigan: LE Phil Sharpe 1–16, RE Elmer Madar 1–14, QB George Ceithaml 1–13. Notre Dame: LE-2 John Yonakor 3–57, RE George Murphy 2–33, LE Bob Dove 1–7.

INTERCEPTIONS—Michigan: Paul White 2, Bob Wiese. Notre Dame: Creighton Miller.

FUMBLE RECOVERIES—Michigan: Elmer Madar, Bob Kolesar. Notre Dame: Bob Dove.

Team statistics

CATEGORY	Michigan	Notre Dame
1st downs	19	15
Rushing att–yds	79–319	39–170
Passing c/a, yds	3/9, 43	6/14, 78
Total plays–yds	88–362	55–248
Avg gain per play	4.0	4.4
Penalty yards	30	12

1943

Notre Dame	7	14	14	0	35
Michigan	0	6	0	6	12

1st quarter

ND: LHB Creighton Miller, 66-yard run. Angelo Bertelli converted. 9:15 remaining.

2nd quarter

M: FB Bill Daley, 4-yard plunge. Merv Pregulman missed conversion. 12:00.
ND: LHB-2 Fred Earley, 70-yard pass from QB Angelo Bertelli. Bertelli converted. 10:30.
ND: FB Jim Mello, 2-yard burst. Bertelli converted. 1:30.

3rd quarter

ND: QB Angelo Bertelli, 2-yard sneak. Bertelli converted. 12:45.
ND: LHB Creighton Miller, 16-yard pass from QB Angelo Bertelli. Bertelli converted. 0:00*.

4th quarter

M: WB Paul White, 13-yard pass from TB-2 Elroy Hirsch. Merv Pregulman missed conversion. 0:00*.
*–The electric scoreboard clock malfunctioned in the third quarter, and about 23 minutes was played before the teams switched ends for the fourth quarter, which was reduced to 7 minutes in length.

Attendance at Michigan Stadium: 86,688.

Individual statistics

Unlike 1942, no newspapers in 1943 provided complete play-by-play accounts of this game—hence most individual statistics could not be compiled. Two accounts, though, provided rushing statistics:

RUSHING—Notre Dame: LHB Creighton Miller 10–159, FB Jim Mello 16–94, LHB-2 Fred Earley 2–17, RHB-2 Johnny Lujack 3–12, FB-2 Vic Kulbitski 3–12, RHB Julie Rykovich 6–4, QB Angelo Bertelli 2–2. Michigan: FB Bill Daley 24–135, WB Paul White 17–34, TB-2 Elroy Hirsch 4–24, QB Bob Wiese 8–14.

Team statistics

CATEGORY	Michigan	Notre Dame
1st downs	15	13
Rushing att–yds	50–210	45–282
Passing c/a, yds	6/17, 89	5/8, 138
Total plays–yds	67–299	53–420
Avg gain per play	4.5	7.9
Penalties–yds	5–41	5–62

1978

Michigan	0	7	7	14	28
Notre Dame	7	7	0	0	14

1st quarter

ND: TE Dennis Grindinger, 6-yard pass from QB Joe Montana. PK Joe Unis converted. 13:07 remaining.

2nd quarter

M: QB Rick Leach, 4-yard option run. PK Gregg Willner converted. 9:39.

ND: HB Vagas Ferguson, 4-yard plunge. Unis converted. 5:21.

3rd quarter

M: TE Doug Marsh, 5-yard pass from QB Rick Leach. Willner converted. 3:29.

4th quarter

M: TE Doug Marsh, 17-yard pass from QB Rick Leach. Willner missed conversion wide left. 14:55.

M: WR Ralph Clayton, 40-yard pass from QB Rick Leach. Leach tackled for loss on two-point conversion attempt. 9:18.

M: DT Curtis Greer, tackled ND QB Joe Montana in the end zone for a safety. 1:08.

Temperature 66 degrees, wind E at 5 mph, sunny and dry.

Attendance at Notre Dame Stadium: 59,075.

Individual statistics

RUSHING—Michigan: TB Harlan Huckleby 22–96, FB Russell Davis 14–39, QB Rick Leach 9–21, FB-2 Lawrence Reid 5–17, TB-2 Roosevelt Smith 4–13, WR Ralph Clayton 3–(–1). Notre Dame: FB Jerome Heavens 16–75, HB Vagas Ferguson 23–72, QB Joe Montana 4–3, FL-2 Mike Courey 2–(–7).

PASSING—Michigan: QB Rick Leach 8/20, 0 int, 3 TD, 110 yards. Notre Dame: QB Joe Montana 16/29, 2 int, 1 TD, 192 yards.

RECEIVING—Michigan: TE Doug Marsh 4–49, WR Ralph Clayton 2–60, FB Russell Davis 2–1. Notre Dame: HB Vagas Ferguson 3–16, SE Kris Haines 2–39, SE Dave Condeni 2–25, TE Dean Masztak 2–23, TE Dennis Grindinger 2–23, TE Nick Vehr 1–23, HB-2 Jim Stone 1–16, FB-2 Dave Mitchell 1–11.

TACKLES LEADERS—Michigan: ILB Ron Simpkins 15, OLB Tom Seabron 13. Notre Dame: MLB Bob Golic 26, LLB Steve Heimkreiter 17.

INTERCEPTIONS—Michigan: ILB Jerry Meter, CB Mike Harden.

FUMBLE RECOVERIES—Michigan: DT Curtis Greer, CB Gerald Diggs. Notre Dame: DE Scott Zettek.

Team statistics

CATEGORY	Michigan	Notre Dame
1st downs	18	18
Rushing att–yds	57–185	45–143
Passing c/a, yds	8/20, 110	16/29, 192
Total plays–yds	77–295	74–335
Avg gain per play	3.8	4.4
Penalties–yds	3–18	8–80

1979

Notre Dame	3	3	6	0	12
Michigan	3	7	0	0	10

1st quarter
M: PK Bryan Virgil, 30-yard field goal. 7:35 remaining.
ND: PK Chuck Male, 40-yard field goal. 2:27.

2nd quarter
M: TB Stan Edwards, 1-yard dash. PK Bryan Virgil converted. 10:48.
ND: PK Chuck Male, 44-yard field goal. 4:48.

3rd quarter
ND: PK Chuck Male, 22-yard field goal. 8:21.
ND: PK Chuck Male, 39-yard field goal. 3:46.

4th quarter
No scoring.

Temperature 68 degrees, wind W at 12 mph, sunny and dry.
Attendance at Michigan Stadium: 105,111.

Individual statistics
RUSHING—Notre Dame: HB Vagas Ferguson 35–118, FB John Sweeney 1–3, FB-2 Ty Barber 1–3, QB-2 Tim Koegel 1–(–2), QB Rusty Lisch 5–(–8). Michigan: TB Stan Edwards 22–72, QB B.J. Dickey 14–68, FB Lawrence Reid 7–28, QB-2 John Wangler 1–7, WR-2 Anthony Carter 1–(–3).

PASSING—Notre Dame: QB Rusty Lisch 5/10, 1 int, 0 TD, 65 yards; QB-3 Mike Courey 0/1, 1 int; HB-2 Jim Stone 0/1, 0 int. Michigan: QB B.J. Dickey 9/18, 1 int, 0 TD, 106 yards; QB-2 John Wangler 3/6, 0 int, 0 TD, 28 yards.

RECEIVING—Notre Dame: TE Dean Masztak 3–30, SE Tony Hunter 1–31, HB Vagas Ferguson 1–4. Michigan: TE Doug Marsh 4–46, TB Stan Edwards 3–20, WR Alan Mitchell 2–30, WB Ralph Clayton 2–15, WR-2 Anthony Carter 1–23.

TACKLES LEADERS—Notre Dame: SS Steve Cichy 13, MLB Bob Crable 12. Michigan: ILB Andy Cannavino 14, DT Curtis Greer 13.

INTERCEPTIONS—Notre Dame: CB Dave Waymer. Michigan: OLB Mel Owens, CB Mike Jolly.

FUMBLE RECOVERIES—Notre Dame: LE John Hankerd, RLB-2 Tony Beldin. Michigan: DT Curtis Greer.

Team statistics

CATEGORY	Michigan	Notre Dame
1st downs	16	7
Rushing att–yds	45–172	43–114
Passing c/a, yds	12/24, 134	5/12, 65
Total plays–yds	69–306	55–179

Avg gain per play		4.4		3.2
Penalties–yds		4–28		3–45

1980

Michigan	0	14	7	6	27
Notre Dame	0	14	6	9	29

1st quarter
No scoring.

2nd quarter
ND: HB Phil Carter, 6-yard burst. PK Harry Oliver converted. 13:05 remaining.
ND: WR Pete Holohan, 10-yard pass from QB Mike Courey. PK Harry Oliver converted. 5:00.
M: TB Larry Ricks, 8-yard pass from QB-2 John Wangler. PK Ali Haji-Shiekh converted. 1:50.
M: TE Norm Betts, 9-yard pass from QB-2 John Wangler. PK Ali Haji-Shiekh converted. 0:31.

3rd quarter
M: FB Stan Edwards, 2-yard plunge. PK Ali Haji-Shiekh converted. 11:57.
ND: CB John Krimm, 49-yard interception return. PK Harry Oliver missed conversion wide left. 1:03.

4th quarter
ND: HB Phil Carter, 4-yard smash. QB Mike Courey's 2-point conversion pass incomplete. 3:03.
M: TE-2 Craig Dunaway, 1-yard pass from QB-2 John Wangler. Wangler's 2-point conversion pass incomplete. 0:41.
ND: PK Harry Oliver, 51-yard field goal. 0:00.

Temperature 78 degrees, wind S-SW at 15 mph, sunny but muggy.
Attendance at Notre Dame Stadium: 59,075.

Individual statistics
RUSHING—Notre Dame: HB Phil Carter 30–104, FB John Sweeney 2–11, QB Mike Courey 6–11, FB-2 Pete Buchanon 3–6, HB-2 Jim Stone 2–4. Michigan: TB Lawrence Ricks 14–90, TB-2 Butch Woolfolk 9–72, FB Stan Edwards 12–40, QB Rich Hewlett 9–32, FB-2 Jerald Ingram 1–2, QB-2 John Wangler 2–0.

PASSING—Notre Dame: QB Mike Courey 6/13, 2 int, 1 TD, 62 yards; QB-2 Blair Kiel 2/4, 0 int, 0 TD, 14 yards; SE Tony Hunter 1/1, 0 int, 0 TD, 31 yards. Michigan: QB-2 John Wangler 11/19, 1 int, 3 TDs, 98 yards; QB Rich Hewlett 1/5, 0 int, 0 TD, 11 yards.

RECEIVING—Notre Dame: SE Tony Hunter 3–32, TE Dean Masztak 3–25, WR Pete Holohan 2–41, HB Phil Carter 1–9. Michigan: WR Anthony Carter

2–30, FB Stan Edwards 2–22, TE Norm Betts 2–17, TB Lawrence Ricks 2–17, FB-2 Jerald Ingram 2–10, TB-2 Butch Woolfolk 1–12, TE-2 Craig Dunaway 1–1.

TACKLES LEADERS—Notre Dame: MLB Bob Crable 19, DT Don Kidd 10. Michigan: ILB Andy Cannavino 13, ILB Paul Girgash 10, SS Jeff Reeves 10.

INTERCEPTIONS—Notre Dame: CB John Krimm. Michigan: CB Marion Body 2.

FUMBLE RECOVERIES—Notre Dame: CB Dave Duerson.

Team statistics

CATEGORY	Michigan	Notre Dame
1st downs	17	4
Rushing att–yds	47–221	42–127
Passing c/a, yds	12/24, 109	9/18, 107
Total plays–yds	71–330	60–234
Avg gain per play	4.6	3.9
Penalties–yds	3–47	5–39

1981

Notre Dame	0	0	0	7	7
Michigan	0	7	12	6	25

1st quarter

No scoring.

2nd quarter

M: WR Anthony Carter, 71-yard pass from QB Steve Smith. PK Ali Haji-Shiekh converted. 12:08 remaining.

3rd quarter

M: WR Anthony Carter, 15-yard pass from QB Steve Smith. PK Ali Haji-Shiekh conversion muffed at placement. 6:22.

M: TB-2 Lawrence Ricks, 1-yard burst. WR Anthony Carter run stopped short of goal line on 2-point conversion attempt. 1:12.

4th quarter

M: QB Steve Smith, 6-yard option run. PK Ali Haji-Shiekh converted. 12:35.

ND: TE Dean Masztak, 8-yard pass from QB Tim Koegel. PK Harry Oliver converted. 7:42.

Temperature 67 degrees, wind SW at 17 mph, sunny and dry.

Attendance at Michigan Stadium: 105,888.

Individual statistics

RUSHING—Michigan: TB Butch Woolfolk 23–139, QB Steve Smith 8–64, FB Stan Edwards 10–52, TB-2 Lawrence Ricks 11–40, FB-2 Jerald Ingram 2–6, TB-3 Kerry Smith 2–7, TB-5 Rick Rogers 1–6, TB-4 Brian Mercer 1–2, WR Anthony Carter 1–(–12). Notre Dame: TB Greg Bell 11–43, TB-2 Phil

Carter 9–32, FB Larry Moriarty 4–15, WB Tony Hunter 7–11, FB-2 John Sweeney 1–1, QB-2 Blair Kiel 1–(–9), QB Tim Koegel 5–(–23).

PASSING—Michigan: QB Steve Smith 4/15, 2 int, 2 TD, 103 yards. Notre Dame: QB Tim Koegel 10/22, 1 int, 1 TD, 139 yards; * Dave Condeni 1/1, 0 int, 0 TD, 4 yards; QB-2 Blair Kiel 0/2, 0 int; WB Tony Hunter 0/1, 1 int. *–Holder on placekicks, threw after fake field goal.

RECEIVING—Michigan: WR Anthony Carter 3–99, TB Butch Woolfolk 1–4. Notre Dame: WB Tony Hunter 5–72, TE Dean Masztak 3–44, SE Mike Boushka 1–13, SE-2 Dave Condeni 1–10, FB-2 John Sweeney 1–4.

TACKLES LEADERS—Michigan: ILB Mike Boren 10, SS Keith Bostic 9. Notre Dame: MLB Bob Crable 20, WLB Mark Zavagnin 9.

INTERCEPTIONS—Michigan: FS Tony Jackson. Notre Dame: CB John Krimm, FS-2 Joe Johnson.

FUMBLE RECOVERIES—None.

Team statistics

CATEGORY	Michigan	Notre Dame
1st downs	19	12
Rushing att–yds	59–304	38–70
Passing c/a, yds	4/15, 103	11/26, 143
Total plays–yds	74–407	64–213
Avg gain per play	5.5	3.3
Penalties–yds	8–67	2–19

1982

Michigan	0	0	7	10	17
Notre Dame	3	10	10	0	23

1st quarter

ND: PK Mike Johnston, 35-yard field goal. 12:38 remaining.

2nd quarter

ND: FB Larry Moriarty, 24-yard run. PK Mike Johnston converted. 14:01.

ND: PK Mike Johnston, 37-yard field goal. 0:02.

3rd quarter

M: WR Anthony Carter, 72-yard punt return. PK Ali Haji-Shiekh converted. 13:10.

ND: PK Mike Johnston, 41-yard field goal. 7:22.

ND: TB-2 Greg Bell, 10-yard burst. PK Mike Johnston converted. 1:55.

4th quarter

M: PK Ali Haji-Shiekh 42-yard field goal. 13:00.

M: TB-2 Rick Rogers, 39-yard deflected pass from QB Steve Smith. PK Ali Haji-Shiekh converted. 7:38.

Temperature 55 degrees, wind light and variable, clear and dry.

Attendance at Notre Dame Stadium: 59,075.

Individual statistics

RUSHING—Notre Dame: FB Larry Moriarty 16–116, TB-2 Greg Bell 20–95, TB Phil Carter 14–56, FB-2 Mark Brooks 3–10, QB Blair Kiel 2–1. Michigan: TB Lawrence Ricks 13–47, TB-2 Rick Rogers 6–19, WR Anthony Carter 1–11, FB Greg Armstrong 2–4, FB-2 Ed Garrett 1–2.

PASSING—Notre Dame: QB Blair Kiel 15/22, 0 int, 0 TD, 141 yards. Michigan: QB Steve Smith 12/21, 1 int, 1 TD, 186 yards.

RECEIVING—Notre Dame: TE Tony Hunter 7–76, SE Joe Howard 2–31, TB-2 Greg Bell 2–13, FB Larry Moriarty 2–7, TB Phil Carter 1–5, SE-2 Milt Jackson 1–9. Michigan: SE Vince Bean 4–64, TE Craig Dunaway 4–45, WR Anthony Carter 2–34, TB-2 Rick Rogers 1–39, TB Lawrence Ricks 1–4.

TACKLES LEADERS—Notre Dame: WLB Mike Larkin 11, SLB Rick Naylor 9. Michigan: ILB Paul Girgash 18, CB Jerry Burgei 14.

INTERCEPTIONS—Notre Dame: CB Dave Duerson.

FUMBLE RECOVERIES—Notre Dame: MLB Mark Zavagnin. Michigan: SS Keith Bostic.

Team statistics

CATEGORY	Michigan	Notre Dame
1st downs	14	22
Rushing att–yds	36–41	55–288
Passing c/a, yds	12/21, 186	15/22, 141
Total plays–yds	57–227	77–419
Avg gain per play	4.0	5.4
Penalties–yds	3–15	7–66

1985

Notre Dame	3	6	3	0	12
Michigan	0	3	14	3	20

1st quarter

ND: PK John Carney, 34-yard field goal. 3:05 remaining.

2nd quarter

ND: PK John Carney, 31-yard field goal. 9:47.

 M: PK Mike Gillette, 21-yard field goal. 1:04.

ND: PK John Carney, 47-yard field goal. 0:08.

3rd quarter

 M: QB Jim Harbaugh, 10-yard QB draw. PK Mike Gillette converted. 13:20.

ND: PK John Carney, 25-yard field goal. 8:14.

 M: FB Gerald White, 3-yard run. PK Mike Gillette converted. 1:12.

4th quarter

 M: PK Mike Gillette, 23-yard field goal. 5:12.

Temperature 67 degrees, wind N-NE at 15 mph, sunny and dry.

Attendance at Michigan Stadium: 105,523.

Individual statistics

RUSHING—Michigan: TB Jamie Morris 23–119, QB Jim Harbaugh 9–60, FB-2 Bob Perryman 9–28, TB-2 Thomas Wilcher 4–18, FB Gerald White 6–16, WR Erik Campbell 1–10. Notre Dame: TB Allen Pinkett 22–89, FB Frank Stams 5–13, SE Tim Brown 1–7, TB-2 Alonzo Jefferson 2–7, QB Steve Beuerlein 9–(–9).

PASSING—Michigan: QB Jim Harbaugh 7/17, 0 int, 0 TD, 74 yards. Notre Dame: QB Steve Beuerlein 11/23, 1 int, 0 TD, 160 yards.

RECEIVING—Michigan: TB Jamie Morris 3–24, WR-2 Gilvanni Johnson 1–17, FB Gerald White 1–15, SE Paul Jokisch 1–11, FB-2 Bob Perryman 1–7. Notre Dame: WR-2 Reggie Ward 2–37, SE Tim Brown 2–32, TB Allen Pinkett 2–29, SE-2 Pat Cusack 1–19, TE-2 Joel Williams 1–15, TE Tom Rehder 1–14, WR Tony Eason 1–11, FB Frank Stams 1–3.

TACKLES LEADERS—Michigan: ILB Andy Moeller 15, DT Mike Hammerstein 13. Notre Dame: MLB Tony Furjanic 12, FS Steve Lawrence 11.

INTERCEPTIONS—Michigan: SS-2 Doug Mallory.

FUMBLE RECOVERIES—Michigan: OLB Dieter Heren. Notre Dame: CB Troy Wilson, DT Greg Dingens.

Team statistics

CATEGORY	Michigan	Notre Dame
1st downs	21	15
Rushing att–yds	52–251	39–97
Passing c/a, yds	7/17, 74	11/23, 160
Total plays–yds	69–325	62–257
Avg gain per play	4.7	4.1
Penalties–yds	2–13	3–33

1986

Michigan	7	3	14	0	24
Notre Dame	7	7	6	3	23

1st quarter

ND: WR Tim Brown, from backfield, 3-yard dash. PK John Carney converted. 4:34 remaining.

  M: TB Jamie Morris, 8-yard run. PK Pat Moons converted. 0:33.

2nd quarter

ND: TB Mark Green, 1-yard run. PK John Carney converted. 8:08.

  M: PK Pat Moons 23-yard field goal. 0:52.

3rd quarter

  M: TB Jamie Morris, 1-yard run off option. PK Pat Moons converted. 8:57.

  M: TB Jamie Morris, 27-yard pass from QB Jim Harbaugh. PK Pat Moons converted. 8:51.

ND: TE Joel Williams, 3-yard pass from QB Steve Beuerlein. PK John Carney missed conversion wide left. 3:10.

4th quarter
ND: PK John Carney 25-yard field goal. 4:26.

Temperature 75 degrees, wind NW 10–12 mph, mostly sunny and dry. Attendance at Notre Dame Stadium: 59,075.

Individual statistics
RUSHING—Michigan: TB Jamie Morris 23–77, FB Gerald White 8–35, FB-2 Bob Perryman 10–29, WR John Kolesar 1–11, QB Jim Harbaugh 6–2. Notre Dame: WR Tim Brown 12–65, TB Mark Green 12–57, SE-2 Reggie Ward 3–20, TB-2 Anthony Johnson 2–16, FB Pernell Taylor 5–16, QB Steve Beuerlein 4–13, TB-3 Braxston Banks 1–5.

PASSING—Michigan: QB Jim Harbaugh 15/23, 0 int, 1 TD, 239 yds. Notre Dame: QB Steve Beuerlein 21/33, 1 int, 1 TD, 263 yds.

RECEIVING—Michigan: WR John Kolesar 4–93, FB Gerald White 3–35, TB Jamie Morris 3–31, SE Paul Jokisch 2–39, TE Jeff Brown 2–30, SE-2 Sean Higgins 1–11. Notre Dame: TB Mark Green 6–79, SE Reggie Miller 3–58, TE Joel Williams 3–26, SE-2 Milt Jackson 3–26, FB Pernell Taylor 2–17, TE-2 Andy Heck 2–9, WR Tim Brown 1–32, WR-2 Reggie Ward 1–16.

TACKLES LEADERS—Michigan: ILB Andy Moeller 13, DT Mark Messner 10. Notre Dame: ILB Mike Kovaleski 17, DT Robert Banks 12.

INTERCEPTIONS—Michigan: CB David Arnold.

FUMBLE RECOVERIES—Michigan: SS Doug Mallory 2, FS Tony Gant. Notre Dame: ILB Wes Pritchett.

Team statistics

CATEGORY	Michigan	Notre Dame
1st downs	20	27
Rushing att–yds	48–154	39–192
Passing c/a, yds	15/23, 239	21/33, 263
Total plays–yds	71–393	72–455
Avg gain per play	5.5	6.3
Penalties–yds	4–29	4–23

1987

Notre Dame	10	0	7	9	26
Michigan	0	0	7	0	7

1st quarter
ND: PK Ted Gradel, 44-yard field goal. 2:39 remaining.
ND: WR Tim Brown, 10-yard pass from QB Terry Andrysiak. PK Ted Gradel converted. 1:26.

2nd quarter
No scoring.

3rd quarter
ND: FB Braxston Banks, 1-yard plunge. PK Ted Gradel converted. 2:24.
 M: SE Greg McMurtry, 12-yard pass from QB Demetrius Brown. PK Mike Gillette converted. 0:03.

4th quarter
ND: PK Ted Gradel, 38-yard field goal. 8:59.
ND: TB-2 Ricky Watters, 18-yard run. QB Terry Andrysiak's 2-point conversion pass attempt intercepted. 6:14.

Temperature 75 degrees, wind E-SE at 10–15 mph, mostly sunny.
Attendance at Michigan Stadium: 106,098.

Individual statistics
RUSHING—Notre Dame: TB Mark Green 12–46, FB-3 Anthony Johnson 11–41, TB-3 Tony Brooks 6–22, TB-2 Ricky Watters 3–21, QB Terry Andrysiak 9–20, FB Braxston Banks 6–19, TB-4 Alonzo Jefferson 1–12, FB-2 Pernell Taylor 5–10, WR Tim Brown 5–5, QB-2 Steve Belles 1–3. Michigan: TB Jamie Morris 19–128, QB Demetrius Brown 4–38, FB Phil Webb 5–19, FB-2 Jarrod Bunch 2–6, QB-2 Michael Taylor 1–(–2).

PASSING—Notre Dame: QB Terry Andrysiak 11/15, 1 int, 1 TD, 137 yards. Michigan: QB Demetrius Brown 4/15, 3 int, 1 TD, 54 yards; QB-2 Michael Taylor 4/8, 1 int, 0 TD, 72 yards.

RECEIVING—Notre Dame: WR Tim Brown 3/40, TB Mark Green 3–22, SE-2 Ray Dumas 1–25, TE-2 Frank Jacobs 1–23, TE Andy Heck 1–17, TB-3 Tony Brooks 1–9, FB Braxston Banks 1–1. Michigan: SE-2 John Kolesar 2–38, TE-2 Derrick Walker 2–34, SE Greg McMurtry 2–16, TE Jeff Brown 1–33, FB Phil Webb 1–5.

TACKLES LEADERS—Notre Dame: ILB Ned Bolcar 9, SS George Streeter 5. Michigan: DT Mark Messner 14, ILB Andree McIntyre 13.

INTERCEPTIONS—Notre Dame: FS Corny Southall 2, ILB Wes Pritchett, OLB Cedric Figaro.

FUMBLE RECOVERIES—Notre Dame: CB Stan Smagala, DT-3 George Williams, DT Jeff Kunz.

Team statistics

CATEGORY	Michigan	Notre Dame
1st downs	17	19
Rushing att–yds	31–189	59–199
Passing c/a, yds	8/23, 126	11/15, 137
Total plays–yds	54–315	74–336
Avg gain per play	5.8	4.5
Penalties–yds	3–25	8–56

1988

Michigan	0	7	7	3	17
Notre Dame	10	3	0	6	19

1st quarter

ND: WR Ricky Watters 81-yard punt return. PK Reggie Ho converted. 10:11 remaining.

ND: PK Reggie Ho, 31-yard field goal. 0:35.

2nd quarter

ND: PK Reggie Ho, 38-yard field goal. 14:47.

M: TB Leroy Hoard, 1-yard leap. PK Mike Gillette converted. 8:29.

3rd quarter

M: QB Michael Taylor, 1-yard bootleg. PK Mike Gillette converted. 4:44.

4th quarter

ND: PK Reggie Ho, 26-yard field goal, 14:17.

M: PK Mike Gillette, 49-yard field goal, 5:39.

ND: PK Reggie Ho, 26-yard field goal, 1:13.

Temperature 72 degrees, wind SW at 5 mph, clear and dry.

Attendance at Notre Dame Stadium: 59,075.

Individual statistics

RUSHING—Notre Dame: TB Mark Green 18–68, QB Tony Rice 7–52, FB-2 Anthony Johnson 7–49, TB-2 Tony Brooks 7–48, FB Braxston Banks 3–10, WR Ricky Watters 1–(–1). Michigan: TB-2 Tony Boles 25–83, QB Michael Taylor 10–20, TB Leroy Hoard 11–19, FB Jarrod Bunch 4–12, TB-3 Tracy Williams 2–5.

PASSING—Notre Dame: QB Tony Rice 3/12, 1 int, 0 TD, 40 yards. Michigan: QB Michael Taylor 8/11, 0 int, 0 TD, 74 yards.

RECEIVING—Notre Dame: SE Steve Alaniz 1–23, TB-2 Tony Brooks 1–18, TB Mark Green 1–(–1). Michigan: SE Chris Calloway 2–28, SE-2 Greg McMurtry 2–27, TB Leroy Hoard 2–11, WR John Kolesar 1–5, TB-2 Tony Boles 1–3.

TACKLES LEADERS—Notre Dame: ILB Mike Stonebreaker 19, DT George Williams 9. Michigan: ILB John Milligan 9, 4 with 7.

INTERCEPTIONS—Michigan: CB David Key.

FUMBLE RECOVERIES—Notre Dame: DE Arnold Ale. Michigan: OLB Bobby Abrams.

Team statistics

CATEGORY	Michigan	Notre Dame
1st downs	13	15
Rushing att–yds	52–139	43–226
Passing c/a, yds	8/11, 74	3/12, 40
Total plays–yds	63–213	55–266

Avg gain per play	3.4	4.8
Penalties–yds	3–30	3–24

1989

Notre Dame	0	7	10	7	24
Michigan	0	6	0	13	19

1st quarter
No scoring.

2nd quarter
ND: FB Anthony Johnson, 6-yard pass from QB Tony Rice. PK Craig Hentrich converted. 5:05 remaining.
  M: WR Chris Calloway, 9-yard pass from QB Michael Taylor. PK J.D. Carlson missed conversion, hitting left upright. 0:25.

3rd quarter
ND: WR Raghib Ismail, 89-yard kickoff return. PK Craig Hentrich converted. 14:49.
ND: PK Craig Hentrich, 30-yard field goal. 4:28.

4th quarter
  M: TE Derrick Walker, 5-yard pass from QB-2 Elvis Grbac. Grbac's two-point conversion pass incomplete. 12:58.
ND: WR Raghib Ismail, 92-yard kickoff return. PK Craig Hentrich converted. 12:46.
  M: SE Greg McMurtry, 4-yard pass from QB-2 Elvis Grbac. PK J.D. Carlson converted. 4:08.

  Temperature 63 degrees, wind NE at 7–15 mph, rainy and slick.
  Attendance at Michigan Stadium: 105,912.

Individual statistics
  RUSHING—Notre Dame: FB Anthony Johnson 20–80, QB Tony Rice 18–79, TB-2 Rodney Culver 7–35, WR Raghib Ismail 4–14, TB Ricky Watters 5–5. Michigan: TB Leroy Hoard 15–56, TB-2 Tony Boles 5–17, FB Jarrod Bunch 5–12, QB Michael Taylor 6–11, WR-2 Desmond Howard 1–6, QB-2 Elvis Grbac 2–(–8).
  PASSING—Notre Dame: QB Tony Rice 1/2, 0 int, 0 TD, 6 yards. Michigan: QB-2 Elvis Grbac 17/22, 0 int, 2 TDs, 134 yards; QB Michael Taylor 5/6, 0 int, 1 TD, 44 yards; TB Leroy Hoard 0/1, 0 int.
  RECEIVING—Notre Dame: FB Anthony Johnson 1–6. Michigan: WR Chris Calloway 7–72, SE Greg McMurtry 4–51, FB Jarrod Bunch 4–8, TB Leroy Hoard 3–12, TE Derrick Walker 2–12, WR-2 Desmond Howard 1–17, TB-2 Tony Boles 1–6.
  TACKLES LEADERS—Notre Dame: ILB Ned Bolcar 12, SS D'Juan Francisco 9. Michigan: ILB J.J. Grant 10, DT Chris Hutchinson 10.

INTERCEPTIONS—None.

FUMBLE RECOVERIES—Notre Dame: DE Scott Kowalkowski.

Team statistics

CATEGORY	Michigan	Notre Dame
1st downs	15	13
Rushing att–yds	34–94	54–213
Passing c/a, yds	22/28, 178	1/2, 6
Total plays–yds	62–272	56–219
Avg gain per play	4.4	3.9
Penalties–yds	8–70	5–45

1990

Michigan	3	7	14	0	24
Notre Dame	14	0	0	14	28

1st quarter

ND: QB Rick Mirer, 2-yard option run. PK Craig Hentrich converted. 11:28 remaining.

M: PK J.D. Carlson, 38-yard field goal. 7:01.

ND: TB-2 Tony Brooks, 2-yard run. PK Craig Hentrich converted. 1:59.

2nd quarter

M: SE Desmond Howard, 44-yard pass from QB Elvis Grbac. PK J.D. Carlson converted. 3:56.

3rd quarter

M: TB-2 Allen Jefferson, 1-yard dash. PK J.D. Carlson converted. 7:49.

M: SE Desmond Howard, 25-yard pass from QB Elvis Grbac. PK J.D. Carlson converted. 7:33.

4th quarter

ND: FB Rodney Culver, 1-yard plunge. PK Craig Hentrich converted. 12:59.

ND: WR-2 Adrian Jarrell, 18-yard pass from QB Rick Mirer. PK Craig Hentrich converted. 1:40.

Temperature 63 degrees, winds calm, increasing cover and humid.

Attendance at Notre Dame Stadium: 59,075.

Individual statistics

RUSHING—Notre Dame: FB Rodney Culver 19–95, WR Raghib Ismail 6–50, TB Ricky Watters 7–41, TB-2 Tony Brooks 8–36, QB Rick Mirer 10–12. Michigan: TB Jon Vaughn 22–201, FB Jarrod Bunch 11–33, TB-2 Allen Jefferson 4–21, QB Elvis Grbac 2–8, SE Desmond Howard 1–(–10).

PASSING—Notre Dame: QB Rick Mirer 14/23, 1 int, 1 TD, 165 yards. Michigan: QB Elvis Grbac 17/30, 2 int, 2 TDs, 190 yards.

RECEIVING—Notre Dame: WR Raghib Ismail 4–42, SE Tony Smith 3–24, WR-2 Adrian Jarrell 2–26, FB Rodney Culver 2–8, SE-2 Lake Dawson 1–45,

TB Ricky Watters 1–17, TE Derek Brown 1–3. Michigan: SE Desmond Howard 6–133, TB Jon Vaughn 6–41, FB Jarrod Bunch 3–(–5), WR Derrick Alexander 2–21.

TACKLES LEADERS—Notre Dame: ILB Mike Stonebreaker 10, NG Chris Zorich 9. Michigan: ILB John Milligan 14, SS Tripp Welborne 9.

INTERCEPTIONS—Notre Dame: ILB Mike Stonebreaker, CB Reggie Brooks. Michigan: FS Vada Murray.

FUMBLE RECOVERIES—Notre Dame: SS Greg Davis. Michigan: DT Mike Evans, DT T.J. Osman.

Team statistics

CATEGORY	Michigan	Notre Dame
1st downs	22	23
Rushing att–yds	40–253	50–234
Passing c/a, yds	17/30, 190	14/23, 165
Total plays–yds	70–443	73–399
Avg gain per play	6.3	5.3
Penalties–yds	4–31	5–31

1991

Notre Dame	0	7	7	0	14
Michigan	3	14	0	7	24

1st quarter

M: PK J.D. Carlson, 22-yard field goal. 10:54 remaining.

2nd quarter

M: SE Desmond Howard, 29-yard end-around. PK J.D. Carlson converted. 9:58.

M: TB Ricky Powers, 16-yard burst. PK J.D. Carlson converted. 1:49.

ND: FB Jerome Bettis, 3-yard pass from QB Rick Mirer. PK Craig Hentrich converted. 0:17.

3rd quarter

ND: SE Tony Smith, 35-yard pass from QB Rick Mirer. PK Craig Hentrich converted. 6:47.

4th quarter

M: SE Desmond Howard, 25-yard pass from QB Elvis Grbac. PK J.D. Carlson converted. 9:02.

Temperature 77 degrees, wind S-SE at 15–20 mph, overcast but dry. Attendance at Michigan Stadium: 106,138.

Individual statistics

RUSHING—Michigan: TB Ricky Powers 38–164, FB Bernie Legette 11–39, SE Desmond Howard 1–29, TB-2 Tyrone Wheatley 3–5, QB Elvis Grbac 2–(–4).

Notre Dame: FB Jerome Bettis 8–28, TB-3 Willie Clark 2–22, QB Rick Mirer 6–13, TB Rodney Culver 6–10, TB-2 Tony Brooks 6–5.

PASSING—Michigan: QB Elvis Grbac 20/22, 0 int, 1 TD, 195 yards. Notre Dame: QB Rick Mirer 13/25, 1 int, 2 TDs, 234 yards.

RECEIVING—Michigan: SE Desmond Howard 6–74, WR Yale Van Dyne 6–56, TE Dave Diebolt 3–25, TB-2 Tyrone Wheatley 1–10, WR-2 Walter Smith 1–8, TB Ricky Power 1–8, FB Bernie Legette 1–8, SE-2 John Ellison 1–6. Notre Dame: SE Tony Smith 5–121, TE Derek Brown 4–70, FB Jerome Bettis 2–15, WR Lake Dawson 1–20, TB Rodney Culver 1–8.

TACKLES LEADERS—Michigan: ILB Erick Anderson 9, FS Corwin Brown 6. Notre Dame: SLB Demetrius DuBose 14, SS Greg Davis 12.

INTERCEPTIONS—Michigan: CB Lance Dottin.

FUMBLE RECOVERIES—Michigan: ILB Erick Anderson.

Team statistics

CATEGORY	Michigan	Notre Dame
1st downs	26	14
Rushing att–yds	55–233	28–78
Passing c/a, yds	20/22, 195	13/25, 234
Total plays–yds	77–428	53–312
Avg gain per play	5.5	5.8
Penalties–yds	3–21	4–35

1992

Michigan	0	7	3	7	17
Notre Dame	7	0	0	10	17

1st quarter
ND: TB Reggie Brooks, 20-yard run off option. PK Craig Hentrich converted. 5:22 remaining.

2nd quarter
M: TB-2 Tyrone Wheatley, 27-yard pass from QB Elvis Grbac. PK Peter Elezovic converted. 0:57.

3rd quarter
M: PK Peter Elezovic, 28-yard field goal. 6:17.

4th quarter
M: SE-2 Derrick Alexander, 30-yard pass from QB Elvis Grbac. PK Peter Elezovic converted. 14:54.
ND: FB Jerome Bettis, 2-yard smash. PK Craig Hentrich converted. 11:23.
ND: PK Craig Hentrich, 32-yard field goal. 5:28.

Temperature 69 degrees, wind SW at 11 mph, sunny and dry.
Attendance at Notre Dame Stadium: 59,075.

Individual statistics

RUSHING—Michigan: TB–3 Jesse Johnson 15–66, TB Ricky Powers 8–30, TB-2 Tyrone Wheatley 6–27, FB Bernie Legette 3–12, QB Elvis Grbac 2–4, SE-2 Derrick Alexander 1–1. Notre Dame: FB Jerome Bettis 15–82, TB Reggie Brooks 13–69, QB Rick Mirer 7–54, TB-2 Lee Becton 7–44, WR-3 Mike Miller 1–(–12).

PASSING—Michigan: QB Elvis Grbac 17/28, 3 int, 2 TDs, 242 yards. Notre Dame: QB Rick Mirer 14/26, 0 int, 0 TD, 161 yards.

RECEIVING—Michigan: SE-2 Derrick Alexander 6–92, WR Walter Smith 4–70, TE Tony McGee 4–39, TB-2 Tyrone Wheatley 1–27, FB Bernie Legette 1–14, TB-3 Jesse Johnson 1–0. Notre Dame: SE Lake Dawson 6–89, SE-2 Clint Johnson 3–22, FB Jerome Bettis 2–25, TE Irv Smith 2–18, WR-3 Mike Miller 1–7.

TACKLES LEADERS—Michigan: FS Corwin Brown 11, CB Coleman Wallace 11. Notre Dame: CB Greg Lane 8, FS Jeff Burris 8.

INTERCEPTIONS—Notre Dame: CB Tom Carter, ILB Brian Ratigan, FS Jeff Burris.

FUMBLE RECOVERIES—Michigan: ILB Marcus Walker, OLB Martin Davis, ILB Steve Morrison.

Team statistics

CATEGORY	Michigan	Notre Dame
1st downs	18	25
Rushing att–yds	35–136	43–237
Passing c/a, yds	17/28, 242	14/26, 161
Total plays–yds	63–378	69–398
Avg gain per play	6.0	5.8
Penalties–yds	5–30	6–37

1993

Notre Dame	10	14	3	0	27
Michigan	3	7	0	13	23

1st quarter

ND: QB Kevin McDougal, 43-yard option run. PK Kevin Pendergast converted. 11:55 remaining.

 M: PK Peter Elezovic, 32-yard field goal. 6:03.

ND: PK Kevin Pendergast, 24-yard field goal. 2:36.

2nd quarter

ND: WR-2 Mike Miller, 56-yard punt return. PK Kevin Pendergast converted. 10:17.

 M: TB Tyrone Wheatley, 1-yard plunge. PK Peter Elezovic converted. 1:13.

ND: QB Kevin McDougal, 11-yard scramble. PK Kevin Pendergast converted. 0:06.

3rd quarter
ND: PK Kevin Pendergast, 19-yard field goal. 6:52.

4th quarter
M: TB Tyrone Wheatley, 4-yard run. PK Peter Elezovic converted. 14:57.
M: WR-2 Mercury Hayes, 13-yard pass from QB Todd Collins. Collins's 2-point conversion pass incomplete. 0:34.

Temperature 62 degrees, wind W-NW at 15–20 mph, partly sunny, dry. Attendance at Michigan Stadium: 106,851.

Individual statistics
RUSHING—Notre Dame: QB Kevin McDougal 9–66, TB Lee Becton 17–66, FB Ray Zellars 12–18, WR Lake Dawson 1–8, CB/TB-3 Jeff Burris 3–4, TB-2 Randy Kinder 3–1, FB-2 Marc Edwards 1–0. Michigan: TB Tyrone Wheatley 25–146, TB-3 Ed Davis 3–13, TB-2 Ricky Powers 2–6, QB Todd Collins 4–(–14).

PASSING—Notre Dame: QB Kevin McDougal 12/21, 0 int, 0 TD, 208 yards. Michigan: QB Todd Collins 22/37, 3 int, 1 TD, 251 yards.

RECEIVING—Notre Dame: WR Lake Dawson 3–64, SE Clint Johnson 2–56, SE-2 Derrick Mayes 2–34, FB Ray Zellars 2–17, TB Lee Becton 2–14, WR-2 Mike Miller 1–23. Michigan: WR Mercury Hayes 6–96, SE Amani Toomer 5–58, WR-2 Walter Smith 4–34, TB Tyrone Wheatley 3–39, TE Pierre Cooper 2–10, SE-2 Felman Malveaux 1–9, TE-2 Mark Burkholder 1–5.

TACKLES LEADERS—Notre Dame: WLB Pete Bercich 13, MLB Justin Goheen 9. Michigan: SS Shonte Peoples 12, ILB Steve Morrison 11.

INTERCEPTIONS—Notre Dame: FS Jeff Burris 2, CB Bobby Taylor.

FUMBLE RECOVERIES—None.

Team statistics

CATEGORY	Michigan	Notre Dame
1st downs	19	19
Rushing att–yds	34–151	46–163
Passing c/a, yds	22/37, 251	12/21, 208
Total plays–yds	71–402	67–371
Avg gain per play	5.7	5.5
Penalties–yds	4–34	5–40

Appendix
Team, individual, and coaching records for series

Team records, game (1942–1993)

Most 1st downs
Notre Dame, 1986	27
Michigan, 1991	26
Notre Dame, 1992	25
Notre Dame, 1990	23
Notre Dame, 1982	22
Michigan, 1990	22

Most rushing yards
Michigan, 1942	319
Michigan, 1981	304
Notre Dame, 1982	288
Notre Dame, 1943	282
Michigan, 1990	265

Most passing yards
Notre Dame, 1986	263
Michigan, 1993	251
Michigan, 1992	242
Michigan, 1986	239
Notre Dame, 1991	234

Most total yards
Notre Dame, 1986	455
Michigan, 1990	443
Michigan, 1991	428
Notre Dame, 1943	420
Notre Dame, 1982	419

Highest average gain per play
Notre Dame, 1943	7.9
Michigan, 1990	6.328
Notre Dame, 1986	6.319
Michigan, 1992	6.0
Notre Dame, 1991	5.9

Individual records, game (1942–1993)

Most rushing yards
Jon Vaughn, M–90	201
Ricky Powers, M–91	164
Creighton Miller, ND–43	159
Tyrone Wheatley, M–93	146
Butch Woolfolk, M–81	139

Most rushing attempts
Ricky Powers, M–91	38
Vagas Ferguson, ND–79	35
Phil Carter, ND–80	30
Bob Wiese, M–42	26
Tony Boles, M–88	25
Tyrone WHeatley, M—93	25

Most rushing TDs

Creighton Miller, ND–42	2
Tom Kuzma, M–42	2
Phil Carter, ND–80	2
Jamie Morris, M–86	2
Kevin McDougal, ND–93	2
Tyrone Wheatley, M–93	2

Most passing yards

Steve Beuerlein, ND–86	263
Todd Collins, M–93	251
Elvis Grbac, M–92	242
Jim Harbaugh, M–86	239
Rick Mirer, ND–91	234

Most pass attempts

Todd Collins, M–93	37
Steve Beuerlein, ND–86	33
Elvis Grbac, M–90	30
Joe Montana, ND–78	29
Elvis Grbac, M–92	28

Most pass receptions

Tony Hunter, ND–82	7
8 with	6

Most TD pass receptions

Doug Marsh, M–78	2
Anthony Carter, M–81	2
Desmond Howard, M–90	2
Many with	1

Most tackles (since '78)

Bob Golic, ND–78	26
Bob Crable, ND–81	20
Bob Crable, ND–80	19
Mike Stonebreaker, ND–88	19
Paul Girgash, M–82	18

Most TDs by rush/catch/runback

Jamie Morris, M–86	3
11 with	2

Most TDs passing

Rick Leach, M–78	3
John Wangler, M–80	3
Angelo Bertelli, ND–43	2
Steve Smith, M–81	2
Elvis Grbac, M–89–90–92	2
Rick Mirer, ND–91	2

Most pass completions

Todd Collins, M–93	22
Steve Beuerlein, ND–86	21
Elvis Grbac, M–91	20
Elvis Grbac, M–89–90–92	17

Most pass-receiving yards

Desmond Howard, M–90	133
Tony Smith, ND–91	121
Anthony Carter, M–81	99
Mercury Hayes, M–93	96
John Kolesar, M–86	93

Most field goals

Chuck Male, ND–79	4
John Carney, ND–85	4
Reggie Ho, ND–88	4
Mike Johnston, ND–82	3
Mike Gillette, M–85	2
Ted Gradel, ND–87	2
Kevin Pendergast, ND–93	2

Most interceptions

Paul White, M–42	2
Marion Body, M–80	2
Corny Southall, ND–87	2
Jeff Burris, ND–93	2
Many with	1

Individual records, career (1942–1993)

Most rushing yards

Jamie Morris, M–85–87	324
Creighton Miller, ND–42–43	236
Butch Woolfolk, M–80–81	211
Jon Vaughn, M–90	201
Ricky Powers, M–91–93	200

Most rushing attempts

Jamie Morris, M–85–87	65
Vagas Ferguson, ND–78–79	58
Phil Carter, ND–80–82	53
Ricky Powers, M–91–93	48
Stan Edwards, M–79–81	44

Most rushing TDs

Creighton Miller, ND–42–43	3
Jamie Morris, M–85–87	2
Tom Kuzma, M–42	2
Phil Carter, ND–80–82	2
Stan Edwards, M–79–81	2
Ricky Watters, ND–87–90	2
Kevin McDougal, ND–93	2
Tyrone Wheatley, M–91–93	2

Most TDs by rush/catch/runback

Creighton Miller, ND–42–43	4
Desmond Howard, M–89–91	4
Anthony Carter, M–79–82	3
Jamie Morris, M–85–87	3
Tyrone Wheatley, M–91–93	3

Most passing yards

Elvis Grbac, M–89–92	761
Rick Mirer, ND–90–92	560
Steve Beuerlein, ND–85–86	423
Jim Harbaugh, M–85–86	313
Steve Smith, M–81–82	289

Most TDs passing

Elvis Grbac, M–89–92	7
Angelo Bertelli, ND–42–43	3
Rick Leach, M–78	3
John Wangler, M–80	3
Steve Smith, M–81–82	3
Rick Mirer, ND–90–92	3

Most pass attempts

Elvis Grbac, M–89–92	102
Rick Mirer, ND–90–92	74
Steve Beuerlein, ND–85–86	56
Jim Harbaugh, M–85–86	40
Todd Collins, M–93	37

Most pass completions

Elvis Grbac, M–89–92	71
Rick Mirer, ND–90–92	41
Steve Beuerlein, ND–85–86	32
Jim Harbaugh, M–85–86	22
Todd Collins, M–93	22

Most pass receptions

Tony Hunter, ND–79–82	16
Desmond Howard, M–89–91	13
Dean Masztak, ND–78–81	11
Lake Dawson, ND–90–93	11
Mark Green, ND–86–88	10

Most pass-receiving yards

Desmond Howard, M–89–91	224
Lake Dawson, ND–90–93	218
Tony Hunter, ND–79–82	211
Anthony Carter, M–79–82	186
Tony Smith, ND–90–91	145

Most TD pass receptions

Desmond Howard, M–89–91	3
Doug Marsh, M–78	2
Anthony Carter, M–79–81	2
Greg McMurtry, M–86–89	2
Many with	1

Most field goals

John Carney, ND–85–86	5
Chuck Male, ND–79	4
Mike Gillette, M–85–88	4
Reggie Ho, ND–88	4
Mike Johnston, ND–82	3

Most tackles (since '78)		*Most interceptions*	
Bob Crable, ND–79–81	51	Jeff Burris, ND–90–93	3
Mark Messner, M–85–88	38	Paul White, M–42–43	2
Paul Girgash, M–80–82	34	Marion Body, M–80–82	2
Mike Stonebreaker, ND–88,90	29	John Krimm, ND–79–81	2
Andy Moeller, M–85–86	28	Corny Southall, ND–86–88	2

Individual records, career (1888–1909)

Rushing touchdowns		*Field goals*	
William Caley, M–98	3	Dave Allerdice, M–08–09	4
Joseph Maddock, M–02	3	(Only kicker in this era to	
James Duffy, M–88	2	have made a field–goal attempt.	
William Ball, M–88	2	He hit 3 in '08 and 1 in '09.)	
Pete Vaughan, ND–08–09	2		
Many with	1		

Coaches' records

MICHIGAN	*YEARS*	*W*	*L*	*T*	*Pct.*
Gustave Ferbert	1898–99	2	0	0	1.000
Biff Lea	1900	1	0	0	1.000
Fielding Yost	1902, 08–09	2	1	0	.667
Fritz Crisler	1942–43	1	1	0	500
Bo Schembechler	1978–89	4	6	0	.400
Gary Moeller	1990–	1	2	1	.375
NOTRE DAME	*YEARS*	*W*	*L*	*T*	*Pct.*
Frank Hering	1898–99*	0	2	0	.000
Pat O'Dea	1900	0	1	0	.000
James Faragher	1902	0	1	0	.000
Victor Place	1908	0	1	0	.000
Shorty Longman	1909	1	0	0	1.000
Frank Leahy	1942–43	1	1	0	.500
Dan Devine	1978–80	2	1	0	.667
Gerry Faust	1981–82, 85	1	2	0	.333
Lou Holtz	1986–	5	2	1	.688

*– James McWeeney is listed as the official coach of record for Notre Dame in 1899, but newspaper clippings indicate Frank Hering (ND's head coach the three previous years) was still in charge, at least for Michigan game preparations.

Appendix
Comparative all-time
accomplishments

Highest all-time winning percentage, Division I-A

1. Notre Dame	723	211	41	.763
2. Michigan	739	242	36	.744
3. Alabama	691	237	44	.734
4. Oklahoma	659	240	52	.720
5. Texas	687	273	32	.709

(Through 1993)

Most all-time victories, Division I-A

1. Michigan	739
2. Notre Dame	723
3. Alabama	691
4. Texas	687
5. Penn State	674

(Through 1993)

Most all-time national championships, Division I-A

1. Notre Dame	12	(1919–24–29–30–43–46–49–53–66–73–77–88)
2. Michigan	9	(1901–02–03–04–18–23–33–47–48)
3. Alabama	7	(1925–26–61–65–78–79–92)
4. Southern Cal	5	(1931–32–62–67–72)
Oklahoma	5	(1955–56–74–75–85)
Minnesota	5	(1934–35–36–40–41)

(According to the National Championship Foundation, which includes titles won before the writers and coaches polls began. Through 1993).

Most times ever ranked in the AP poll

1. Notre Dame	566
2. Michigan	535
3. Oklahoma	515
4. Ohio State	514
5. Alabama	498

(Through 1993)

Most consensus All-American selections, Division I-A

1. Notre Dame   90
2. Michigan   65
3. Southern Cal   57
4. Ohio State   53
5. Oklahoma   52

(Through 1992)

Notes

By chapter and section, the following notes list where information was gathered for this book. On occasion, these notes also expand on points made in the text, or reference in detail those portions of the text that refute common perceptions or previously published contentions.

The principal sources for this book were: (1) the athletic archives at the University of Michigan and the University of Notre Dame, both of which include a mass of correspondence and business records; (2) more than 30 interviews; (3) various student and local newspapers, plus clippings found in the many scrapbooks of Fielding Yost and Fritz Crisler at Michigan; (4) select books on college football in general, and on Notre Dame and Michigan in particular.

The University of Michigan's athletic archives are located at the Bentley Historical Library. Correspondence is referenced here by date, folder, box number, collection, followed by the abbreviation BHL-UM (for Bentley Historical Library–University of Michigan). The following collections are cited:

UM-BICIA (University of Michigan Board in Control of Intercollegiate Athletics)
CB (Charles Baird)
FHY (Fielding Harris Yost)
JFL (James Frederick Lawton)
EHR (Earl Henry [Spide] Rathbun)
JOM (James Orin Murfin)
HOC (Herbert Orin [Fritz] Crisler)

Similarly, the University of Notre Dame Archives (located on the sixth floor of the Hesburgh Library) house that school's athletic correspondence and records. Such are referenced here by date, collection code, box number/folder number or description, and followed by the abbreviation UNDA (for University of Notre Dame Archives). The following collections are cited:

UADR (University Athletic Director's Records, 1909–29)
UABM (University Athletic Business Manager, 1900–1940)
UFBA (University Faculty Board of Control of Athletics, 1902–20)
UVMU (University Vice President Michael Mulcaire, 1928–1933)
UVOC (University Vice Presidents J. Hugh O'Donnell and John J. Cavanaugh, 1934–46)
PATH (Notre Dame Athletics Collection Printed Material)
UPCO (University President: Charles L. O'Donnell, CSC, 1928–34)

1. Overview

The iceberg quote was in Francis Wallace's *Knute Rockne,* New York, 1960, page 187.

In 1981, the National Championship Foundation was founded by Mike Riter in an attempt to settle the squabbles of yesteryear. A 13-member panel investigated the records and accomplishments of the strongest teams in the country every year since 1869, and it came up with a definitive list of champions. According to the Foundation's findings, Notre Dame has won 12 titles (1919–24–29–30–43–46–49–53–66–73–77–88) and Michigan nine (1901–02–03–04–18–23–33–47–48). The next closest Division I-A school is Alabama with seven.

Frank Leahy's comment about perfection was in Wells Twombley's book, *Shake Down the Thunder: The Official Biography of Notre Dame's Frank Leahy,* Radnor, Pa., 1974, page 183.

2. Prehistory

The schools

The primary source for background on the University of Michigan was *History of the University of Michigan,* by Burke A. Hinsdale, Ann Arbor, 1906.

O.W. Stephenson's *Ann Arbor: The First Hundred Years,* Ann Arbor, 1927, described how the city got its odd name. The first settlers to this area along the Huron River were Elisha Rumsey and John Allen in 1824. Each of their wives was named Ann. The couples built an arbor of small trees, grapevines, and bushes, and the men decided to call not only the arbor but the entire plot of land they surveyed, "Ann's Arbor"—in honor of their better halves. The sprouting village, when organized, adopted the name Ann Arbor.

In the 1880s, Michigan and Harvard traded the title of largest college on the continent. The November 20, 1886, edition of the Michigan student weekly, *The Chronicle,* reported that Michigan's enrollment had reached 1,500, second nationally only to Harvard. On December 15, 1888, *The Chronicle* said Michigan's student body size had surpassed Harvard's.

Michigan was the first college in America to offer an entire course of electives, according to *The Chronicle* on October 23, 1886. This liberal curriculum was a point of pride among Michigan students.

In its September 8, 1888, edition, the Notre Dame student newspaper, *The Scholastic,* reprinted an *Ypsilanti Sentinel* story that described how Notre Dame was, "in all respects . . . exactly the opposite of the University of Michigan."

Notre Dame is now run by a lay board of trustees.

The story of how Father Sorin founded Notre Dame is in Rev. Arthur J. Hope's *Notre Dame: One Hundred Years,* Notre Dame, Ind., 1948.

Notre Dame's primitive academic structure of the 1800s was well described in a dissertation by Philip S. Moore, C.S.C., entitled, *Academic Development, University of Notre Dame: Past, Present and Future,* privately printed, Notre Dame, Ind., 1960.

The holier-than-thou academic attitude adopted by such Western Conference schools as Michigan was vividly illustrated in (1) Sperber, pages 19–20; and (2) *The Chronicle* of October 23, 1887, which in the following excerpt revealed the utter disdain at Michigan for demoninational schools:

> Presbyterians of the state propose to found a denominational college. . . . Every friend of the University [of Michigan] or, indeed, of higher education, will sincerely wish them total failure in their attempt. The state now has too many little denominational schools—institutions whose very existance is a bane to modern culture but who tenaciously exist by means of their sectarianism and the vanity of some unlettered *Croesus.* . . . They slur higher education in giving their degrees for a minimum of work in quality and quantity.

Champions of the West

This early history of Michigan football was culled in part from Will Perry's *The Wolverines: A Story of Michigan Football,* Huntsville, Ala., 1974, pages 20–29, and from

The University of Michigan Football Scrapbook, by Richard M Cohen, Jordan A. Deutsch, and David S. Neft, Indianapolis/New York, 1978, pages 9–12.

A Chronology of Changes in Collegiate Football Rules, 1873–1954, a dissertation by Lawrence James Green, State University of Iowa, 1955, is an outstanding source for determining how the game evolved, year by year.

Through 1896, Michigan was the only western school ever brave enough to travel East to play Harvard, Yale, or Princeton. (Source: *The Michigan Alumnus,* December 1896 edition.)

3. Carefully taught: 1887–88

I. Fall term, '87

Notre Dame's unique, early brand of football was described in a letter from George W. DeHaven to Fielding H. Yost, October 21, 1939, "Papers 1939 October (1)" folder, Box 25, UM-BICIA, BHL-UM. All other quotes from DeHaven in this chapter were found in that letter.

Life and attitudes in 1880s America were fully described in an article in the January 1988 issue of *National Geographic* magazine.

The November 16, 1889, issue of *The Chronicle* indicated Harless went by the name of Billy, not William.

Notre Dame and Michigan registry records, and Michigan alumni records, supplied much of the background on Harless and DeHaven. The Chicago Historical Society located the homes of their families as being in the downtown area.

The *Scholastic*s of 1884–85 and 1885–86 regularly listed the athletic and recreational activities of Harless and DeHaven. The April 17, 1886, edition said both were members of the Evangeline rowing team, and the June 30 edition reported this team's campus victory.

The background on Patrick Connors/Brother Paul was found in his obituary in *The Scholastic,* December 16, 1893. During the late 1880s, *The Scholastic* was forever reporting on Brother Paul's integral role in the campus athletic scene.

The *Cornell Sun*'s stinging comment was reprinted in *The Scholastic,* October 16, 1886.

Harless's and DeHaven's athletic activities at Michigan were described by DeHaven in his letter to Yost, and were corroborated in the following editions of *The Chronicle:* November 6 and 20, 1886; May 31, 1887; and November 12, 1887.

The story of how the game was arranged was pieced together from reports in *The Scholastic* (October 29 and November 19, 1887) and from DeHaven's recollections to Yost.

The arrangement of Michigan's game in Chicago against Northwestern, and its subsequent cancellation, were described in an untitled, apparently unpublished early history of Michigan football found in the "Manuscripts and Articles/Fielding H. Yost & Career (1)" folder, Box 1, JFL, BHL-UM.

In his letter to Yost, DeHaven said Brother Paul told him the Notre Dame boys had "practiced our game from a book." Yet when Michigan arrived, the Notre Damers asked to mix the teams "so they would get the idea." DeHaven also said Ann Arbor merchants paid for the Wolverines' trips, but *The Chronicle* on November 26, 1887, said students chipped in $150 on this one.

The chronology of Michigan's trip, from Ann Arbor to Notre Dame to Chicago and back, plus the two games played along the way, was pieced together from subsequent stories in the November 26, 1887, issues of *The Chronicle* and *The Scholastic.*

Harry Jewett's American record of 44 feet, 8¼ inches in the "hop, step, and jump" was set in Detroit on August 17, 1890, and reported in the September 27, 1890, edition of *The Scholastic*. James E. Duffy's record 55-yard field goal was listed in a *New York Times* story on October 18, 1916.

Rev. Bernard J. Ill, then a 15-year-old student, recalled the Michigan players' request for Notre Dame to tone it down in a story in the *South Bend Tribune*, November 13, 1942.

Frank Fehr's comment about the "practice game" was made to the *South Bend Tribune*'s Joe Doyle in the 1950s and reprinted in that paper on September 17, 1978.

Additional details of the Harvard game came from the *Chicago Tribune* story of November 25. The Chicago Historical Society provided proof of the Harvard School's existence and early athletic prowess.

Fehr's comment about the need to become organized was also made to Doyle in the 1950s and was reprinted in Doyle's book, *Fighting Irish: A Century of Notre Dame Football*, Charlottesville, Va., 1987, page 34.

The formation of Notre Dame's Rugby Football Association was described in the December 3, 1887, edition of *The Scholastic*.

II., III. Spring term, '88

The January 1988 edition of *National Geographic* described the harshness of the 1888 winter.

The Scholastic, in its January 21–April 28 editions, was the sole source for all information on Notre Dame's winter fundraisers and spring football activities—likewise *The Chronicle* for Michigan football preparations in that time frame.

The Scholastic provided additional detail on how the games were arranged in the March 24 and 31 issues.

Details of Michigan's trip, and the game accounts, were pooled from the April 21 and 28 editions of *The Scholastic*, the April 21 edition of the *South Bend Tribune*, and the April 28 issue of *The Chronicle*.

John W. Heisman—a famous coach in the early 1900s and namesake for the famous trophy—played at Brown and Penn from 1887 to 1891, and he described how arguments continually delayed games in a story reproduced in Richard Whittingham's *Saturday Afternoon: College Football and the Men Who Made the Day*, New York, 1985, page 18.

Green's rules dissertation helped describe how touchdowns and conversions were scored in 1888.

The *South Bend Tribune* account of the Friday game reported that "some money changed hands on the result, many having wagered Notre Dame would not make a score."

Brother Leander was the campus prefect who remembered that Notre Dame split the weekend series; this was reported in the October 3, 1907, edition of the *South Bend Tribune*.

Michigan's "favorable impression" was reported in the April 28 edition of *The Scholastic*.

Michigan alumni records and the Chicago Historical Society supplied information about what Harless and DeHaven did in adulthood.

Sadness draped the Notre Dame campus when Brother Paul died, as described in his obit in *The Scholastic,* December 16, 1893.

4. Michigan and its pesky kid brother: 1888–1900

Homebodies

Michigan's snub on Thanksgiving 1888 weekend was discussed in *The Scholastic* on December 4, 1888.

The Scholastic and *The Chronicle* were always reprinting views and news from other colleges' papers in this time. Michigan generally couldn't stand to be downtrodden by snotty Easterners, just as Notre Dame challenged any unfavorable comment made by a snotty state university in the West.

Through 1909, *The Scholastic* always made the biggest deals out of those athletic contests against Michigan. In the late 1880s, Notre Dame was especially hung up on Michigan. When the Wolverines closed their 1889 season disastrously (with back-to-back shellackings from Cornell and the Chicago Athletic Association), *The Scholastic* crowed on December 7, 1889, that it was "a continuance of work begun by Notre Dame."

🏈   🏈   🏈

On November 14, 1891, *The Scholastic* reported that "football is the order of the day. . . . The eleven must get to work! Only 11 days more." Eleven days more being November 25. Nothing more, however, was ever written about the game with Michigan, or why it didn't come off.

🏈   🏈   🏈

Nowhere was a single document found to prove conclusively that a travel ban was in effect from 1892 to 1897. In fact, no other Notre Dame football books have ever mentioned it. But there can be little doubt a ban indeed was in place. In 1894, Notre Dame's Brother Hugh had to turn down a request to play the Wolverines in Battle Creek because, as he informed Michigan grad manager of athletics, Charles Baird, "the faculty will not permit the team to travel, hence they cannot play anywhere but upon their own grounds" (letter, July 28, 1894, "June 1894–July 1894" folder, Box 1, CB, BHL-UM). And because Notre Dame played only two road games in that six-season span, one should naturally presume this faculty edict was not limited to just 1894.

The "kill the fighting Irish" story was in the *1989 Notre Dame Football Guide,* page 342. The January 1930 edition of *The Notre Dame Alumnus,* page 140, said athletics were always "in the red" prior to Jesse Harper's time (1913).

The exploits of, and crackdown on, the Michigan football team in the early 1890s was pieced together from: various stories in *The Chronicle* in 1889 and in its successor, *The Michigan Daily,* in 1890 and '91; the January 1897 edition of *The Michigan Alumnus,* pages 84–86; and Perry, pages 32–33.

Carefully coached

An example of *The Scholastic*'s routine praise of the Wolverine baseball team's sportsmanship was in the April 23, 1892, edition: "The gentlemanly behavior of the visiting team attracted universal commendation." This feeling was usually reciprocated. That year *The Michigan Daily* wasn't even upset over the "importation of four or five professional players by Notre Dame for the express purpose of downing the Univ.

of Michigan team," and *The Daily* in fact called it "the highest tribute paid to the Michigan nine on its Western trip."

The story about James Kivlan was in Gene Schoor's *100 Years of Notre Dame Football*, New York, 1987, page 22. T.D. Mott, Jr.'s, letter to Baird, September 24, 1894, is in "September 1894" folder, Box 1, CB, BHL-UM.

Today, James L.D. Morrison is incorrectly listed in Notre Dame records as J.L. Morison. His letter to Baird, October 7, 1894, is in "October 1894" folder, Box 1, CB, BHL-UM. Morrison's "indefatigable" teaching was reported in the October 13, 1894, edition of *The Scholastic*. His departure for Hillsdale was announced in the October 20, 1894, edition.

In fall 1895, *The Scholastic* failed ever to mention H.G. Hadden's playing days with the Wolverines, and that must be why Notre Dame historians have never reported it.

The story of Hadden's hiring, coaching, and abrupt departure was in *The Scholastic*, issues September 14, October 26, November 2, November 9, and November 16.

Hadden wrote Charles Baird on October 11 that his parents wouldn't let him leave Chicago. That letter is in "October 1895" folder, Box 1, CB, BHL-UM. Hadden's tour of the East was mentioned in *The Scholastic* of October 26. The Michigan alumnus who complained that Hadden had "evidently deserted his colors" was Harry M. Bates, in a letter to Baird on October 23, 1895, "October 1895" folder, CB, BHL-UM.

The Naughty Nineties

The sad state of precrackdown college football in the Midwest was best described in *The Michigan Alumnus*, January 1897, pages 84–86, and January 1898, pages 108–109.

The formation of the Western Conference, and its charter regulations, were chronicled in *The Big Ten* by Kenneth L. (Tug) Wilson and Jerry Brondfield, Englewood Cliffs, N.J., 1967, pages 50–53.

The *South Bend Tribune*'s recollection of Notre Dame's "little respect for amateurs" was in the September 17, 1898, edition.

Notre Dame's reform measures were discussed in Doyle, page 38. Frank Hering's dual coaching role was reported in the *South Bend Tribune*, September 29, 1898.

The story of Michigan's tramp player in 1897 was in *The Michigan Alumnus*, January 1898, pages 108–109.

IV. Michigan . . . convincingly, '98

The Michigan Alumnus, in its December 1898 edition, had this to say of the worst-to-best scheduling scenario:

The November games are, of course, the most important, as during this month the Varsity meets all those colleges which are thought as having any effect in determining the position which a team is to occupy in the race for Western championship honors.

Michigan, for one, continued to schedule in a worst-to-best fashion through the 1920s.

The Michigan Daily's concern about Notre Dame's prowess was printed October 21, 1898. The quote about Notre Dame trying to "clinch her claim," and the South Bend betting odds, were printed in the *South Bend Tribune*, October 22, 1898.

Game details were culled from the October 23 editions of *The Michigan Daily*, the *Detroit News*, and the *Detroit Free Press;* the October 24 issue of the *South Bend Tribune;* the October 29 issue of *The Scholastic;* and the November 1898 edition of *The Michigan Alumnus*.

Rev. John Cavanaugh's letter to Michigan authorities was printed in *The Michigan*

Daily, November 2, 1898. The next day, the *Daily* commended Cavanaugh's actions in an editorial.

V. Getting a line on Notre Dame, '99

The epoch was noted by *The Scholastic* in its Easter 1899 edition.

The *South Bend Tribune* quote about Notre Dame's "grim determination" appeared in the October 18, 1899, edition. *The Michigan Daily*'s grim forecast was on October 17.

Details of the "Businessmen's Game" were in the untitled, apparently unpublished early history of Michigan football, previously noted.

Game details were pieced together from the October 19 editions of *The Michigan Daily,* the *South Bend Tribune,* the *Detroit News,* and the *Detroit Free Press;* the October 21 issue of *The Scholastic;* and the November 1899 edition of *The Michigan Alumnus.*

The "hoo-doo" quote also appeared in the October 21 issue of *The Scholastic.*

VI. Another slipup, '00

Game details were culled from the November 18 editions of *The Michigan Daily,* the *Detroit News,* and the *Detroit Free Press;* the November 19 issue of the *South Bend Tribune;* the November 24 issue of *The Scholastic* (in which the quote about Red Salmon also appeared); and the December 1898 edition of *The Michigan Alumnus.*

This quote appeared in the March 31, 1900, edition of *The Scholastic.*

5. Undercurrents of ill will: 1901–08

Fielding H. Yost

Much of the background on Yost was found in *Fielding Yost's Legacy to the University of Michigan,* by John Behee, Ann Arbor, 1971—an exhaustive, scholarly study of Yost's 40-year tenure at Michigan.

The one year Yost didn't coach from 1901 to 1926 was 1924. On page 26, Behee reported Yost was hired in 1901 at a salary of $2,300—twice the annual pay of a full-time professor at Michigan.

Ring Lardner made his remark about Yost's personality in a letter to M.L. Burton, president of the University of Michigan. Lardner repeated these comments in a May 23, 1921, letter to someone listed only as "Carl," and a copy of that letter is in "1921 May (2)" folder, Box 4, UM-BICIA, BHL-UM.

Edwin Pope's comments about Yost were reprinted in Behee, page 46. The anecdote about Yost's fishing trip was found in the draft manuscript of J. Fred Lawton's book, *"Hurry Up" Yost in Story and Song,* in "Yost, Fielding H. (1)" folder, Box 2, JFL, BHL-UM. Grantland Rice wrote his "heart, soul, brain, and tongue" remark in his April 29, 1941, column that appeared in the *Detroit Free Press.*

Yost's .826 winning percentage remains the sixth all-time highest among all Division I-A coaches, according to the *Official 1993 NCAA Football Guide.*

Off the track

The transformation of the W.I.A.A. into the I.C.A.A. was generally described in Wilson and Brondfield, pages 60–61. The controversy that followed this reorganization was detailed in *The Michigan Daily* in the following editions of 1901: January 30, February 14 (which also had the Dan Murphy quote), February 26, and February 28. *The Scholastic* stated Notre Dame's stand in its March 23 issue.

The Western Conference's indifferent attitude toward Notre Dame in these early years was described in Sperber, pages 18–20, 41–42. *The Michigan Daily,* on March 24, 1898, reported Michigan's opposition to Notre Dame entering the W.I.A.A.

It was at an A.A.U. track meet in the East where a Notre Dame player was ruled ineligible, according to the *Detroit News* on February 23, 1901.

The *South Bend Sunday News* reported on September 21, 1902, that Michigan and Chicago "have, in the last two years, severed athletic relations with Notre Dame, in fact, prohibited its athletes from taking part in the Conference meet in Chicago last spring on a minor charge of professionalism." This report was reprinted in *The Scholastic* on October 4, 1902.

Harry M. Bates to M.A. Quinlan, March 15, 1902, is in the "Correspondence" folder, UFBA, UNDA. Notre Dame's desire to strictly abide by conference rules in 1902—and its applications for admission into the conference both in November 1902 and November 1903—are discussed in the minutes of the Board of Control, located in the "Minutes Book, 1902–16," UFBA, UNDA.

The end of the Big Nine's boycott of Notre Dame, and the resumption of the Michigan football series, was reported in the March 1, 1902, edition of *The Scholastic.*

VII. A most magnificent struggle, '02

Both *The Scholastic* on March 1, 1902, and *The Michigan Daily* on March 11, 1902, listed Ann Arbor as the original site of the 1902 game.

Michigan alumni in Grand Rapids had successfully lobbied to have Michigan and Cornell play a baseball game there in June 1899, and the Michigan Athletic Association cleared $300 (*Michigan Daily,* June 8, 17, and 21, 1899). That summer, the site of the Michigan–Notre Dame football game was moved to Grand Rapids. But for some reason, on September 26 the Michigan Board in Control moved it back to Ann Arbor, as documented in the board minutes, Volume 1, Dec. 1893–March 1900, Box 48, UM-BICIA, BHL-UM.

Similarly, the Toledo alumni induced Michigan officials to move the June 1902 Michigan-Cornell baseball game to Toledo. On June 4 *The Michigan Daily* said these alums had "previously felt themselves neglected." The baseball game was a success, as reported in the June 15 edition of the *Detroit News-Tribune.*

A reporter from the *Toledo Bee* indicated to Baird that Notre Dame's and Michigan's alumni in Toledo were of similar size. This letter, October 3, 1902, is in "Papers 1902 October" folder, Box 1, UM-BICIA, BHL-UM.

The state of Notre Dame's team before the game was mentioned in the October 11, 1902, edition of *The Scholastic.*

Game details were pieced together from the October 19, 1902, editions of *The Michigan Daily,* the *Detroit News-Tribune,* and the *Detroit Free Press;* the October 20 edition of the *South Bend Tribune;* the October 25 issue of *The Scholastic;* the November 1902 issue of *The Michigan Alumnus;* and from the recollections of spectator Aaron B. Cohn, who wrote a detailed piece for the *Toledo Blade* 50 years later, on November 16, 1952. A clipping of this story was found in the Notre Dame Sports Information Department's files.

Willie Heston's contention that he scored 92 touchdowns was made to Michigan alumnus Spide Rathbun in an undated correspondence, "Rose Bowl contracts, 1906, 1921; information on football scores, 1879–1902" folder, Box 1, EHR, BHL-UM. "I tried to keep an accurate count when they started to run up," Heston wrote. "Not that it makes any great difference . . . but I like to be accurate about it."

O'Malley's chicanery, Yost's subsequent complaints, and the officials' resultant actions were detailed in the *Detroit Free Press*'s game report.

From 1893 to 1902, 654 known serious injuries were attributed to college football, and football at all levels had caused 68 deaths nationwide from 1901 to 1904 (Behee, pages 59–61). The November 25, 1906, edition of the *Chicago Tribune* noted that the number of Americans killed playing football that year was 11, down from 18 in 1905. The writer of this story seemed impressed that in 1906 "not one fatality has occurred in the game played by the larger American colleges."

The *Detroit News* game account said Herrnstein suffered two "ugly gashes" around his eyes, yet after being bandaged almost to the point of blindness, he continued playing. The Redden-Lonergan slugging incident was reported in the *Detroit Free Press* game report.

Baird's comment about the crowd size was made to the *Toledo Blade* afterward and reprinted in Cohn's 1952 account.

A lasting first impression

Baird's numerous scheduling consultations with alumni in the mid- to late-1890s are in Box 1, CB, BHL-UM.

It appears all the scheduling pleas sent to Michigan from other schools prior to the 1901 and 1903 seasons remain in file folders for these years in Box 1, UM-BICIA, BHL-UM. It is clear, from both the wording and sheer volume of these requests, that Baird and Yost could easily afford to be choosy.

Byrne M. Daly's letters to Baird (March 13, March 18, and May 3, 1903) are in the "Papers 1903 March–April" and "Papers 1903 May–June" folders, Box 1, UM-BICIA, BHL-UM.

In 1903, Baird did not yet make carbon copies of his outgoing letters, and Notre Dame athletic correspondence—housed in that school's archives—dates back only to 1909. So there is no way to know conclusively what Baird said in his return letters to Daly. There can be no doubting, however, that Baird sought Yost's approval for scheduling Notre Dame—then didn't get it. If Baird himself had had concerns about scheduling Notre Dame, he certainly would not have offered Daly the two dates in his first reply. What's more, the concerns he cited to Daly in his second reply (Notre Dame's snap interference and slugging in the 1902 game) have Yost's name written all over them.

The minutes of the Michigan Board in Control indicate when Beloit and Drake filled the Wolverines' final two vacancies, in Volume 2, Oct. 1, 1900–Nov. 4, 1910, Box 48, UM-BICIA, BHL-UM.

Best way out of a bad matter

The events surrounding the national rules changes, and Michigan's fight with the Western Conference from 1906 to 1908 on policy matters, were discussed in outstanding detail by Behee, pages 59–74.

The *Ann Arbor Daily Times News* quote appeared on November 5, 1910.

At the April 8, 1907, meeting of the Michigan Board in Control, athletic director Baird submitted for ratification an October 19 game against Notre Dame. At the April 23 board meeting, "it was moved and carried that the director of outdoor athletics be permitted to schedule proposed football games with Notre Dame University and Wabash College" (Volume 2, Oct. 1, 1900–Nov. 4, 1910, Box 48, UM-BICIA, BHL-UM).

Unfortunately, no other references either to the scheduling or canceling of this 1907 game—after a wide, painstaking search—were found anywhere. It seems quite likely, then, that Michigan athletic director Baird pulled the plug on the game before he ever approached Notre Dame officials about scheduling it. That would explain why nothing was ever written about negotiations in *The Scholastic* or the *South Bend Tribune,* even in retrospect.

The *Indianapolis Star,* in its October 13–19 editions, reported that 4,000 people at an astronomical price of $5 a head were due to attend the Michigan-Wabash game on October 19. Michigan was guaranteed half the take—$10,000. Conversely, the Wolverines could have perhaps drawn 5,000 for a home game against Notre Dame, and at the usual ticket price of 50 cents a head that would have grossed only $2,500—before Notre Dame's cut. So if the October 19 vacancy came down to either Notre Dame at home or Wabash at Indianapolis, the latter simply would have been too lucrative for Michigan to turn down.

VIII. Time was on Michigan's side, '08

Game details were pieced together from the October 18, 1908, editions of *The Michigan Daily,* the *Detroit News-Tribune,* and the *Detroit Free Press;* the October 19 edition of the *South Bend Tribune;* the October 24 issue of *The Scholastic;* and the November 1908 issue of *The Michigan Alumnus.*

Harry (Red) Miller's recollection of the disputed play involving Paul McDonald was in Gene Schoor's *A Treasury of Notre Dame Football,* New York, 1962, page 18.

Yost's quote on the importance of the kicking game was in the *Los Angeles Examiner,* April 10, 1935. A clipping of this story is in a scrapbook of Yost's, Box 45, UM-BICIA, BHL-UM.

Postgame quotes were culled from the above game reports.

6. Disintegration: 1909–10

IX. Red-letter day, '09

E.A. Batchelor's story appeared in the November 7, 1909, edition of the *Detroit Free Press.* The official origin of the moniker "Fighting Irish" has forever been disputed. The *Detroit Free Press,* though, popularized the nickname with continued references in stories and headlines over at least the next year. According to the *1990 Notre Dame Football Guide,* page 338, the nickname wasn't officially embraced by the school until 1927.

Pregame perspective was extracted from the following newspapers in their November 2–6, 1909, editions: the *South Bend Tribune,* the *Chicago Tribune,* the *Detroit News,* the *Detroit Free Press,* the *Ann Arbor Daily Times News, The Scholastic,* and *The Michigan Daily.* Also helpful were: Chet Grant's *Before Rockne at Notre Dame,* South Bend, 1978, pages 105–120; clippings from other Ann Arbor/Detroit newspapers circa September and October 1909, pasted in one of Yost's scrapbooks, Box 45, UM-BICIA, BHL-UM.

Longman's "hiding" of Red Miller against Pittsburgh, and the ruse of not using his pet pass plays, was described in a retrospective story in the *Ann Arbor Daily Times News* on November 3, 1910.

Game details and postgame quotes were culled from the November 7, 1909, editions of the *Chicago Tribune, The Michigan Daily,* the *Detroit News-Tribune,* and the *Detroit Free Press;* the November 8 editions of the *South Bend Tribune* and *Ann Arbor Daily Times News;* the November 13 issue of *The Scholastic;* and the December 1909 issue of *The Michigan Alumnus.*

Miller's recollections of the game were in Schoor's *A Treasury of Notre Dame Football,* pages 20–21.

The story of Vaughan's plunge leaving "the mark of the goal post . . . clearly on the back of his jersey" was in Wallace's *Knute Rockne,* pages 37–38. The story of Vaughan knocking the goalpost over with his head was often told by Rev. Matthew Walsh when he was vice president a decade later, according to Grant, page 136.

Vaughan's "fighting Irish" plea was found in the *1990 Notre Dame Football Guide,* page 338.

Yost's "kicking game" was described in general by H.G. Salsinger in the *Detroit News,* November 28, 1926, and in detail beginning on page 78 of Yost's "Football Notes" binder, Box 42, UM-BICIA, BHL-UM. An undated clipping from the *Columbus Citizen,* circa 1931 (in outsize scrapbook "1928–35," FHY, BHL-UM) also summarized his approach—which can be corroborated by any newspaper play-by-play account of virtually any Michigan game between 1901 and 1926.

Miller's recollection of meeting Yost was in Schoor's *A Treasury of Notre Dame Football,* page 21.

Who's No. 1?—'09

The chronology of the great western football debate of 1909 was pieced together from stories in the following newspapers, between November 7, 1909, and January 17, 1910: *The Scholastic, The Michigan Daily,* the *South Bend Tribune,* the *Chicago Tribune,* the *Detroit Free Press,* the *Detroit News-Tribune,* the *Ann Arbor Daily Times News.*

Yost's quote before the Minnesota game was made to the *Detroit News-Tribune* on Monday, November 15. His "practice was what we wanted" quote appeared in the November 22 edition of the *South Bend Tribune.* His quote about Michigan winning the games that counted came from the November 26 issue of the *Detroit Free Press,* and remarks about his all-western selections appeared in the November 23 edition of that paper.

The December 25 issue of *Collier's* reported that after Notre Dame's tie with Marquette, "few of those who control the destinies of football in the West were willing to concede that Notre Dame won the Western championship." Walter Camp's selections and comments were in the November 28 issue of the *Detroit News-Tribune.* On December 21, the *Detroit News-Tribune* reported that *Baseball Magazine* (commonly known as "Outdoor" magazine) in its January edition ranked the top eight teams nationally, and Michigan was placed third behind Yale and Harvard; Notre Dame did not even make the list.

Chet Grant devoted about a third of his book, *Before Rockne at Notre Dame,* to Notre Dame's 1909 season. He argued Notre Dame's merits as champion of the West and quoted numerous newspaper commentaries for backing. But all the accolades Grant cited were bestowed *before* Notre Dame's tie with Marquette. By December, most critics had changed their minds and awarded Michigan the mythical title. Grant made no mention of this.

The *Cleveland Plain-Dealer* was one of the prominent voices that continued to back Notre Dame, as reported in the November 29 issue of the *South Bend Tribune.*

The "contraband cargo" quip appeared December 3 in the *Chicago Tribune,* and was reprinted in *The Scholastic* on December 19.

In a September 28, 1907, story, the *South Bend Tribune* explained why Notre Dame was about to stop complying with the strict conference rules. Michigan's rules of this era were clearly described in the board minutes, Volume 2, Oct. 1, 1900–Nov. 4, 1910, UM-BICIA, BHL-UM.

The "considerable laughter around Ann Arbor" was reported in December 12 in the *Detroit News-Tribune.* George J. Finnigan's poem appeared in *The Scholastic*'s November 27 issue, which was devoted almost entirely to Notre Dame's championship season—an unprecedented emphasis on athletics in the student newspaper.

Mucker spirit

The story about the unidentified Notre Dame player saying he had played "nine years" was printed by the *Detroit News-Tribune* on November 6, 1910.

The saga of how this game was scheduled, how relations between the schools completely soured in the spring, and how the 1910 cancellation ultimately came about, was pieced together principally from (1) reams of stories printed between November 1909 and November 1910 in all the Detroit, Ann Arbor, South Bend, Chicago, and campus newspapers previously referenced, and (2) reams of athletic correspondence between the two schools found in the archives at both universities. The task of unraveling this age-old mystery was made easy by the fact that nearly every vital correspondence between these schools in 1910 remains in the archives at the University of Michigan (in the form of Michigan copies, Notre Dame originals). Contents of the few important correspondences that didn't survive were discussed in postcancellation newspaper reports.

Unless otherwise noted, all letters and telegrams quoted in the text sent to or from Michigan can be found in the massive "Notre Dame, 1910–1945" folder, Box 36, UM-BICIA, BHL-UM.

The quote about there being "no glory" for a conference school to beat Notre Dame was printed February 25, 1911, in *The Scholastic*.

The January 15 excerpt from the Notre Dame Board of Control minutes is in the "Minutes Book, 1902–16," UFBA, UNDA. The events of Curtis's trip to Ann Arbor were rehashed after the cancellation in various newspaper reports, especially the November 8 and 9, 1910, editions of the *South Bend Tribune*. Notre Dame has the only surviving copy of the game contract, and it is in "Contracts-Football-M" folder, UABM, UNDA.

Longman's rehiring was announced January 26, 1910. Doug Roby recounted the story about Longman parading his dog around Ann Arbor in an interview at his home on July 31, 1990. Longman's comment about having it "rubbed in" on him is in F.C. Longman to (Ed) Lynch, April 7, 1910, UADR 1/61, UNDA.

Details of the Notre Dame–Michigan baseball game in Ann Arbor, and the conference track meet in Urbana, appeared in all the relevant newspapers on June 5, 1910. California's protest of Dimmick and Philbrook was discussed in greater detail in November 1910. *The Scholastic*'s "hundredth time" quotation was extracted from that part of the November 12 editorial which recounted the infamous June weekend.

The two ex-Wolverines who coached out West were Fred Norcross at Oregon State from 1906 to 1908, and Ev Sweeley at Washington State in 1904 and 1905. Stan Borleske played football and baseball as a freshman at Whitman College in Walla Walla, Wash., in the 1907–08 school year, according to the student yearbook, *Waiilatpu '09, Volume III*. He appeared with Dimmick and Philbrook in the '07 football team photo.

The Michigan board minutes from the key October 4 meeting do not indicate that Bartelme was instructed to investigate the Notre Dame trio. The fact that he started a vigorous investigation the very next day, however, is strong evidence that he was.

The only key correspondences not located in either school's archives are the ultimatum Michigan wired Notre Dame on November 3, the special-delivery letter Notre Dame sent Michigan that night, and Michigan's final wire to Notre Dame on November 4. Newspaper reports, however, later discussed the contents of these communications.

Yost denied having "anything whatsoever" to do with the cancellation, in a letter to his secretary, Andrew Baker, January 27, 1936, "Papers 1936 January (1)" folder, Box 21, UM-BICIA, BHL-UM. Bartelme disputed this in a letter to Baker, March 2, 1936, "Papers 1936 February (1)" folder, Box 21, UM-BICIA, BHL-UM. Yost's "sweet chance" comment was printed in the November 7, 1910, edition of the *Ann Arbor Daily Times News*.

The Notre Dame team's options for train travel on Friday, November 4 were indicated in F.C. Noble, ticket agent, to James S. Hope, October 29, 1910, UADR 1/93, UNDA.

●　●　●

The Michigan Daily's editorial appeared November 5, while *The Scholastic*'s was printed November 12.

Bartelme's recollection about Crumley appeared in the same letter to Baker, noted above. The hazy recollection told to Francis Wallace appeared in his book, *The Notre Dame Story*, New York, 1949, page 51. The playing histories of all Notre Dame players of that era were found in the *1990 Notre Dame Football Guide*. Knute Rockne's remembrances of Foley first appeared in his ghost-written autobiography, and were reproduced in *Knute Rockne: His Life and Legend*, by Robert Quackenbush and Mike Bynum, Chicago, 1988, pages 54–55. Philbrook's efforts with regard to Clinnen are in Geo. W. Philbrook to Mr. Jas. Hope, September 14, 1910, UADR 1/105, UNDA.

Stan Borleske's banishment due to "summer baseball" was reported in the *Waiilatpu '09, Volume IV*. The letter supporting Harry Curtis's contention is F.C. Longman to [Ed] Copper [Lynch], April 28, 1910, UADR 1/61, UNDA. That "Copper" was Ed Lynch was indicated in his bio on page 185 of the November 27, 1909, edition of *The Scholastic*. Edythe Longman's charge against Yost was leveled in the *Detroit News*, January 25, 1936. Edwin Pope's remark about Yost's early recruiting tactics was reprinted in Behee, page 107.

7. "Do not favor Notre Dame game": 1911–17

Pitt was viewed as a renegade school, in both the East and the West, right up until about 1940. Conference schools, meanwhile, refused to schedule St. Louis and Marquette. The lack of respect given the latter school was made clear in William E. Cotter to Jesse C. Harper, December 18, 1912, UADR 3/32, UNDA.

Michigan Agricultural College's boycott of Notre Dame was indicated in Harper to J.F. Macklin, December 14, 1912, UADR 3/52, UNDA. Notre Dame's desire to come clean and the abysmal failures of the grad managers were detailed in two letters from Cotter to Harper, December 16, 1912, and December 18, 1912, UADR 3/32, UNDA.

A bio of Harper appeared in *The Scholastic*, November 24, 1917. His remark about "tackling a big job" was in the above-noted letter to Macklin. Cotter urged Harper to try to resume relations with Michigan in his December 18 letter. The conference's ban against playing Michigan was discussed in Behee, page 77, and the hesitance of Ivy League powers to play the Wolverines was noted in many letters throughout Box 1, JOM, BHL-UM.

Harper's initial scheduling pleas to Michigan are in Harper to Bartelme, December 11, 1912, UADR 3/49, UNDA; Harper to Bartelme, January 14, 1913, UADR 3/49, UNDA.

No copies remain, either at Notre Dame or Michigan, of Harper's letter to Michigan in December 1913, but the Michigan board minutes (Volume 3, June 1, 1910–June 2, 1927, Box 48, UM-BICIA, BHL-UM) explain why and when Michigan resumed relations.

Harper's request to play Michigan at Comiskey Park is in Harper to Bartelme, November 19, 1914, UADR 4/83, UNDA.

Michigan officials discussed adding Notre Dame to the 1915 football schedule in these letters located in "Correspondences 1914, November–December" folder, Box 1, JOM, BHL-UM: Bartelme to James E. Duffy, December 19, 1914; Murfin to Bartelme, December 21, 1914; Duffy to Bartelme, December 22, 1914; Bartelme to Murfin, December 22, 1914 (which includes a copy of Bartelme to Duffy, December 22, 1914, in which Bartelme reprints Yost's telegram verbatim); and Murfin to Bartelme, December 23, 1914.

That Harper had won over Bartelme is plainly evident in the way Bartelme closed his letter to Harper, September 27, 1917, UADR 5/197, UNDA: "Trusting Notre Dame will have every success in all branches of athletics, and with very kindest personal regards, I am, Yours sincerely, P.G. Bartelme."

🏈   🏈   🏈

The "Yielding Fost" satire appeared in the December 13, 1913, edition of *The Scholastic.*

8. The hillbilly vs. the likeable fellow: 1918–31

Personal antagonism

Knute Rockne described his "first big thrill" in football in an excerpt from his ghost-written autobiography reprinted in Bynum and Quackenbush, page 167. Yost's first tragic moment—and other details of the 1905 Michigan-Chicago game—were described in an unidentified clipping in Coehn, Deutsch, and Neft, page 35. For years, this game was remembered as the greatest football spectacle ever staged in the West. A who's who of soon-to-be famous football men was present at Marshall Field that day. In addition to Stagg, Yost, and Rockne, there was legendary writer Ring Lardner, Maroons players Jesse Harper and Walter Eckersall, and Wolverine Shorty Longman.

The "personal antagonism" quote was in Wallace's *Knute Rockne,* page 38.

General background on Rockne was culled, in part, from Sperber; Wallace's *Knute Rockne;* and Ken Rappaport's *Wake Up The Echoes,* Tomball, Tex., 1988. Will Rogers's quote appeared in Bynum and Quackenbush, page 5. Rockne's "ox-knuckled" and "bovine expressions" quotes were also in Bynum and Quackenbush, page 157. The *Liberty* magazine article of October 20, 1934, titled "The Svengalis of Football," was found in outsize scrapbook "1928–35," FHY, BHL-UM.

Yost's book was *Football for Player and Spectator,* Ann Arbor, 1905. His recollection about the 1922 Ohio State game was in a letter to Doug Roby, May 15, 1939, "Papers 1939 May (2)" folder, Box 24, UM-BICIA, BHL-UM. Further testament to Yost's binding ability as coach was in Friedman's *Liberty* magazine article, and in Lawton.

The *New York Telegraph* on October 15, 1926, reported that Yost was "far and away the wealthiest coach in the country." This clipping is in outsize scrapbook "1924–28," FHY, BHL-UM. It was Michigan alumnus James Murfin, the Detroit circuit-court judge, who told Yost he had "no equal" as an advocate, in Behee, page 157.

Yost's lack of humor was perfectly illustrated in the following excerpt from the draft manuscript of Lawton (in "Yost, Fielding H. [1]" folder, Box 2, JFL, BHL-UM):

> No joke on Yost was ever funny—to Yost. Germany Schulz throws light on this when he tells of taking the coach for a ride in his car. One of those old-time Interurban [train] cars whizzed by them on the tracks beside the road. Yost said, "Dutchman, those Interurbans sure go fast!" With a straight face, Schulz replied, "Yes, but they're hard to steer." Silence for 30 seconds. Yost was concentrating. Then he dug his elbow in Germany's ribs, and drawled, seriously, "What d'ye mean—hard to steer?"

Rockne evidently was perplexed by Yost's seriousness, because *Detroit News* columnist H.G. Salsinger recalled that Rockne once said "a man without a sense of humor could never be a successful football coach. Yost was the exception." This undated story was in a clippings folder in Box 2, JFL, BHL-UM.

The story and quotes from the 1925 banquet in New York were in the *New York Times,* December 1.

Yost's assessment of Rockne was made in a letter to W.W. Campbell of the University of California, March 14, 1925, "Papers, 1925, March (2)" folder, Box 7, UM-BICIA, BHL-UM.

The thread is slashed

Yost and Rockne chummed together at a lawyers-club banquet, along with Boston College coach Maj. Frank Cavanaugh, on December 29, 1922, as reported the next day in the *New York Sun.*

Yost's role in Northwestern's pitch to Rockne was indicated in two letters after the fact: O.F. Long to Yost, January 7, 1922, and Yost to O.F. Long, January 9, 1922, "1922 January (1)" folder, Box 4, UM-BICIA, BHL-UM. Long thanked Yost "for a lot of good help in the matter."

Detroit News columnist Salsinger, probably on Rockne's suggestion, urged Yost to hire former Notre Dame player Johnny Mohardt as an assistant, in a letter March 5, 1922, "1922 March (2)" folder, Box 4, UM-BICIA, BHL-UM. Rockne pitched Barry Holton as an assistant in a letter to Yost, July 17, 1922, "1922 July (1)" folder, Box 5, UM-BICIA, BHL-UM.

Yost discussed his inferiority complex with eastern teams in a letter to alumnus Murfin, February 26, 1917, "Correspondences, 1917 January–February" folder, Box 1, JOM, BHL-UM. In another letter, to H.W. Blakeslee of the Associated Press, December 21, 1922, "1922 December (2)" folder, Box 5, UM-BICIA, BHL-UM, Yost wrote:

> Under "Equality of Competition" I am trying to sell the idea of equal opportunity in competition, which means the same eligibility rules, same number of games, etc., for all competitors. No doubt you will remember how for 10 years Michigan competed under the present strict rules with those institutions who played freshmen, transfer students, and four-year men, and I certainly know the disadvantages of such a handicap.

Yost's 1917 letter to Murfin carried his "hitched in the same kind of harness" remark. In a January 27, 1913, letter to Joe H. Maddock, a member of the 1902–03 Michigan Point-A-Minute teams, Yost said "with the three-year limit, small schedules, and small opportunity for development, we have practically no class whatsoever as compared with [your] teams," and he went on to cite stricter rules as reasons Michigan was not finding much success against eastern teams ("Papers 1913 [5]" folder, Box 1, FHY, BHL-UM). As well, in the December 2, 1913, edition of the *Detroit Free Press,* Yost maintained that "gridiron ability depends so largely on experience."

Yost's "fair field and no favors" quote was made in a letter to Hugh S. Fullerton of the *Chicago Tribune,* January 20, 1923, "Papers 1923 January (2)" folder, Box 5, UM-BICIA, BHL-UM.

The chronology of events at the 1923 Big Ten track and field championships, and the controversy that followed, were all pieced together from the following reports: the June 3–6 and 13–14, 1923, editions of *The Michigan Daily,* the *South Bend Tribune,* the *Detroit News,* the *Detroit Free Press,* the *Ann Arbor Times News,* the *Daily Illini,* and the *Chicago Tribune;* and the June 7, 1923, edition of *The Michigan Alumnus.*

The remaining details were culled from the vital letters between these men: Rockne to Yost, June 14, 1923; Yost to Rockne, June 18, 1923; Rockne to Yost, June 26, 1923; and Yost to Rockne, July 5, 1923—all of which are in "Papers 1923 June" folder, Box 5, UM-BICIA, BHL-UM.

The *Daily Illini* commented in its editorial of June 14, 1923, that "we doubt if it was quite discreet for a man high in Michigan athletic circles to inform a visiting coach that he did not want his 'dirty Irish' on Ferry Field again."

Yost's comment about the "faith" and "honor" in his opponents was made in a letter to Minnesota coach Henry L. Williams, January 7, 1921, "Papers 1920 December" folder, Box 3, UM-BICIA, BHL-UM.

The Ku Klux Klan's rise in the 1920s, and the problems that presented to Notre Dame, were well documented in Sperber, pages 134, 158–162.

● ● ●

That Yost never forgave Rockne for his betrayal was confirmed in H.G. Salsinger to Rockne, November 23, 1925, UADR 19/52, UNDA. Salsinger tried to answer for Rockne why Yost had it in for him:

I made various inquiries and I will give you frankly the result of this investigation. There was a track meet at Ann Arbor, it seems, where a dispute arose between Michigan and Illinois. It involved the result of the meet, I am told. You took sides with Gill of Illinois, and Yost became seriously offended. He has not gotten over it. I was told that he had not forgiven you.

Muckraking

Yost's suggestion that the Western Conference hire a commissioner in 1922 was in Behee, page 167. Sperber reported that by advertising in John L. Griffith's *The Athletic Journal,* Rockne always got a sympatic ear from the commissioner (pages 190–193).

● ● ●

In Rockne to E.P. Trueblood, January 3, 1928, UADR 11/42, UNDA, Rockne said Notre Dame had "five hundred and four boys in football uniforms last year, including all the intramural teams." The November 5, 1926, edition of *The Scholastic* reported the Brownson Hall "Bearcats" had defeated the Battle Creek (Mich.) College team, 7–6, the week before.

Yost's diatribe to Griffith, December 23, 1926, is in "Papers 1926 December (4)" folder, Box 9, UM-BICIA, BHL-UM.

Rockne's "Kreisler/Paderewski" quote was in the same letter to E.P. Trueblood. Allison Danzig's story appeared in the *New York Times* on December 10, 1929.

Yost indicated his refusal to play Pop Warner's teams in a letter to Phil Bartelme, February 20, 1913, "Papers, 1913 (3)" folder, Box 1, FHY, BHL-UM. Wrote Yost: "I believe—between you and I—that Warner does not in any way discourage professionalism among his men. . . . I do not believe in competition with [his Carlisle teams]."

● ● ●

Rockne's letter about "Michigan propaganda" was sent to Pat Malloy, April 22, 1929, UADR 15/120, UNDA. His remark about "one of the Big Ten universities" questioning ND's eligibility standards was found in an unidentified clipping, in UADR 16/59, UNDA. Jesse Harper's letter to Rockne was dated April 26, 1927 (UADR 13/33, UNDA).

The Wurzer-Yost letters (Wurzer to Yost on May 3, 1928, Yost to Wurzer on May 17, 1928, and Wurzer to Yost on June 5, 1928) are in the "Notre Dame, 1910–1945" folder, Box 36, UM-BICIA, BHL-UM. The information about Boeringer's past was provided by Minnesota athletic director F.W. Luehring, February 9, 1927, "Papers 1926 February (1)" folder, Box 9, UM-BICIA, BHL-UM. The uncirculated copies of the Wurzer-Yost letters remain in the "Notre Dame, 1910–1945" folder.

Notre Dame's eligibility rules, circa April 1924, are published as "Constitution Bylaws and Regulations of the Faculty Board of Control of Athletics at the University of Notre Dame" (Notre Dame, 1925), a copy of which is found in PATH, UNDA. They are nearly identical—often word for word—to those in the official 1925 rulebook of the Western Conference, "UM Board in Control of intercollegiate athletics; Papers, Misc." folder, Box 7, HOC, BHL-UM. Sperber's account of Rockne and the flunked-out half-back was on page 300.

The Brooker incident was pieced together from the following letters: Griffith to Yost, February 26, 1925, "1925 February (1)" folder, Box 7, UM-BICIA, BHL-UM; Rockne to Griffith, March 17, 1925, UADR 12/81, UNDA; Yost to Griffith, April 28, 1925, "1925 April (2)" folder, Box 7, UM-BICIA, BHL-UM; and Griffith to Yost, April 30, 1925; "1925 April (2)" folder, Box 7, UM-BICIA, BHL-UM—and also from the April 24 and 28, 1925, editions of *The Michigan Daily.*

The Michigan board ruled on Vick on February 9, 1924 (Minutes, Volume 3, June 1, 1910–June 2, 1927, Box 48, UM-BICIA, BHL-UM).

● ● ●

The conference's actions against pro athletes were discussed in retrospect in a letter from Michigan Board in Control chairman, Ralph Aigler, to Yost, February 9, 1925, "1925 February (3)" folder, Box 7, UM-BICIA, BHL-UM.

College football players playing in pro games on Sundays was a particular problem for many schools, including Michigan, in the mid-1910s, according to the following letters: F.M. Church to James Murfin on November 9, 1915, Murfin to Aigler on November 10, 1915, Murfin to Church on November 10, 1915, and Church to Murfin on November 11, 1915 ("Correspondences, 1915 November–December" folder, Box 1, JOM, BHL-UM).

Details of the Taylorville-Carlinville incident were in Sperber, pages 120–125, and in Jerry Brondfield's *Rockne: The Coach, the Man, the Legend,* New York, 1976, pages 105–112.

Hunk Anderson's recollection of the Rockne-Stagg-Yost meeting was in his memoirs, *Notre Dame, Chicago Bears, and Hunk,* co-written by Emil Klosinski, Oviedo, Fla., 1976, pages 69–70.

Yost's actions against Dick Hanley were discussed in the following letters: Rockne to Pop Warner, March 22, 1927, UADR 21/72; and Yost to Griffith on April 15, 1927, Griffith to Yost on April 20, 1927, Tug Wilson to Griffith on April 22, 1927, and Griffith to Yost on April 26, 1927, "1927 April (2)" folder, Box 9, UM-BICIA, BHL-UM.

● ● ●

The term "organized recruiting" was defined by Commissioner Griffith, in a "Statement on recruiting," UADR 21/106, UNDA.

The Carnegie Report's criticisms of Michigan were summarized by Behee, pages 107–109, and detailed in a letter from Howard J. Savage of the Carnegie Foundation to University of Michigan president C.C. Little, April 17, 1929, "April 1929 (3)" folder, Box 12, UM-BICIA, BHL-UM. The report's criticisms of Notre Dame were summarized in the November 1929 issue of *The Notre Dame Alumnus.*

Yost denied the report's charges, telling *Detroit Daily Illustrated* on October 24, 1929, that "I know of no such system of agents operating either on or off campus to recruit athletes for the University of Michigan, and I would be glad to have any information regarding the same." (This clipping is in the "Carnegie Report on football, 1927–31" folder, Box 34, UM-BICIA, BHL-UM.) *The Notre Dame Alumnus* reported that "the extent to which Notre Dame athletes are 'taken care of' can be determined by a very brief conversation with Mr. Rockne."

Ralph Aigler defended the Michigan athletic department in the Board in Control's annual report to the Board of Regents, September 1929–June 1930, "Annual Reports, 1912–32" folder, Box 32, UM-BICIA, BHL-UM.

Griffith's "sane and sound basis" comment was in Behee, page 109, and his conclusion about there being no organized recruiting at Michigan was made to Aigler, November 6, 1929, "1929 November (3)," Box 13, UM-BICIA, BHL-UM.

Behee described the stepped-up recruiting efforts at Michigan in 1919–20 (pages 84–89), and the following letters revealed Yost knew about all the chicanery: Bob Clancy to Yost on August 5, 1920 ("Papers 1920 August" folder, Box 3, UM-BICIA, BHL-UM); and Clancy to Yost on January 28, 1921, Clancy to Yost February 7, 1921 ("1921 January [1]" folder, Box 4, UM-BICIA, BHL-UM).

On May 25, 1927, Griffith sent Rockne a copy of the letter he had sent to Yost regarding Rockne's charge about the lot of land in Detroit (UADR 12/84, UNDA). Yost's close friendship with Irvin (Cy) Huston was evident in: Huston to Yost, March 27, 1928, "1928 March (1)" folder, Box 10, UM-BICIA, BHL-UM; and Yost to Huston, April 18, 1928, "1928 Apil (3)" folder, Box 10, UM-BICIA, BHL-UM.

The quote from Twombley was on page 97. Rockne's involvement in securing jobs for star athletes was detailed in Sperber, pages 251–253. Leahy's recollection about Rockne's "appalling" recruiting tactics was in Twombley, page 126.

Rockne's "bird-dog" system was discussed in Sperber, pages 141–142, 245–250.

A shift of philosophies

Early forms of the shift, and its evolution up to the Rockne years, were described in Michael R. Steele's *Knute Rockne: A Bio-Bibliography,* Westport, Conn., 1983, pages 184, 256–257; in Whittingham, pages 23 and 26; in *The Michigan Alumnus,* December 1910, pages 140–141 (which diagrammed the strange variations of the Minnesota shift); and in Wilson and Brondfield, pages 78–79.

The workings of the Rockne shift, and general descriptions of how he reacted to the rules crackdowns, were described in Steele, pages 27–29, 45, 129, 153, 158, 176–177, 181, 247, 233; Brondfield, pages 113–116; and in *Out of Bounds: An Anecdotal History of Notre Dame Football,* by Mike Bonifer and Larry Weaver, Blue Earth, Minn., 1978, pages 48–49. Rockne's quote about momentum was in Brondfield, pages 114–115. His "smart football" remark was captured by a Newsreel film crew at practice in 1930.

Yost's "we never shift" remark was printed February 11, 1934, in the *Atlanta Constitution* (clipping in outsize scrapbook "1928–35," FHY, BHL-UM). Sources for workings of Yost's offensive system were listed previously. Salsinger's "best authorities" assertion appeared November 28, 1926, in the *Detroit News.*

Yost's letter to Walter Camp, March 6, 1922, is in "1922 March (1)" folder, Box 4, UM-BICIA, BHL-UM. His letter to Walter Eckersall, November 22, 1926, is in "Papers 1926 November (1)" folder, Box 8, UM-BICIA, BHL-UM.

Rockne's recollection that Meyer penalized Notre Dame 95 yards to Northwestern's 0 is in a letter to Colorado football coach Fred Dawson, March 12, 1927, UADR 10/140, UNDA. The *South Bend Tribune* game story of October 24, 1926, reported the 75–45 ratio. Rockne's quote about this being the "only time" he was sore at an official was in a letter to K.L. (Tug) Wilson, November 10, 1926, UADR 21/127, UNDA.

Any game summary from the first half of the century will list officials by school. The workings of the Western Conference officials committee, and Rockne's opposition to "Yost" choosing them for his games, was fervently argued in his letter to Griffith, February 9, 1925, UADR 12/80, UNDA. Rockne mentioned his "suckhole" comment to Griffith, November 5, 1926, UADR 12/83, UNDA. Dawson was the coach Rockne warned against using Morton, in the above noted letter.

Stagg indicated his concerns to the Associated Press, which were carried in the November 4, 1926, edition of *The Michigan Daily*. Griffith's soothing letter to Rockne, November 3, 1926, is in UADR 12/83, UNDA—and his plea to Yost, same date, is in "Papers November (2)" folder, Box 8, UM-BICIA, BHL-UM.

That Mark Kelly was a friend of Rockne's is indicated in the following letters: E.C. Henderson to Rockne, May 8, 1923 (UADR 19/134, UNDA); and Rockne to Kelly on April 8, 1929, Kelly to Rockne on April 12, 1929, and Rockne to Kelly on April 23, 1929, UADR 14/53, UNDA. Kelly's story in the *Los Angeles Examiner* appeared January 10, 1927 (clipping in outsize scrapbook "1924–28," FHY, BHL-UM). Sperber explained why Rockne had to be in Chicago for Christy Walsh, pages 218–221.

On November 15, 1926, after reading that Notre Dame's second team defeated Western State Normal (Mich.), Yost decided to find out, once and for all, what competition and scholastic rules Rockne was working under, and he sent Griffith a long list of questions ("Papers 1926 November [2]" folder, Box 8, UM-BICIA, BHL-UM). Because Griffith dated his response November 26—the first day of the Big Ten meetings in Chicago—and because Griffith got Rockne himself to answer the questions (one answer said "this year we are playing ten games"), it's most likely Rockne was given these questions in advance of the meeting. The Griffith/Rockne response to Yost is in "Notre Dame, 1910–1945" folder, Box 36, UM-BICIA, BHL-UM.

The *South Bend Tribune* reported on November 26, 1926, that the conference might force members to play a minimum of four games a season against one another. Rockne told Joseph H. Thompson on November 12, 1926 (UADR 20/48, UNDA), that it was "imperative that I get three conference [games for 1927]."

The events of the two-day conference meetings were culled from the following newspapers, November 27–30: the *Chicago Tribune*, the *South Bend Tribune*, the *Detroit Free Press*, the *Detroit News*, and *The Michigan Daily*.

Rockne's letter to Gus Dorais was dated January 28, 1927, UADR 10/189, UNDA. His letter in reference to a "bitter" Yost was to H.J. Koehler, February 25, 1927, UADR 20/107, UNDA, and he wrote E.K. Hall on February 28, 1927, UADR 13/10, UNDA.

News of the rules committee's decison was reported March 6, 1927, in such papers as the *New York Times*, the *Detroit Free Press*, and the *Detroit News*. Rockne mentioned his "all we need to do" suggestion to Wilbur S. Eaton of Mount St. Charles College in Montana, March 22, 1927, UADR 11/61, UNDA. To another shift disciple, James Phelan of Purdue, Rockne wrote, "I don't believe our shift is interfered with in any way" (March 10, 1927, UADR 17/165, UNDA).

H.G. Salsinger, in the November 29 edition of the *Detroit News*, discussed how Rockne combatted the 1930 rule clarification: He drilled the backfield so well that its stop was repeatedly timed to be no less than 1.1 seconds, and usually no longer than 1.2 seconds. Rockne outlined his position on the lack of representation of "shift" coaches on the rules committee, and made his Boston Tea Party remark, in his so-called autobiography, reprinted in Bynum and Quackenbush, pages 157–158.

The *Detroit Saturday Night* article about the 1925 Michigan-Minnesota game appeared in the November 28, 1925, issue, and was found in outsize scrapbook "1928–35," FHY, BHL-UM.

Rockne's comment about being "unable to satisfy our enemies" was also made during the 1930 newsreel clip from practice.

Michigan Stadium, Jr.

Behee provided a detailed chronology of how Yost won approval for Michigan Stadium, how he had such an integral role in its construction, and how he helped come up with the financing scheme, pages 145–171. Additional information on design was in the *Chicago Herald and Examiner,* May 3, 1927 (clipping in outsize scrapbook "1924–28," FHY, BHL-UM). The legend of Yost's phantom seat was mentioned in a souvenir book published by the University of Michigan Football Centennial Committee in 1979, *University of Michigan Football: The First 100 Years,* page 24, and corroborated in an interview with Michigan athletic director Jack Weidenbach in his office at the University of Michigan on June 25, 1992.

Rockne's desire for a larger stadium was in Anderson and Klosinksi, pages 75–77, and Sperber, pages 88, 95, 268–272.

The formation of the two stadium committees was described in the January 1928 edition of *The Notre Dame Alumnus,* page 201. The following letters are in "1927 December (1)" folder, Box 10, UM-BICIA, BHL-UM: A.R. Erskine to Clarence Cook Little, December 19, 1927; Little to Erskine, December 22, 1927; Yost to Erskine, December 27, 1927; and Erskine to Yost, December 28, 1927.

That Rev. James Burns urged Rockne and Rev. Thomas Steiner to inspect Michigan Stadium was indicated afterward, in Steiner's report to Burns, March 30, 1928, UABM "Stadium" folder, UNDA. Rockne and Tad Wieman had their initial discussions in: Rockne to Wieman, October 4, 1927; Wieman to Rockne, October 6, 1927; and Rockne to Wieman, October 11, 1927, UADR 21/121, UNDA (the latter of which contained Rockne's "I hate to bother" remark). H.G. Salsinger, in his letter informing Rockne why Yost still had it in for him (noted earlier), also mentioned Harry Tillotson's admiration. Philip Pack apologetically wrote Rockne for tickets to the 1927 ND-USC game in Chicago and was extremely thankful to have been obliged by Rockne himself (Pack to Rockne, November 14, 1927; Rockne to Pack (telegram), November 16, 1927; Pack to Rockne, November 22, 1927, UADR 17/129, UNDA).

Regarding his and Rockne's trip to Ann Arbor, Steiner reported to Burns (March 30, 1928, UABM "Stadium" folder, UNDA) exactly how cordial Tad Wieman had been, and described everything Wieman had given them access to—and included a detailed breakdown of all Michigan Stadium construction costs.

Yost's secretary, Andrew Baker, wrote on March 19, 1928, that Yost was "absent on a trip through North Carolina, South Carolina, Georgia, and Tenn., and will not return to Ann Arbor until about April 16th" (in a letter to Irving K. Pond, "1928 March (3)" folder, Box 10, UM-BICIA, BHL-UM). The souring of the Yost-Wieman relationship, and Yost's apparent lingering bitterness against him, was in Behee, pages 99–101, 104.

Rockne sent his thank-you to Wieman on March 29, 1928, UADR 21/121, UNDA.

The Notre Dame Alumnus reported Notre Dame's decision to indeed build a stadium in its May 1928 edition, page 271. Additional details regarding construction and finance were in the September 1929 issue of *The Notre Dame Alumnus,* and in "Stadium Publicity Committee" folder UABM, UNDA. By 1928, the Osborn Engineering Company of Cleveland had 23 years of experience in designing sports stadiums, such as Comiskey Park, Yankee Stadium, the Polo Grounds, and the football stadiums at Indiana, Purdue, and Minnesota. Notre Dame had in its possession a schematical diagram of the original parking scheme around Michigan Stadium ("Stadium Traffic" folder UABM, UNDA) but it was Rockne who devised same for Notre Dame Stadium (*Chicago Tribune,* October 4, 1930).

Rockne wrote A.S. Murphy of The Pacific Lumber Company of Scotia, Calif., March 19, 1929 (UADR 16/121, UNDA) that Notre Dame had "in mind doing the same as Michigan, namely, using your Redwood for seats on account of their durability."

The Rev. Charles O'Donnell–Yost letters (October 2 and October 7, 1930) are in "Notre Dame, 1910–1945" folder, Box 36, UM-BICIA, BHL-UM.

Summing up

Rockne's "take Michigan with a big score" comment was made to Minnesota coach C.W. (Doc) Spears, November 17, 1927, UADR 16/90, UNDA. Yost's anxiousness for Southern Cal to have beaten Notre Dame was made to Trojans coach Howard Jones, November 18, 1929, "1929 September (2)" folder, Box 13, UM-BICIA, BHL-UM.

Rockne's New Year's Eve 1929 rocket was to M.J. McGuire, UADR 15/55, UNDA.

Yost's comments about Rockne's death were made in the April 1, 1931, editions of *The Michigan Daily,* the *Detroit Free Press,* the *Detroit News,* the *South Bend Tribune,* and the *Ann Arbor News.*

In a memorandum to all conference athletic directors the day after Rockne died, Commissioner Griffith indicated that "unless you advise me" otherwise, he was sending flowers to Rockne's funeral in their collective names ("Papers 1931 April [2]" folder, Box 15, UM-BICIA, BHL-UM). Yost apparently did not object. The mass of condolences sent Bonnie Rockne, Knute's widow, is listed in UPCO, Box 10, UNDA. The list of coaches' contributions to the Knute Rockne Memorial Fund is in "Lists of Rockne Condolences, Honorary Pallbearers, etc." folder, UPCO Box 10, UNDA.

Rockne's *The Four Winners* was published in New York in summer 1925, shortly after his feud with Yost had really fired up. The description of Coach Smith was on pages 135 and 146, and Elmer's reevaluation of Smith was on 248.

Rockne's "Kluxer minds" comment was made to M.J. Donnelly, October 18, 1926, UADR 10/183, UNDA, and he called Yost a "hillbilly" in his letter to Pat Malloy on April 22, 1929, UADR 15/120, UNDA.

Yost's remark about Catholic schools being a "rather independent lot" was made in his assessment of Rockne, to W.W. Campbell of the University of California, previously noted. In late November, Michigan was under tremendous pressure from Detroit mayor Frank Murphy, Michigan governor Fred W. Green, and local newspapers to play the University of Detroit in a charity game. The Michigan Board in Control declined, citing the conference's previous denial of a charity game between Chicago and Northwestern (Volume 5, March 1927–Jan. 1938, Box 49, UM-BICIA, BHL-UM). Rockne's conversion to Catholicism was in Steele, page 33.

Jay Wyatt's story was in Mary Stuhldreyer's *Many a Saturday Afternoon,* New York, 1964, pages 72–73.

9. Smoothing out the frictions: 1931–41

The Yost/John Nicholson letters, May 25 and May 28, 1931, are in the "Notre Dame, 1910–1945" folder, Box 36, UM-BICIA, BHL-UM.

Details of Harry Kipke's appearance at the Notre Dame football banquet were in the January 15–18, 1933, editions of the *South Bend Tribune,* the *Chicago Tribune,* the *Detroit News,* the *Detroit Free Press,* and *The Michigan Daily.* Jimmy Crowley's quote appeared in the *South Bend Tribune* on January 17. The *Detroit Free Press,* on the 18th, reported Kipke's willingness to return more frequently to Notre Dame.

The following also appeared on the 18th: the "Kipke" headline atop the *Detroit News* sports section; the "Wolverine-Irish" headline in *The Michigan Daily;* Hunk Anderson's and Jesse Harper's quotes in the *Detroit Free Press;* and Yost's evasive answers and Kipke's "personally would favor" comment in the *Detroit News.* The scheduling meeting called by Yost, which killed all the speculation, was described on January 21 by the *Detroit Free Press* and the *Chicago Tribune.* Frank MacDonnell of the *Detroit*

Times appears to have been the only Detroit-area writer who publicly questioned Yost's stance in January 1933.

Fred DeLano's columns were given prominent play in the January 12 and 19, 1936, editions of *The Michigan Daily*. Rev. John O'Hara's move to put Notre Dame a step ahead of the conference was in Sperber, page 448.

Between January 21 and 28, all the dailies in Detroit, Ann Arbor, Chicago, and South Bend ran speculative and reflective stories. The sentiments of Notre Dame's Rev. J. Hugh O'Donnell and Elmer Layden appeared in the *Detroit News* on January 22. Letters between Yost and Andrew Baker (January 22, January 27, and January 30, 1936) are in "Papers 1936 January (1)" folder, Box 21, UM-BICIA, BHL-UM. Ralph Aigler's comment was in the *Ann Arbor News* on January 27. Andrew Reid's letter to Yost, February 3, 1936, is in "1936 February (1)" folder, Box 21, UM-BICIA, BHL-UM.

Arch Ward, sports editor of the *Chicago Tribune,* reported on January 16, 1933, that the Depression was forcing schools everywhere to resume old rivalries.

The following letters are in the "Notre Dame, 1910–1945" folder, Box 36, UM-BICIA, BHL-UM: Bernard Weadock to Yost on October 13, 1936; Yost to Layden on October 22; Layden to Yost on October 28; Weadock telegram to Yost on October 28; Yost to Weadock on October 29; Yost to Layden on October 29; Yost to Weadock on November 2; and Yost to Layden on November 2.

Pertinent details of Harry Kipke's selection of Hunk Anderson as line coach were found in the February 20, 1937, edition of the *Detroit News* and in the next day's editions of the *South Bend Tribune* and *The Michigan Daily.* Yost explained that he left it to Kipke to find his own assistant in a letter to E.R. (Butch) Slaughter, February 24, 1937, "1937 February (2)" folder, Box 21, UM-BICIA, BHL-UM. H.G. Salsinger's letter to Aigler, February 22, 1937, is in "1937 February (1)" folder, Box 21, UM-BICIA, BHL-UM.

Layden's letter to Yost regarding his "splended handling" of the conference meeting was on May 24, 1937, "Notre Dame, 1910–1945" folder, Box 36, UM-BICIA, BHL-UM. Yost arranged tickets again for Weadock in letters found in the same folder: Yost to Layden on November 1, 1937; Layden to Yost on November 3; and Yost to Layden on November 4.

Layden's recollections about dealing with elder athletic directors was in his autobiography, co-written with Ed Snyder, *It Was a Different Game: The Elmer Layden Story,* Englewood Cliffs., N.J., 1969, pages 123–129.

That Yost and Layden talked by phone on November 30, 1937, was reported in the *South Bend Tribune* on December 2. Michigan issued a statement for release at 6 P.M. on December 1, 1937, regarding the resumption of athletics with Notre Dame, and this press release can be found in the "Notre Dame, 1910–1945" folder, Box 36, UM-BICIA, BHL-UM. All the dailies in Detroit, Ann Arbor, Chicago, and South Bend played up this story between December 2 and 6.

The chronology of Kipke's firing and Fritz Crisler's hiring as Michigan head football coach was detailed in Behee, pages 101–104. Hunk Anderson, incidently, had left Michigan immediately after the season to become line coach at the University of Cincinnati (according to Anderson and Klosinski, page 118).

Layden's telegram to Yost (9:59 P.M., April 29, 1939, "1939 Papers [1]" folder, Box 5, FHY, BHL-UM) read:

My congratulations to you on your birthday. I am sure the years in retrospect should afford most satisfying memories for you. And your contribution to the game and to life should provide a most happy day. May many more birthdays be yours. Regards,

Elmer F. Layden

Yost's return telegram on May 15, 1939, is also in "1939 Papers (1)" folder, Box 5, FHY, BHL-UM.

The first mention in Yost's correspondences of his plan to visit Layden at Notre Dame was to former Wolverine Kenneth T. Knode, a South Bend physician, on July 12, 1939, "Papers 1939 July (1)" folder, Box 24, UM-BICIA, BHL-UM. Knode, an active Michigan alumnus living in South Bend, indicated he was "delighted" by the prospect of the Old Man's visit in a letter to Yost, September 25, 1939, "Papers 1939 October (3)" folder, Box 25, UM-BICIA, BHL-UM.

Details of Yost's visit were in the September 30–October 2, 1939, editions of the *South Bend Tribune,* and in the following letters: Yost to Knode on October 3, 1939, and Knode to Yost on October 6, 1939, "Papers 1939 October (3)" folder, Box 25, UM-BICIA, BHL-UM. That Yost was still raving about Layden's hospitality a week later was reported in an undated clipping of the *South Bend Tribune,* found in the "Notre Dame, 1910–1945" folder, Box 36, UM-BICIA, BHL-UM. What's more, Yost told ex-Wolverine Edwin J. Bennett of South Bend that he "enjoyed this trip very much—every minute of it," in a letter, October 3, 1939, "Papers 1939 October (5)" folder, Box 25, UM-BICIA, BHL-UM.

The astute Salsinger reported in the December 29, 1937, edition of the *Detroit News* that "Michigan alumni are opposed to scheduling a game with Notre Dame, and Notre Dame alumni are opposed to scheduling one with Michigan. There are many reasons why neither side is in favor of a game. Six or seven years from now, yes, but now, no."

Slezak recalled his friendship with Yost as an undergraduate at Michigan, his being pursued and hired by Notre Dame, and his role as middle-man in Yost's and Layden's negotiations, in telephone interviews on November 28 and 29, 1990, and January 18, 1991.

The *New York Times* reported the University of Chicago's decision to drop football on December 22, 1939. Aigler's statement regarding scheduling was found in *The Michigan Daily* on January 6, 1940. Michigan scheduled California for the 1940 vacancy on January 29. Crisler indicated the "terrific pressure" to play the University of Detroit to alumnus Ralph O. Rychener, January 18, 1940, "1940 January (3)" folder, Box 25, UM-BICIA, BHL-UM.

Regarding political pressure on Michigan to play Notre Dame, Salsinger also reported in his December 29, 1937, article in the *Detroit News* that "political influences were reflected in the resumption of [Michigan's] athletic relations with Notre Dame. It is known that at least one politician demanded that Michigan include Notre Dame on the football schedule." What's more, Rev. Edmund Joyce, who years later became Notre Dame's executive vice president, said in an interview for this book on March 12, 1991, that it was his understanding that the governor of Michigan had lobbied hard for a football resumption.

Nowhere was a single document found to specifically indicate a power struggle existed between Crisler and Yost, but there can be little doubting this assertion. It was Yost who arranged Cal for the 1940 vacancy, and Crisler consequently indicated his "disappointment" that Pittsburgh didn't get the date in a letter to Pitt athletic director Jimmy Hagan, February 5, 1940, "1940 February (2)" folder, Box 25, UM-BICIA, BHL-UM. Crisler further stated to Hagan that "as yet, we haven't closed any dates for 1941 or 1942, and I personally would be delighted if we could work something out with you." Almost two months later, Crisler was so sure Pitt would get the '41 and '42 vacancies, he discussed with Hagan the specific dates that would be best for "our games" (in a letter, March 28, 1940, "1940 March [3]" folder, Box 25, UM-BICIA, BHL-UM). So it certainly wasn't Crisler's idea to schedule Notre Dame, especially not for '42. That Notre Dame, in the end, was given the home-and-home deal—and not Pitt—certainly wouldn't have been Crisler's idea either. Finally, if Yost and Crisler had been pursuing replacement opponents together, amicably and cooperatively, Crisler wouldn't have been offering the '41 and '42 dates to Pittsburgh when Yost, at the same time, was arranging for Notre Dame to get the '42 date. Thus, it's quite obvious Yost and Crisler weren't together on this at all.

The minutes from the April 20 and May 8 meetings of the Michigan Board in Control are in Volume 6, February 1939–June 1950, Box 49, UM-BICIA, BHL-UM. The minutes of the May 8 and June 1, 1940, meetings of the Notre Dame Board of Control are in UVOC 4/48, UNDA.

The announcement of the football resumption was splashed across the tops of various sports sections in Detroit, Ann Arbor, Chicago, and South Bend. Layden's "biggest triumph" quote was in Layden and Snyder, page 125. Yost thanked Slezak on May 28, 1940, "Notre Dame, 1910–1945" folder, Box 36, UM-BICIA, BHL-UM. Cavanaugh's qualifying press release was printed in the May 26, 1940, edition of the *South Bend Tribune.*

Francis Wallace's recollection of the 1940 Heisman Trophy dinner and Yost's 1939 trip to Notre Dame appeared in his book, *Knute Rockne,* pages 186–187.

Layden's "winding up our careers" letter to Yost was on February 15, 1941, "Notre Dame, 1910–1945" folder, UM-BICIA, BHL-UM.

Yost's letter to Slezak following the 1942 game, November 19, 1942, and his letter to Homer Hattendorf on November 20, 1942, are both in "Papers 1942 November (1)" folder, Box 28, UM-BICIA, BHL-UM.

Details of Yost's death were in the August 21, 1946, editions of the various daily newspapers.

Louis B. Hyde assessed the change in Yost from 1901 to 1941 in a letter to Michigan publicity manager Philip Pack, September 30, 1940, "Papers 1940 September (4)" folder, Box 26, UM-BICIA, BHL-UM.

10. Wartime blitzes: 1942–43

H.O. (Fritz) Crisler

That Crisler was a shrewd negotiator and power broker was clearly evident from a variety of sources, including: (1) his letters (stored in HOC and UM-BICIA Boxes 23–35, at the Bentley Historical Library at the University of Michigan); (2) his actions on various committees over the years; and (3) Pete Waldmeir, in an insightful telephone interview on February 8, 1991. Waldmeir was a sportswriter at the *Detroit News* from the 1950s to the 1970s.

General background on Crisler's life before coming to Michigan in 1938 was found in Perry, pages 156–161, and in Wilson and Brondfield, pages 274–277.

Throughout his 27 years as athletic director, Crisler employed only three baseball coaches, three hockey coaches, two football coaches (following his own retirement from that post in early 1948), two track coaches, two swimming coaches, and essentially only one wrestling coach.

Crisler described the general workings of his single-wing offense in his own book, *Modern Football: Fundamentals and Strategy,* New York, 1949. Art Valpey, an assistant coach at Michigan in the 1940s, provided detailed descriptions of the single wing in a letter to this author, February 2, 1991, and in two telephone interviews on January 21 and February 13, 1991.

Don Lund, a Wolverine halfback from 1942 to 1944, described the mechanical repetition that Crisler stressed, in an interview in his office at the University of Michigan on July 3, 1990. Lund recalled that at the beginning of fall practice, all Crisler would teach was the correct positioning of each player for each play, "and you'd start with that foundation and build on it," Lund remembered. Crisler described his unemotional approach to the game in his book, pages 254–256. His "higher sensibilities" remark was reprinted in the *Ann Arbor News*, May 24, 1968, and his disdain for pregame tirades was on page 254 of his own book.

Frank Leahy

The story of Rockne introducing Crisler to Leahy was in Twombley, page 145.

General background on Leahy was culled largely from Twombley's definitive biography, but also helpful were: *Many Autumns Ago: The Frank Leahy Era at Boston College and Notre Dame,* edited by Mike Bynum, Greenwich, Conn., 1988, pages 3–26; and Francis Wallace's *Notre Dame from Rockne to Parseghian,* New York, 1966, pages 97–117.

The National Championship Foundation credits Leahy with having won four national titles, but in the years 1943–46–49–53.

X. Michigan runs amok, '42

Unless otherwise indicated, all details about the immense pregame buildup and the game itself were pieced together from stories in the following dailies between November 8 and 16, 1942: the *Chicago Tribune,* the *South Bend Tribune,* the *Detroit News,* the *Detroit Free Press,* the *Ann Arbor News,* and *The Michigan Daily.*

That Crisler introduced so many new defensive schemes was indicated in a telephone interview with quarterback George Ceithaml on November 8, 1993.

In his own book, Leahy called Angelo Bertelli "the greatest passer in football" (page 145). That Leahy took the team to Knute Rockne's grave was confirmed by Ed (Moose) Krause in an interview in his office at the University of Notre Dame on August 1, 1990. Krause died on December 11, 1992.

Yost's quote about the wildness of the game was in the *Detroit News* on November 15, 1942. The old scribe's quote about it being worth the wait was in the November 16, 1942, issue of the *Detroit News.*

Ceithaml recalled the Harry Wright incident and the events at halftime in his November 8, 1993, interview. Albert (Ox) Wistert's recollections about halftime were found in a story in the September 10, 1975, edition of the *South Bend Tribune.*

The coaches' postgame comments were printed in the November 15, 1942, edition of the *Detroit Free Press.*

Michigan lost the next week to Ohio State and finished the season 7–3 with a No. 9 ranking in the AP poll. Notre Dame wound up 7–2–2 and finished No. 6.

● ● ●

Fred DeLano and Joe Petritz discussed the missing game in these letters: Petritz to DeLano, September 10, 1942, "Papers 1942 September (2)" folder, Box 28, UM-BICIA, BHL-UM; and DeLano to Petritz, "Papers 1942 November (2)" folder, Box 28, UM-BICIA, BHL-UM.

XI. Miller time again, '43

Unless otherwise indicated, all details about the pregame buildup and the game itself were pieced together from stories in the following dailies between October 3 and 11, 1943: the *Chicago Tribune,* the *South Bend Tribune,* the *Detroit News,* the *Detroit Free Press,* the *Ann Arbor News,* and *The Michigan Daily.*

Dozens of letters of Crisler's in 1943 (stored in Box 29, UM-BICIA, BHL-UM) helped explain how the "lend-lease" system worked.

Crisler's glum forecast was made to George Ceithaml, October 8, 1943, "Papers 1943 October (2)" folder, Box 29, UM-BICIA, BHL-UM.

Miller recalled details of the game in a telephone interview on November 8, 1993. Lund's wisecrack about his "jock strap" was made in his July 3, 1990, interview. Lund and Miller later became golfing buddies—as did many Wolverines and Fighting Irish players of this generation, according to Miller. The working of the "48-blind" play was described by Miller in his interview.

Hunk Anderson recalled chiding Leahy for using an ineffective defense against Michigan in '42, in Anderson and Kosinski, pages 138–139. Krause recalled ND's hit-the-faking-back-regardless strategy in his August 1, 1990, interview.

The coaches' postgame comments were printed October 10, 1943, in the *Detroit Free Press*. Crisler's postgame I-told-you-so was to Archie Kodros, October 18, 1943, "Papers 1943 October (2)" folder, Box 29, UM-BICIA, BHL-UM.

Notre Dame finished the season 9–1 and won the national championship—its first since 1930. Michigan finished 8–1, tied Purdue for the Big Nine championship, and placed third in the final AP poll.

11. The Crisler dodge: 1943–68

On hold again

Charles Wattles, as representative of the University of Michigan Club of South Bend, had urged Yost to schedule Notre Dame in football, in a letter December 8, 1926, "Papers 1926 December (2)" folder, Box 9, UM-BICIA, BHL-UM.

Crisler's letter to Wattles, November 27, 1942, is in "Papers 1942 November (1)" folder, Box 28, UM-BICIA, BHL-UM. Valpey recalled events at the 1942 Notre Dame banquet in his interviews and letter, previously noted.

Notre Dame vice president Rev. John J. Cavanaugh, in a letter to Leahy on February 26, 1943 (UVOC 5/12, UNDA), indicated the schools "we should attempt to schedule" were, in this order: (1) Michigan, (2) Ohio State, (3) Minnesota, (4) Penn State, (5) Stanford, and (6) California.

Cavanaugh's letter to Crisler, October 13, 1943, is in UVOC 5/39, UNDA.

The dailies began speculating as to further Michigan–Notre Dame football relations in the days leading up to the 1943 game. The speculation reached its zenith in December. Details of the Detroit banquet were printed in the December 18–19 editions of the *Detroit Free Press* and *Detroit News*, while Crisler's comment to AP was printed in the December 19, 1943, edition of the *South Bend Tribune*. Dale Stafford put forth his theory in the December 20, 1943, edition of the *Detroit Free Press*. Roscoe Bennett's column appeared in the December 21, 1943, edition of the *Grand Rapids Press*, and the politics that prompted it were explained in letters from Bots Thompson to Crisler, December 23, 1943, and Crisler to Thompson, January 6, 1944. Crisler thanked Bennett, January 6, 1944. All of these letters are in "Papers 1944 January" folder, Box 29, UM-BICIA, BHL-UM.

The minutes of the October 4, 1946, meeting of the Michigan Board are in Volume 6, February 1939–June 1950, Box 49, UM-BICIA, BHL-UM.

Crisler's letter to John L. Griffith was on March 4, 1944, "Papers 1944 March" folder, Box 29, UM-BICIA, BHL-UM. That Crisler even made a carbon copy of this letter is astounding considering what he asked Griffith to do with the original. Even more puzzling is why Crisler didn't throw out this carbon along with almost all of the others from this era.

Who's No. 1?—'47

The national championship recognition given Notre Dame and Michigan by the various selectors and systems was found on page 312 of the *1990 Notre Dame Football Guide.* That *College Football Illustrated* picked Michigan was reported on January 7, 1948, in the *South Bend Tribune.* The National Championship Foundation picked Michigan by virtue of having won the special postbowl AP poll.

The postwar fortunes begun at Michigan and Notre Dame in 1946 and continuing into 1947 were discussed, respectively, in Perry (pages 205–213) and in Rappaport (page 256–271). Additional perspective on the 1947 Michigan and Notre Dame teams was gathered from various early October editions of *The Michigan Daily,* the *Detroit News,* the *Ann Arbor News,* and the *Chicago Tribune.* Crisler's use of offensive and defensive platoons was in Perry, pages 200–204, 212.

The season chronology, including the weekly results of the AP poll, was pieced together from various newspaper reports, principally in *The Michigan Daily,* between October 13 and December 3, 1947, and from the January 2–7 editions of *The Michigan Daily,* the *South Bend Tribune,* the *Ann Arbor News,* the *Chicago Tribune,* the *Detroit News,* and the *Detroit Free Press.*

Jimmy Baird's contention that having black players hurt Michigan in the AP poll was in a letter to Crisler, November 12, 1947, "Football schedules 1947" folder, Box 35, UM-BICIA, BHL-UM.

The Heisman Trophy balloting results were on page 306 of the *1990 Notre Dame Football Guide.* Notre Dame placed two players on the first-team AP All-America team, one on the second, and one on the third. Michigan placed one player on the first team, two on the second, and one on the third.

The *Atlanta-Journal* "Super Bowl" headline was reprinted in Bill Cromartie's *The Big One: Michigan vs. Ohio State,* West Point, N.Y., 1981, page 173. News that the Great Lakes Bowl of Cleveland had offered bids to Notre Dame and Michigan hit the papers on October 17, 1947.

The following letters all are in "Football schedules 1947" folder in Box 35, UM-BICIA, BHL-UM: R.P. Dryer to Crisler, November 26, 1947, in which he included a copy of a letter from someone in Pensacola, Fla., championing a game to benefit the March of Dimes; John W. Miller to Crisler (undated), in which he dangled the idea of a million-dollar gate in Philadelphia; and Robert C. Main to Crisler (undated), in which he suggested Soldier Field as the site with $20 tickets.

Fuller Warren's movement in Florida was reported January 5, 1948, in the *South Bend Tribune.*

The *Detroit Free Press* and the *South Bend Tribune,* and probably every other daily newspaper in the country, carried in-depth coverage of the special postseason AP poll in the January 3–4–6 editions. Lyall Smith's and Jim Costin's columns appeared in the January 4 editions. These additional statistics supporting Michigan appeared in the *Maize and Blue Book,* put out by the National Championship Foundation: the Wolverines led the nation in 1947 in total offense (412.7 yards per game), in passing offense (173.9 yards per game), and in scoring offense (38.3 yards per game). Crisler's and Leahy's diplomatic responses to the special AP poll, and their thoughts on a 1947 Michigan–Notre Dame matchup, appeared in the January 6 edition of the *South Bend Tribune.*

United Press published the results of its poll the next day.

Leahy's comment about playing Michigan "any time, on any Saturday, during any fall" appeared prominently in midwestern papers on October 14, 1947.

Personal antagonism II

Leahy's lack of popularity among other coaches, and his poor social skills, were best described in Twombley, pages 244–245, and in Wallace's *Notre Dame From Rockne to Parseghian,* pages 97, 116–117. Wallace's comparison of Rockne and Leahy was in his book, *The Notre Dame Story,* New York, 1949.

Crisler's quote in the *Detroit Times* was reprinted on page 242 of Twombley. Red Grange's praise of Leahy was reprinted in Twombley, page 249. Leahy's recollection of his scheduling pleas to Crisler was in Twombley, pages 242–243.

A story in the October 26, 1948, edition of the *Detroit News* carried Crisler's "we couldn't fit Notre Dame in" quote.

🏈   🏈   🏈

Details of Notre Dame's "sucker shift" against Southern Cal in 1952, and Leahy's quotes about it being "standard procedure" and about Crisler being the "original genius" at the sucker shift, were in Twombley, pages 269–270. Crisler's variation of the tactic was described in Austen Lake's column in the *Boston Evening American* on December 3, 1952 (this clipping is in "Clippings and scrapbooks, loose scrapbook material" folder, Box 7, HOC, BHL-UM). Wrote Lake:

> Fritz's teams would, once or twice each game, wipe out the one-second pause required after a shift. . . . But Princeton did it only when it needed a few yards near the opposing goal. Result—they'd catch the rival linemen drifting to adjust positions and bang 'em when off-balance. . . . Smart old Fritz relied on the frailty of human nature, figuring the officials would say, "Oops! Fast shift!", then while they gnawed their squawkers in uncertainty, they'd add, "Aw well, they've been honest up to now. I'll wait till next time." But there wouldn't BE any NEXT time! So Fritz got what he wanted.

Leahy's tryouts for scholarship candidates, and Rev. Edmund Joyce's statement, were discussed in a story written by Leahy for *Look* magazine, March 23, 1954, issue— which was reprinted in Schoor's *A Treasury of Notre Dame Football,* page 197.

The story of the "Fainting Irish," and the ensuing outlash against Leahy that led to his retirement, were described in Twombley, pages 276–285; in Rappaport, pages 304–305; and in the *Look* magazine article reprinted in Schoor.

Leahy defended the use of faked injuries in the *Look* magazine article, on page 195 of Schoor.

Gene Leahy's letter to Crisler is undated but appears to have been written within days of the feigned injuries incident. It, along with Crisler's reply, can be found in "Squawks, 1950–57" folder, Box 1, HOC, BHL-UM. The NCAA rules committee's press release on January 13, 1954, is in "NCAA Football Rules Committee correspondences, 1954–57" folder, Box 4, HOC, BHL-UM. The feigned-injury incident served "to discredit [Leahy] until the moment of his death," asserted Twombley, page 276.

Gene Leahy's follow-up letter to Crisler is also in "Squawks, 1950–57" folder, Box 1, HOC, BHL-UM.

Unlike Yost, Crisler did not keep the majority of his correspondence. In fact, Crisler kept few of his letters from the entire decade of the 1950s. In those, there was nothing to indicate he acted against Leahy on spite.

At cross-purposes

Unless otherwise noted, all quotes and most information in this section were provided to the author in the following interviews:

• Rev. Edmund Joyce, in his office at the University of Notre Dame, on March 12, 1991.

• Ed (Moose) Krause, in his office at the University of Notre Dame, on August 1, 1990.
• Pete Waldmeir, via telephone on February 8, 1991.
• Don Canham, in his Ann Arbor office, on July 13, 1990.
• Bump Elliott, via telephone on October 6, 1993.
• Cliff Keen, via telephone on January 22, 1991. Keen died on May 11, 1991.
• Dave Strack, via telephone on November 5, 1990.
• Don Lund, in his office at the University of Michigan, on July 3, 1990.
• Scott Crisler, via telephone on November 7, 1990.
• Doug Roby, via telephone on January 21, 1991. Roby died on March 31, 1992.

For the purposes of this section, Canham was a track coach, Elliott was a football coach, Keen was the wrestling coach, Strack was a basketball coach, and Lund was a baseball coach at Michigan at various times during Crisler's reign as athletic director.

Crisler and Joyce may not have ever engaged in conversation, but they were at opposite ends of a dispute that nearly fractured the NCAA during the 1954–55 school year. At issue was the NCAA's television policy.

Crisler, as the Big Ten's official representative on this matter, and a few other power brokers in the NCAA wanted a policy with more regional emphasis—that is, fewer games shown nationally and more shown regionally, thus allowing various conferences to control their own destinies in their respective regions. Such a policy would have allowed Crisler and the Big Ten to not only limit Notre Dame's exposure nationally but reduce it regionally in the Midwest. Notre Dame's Father Joyce, meanwhile, had long been championing a plan to eliminate television restrictions entirely, because the Fighting Irish could certainly command more than the one national appearance allowed per year.

In September 1954, NFL commissioner Bert Bell labeled Crisler and a few other power brokers in the NCAA "selfish men" who had "banded together to keep Notre Dame in the same boat with them." Crisler and others argued that more national exposures for big schools would kill attendance at small-college games. "They hide behind that 'protect the small college' stuff," Bell countered, "but you don't notice them scheduling small colleges to help out, do you?" (Source: the *Detroit Free Press,* September 22–23, 1954.)

This divisive issue reached crisis proportions at the January 1955 NCAA convention. Crisler, representing the Big Ten, and with backing from the Pacific Coast Conference (forerunner of the Pac-10), addressed the convention on January 6. In a "quiet, disarming tone of voice" Crisler proposed a universal plan that would continue to limit a school's national appearances to one, but allow for two regional appearances. Under this plan, the Big Ten would stand a far better chance of competing against Notre Dame for midwestern air time. Crisler hinted that the Big Ten was prepared to break away from the NCAA, if need be, to get its way. This "startled" the floor, *The Michigan Daily* reported, because many felt the Big Ten's withdrawal from the NCAA would mean "the entire organization would collapse." But the next day, the Big Ten's plan was rejected, and the conference was more or less forced to back a compromise that answered some, but not all, of its regional concerns. The NCAA liberalized the national telecast rule to allow one appearance per year per network. (Sources: the *New York Times,* January 7–8, 1955; and *The Michigan Daily,* January 7, 1955.)

Krause's quote in *Sports Illustrated* was in the October 2, 1978, edition, page 72. Canham, Lund, Keen, and Strack all cited the Big-Ten-comes-first theory as Crisler's main reason for not scheduling Notre Dame.

Between December 1948 and February 1949, Michigan State was so miffed about being unable to contract home-and-home games with Michigan, it went public with its discontent. Still, Crisler held out to have the majority of games played in Ann Arbor. Michigan State continued to demand an alternation of sites. It wasn't until Crisler announced Michigan was prepared to drop the Spartans off all future schedules that State submitted, grudgingly, to the uneven arrangement—another classic Crisler power play. But by 1959, the Big Ten had mandated home-and-home arrangements between member schools. (Source: various clippings in "outsize scrapbook 1948–57," HOC, BHL-UM.)

That Notre Dame was offering 32 full athletic scholarships in 1947 was indicated in Twombley, pages 258–260. Big Ten rules covering these issues in the '40s and '50s were in Wilson and Brondfield, pages 449–451, and in an article in the *Detroit News* on December 1, 1957.

According to Wallace in his book, *Notre Dame From Rockne to Parseghian,* page 99, Layden had not been allowed to recruit off campus. "Leahy was no longer restricted so tightly," Wallace wrote, "which obviously meant that the administration had been sold, probably by Leahy, on the theory that if you wanted a coach to successfully meet the competition on the field, he must first meet the competition off the field on at least even terms." The landmark Conference recruiting rules of 1927, which banned off-campus recruiting, were described in Ralph Aigler's report to the Board of Regents after the 1929–30 season, previously referenced.

Big Ten schools confessed their pre-1957 sins in a 24-page report that culminated eight months of internal investigations. Among the findings: 95 percent of all football players were "actively" recruited; some schools had bogus job programs; and conference athletes had received some $300,000 in direct scholarship aid. (Source: *Detroit Free Press,* October 16, 1956.)

Crisler discussed his distaste for recruiting and subsidizing in the December 1, 1957, *Detroit News* article. "I don't think any good at all comes out of recruiting," he said. "Of course, I realize I stand pretty much alone in this thinking." Bump Elliott, Michigan head coach from 1959 to 1968, indicated in his interview that the Big Ten's restriction of providing aid based solely on need, circa 1957–61, "was a terrible disadvantage . . . because nobody else at the time had it in the NCAA, outside of maybe the Ivy League schools." Crisler was a proponent of this limitation, and he steadfastly refused to budge from that stance, even if it harmed Michigan's success. "I argued the point at the time that it would kill us in recruiting," Elliott recalled, "and it certainly did."

Crisler helped strike down two-platoon football in January 1953 because he foresaw its problems, his son Scott said in his interview. Crisler's concerns on this line were also mentioned in an unidentified clipping, circa 1975, in "Clippings and scrapbooks, loose scrapbook material, (1)" folder, Box 7, HOC, BHL-UM.

Leahy's pregame speech was in Twombley, page 221. Scott Crisler, Don Canham, and Pete Waldmeir emphatically asserted Crisler had nothing against Catholics from a traditional, bigoted standpoint.

Doug Roby, a star Wolverine in the early '20s, was an alumni member of the Michigan Board in Control in the '40s. He recalled there being a religious sentiment against Notre Dame even among board members. "I think it was, you know, anti-Catholic," Roby said in his interview. The alumnus's letter about "public opinion" was dated January 22, 1940, "1940 January (3)" folder, Box 25, UM-BICIA, BHL-UM.

Robert Stierwalt's letter to Crisler is undated, in the "Squawks, 1940–49" folder, Box 1, HOC, BHL-UM.

12. Utmost respect: 1968–77

Background on Don Canham was found in Cohen, Deutsch, and Neft, pages 181 and 232; and in Perry, pages 337–339. That Michigan was projecting a $139,000 deficit for 1968–69 was reported in the *Detroit News* on September 23, 1969.

The chronology of the resumption was pieced together from the following interviews:
- Don Canham, in his Ann Arbor business office on July 13, 1990; and via telephone on November 2, 1990, and February 11, 1992.
- Rev. Edmund Joyce, previously noted.
- Moose Krause, previously noted.
- Bump Elliott, previously noted.
- Dave Strack, previously noted.
- Bo Schembechler, in his former office at Tiger Stadium, on September 8, 1991.
- Ara Parseghian, in his South Bend business office, on July 18, 1990.

Other sources for this chronology were: a story in the *Chicago Tribune* on September 22, 1978, and Pete Waldmeir's column in the *Detroit News* on September 23, 1969.

The events surrounding Notre Dame's trip to Ann Arbor in 1970, the effort to perhaps have Michigan and Notre Dame play after the 1970 season, the freshman and JV games in the 1970s, and the 1971 incident involving Krause and Canham, were pieced together from the above interviews. Purdue athletic director George King corroborated the 1971 incident in telephone interviews from West Lafayette, Ind., on October 31 and November 1, 1990.

Canham is generally credited as the athletic director who began the mass marketing of clothing and souvenirs that major colleges so greatly benefit from today. In his interview, Krause gushed over Canham's marketing genius as athletic director.

The extension of the series from 1981 to 1990, and then to 2000, was mentioned in *Sports Illustrated* on October 2, 1978, page 72. In his July 18, 1990, interview, Canham said the handshake agreement through 2000 became a letter agreement.

13. Modern classics: 1978–93

Play-by-play accounts, statistics, and locker-room quotes for the 1978–1993 games were found in the press kits provided by the sports information departments of both schools. Each school's media guides also helped provide the season perspectives provided in these notes.

Unless otherwise noted, and except for the 1980 game, comments from the following coaches were made in these interviews:
- Bo Schembechler, previously noted.
- Lou Holtz, in his office at the University of Notre Dame on June 23, 1992.
- Gary Moeller, in his office at the University of Michigan on June 25, 1992.

XII. The Guts and Glue, '78

Rick Leach provided his recollections about Bob Ufer and the 1978 game in a telephone interview on September 24, 1993.

The Wolverines had opened the week before with a 31–0 blanking of Illinois, while Missouri upset the Irish at Notre Dame, 3–0. Michigan was ranked fifth by AP going in, Notre Dame 14th.

Michigan finished the season 10–2 and ranked fifth in the final AP poll, after its third consecutive Rose Bowl loss, 17–10 to Southern Cal. Notre Dame finished 9–3 and ranked seventh after Joe Montana capped his collegiate career with a remarkable fourth-quarter rally that nipped Houston 35–34 in the Cotton Bowl.

Leach finished fourth in the Heisman Trophy balloting.

XIII. The can't-miss kid, '79

Chuck Male provided his recollections in a telephone interview on December 3, 1993.

Michigan had opened the week before with a 49–7 win at home over Northwestern and was ranked sixth by AP going in. Notre Dame was No. 9.

Schembechler always cringed whenever anyone mentioned that Crable blocked Michigan's last-ditch field-goal attempt. "He didn't block anything! I see Crable now and I say, 'Crable, I made you an All-American,'" Schembechler quipped during his September 8, 1991, interview.

Notre Dame finished the season 7–4, didn't accept a bowl invitation, and failed to make any final top 20 poll. Michigan, too, had a subpar season—finishing 8–4, with a No. 18 AP ranking, after a 17–10 loss to North Carolina in the Gator Bowl.

XIV. The game of the century, '80

Vince Doyle's assessment of this game was found in *Go Blue!: Inside Wolverine Sports* newsletter, Volume 1, Number 2. ABC's decision to televise Notre Dame–Purdue instead of Notre Dame–Michigan was reported in the *Football News* on September 30, 1980.

● ● ●

The events leading up to the game, and many of the quotes in reference to various parts of the game, were found in the *Detroit News,* the *South Bend Tribune,* and the *Chicago Tribune* between September 15 and 21, 1980. Bo Schembechler's quotes about John Wangler's insertion into the game were on pages 112–113 of the book he wrote with Mitch Albom, *Bo: Life, laughs, and lessons of a college football legend,* New York, 1989. The remainder of quotes were included in the postgame press kit.

Michigan recovered from the ND and South Carolina heartbreakers and won its remaining nine games, including a 23–6 win over Washington in the Rose Bowl, to finish fourth in the final AP poll.

Notre Dame, meanwhile, didn't come back down to earth for six weeks. Georgia Tech shocked the 7–0, top-ranked Irish with a 3–3 tie in Atlanta. Notre Dame then crushed Alabama and Air Force to move up to No. 2 in the polls, but season-closing losses to USC and to national champion Georgia in the Sugar Bowl gave the Irish a final record of 9–2–1 and a No. 9 ranking.

XV. Up to the challenge, '81

Ed Muransky recalled the challenges put to the Wolverines in a telephone interview on December 3, 1993.

Michigan had dropped to No. 11 in the AP poll after the Wisconsin game. This was the first regular-season game in college football history to draw a $1-million gate.

Notre Dame, which had opened with a 27–9 victory over LSU, stumbled to a 5–6 record. Michigan finished 9–3, and ranked 12th by AP, after a 33–14 win over UCLA in the Bluebonnet Bowl.

XVI. Redemption at night, '82

Blair Kiel discussed the 1981 and '82 seasons in a telephone interview on December 5, 1993.

Michigan had opened a week earlier with a 20–9 win over Wisconsin.

As it turned out, this was not a memorable season for either school. Notre Dame continued to struggle under Faust, finishing the regular season 6–4–1—despite a 4–0 start—and out of both the AP poll and the bowl picture. Michigan went to the Rose Bowl but lost 24–14 to UCLA, finishing 8–4 and, like ND, out of the AP Top 20.

XVII. The crossroads, '85

Jim Harbaugh's comments were made in a telephone interview on December 8, 1993.

Notre Dame was 13th in the AP poll before the game, while Michigan was unranked.

Michigan capped its comeback season with a 27–23 win over Nebraska in the Fiesta Bowl, to finish 10–1–1 and second in the final AP poll—the Wolverines' highest national ranking since 1948. Notre Dame's season gradually unraveled until the embarrassing finale—a 58–7 drubbing at the hands of powerful Miami. Faust had announced he was leaving Notre Dame before that game, which dropped the Irish to 5–6.

XVIII. Michigan . . . barely, '86

Michigan won its next eight games before being upset by Minnesota 20–17 at Ann Arbor. The Wolverines lost 22–15 to Arizona State in the Rose Bowl to finish 11–2 and ranked eighth in the AP poll. Notre Dame continued to match up well against a slew of strong opponents but also continued finding ways to narrowly lose. The Irish beat Southern Cal 38–37 in their finale to improve to 5–6.

XIX. Carefully played, '87

Before the game, Michigan was ranked ninth in the AP poll, Notre Dame 16th.

Tim Brown became the seventh Notre Dame player to win the Heisman Trophy this year.

Notre Dame won its next seven games before the floor gave way. After the Irish lost 35–10 to Texas A&M in the Cotton Bowl, their record fell to 8–4 and their AP ranking to 17. Michigan beat Alabama 28–24 in the Hall of Fame Bowl to finish 8–4 and 19th in the AP poll.

XX. Razor close, '88

Before the game, Notre Dame was ranked 13th in the AP poll, Michigan ninth.

Reggie Ho's comments were made in a telephone interview on December 11, 1993.

Holtz's quotes about Gillette's last-play kick were on page 127 of the book he wrote with John Heisler, *The Fighting Spirit: A Championship Season at Notre Dame,* New York, 1989.

Notre Dame went on to win its 10 remaining games, then thrashed West Virginia 34–21 in the Fiesta Bowl to capture its first national title since 1977. Michigan beat Southern Cal 22–14 in the Rose Bowl and placed fourth in the final AP poll.

As it turned out, the 1988 national title came down to three nail-biting games between Notre Dame, Michigan, and Miami. Notre Dame beat Michigan 19–17 and Miami 31–30, while the Hurricanes edged Michigan 31–30. Each of these teams didn't lose a single game outside of this round-robin. Miami finished No. 2 in the AP poll.

XXI. Rocket blasts off, '89

Raghib Ismail's and Bo Schembechler's postgame quotes were in the September 17, 1989, edition of the *Detroit News.*

Notre Dame had beaten Virginia 36–13 in the Kickoff Classic. It later extended its winning streak to a school-record 23 games before losing its regular-season finale to eventual national champion Miami, 27–10. The Irish smashed then top-ranked Colorado 21–6 in the Orange Bowl, though, and finished No. 2 in the AP poll. Michigan won its 10 remaining regular-season games but lost to Southern Cal in the Rose Bowl, 17–10, and finished No. 7.

The Rose Bowl was Bo Schembechler's last game as Michigan head coach. He had announced his retirement on December 13, after 21 seasons as head coach of the Wolverines. Schembechler named Gary Moeller, a long-time assistant, as his successor.

XXII. Smashing debuts, '90

Rick Mirer's postgame comment was found in the postgame press kit.

Notre Dame lost three weeks later to Stanford, and Michigan became the new No. 1 team in the AP poll. The Wolverines lost the very next week to Michigan State, however.

Notre Dame finished the season 9–3 and ranked sixth after a 10–9 loss to Colorado in the Orange Bowl. Michigan finished seventh in the final AP poll, also with a 9–3 record, after whipping Mississippi 35–3 in the Gator Bowl.

XXIII. The Catch, '91

The comment about The Catch in *Sports Illustrated* appeared on page 93 of the December 9, 1991, edition.

Michigan was ranked third in the AP poll (after beating Boston College 35–13) and Notre Dame seventh (after a 49–27 win over Indiana) before the game.

This was the first regular-season game in NCAA history to draw a $2-million gate.

Michigan finished the season 10–2 and ranked sixth in the final AP poll after getting blown out in the Rose Bowl by Washington, 34–14. Notre Dame beat Florida 39–28 in the Sugar Bowl to finish 10–3 and 13th in the AP poll.

XXIV. Fit to be tied, '92

Notre Dame was ranked third in the AP poll going in, after opening a week earlier with a 42–7 win over Northwestern. Michigan was opening this week, ranked sixth.

Rick Mirer's, Elvis Grbac's, and Lou Holtz's quotes were found in the postgame press kit.

Holtz recalled his strategy in the final minute in an on-field interview with NBC immediately after the game, and the next morning on CNN's *College Coaches Corner* show.

Notre Dame whipped Texas A&M 28–3 in the Cotton Bowl, capping a 10–1–1 season and garnering a No. 4 ranking in the final AP poll. Michigan beat Washington 38–31 in the Rose Bowl to finish No. 5 in the AP poll with a 9–0–3 record—Michigan's first unbeaten season since 1973.

XXV. All but written off, '93

Notre Dame beat Northwestern 27–12 the week before, while Michigan smashed Washington State 42–14. Lou Holtz made his good/bad comment at a news conference on Wednesday before the game.

Don Yaeger and Douglas S. Looney wrote *Under the Tarnished Dome: How Notre Dame Betrayed Its Ideals for Football Glory*, New York, 1993.

All the postgame quotes were found in the September 12, 1993, edition of the *Detroit News*.

Notre Dame cruised past its next eight opponents before smashing No. 1 Florida State 31–24. But the Irish closed their regular season the following week with a wild 41–39 loss to Boston College, then beat Texas A&M 24–21 in the Cotton Bowl to finish 11–1 and ranked second in the final AP poll. Michigan sputtered through its schedule before winning its last four games convincingly, including a 42–7 whipping of North Carolina State in the Hall of Fame Bowl, to finish 8–4 and ranked 21st by AP.

Postgames report

The records, trends, and stats were included in, or deduced from, information in each school's postgame press kits and football media guides.

14. Extra points

Who's No. 1?—Fight songs

Bill Studwell discussed the Notre Dame and Michigan fight songs in a telephone interview on December 15, 1993. He published his Top 13 list in 1990.

● ● ●

One Michigan record album, *U of M presents . . . the 5 Greatest Games in Wolverine Football History,* Detroit, 1972, gave the most exaggerated story of Charles (Chuck) Widman's touchdown run. The correct version of events was easy to find: in the detailed game story printed in the next edition of *The Michigan Daily,* on November 28, 1898. Widman was a standout in Michigan's victory over Notre Dame that year.

The background on Louis Elbel and how he came to write "The Victors" was found in a story that Michigan alumnus Charles D. Kountz wrote for the *Columbus Citizen* on October 12, 1930 (clipping in "Papers 1930 November [2]" folder, Box 14, UM-BICIA, BHL-UM). Elbel's quotes were found in this story. A story in the *South Bend Tribune* on September 20, 1978, provided additional information on Elbel.

Copyright for the lyrics of "The Victors" is owned by the University of Michigan.

The correct order of the initial public performances of "The Victors" was reported in *The Michigan Daily* from April 5–10, 1899.

The worldliness of "The Victors" was culled from: (1) a page in the "Yost—40 Years at Michigan" scrapbook in Box 7, FHY, BHL-UM; (2) Kuntz's story; (3) a telephone interview with William D. Revelli, Michigan Marching Band director from 1935 to 1971, on December 15, 1993.

Studwell's comments were made in his December 15, 1993, interview. Michigan publications routinely report that John Philip Sousa called "The Victors" the greatest college fight song ever written. The only documentation that could be found was Kountz's *Columbus Citizen* quotation.

● ● ●

The story of how Michael J. Shea and his brother, John, wrote "The Victory March" was pulled together from: Sperber, pages 24–26; a story in the *Chicago Tribune* on September 22, 1978; and Rappaport, page 37.

The copyright holder for the lyrics of "The Victory March" is Edwin H. Morris & Co.

Sperber, on page 25, wrote that Joseph Casasanta rearranged the song's tempo. The Vietnam anecdote was found in the *Chicago Tribune* story of September 22, 1978.

● ● ●

Elbel's quote about the psychology of composing was found in Kountz's story in the *Columbus Citizen.*

Who's No. 1?—Marching bands

The author overheard jibes from the Notre Dame band while taking photos on the Notre Dame sideline during the 1993 game.

Several Michigan band members, in off-the-record discussions, told the author about their view toward the Notre Dame band on January 2, 1990.

🏈　　🏈　　🏈

Background on the Notre Dame band was found in a historical sketch in the university's sports information department files.

🏈　　🏈　　🏈

Background on the Michigan band was found in: (1) an untitled report dated September 28, 1923, "Papers 1923 October (1)" folder, Box 5, UM-BICIA, BHL-UM; (2) in the telephone interview with William D. Revelli, conductor emeritus; and (3) in the historical sketch included in 1993 Michigan–Notre Dame football program.

Michi-Damers

Michigan's 1893 lettermen list was in Cohen, Deutsch, and Neft, page 13.

The Scholastic of November 17, 1894, mentioned the prominent role "Morrison" played against Wabash, including his two touchdowns.

Tom Joyce's tryout attempt at Michigan was described in the September 26, 1907, edition of the *Detroit News.*

🏈　　🏈　　🏈

George Gipp's wild ways, and the chronology of his expulsion and reinstatement in early 1920, were described in *One for The Gipper* by Patrick Chelland, Chicago, 1973, pages 102–111 and 128–137.

The following sources said Michigan and/or Fielding H. Yost was actively wooing Gipp during his expulsion: Chelland, page 137; George Gekas's *Gipper: The Life & Times of George Gipp,* South Bend, Ind., 1987, page 120; Rappaport, page 106; and Anderson and Klosinksi, page 52.

It was Rappaport's account that purported Gipp's two-week stint in Ann Arbor under Fielding Yost. But Coach Yost, from Nashville, continually exchanged letters with Michigan athletic director Phil Bartelme between March 8 and April 29, 1920 (see letters in "Papers 1920 March" and "Papers 1920 April" folders, Box 3, UM-BICIA, BHL-UM). In an April 1 letter to Bartelme, Yost indicated he wouldn't be in Ann Arbor until May 1 and would stay until May 21.

Gipp's great 1920 season, and the chronology of his final days alive, were detailed in Gekas, pages 140–204.

Details of Rockne's famous Gipper speech were reported in Sperber, pages 282–288.

🏈　　🏈　　🏈

That Bernie Kirk was Gipp's favorite receiver was mentioned in Gekas, page 133—as was the outrage among Notre Dame students that Kirk had left for Michigan, and the hot rumor about the "inducement."

Doug Roby provided some of the background on Bernie Kirk in his July 31, 1990, interview. Roby was another Michigan native who had been wooed to Ann Arbor from an out-of-state college. Roby had been playing at Phillips University in Enid, Oklahoma, and, like Kirk, sat out 1920 before playing in 1921 and 1922.

Bob Clancy's first letter to Yost (August 20, 1920) is in "Papers 1920 August" folder, Box 3, UM-BICIA, BHL-UM. His letter on January 28, 1921, is in "1921 January (1)" folder, Box 4, UM-BICIA, BHL-UM.

Because of the First World War, freshmen were allowed to play in 1918. Those who did, such as Kirk, were still allowed to play three more years. That's why Kirk played two years at Notre Dame then two more at Michigan.

Yost's statement to H.G. Salsinger was in a letter, November 9, 1922, "1922 November" folder, Box 5, UM-BICIA, BHL-UM.

The January 3, 1923, edition of *The Michigan Daily* provided details surrounding Kirk's death, including the fact he learned of his selection to Walter Camp's All-America team—surprisingly, as only a second-teamer—on his deathbed.

● ● ●

The *South Bend Tribune* on September 17, 1907, reported Bert Maris's Notre Dame and Michigan affiliations. Ties of other Michi-Damer coaches were discussed previously in this book, or were simply found after a simple check of each school's all-time lists of players and coaches.

Mike Trgovac was reported to have been in tears after the 1980 Notre Dame game during the Michigan Football Network's radio broadcast of the 1981 Rose Bowl, on January 1, 1981. The various comments regarding Trgovac's pregame speech at Ann Arbor in 1993 were reported by the *Associated Press* on September 13, 1993.

15. Nearly uprooted: Today and tomorrow

Bo Schembechler discussed his concerns with the Notre Dame game in his September 8, 1991, interview. The *Detroit Free Press* on September 1, 1989, reported Schembechler was dissatisfied with the placement of the 1997–99 games.

Lou Holtz indicated his belief that a football team makes its greatest improvement between its first and second games in Holtz and Heisler, page 114.

● ● ●

Jack Weidenbach discussed scheduling switches and his view toward Notre Dame in an interview in his office at the University of Michigan on June 25, 1992.

Dick Rosenthal said the schedule agreement was extended in the summer of 1993 on Weidenbach's initiation, in a telephone interview on December 1, 1993. Individual game contracts aren't usually drawn up until a few years beforehand, but "schedule agreements" are now used to ink long-term pacts.

For the dates of future games, see Appendix 1.

● ● ●

Rosenthal and Lou Holtz discussed their views toward Michigan in separate interviews in their respective offices at the University of Notre Dame on June 23, 1992.

Moose Krause said Michigan was ND's biggest game in his August 1, 1990, interview.

Gary Moeller shared his thoughts about the Notre Dame game in his June 25, 1992, interview.

Elvis Grbac was quoted on the 1–10 scenario in the *South Bend Tribune* on August 17, 1991. In fact Grbac picked Notre Dame "without hesitating an instant." George Ceithaml said "beating Notre Dame stays forever!" in a letter to Fritz Crisler, circa 1969, "1969 General Correspondences" folder, Box 1, HOC, BHL-UM.

The preseason college football issue of *The Sporting News,* August 23, 1993, edition, rated Michigan–Notre Dame the top rivalry in the Midwest.

Don Canham made his prediction in his July 18, 1990, interview. Krause recalled President Gerald Ford's remark in his August 1, 1990, interview. Ford was team MVP for Michigan in 1934.

● ● ●

Chris Zorich's comment appeared in the September 13, 1990, edition of the *Detroit Free Press.*

Appendix 1

Sources of statistical information for 1887–1943 games were noted for each game previously. Information for 1978–93 games was found in the postgame press kits.

Appendix 2

All records here were deduced from the game summaries in Appendix 1.

Appendix 3

These comparative accomplishments were found in *The Fighting Irish: 1993 Notre Dame Football* (media guide), pages 351 and 366, except for All-American selections (*1993 NCAA Football* media guide) and national championships (the National Championship Foundation).